Harmful and Undesirable

Harmful and Undesirable

Book Censorship in Nazi Germany

GUENTER LEWY

OXFORD
UNIVERSITY PRESS

OXFORD
UNIVERSITY PRESS

Oxford University Press is a department of the University of Oxford. It furthers
the University's objective of excellence in research, scholarship, and education
by publishing worldwide. Oxford is a registered trade mark of Oxford University
Press in the UK and certain other countries.

Published in the United States of America by Oxford University Press
198 Madison Avenue, New York, NY 10016, United States of America.

Library of Congress Cataloging-in-Publication Data
Names: Lewy, Guenter, 1923- author.
Title: Harmful and undesirable : book censorship in Nazi Germany / Guenter Lewy.
Description: New York, NY : Oxford University Press, 2016. |
Includes bibliographical references and index.
Identifiers: LCCN 2015044227 | ISBN 9780190275280 (hardback) |
ISBN 9780197524282 (paperback)
Subjects: LCSH: Censorship—Germany—History—20th century. | Germany—Politics and
government—1933–1945. | Germany—Intellectual life—20th century. | BISAC: HISTORY /
Europe / Germany.
Classification: LCC Z658.G3 L49 2016 | DDC 363.310943/0904—dc23 LC record available at
http://lccn.loc.gov/2015044227

Books cannot be killed by fire. People die, but books never die. No man and no force can put thought in a concentration camp forever. No man and no force can take from the world the books that embody man's eternal fight against tyranny.

—President Franklin D. Roosevelt,
World War II poster, U.S. Government Printing Office, 1942

CONTENTS

PREFACE

The history of the Third Reich has been studied extensively. Yet, surprisingly, book censorship, an important tool in the Nazi apparatus of dictatorial rule, has received little attention by scholars. In 1960 Dietrich Strothmann brought out the first book-length treatment of National Socialist literary policy, but the work, originally a dissertation, was marred by a failure to consult archival sources. Between 1995 and 2010 the German historian and librarian Jan-Pieter Barbian published three valuable books dealing with the politics of literature in Nazi Germany, which for the first time drew on relevant archival materials to describe the practice of book censorship. An English translation of one of these, *Literaturpolitik im NS-Staat,* appeared in 2013. Barbian's works, however, are more in the nature of reference books to be consulted for specific information than of books to be read. Crammed with detail (one of them is 916 pages long), they fail to provide a sense of narrative or a clear picture of the events involved. The present study aims to fill this gap. It is designed to provide an account of book censorship in the Third Reich within the context of Nazi cultural policy. At the same time, the work also throws an interesting new light on intellectual life during the Nazi era and on some of the major figures of the Nazi regime, such as Martin Bormann, Joseph Goebbels, and Alfred Rosenberg.

In the eyes of the Nazis, German culture had to be purged of its liberal and Marxist elements, with a special target the alleged domination of German culture by Jews. Hitler repeatedly stressed that in this world, human culture and civilization are inseparably bound up with the existence of the Aryan. Recognizing the importance of the printed word, the regime early on sought full control of both the publication and the readership of books. On March 13, 1933, the Nazi stalwart Goebbels was appointed head of the new propaganda ministry, created to achieve the forcible coordination (*Gleichschaltung*) of all those engaged in creative activity. Insofar as it concerned books, the ministry's remit included authors, publishers, bookstores, and libraries. The aim was to get rid of all ideological rivals and achieve the preeminence of National Socialist ideas. Given the importance of the claim for the total domination of the world of culture inherent in Nazi ideology, it is not surprising that book censorship encompassed a large segment of German book production. Between 1933 and 1938, 4,175 book titles were banned, and in the case of 564 authors all of their writings were forbidden. During the twelve years of Nazi rule, a total of 5,485 books were banned. Objectionable categories of books included alleged moral corruption; Marxist, pacifist, or confessional ideas; Jewish authorship; and the catch-all designation of "failure to live up to what was expected in the new Germany."

The sweeping powers granted to Goebbels' propaganda ministry necessarily created conflicts of jurisdiction with other agencies. While all bureaucracies seek to enlarge their turf, the overlapping tasks of state and party organizations that characterized the Nazi regime increased the frequency and vehemence of the bureaucratic rivalry. The conflicts that developed with regard to book censorship were particularly egregious and reveal again how ineptly this alleged super-state was governed—monolithic in theory but polycratic in practice. While Goebbels gradually succeeded in achieving a dominant position, he never was able to bring all aspects of book censorship under his sway.

The control and censorship of books by a multiplicity of state and party organizations resulted in a less than orderly, not to say chaotic, outcome. Libraries, for example, fell under the jurisdiction of both the Ministry of Propaganda and the Ministry of Science and Education. The authors of scholarly works were not required to be members of the Reich Chamber of Literature (Reichsschrifttumskammer), and their activities were regulated by the Ministry of Education. However, the publication of their books was in the hands of publishers who were under the supervision of the Ministry of Propaganda. Acting on the basis of President Hindenburg's "Decree for the Protection of People and State," issued on February 4, 1933, the political police in Bavaria confiscated more than 6,000 titles by 2,293 "Marxist" authors. Searches at publishers and book dealers as well as seizures of books by the Gestapo in the various German states continued during the following years, thus adding another actor to the number of agencies involved with censorship.

Moreover, all these state and party organizations had subsidiary offices on the state, district, and local levels, which often acted on their own initiative. Thus, for example, a Nazi official in the state of Baden, whose affiliation is not identified, on October 19, 1937, is known personally to have ordered the destruction of 2,517 books in the Heidelberg public library. He also had 351 other books moved to the university library, where they were kept in a special storage area for works by Jewish, Marxist, and pacifist authors. Books held in what was called the *Separata*, or "poison cabinet," were made available to scholars and students who could show cause why they needed to consult the literature of the enemy. At some university libraries, zealous directors established an additional category of books named *Secreta*, and these books were no longer listed in the general catalog. Sometimes only librarians considered fully reliable politically were allowed to handle such books.

Several hundred German writers left their homeland after the Nazis' rise to power in 1933. Among these émigrés were some of the best-known figures of German literature, such as Heinrich and Thomas Mann, Kurt Tucholsky, Franz Werfel, and Arnold and Stefan Zweig. Yet there was another group of authors who stayed in Germany and who, it has been said, constituted an "Inner Emigration." Some of these writers concealed the true meaning of their publications by "writing between the lines" and by using allegories or parables. The question of whether there really existed such an inner emigration continues to be debated. I analyze this issue with regard to a number of well-known German writers in a chapter that also provides a vivid picture of what it was like being a writer under the Nazi dictatorship. The ramifications of the regime's book censorship involved more than just bureaucratic procedures. As Robert Darnton has pointed out in his study *Censors at Work*, censorship not only pervades institutions but it also "colors human relations, [and] reaches into the hidden workings of the soul."

I wish to acknowledge my gratitude for the award of a Fulbright Senior Research Grant that made possible four months of research in the Federal Archive in Berlin, including the files of the former Berlin Document Center. I also want to thank the helpful personnel of the Bundesarchiv, many of whom exerted themselves on my behalf well beyond the call of duty. My historian friends Abraham Ascher, Walter Laqueur, and Allan Mitchell read an early draft of this book, and I thank them for their constructive criticism. As it is customary to state, none of the above institutions and individuals are responsible for the opinions and conclusions reached here, which remain my personal responsibility.

PART 1

THE EMERGENCE OF CENSORSHIP

Book Control in the Weimar Republic

Nazi propaganda, both before and after the seizure of power in 1933, portrayed the German literary scene during the Weimar period as a chaotic free-for-all in which individual rights trumped all concepts of beauty and goodness in favor of a corrosive Jewish "cultural bolshevism." In point of fact, the publication of books in the Weimar Republic, denigrated by the Nazis as the *Systemzeit* (time of the system), was not as uncontrolled as Nazi criticism suggested. Article 118 of the Weimar Constitution, adopted in 1919, guaranteed German citizens the right "to express his opinion freely in word, writing, print, image, or otherwise" and announced that "there is no censorship." At the same time, the article noted that "legal measures are permissible" for regulating the cinema as well as "in order to combat trashy and obscene literature." Public exhibitions and performances could be restricted "for the protection of youth." Moreover, the freedoms of Article 118 were guaranteed "within the bounds set by general laws," and several provisions of the penal code could be, and indeed were, used to circumscribe the right to publish freely.[1]

Article 82 of the criminal code punished high treason, conspiracy, and preparation to commit treason as well as the violent overthrow of the constitutional order. Invoking this law, local authorities confiscated books that were said to incite the forceful overturn of the Weimar constitution. The writings of authors of the radical Left in particular were frequently caught in this net. In June 1925 a magistrate's court in Berlin ordered the confiscation of a book of poems *Der Leichnam auf dem Thron* (The Corpse on the Throne) by Johannes R. Becher, a well-known member of the German Communist party, on the grounds that the book encouraged the violent overthrow of the republic. Two months later, Becher himself was indicted for preparing to commit treason by using his novel *Levisite* as a "literary instrument" to incite a revolutionary uprising.[2] Article 66 of the criminal code penalizing blasphemy was used against several writers, including Ernst Glaeser and Kurt Tucholsky.[3]

Another way of silencing politically undesirable writings was to take legal action against libel. An individual could charge that a particular book represented an insult and, if successful, achieve the confiscation and destruction of the offending publication. The Reichswehr (German army) used this weapon in order to suppress a number of pacifist books. Outright pornography was outlawed by Article 184 of the criminal code, and the enforcement of this provision was in the hands of the criminal police. However, because of the federal structure of the Weimar Republic, actual practice varied from state to state. A book could be confiscated in Prussia but be freely sold in Saxony. The police of Bavaria had the reputation of being particularly aggressive.[4] In order to comply with international treaties, the Deutsche Zentralpolizeistelle zur Bekämpfung unzüchtiger Schriften (German Central Police Office for the Struggle against Obscene Publications) in Berlin kept a list of all books confiscated in the country as obscene, the so-called *Polunbi-Katalog*. This list was kept secret and was marked "For official use only."[5]

Despite these strictures, Germany before World War I had been much more liberal than other European nations in the freedom it granted authors to discuss the cultivation of physical health and sexuality. During the Weimar Republic this freedom expanded to such a degree that people of different political persuasions began to regard it as symptomatic of a decadent permissiveness. Article 122 of the Weimar Constitution stipulated that "Young people are to be protected against exploitation as well as against moral, psychological, and physical neglect," and as early as 1920, at the time of the enactment of a film censorship law, there were demands for the passage of legislation to curb the flood of cheap *Groschenhefte* (dime novels) and erotically stimulating publications. Even liberal and progressive pedagogues agreed that something had to be done about the deluge of shoddy and filthy literature. There was opposition from authors and publishers, but finally, six years later, a parliamentary majority could be mustered in support of such legislation. On December 3, 1926, the Reichstag (German Parliament) enacted the Law for the Protection of Youth against Trash and Filth Literature (Gesetz zur Bewahrung der Jugend vor Schund- und Schmutzliteratur). The legislation did not define the meaning of trash and filth; it left it up to inspection offices in Berlin and Munich to decide which publications were to be so designated. Decisions by these two offices could be appealed to a Superior Inspection Office (Oberprüfstelle) in Leipzig. By January 1933 the list consisted of 188 items. Listed publications could not be sold to anyone under the age of eighteen and were not to be advertised or displayed.[6]

The law against trash and filth had the support of the Right, especially of the various elements of the *Völkische* movement, the largest and most radical group in the conservative camp.[7] In fact, for these elements, including the Nazis, the legislation did not go far enough. They had their sights not only on excessively erotic publications but also on the writings of their political opponents on the Left—the books of authors such as Bertolt Brecht, Ernst Glaeser, Heinrich Mann, Ernst Toller, Kurt Tucholsky, and Arnold Zweig.

Prominent in the struggle against what it regarded as antinational, defeatist, and Jewish literature stood the Fighting League for German Culture
(Kampfbund für deutsche Kultur), established in 1928 (first under the name
Nationalsozialistische Gesellschaft für deutsche Kultur) and headed by the
veteran Nazi ideologue Alfred Rosenberg. The founding document of the
Kampfbund, published in May 1928, denounced the "literature hostile to
the German race," which was said to carry out a systematic fight against the
true values of German culture. Instead of strengthening the resistance of
the German people against its enemies, these literati praised "the virtue of
pacifism, cowardice, and racketeering." The appeal called upon the German
people to take up the struggle against *"Verbastardisierung und Vernegerung"*
(Bastardization and Succumbing to the Negroes).[8] Joseph Goebbels, the up-
and-coming master propagandist of the Nazi party, declared in his publication *Der Angriff* that these kinds of writers, spreading nothing but corrosion,
deserved to be put up against a wall and shot.[9]

The opportunity to achieve the suppression of "corrosive" literature presented itself in the state of Thuringia, where on January 23, 1930, the Nazi
leader Wilhelm Frick became minister of the interior and education. Frick
was a lawyer, for a time head of the criminal police in Munich, and a participant in the Nazi Beer Hall Putsch of November 9, 1923. On April 5, 1930, he
issued a decree, "Against the Culture of the Negroes and for German National
Tradition," that included a ban on books such as Erich Maria Remarque's *Im
Westen nichts Neues* (All Quiet on the Western Front) as well as on the film
based on that novel. In December, Frick's ministry published a list of books
described as "national literature" that all public libraries were required to
carry in their collections. In an article published in 1932, Frick took pride in
the work he had been able to do in Thuringia for Germany's spiritual renewal
and against "the Jewish, Marxist, internationalist, pacifist infestation."[10] After
Frick's dismissal on April 1, 1931, many of these measures were revoked, but
when the Nazis in an election on July 31, 1932, again became the strongest
party in the Landtag (state parliament) of Thuringia, Fritz Wächtler, the new
minister of education, could resurrect and continue the practice of censorship
with renewed vigor. After the Nazi assumption of power on January 31, 1933,
Frick became Hitler's minister of the interior.[11]

Article 48 of the Weimar Constitution gave the president the power to pro-
mulgate emergency decrees without the prior consent of the Reichstag (the
national parliament). Also, on March 25, 1930, the parliament enacted a new
version of the 1922 Law for the Protection of the Republic that contained the
right to ban organizations and limit speech.[12] These legal provisions had been
intended to be used in emergencies only, but during the tense and strained
political conditions of the last years of the Weimar Republic they increasingly
became the normal mode of governing. The ministerial bureaucracy from 1930

on now replaced the Reichstag as the real law-giver. The republic became an authoritarian state run by civil servants.[13]

Among the victims of rule by emergency decree were the authors of books, especially writers on the Left. The presidential emergency decree of March 28, 1931, was aimed at limiting freedom of assembly, but it also allowed the banning of books for up to eight months. Another decree, issued on July 17, gave the police the power to confiscate any publication that threatened public safety and order. Still another decree, promulgated on June 16, 1932, forbade publications that endangered the vital interests of the state by spreading untrue or distorted facts or slandered or maliciously brought into contempt the organs or leading officials of the state. Until then such offenses had been adjudicated by the courts. Now the police were given a free hand to apply these provisions as they saw fit. A historian of book censorship during the Weimar Republic concludes that the repressive measures enacted by the Nazi regime from 1933 on had been prepared step by step by the Weimar governments.

The Book Burning of 1933

On January 30, 1933, Adolf Hitler was named chancellor of Germany, and the Nazis began to settle accounts with their political enemies. Functionaries and intellectuals of the Left were rounded up and carted off to improvised prisons, often in the cellars of the Nazi storm troopers' (Sturmabteilung, or SA) local headquarters, where they were brutally beaten, tortured, and in some instances murdered. In Prussia alone, by the end of April, at least 25,000 people had been taken into "protective custody" and incarcerated in newly established concentration camps.[1] Included in these mass arrests were writers who in their works had openly opposed the Nazis, among them Erich Baron, Erich Mühsam, Carl von Ossietzky, and Ludwig Renn. Mühsam was soon murdered; Ossietzky died on May 4, 1938, as a result of serious damage to his health incurred during five years in a concentration camp.

On February 27 the Reichstag building went up in flames, and a former Dutch Communist was caught in the act of arson. The Nazis used the opportunity to create a wave of public hysteria about the Communist peril. On March 23 the Reichstag approved the so-called Enabling Act. The parliament acted without its eighty-one Communist deputies, who had been arrested or gone underground, and under the menacing presence of armed SA and SS troopers, who lined the aisles and surrounded the building. The Law for Removing the Distress of People and Reich gave the cabinet—in effect the chancellor, Hitler—the authority to enact laws and decrees without involving the Reichstag.[2] In a speech that lasted two and one-half hours, Hitler promised to work for a "thorough-going moral renewal" and the preservation of the nation's eternal values. Art and literature would be used in this endeavor. "Blood and race," he proclaimed, "will again become sources of artistic creativity."[3]

By March 1933, Nazi-type "moral renewal" was well under way, with Nazi terror also targeting books. Storm troopers attacked Communist, Social Democratic, and trade union headquarters and their publishing houses and set fire to furniture and files, as well as to the books found there. This book burning did not involve specific authors or titles. Members of the Hitler Youth (Hitlerjugend, or HJ) burned books seized at school and public libraries, and these actions, by contrast, did focus on specific authors considered subversive of the new order, such as Lion Feuchtwanger, Emil Ludwig, Ernst Toller, Erich Maria Remarque, and Kurt Tucholsky. In Düsseldorf, the birthplace of Heinrich Heine, the HJ burned a collection of Heine's poems. At the Karl-Marx-School in Berlin-Neukölln, Nazi youths seized copies of Boccaccio's *Decameron* that were said to be well-thumbed; the stakes in the courtyards of many Berlin schools were reported to be burning for several days. On April 19 HJ leaders in Bavaria called for large rallies to take place on Sunday, May 7, the "Day of Youth," at which Marxist, pacifist, and democratic literature was to be burned. On May 2 they asked the Bavarian Ministry of Education and Cultural Affairs to order public libraries to put these books at the disposal of the HJ. The ministry did not explicitly comply with this request, though on May 4 the newly appointed Nazi minister, Hans Schlemm, did issue an appeal for support of the book purge.[4]

The most systematic and best-organized undertaking to burn undesirable books came from the Deutsche Studentenschaft (DSt)—the nationwide umbrella organization of student councils founded in 1919 as a defender of the economic interests of German and Austrian university students. During the following years the DSt became increasingly enmeshed in the struggle between republican and *völkische* (militant nationalist) students, and by 1931 it had come under the domination of the National Socialist German Students' League (Nationalsozialistischer deutscher Studentenbund), founded in 1926 as a division of the Nazi party. In April 1933 the DSt sought to do its part in the so-called national revolution and thus strengthen its standing in the new state.

On April 6 the executive committee of the DSt established an office for press and propaganda to be headed by the twenty-four-year-old law student Hans Karl Leistritz. Two days later the new office sent out a circular to all affiliated student organizations in which it announced its first plan of action to begin on April 12 with a "campaign of enlightenment" and culminating in the public burning of "Jewish and corrosive literature." All students were to cleanse their own collections of books; student organizations were to see to it that public libraries were purged. The action was described as an answer to the "shameless campaign of world Jewry against Germany." Attached to this letter were 12 *Thesen wider den undeutschen Geist* (12 Theses against the un-German Spirit) that were to be distributed on April 13 as large placards. A shortened version of this letter was sent to some sixty German writers, expected to be sympathetic, who were asked to support the action of the DSt.[5]

The appeal *Wider den undeutschen Geist* called for the purification of the German language and German literature. The most dangerous enemy, it averred, were the Jews and those who were in bondage to the Jews. "The Jew can only think in a Jewish manner. If he writes in German he lies. The German who writes in German but has an un-German mind is a traitor." German students were exhorted to overcome "Jewish intellectualism and the liberal manifestations of decay" connected to it. The German university had to insist that its students and professors have a firm commitment to the life of the German mind. The manifesto ended by reminding students and student organizations to carry out the purge of the public libraries and to burn the collected corrosive literature.[6]

The cleansing of the libraries began promptly. The students of Breslau, the seat of an old and prestigious university, informed the Berlin propaganda office that on April 22 and 23 uniformed and armed students had searched the lending libraries of the city and had seized some 10,000 works of un-German literature. The police had been informed ahead of time and had "protected our endeavor in every way." Most library owners also cooperated. Many had already on their own removed offending books from circulation. In the next few days, the students wrote, they would sort through the books in accordance with the "blacklist" they had just received in order to make the final determination about which books were to be burned.[7] Similar actions took place in other cities. The librarian of the Technical University Braunschweig recalled in his memoirs published after the war that his shelves emerged from the purge "rather thinned out."[8] In Berlin the student raiding parties, driving around in trucks, not only seized books but also went on to destroy and close down the Institute for the Study of Sexuality headed by Magnus Hirschfeld.[9]

The blacklist mentioned by the Breslau students had been compiled by the librarian Wolfgang Hermann, assisted by two other Nazi librarians, Hans Engelhard and Max Wieser. Hermann was a member of the Verband Deutscher Volksbibliothekare (VDV), the Association of German Public Librarians, an organization that welcomed the opportunity to proceed against its rival, the lending libraries. Since 1930 these commercial enterprises had gained an increasing share of readers, especially among the unemployed, and the lending libraries were said to stock "trash and filth." Functioning as a committee of the VDV, the three Nazis quickly progressed from the original endeavor to cleanse the lending libraries to the task of "reorganizing" all Berlin's libraries and purge them of "cultural bolshevism"—Bolshevik, Marxist, and Jewish literature. The work of the committee had the blessing of the Lord Mayor of Berlin, Heinrich Sahm. This elected official was acting under the tutelage of a "State Commissioner" appointed by Hermann Göring, who quickly became the real power in the mayor's office.[10]

In a letter dated April 26, Hermann voiced the expectation that within a day the Prussian government would make his list official,[11] a hope that remained unfulfilled. Hermann provided the list of seventy-one authors of fiction to the propaganda office of the DSt that sent it out to its counterparts at the universities on April 27. The list, Leisritz wrote, was still incomplete. A fuller version as well as a list of books on history and philosophy would follow in the next few days.[12] The blacklist on these topics and the fields of politics, art, religion, and pedagogy was finally completed by May 8, when Hermann sent it to the DSt. The list of objectionable fiction included 131 authors, among them ninety-four German-speaking authors, thirty-seven translated foreign-language authors, and four anthologies. It contained such well-known literary figures as Berthold Brecht, Ilja Ehrenburg, Lion Feuchtwanger, Emil Ludwig, Heinrich and Klaus Mann, John Dos Passos, Arthur Schnitzler, and Arnold and Stefan Zweig. The nonfiction list comprised 190 authors. The lists for politics and history were graced by names such as Max Adler, Otto Bauer, August Bebel, Helen Keller, Ferdinand Lassalle, Karl Marx, V. I. Lenin, and Walther Rathenau.[13]

Hermann also sent copies of the lists to the Berlin public libraries and informed them that some of this corrosive literature would be publicly burned. The date for this "big auto-da-fé" would be announced soon.[14] On May 5 the Association of German Lending Libraries announced that it had agreed to cooperate with the DSt in the action *Wider den undeutschen Geist* and asked the affiliated libraries to remove the books enumerated in the attached list from their inventory. Otherwise there was the danger that these books would be confiscated.[15]

On March 13 Hitler had named his master propagandist Joseph Goebbels to head the new Ministry for Popular Enlightenment and Propaganda (Reichsministerium für Volksaufklärung und Propaganda, or RMfVP). On April 10 the DSt applied to this ministry for a subsidy of RM 600 to defray the cost of printing placards for the action *Wider den undeutschen Geist*. [16] The results of this request are not recorded, but when on May 3 the students asked Goebbels to give the main speech to accompany the ceremonial burning of the books in Berlin a week later—the so-called *Feuerrede* (fire speech)—he agreed.[17] Contrary to many older accounts, this was the extent of Goebbels's involvement in the book burning. He did not initiate it, and, being an astute politician, he may indeed have foreseen that this auto-da-fé of books would do great damage to Germany's reputation abroad.

On May 10 Alfred Bäumler, the newly appointed professor of political pedagogy at the Friedrich-Wilhelm University of Berlin and a protégé of the veteran Nazi leader Alfred Rosenberg, gave his inaugural lecture. Most of the students filling the large auditorium wore SA uniforms. Behind Bäumler's lectern stood a detachment with swastika flags. He ended his lecture with the exhortation not to wait for book bans but to act proactively and burn un-German books. In the evening a torchlight parade of students and trucks loaded with some 20,000 books wended their way to the place before the Opera, where a large pyre of wood had been set up SA and SS bands played German folk songs and marches, and about 40,000 spectators watched the ceremony. The Deutschlandsender, the semiofficial radio station, broadcast the proceedings, which later were also shown in newsreels.[18]

Nine students, who had been allocated books according to nine differ-ent categories, committed the condemned titles to the fire accompanied by appropriate oratory. Thus speaker 1 exclaimed: "Against the class struggle and materialism, for a people's community and an idealistic lifestyle! I hand to the flames the writings of Marx and Kautsky." He was followed by speaker 2, who declared "Against decadence and moral decay, for discipline, moral-ity in family and state! I hand to the flames the writings of Heinrich Mann, Ernst Glaeser, and Erich Kästner." Other callers pronounced judgment against the falsification of German history (Emil Ludwig), against the destructive exaggeration of desires (Sigmund Freud), against un-German journalism of a Jewish-democratic type (Theodor Wolff and Georg Bernhard), against literal betrayal of the soldiers of the world war (Erich Maria Remarque), and against the impudence and presumptuousness that offended the eternal German mind (Kurt Tucholsky and Carl von Ossietzky). Next came the speech of Goebbels, in which he blessed the bonfire and praised the students for standing up for the revolutionary ideas of the new state. When you claim the right to throw

Book burning in Berlin on May 10, 1933. *Courtesy US Holocaust Memorial Museum/ National Archives and Records Administration, College Park, Md.*

literary filth into the flames, he told them, you also have the duty to prepare the way for a truly German spirit.[19]

Similar actions took place in other university towns. In Bonn the burning of books was celebrated by two faculty members—Hans Naumann, a professor of German philology, and Eugen Lüthgen, professor of art history. Naumann congratulated the students for having the courage to burn the books that, if undestroyed, might have misled and threatened them. They were not to worry that an innocent book might end up on the pyre. This was better than if one bad book failed to find its way into the flames.[20] Lüthgen commended the students for fighting the materialist-liberal worldview. "Light the fire and throw into the flames the representatives of the un-German mind."[21]

In Braunschweig the local newspaper announced on May 9 that on the following day the books of certain enumerated authors brought in from the various libraries of the city would be burned. On the evening of this announcement, the Nazi Students' League held a meeting at which a leader proclaimed that the German revolution was just beginning. It was not enough to send a few prominent defenders of the un-German ideology into concentration camps. It was imperative that the last remainders of this false worldview be eradicated. The time of unlimited individual freedom and of the false slogans of liberty, equality, and fraternity was over. The next day, the burning of the books was attended by a large number of special guests, including the chancellor and the senate of the Technical University. The total number of books burned was almost one thousand—117 books from the public library, 240 books from the student union library, and 640 books from the library of the Technical University.[22]

In Göttingen the burning of the books was preceded by a meeting organized by the DSt in the Auditorium Maximum (Great Hall) of the university, which drew a capacity crowd with many more turned away. The newly appointed chancellor of the university, Friedrich Neumann, a professor of German literature, opened the meeting, stressing the importance of what was about to happen. German society had succumbed to the corrosive influence of literati who finally were receiving their due. Writers like Remarque had been bought and read by thousands while those who knew better did not raise their warning voice. Today's action, he noted, would be the beginning of Germany's returning to its true spirit. The main address was delivered by Gerhard Fricke, director of the Institute of Literature and Theatre. All of us, he pronounced, had failed and thus had made the forthcoming act of destruction necessary. The un-German forces had been dominant. Jewish scribblers like Tucholsky had been allowed to ridicule everything that was sacrosanct and unimpeachable. The symbolic act of burning this trash, Fricke concluded, had to be followed by vigilance and building a better Germany: "We wait for the New and we believe in the future." A torch parade led by an SS band then proceeded to a square where the pyre had been erected and the actual burning of the offending books took place.[23] The pattern of professors and university administrators giving their blessing to the barbarity of burning books repeated itself just about everywhere.[24]

On May 16 the propaganda office of the DSt asked the local organizations to send in brief reports on the Action against the Un-German Mind in their university. The effort itself, the letter noted, was not yet finished. During the week of May 22 through 27, students were to visit bookstores and libraries to make sure that the purge of undesirable books had been fully implemented.[25] Meanwhile, book burnings continued, albeit on a reduced scale. For May 19 the HJ of the Koblenz-Trier district planned a burning of corrosive books in the high school libraries in the courtyards of the schools. The governor (Oberpräsident) of the Rhine province asked the principals of the high schools to make these books available and to excuse the students from classes on May 19 between noon and 1 P.M. so that they could attend the burning. In the territory of Baden, too, the HJ announced two weeks of "cultural struggle." In accordance with a list that would follow, the leaders of the HJ were to collect all "filth and trash literature." The general population and all libraries were asked to surrender these books. On June 17 parades would be held in every town, culminating in the ceremonial burning of the condemned books. The HJ, it appears, wanted to prove that its commitment to the fight for a new German culture was as strong as that of the DSt.[26]

Not to be left behind, Rosenberg's Kampfbund für deutsche Kultur, too, organized book burnings, based on its own list of offending books. In Offenbach am Main on May 22 these works included Einstein's *Theory of Relativity*. Some of these burnings took place as late as October 9, 1933.[27] In Dortmund an auto-da-fé of books was arranged by the National Socialist League of Teachers (Nationalsozialistischer Lehrerbund, or NSLB) for May 30, with the detailed preparations made by a former staff member of the city's public library. In Essen the initiative was taken by the National Socialist Shop Cell Organization (Nationalsozialistische Betriebszellenorganisation). At the burning on June 21, the new director of the Essen public libraries, a veteran Nazi party member since the 1920s, referred to the incineration of the "Marxist scribble" as "beautiful, symbolic, and educational."[28]

In 1933 there were ninety-three book burnings in seventy German cities.[29] The total number of books that were thus destroyed is not known, though it must have been substantial. Nazi functionaries praised the burning. The librarian Joachim Kirchner, a stalwart follower of Rosenberg who later was rewarded by being named director of the library of the Ludwig Maximilian University of Munich, defended the burning as a measure necessary to purge the libraries of "corrosive" books and *Asphaltliteratur* (a term used by the Nazis to denigrate literature that dealt with life in the big cities with undue emphasis on loneliness and alienation).[30] Werner Schlegel, an official in the Ministry of Propaganda, called the book burning "a symbol of the revolution, a symbol for the final conquest of intellectual decay, a sign of the victory of the new values. ... Where other nations, according to their respective temperaments, decapitate [England in the 17th century], shoot [Russia], or storm [France in 1789], the German people burn. Fire as a purifying power is an age-old symbol, inseparable from Germanic-German history."[31]

The Nazi functionary's invocation of fire as an old German symbol of cleansing probably referred to an event that had taken place more than one hundred years earlier. Back on October 18, 1817, on the fourth anniversary of the victory over Napoleon, some 500 German students had met at the Wartburg castle in Thuringia and had affirmed the demand for national unity. To the accompaniment of speeches denouncing "foreigners," "cosmopolitans," and "Jews," they had also burned books they considered an impediment to this goal, such as the Napoleonic Code and a history of Germany by the conservative German author August von Kotzebue (who was murdered as an alleged traitor less than two years later by a member of the first student fraternity, the Burschenschaft). It is symptomatic of the intellectual climate of 1933 that a Nazi functionary celebrated book burning as a valuable part of German history.

Not everyone was happy. Looking back at the events of 1933, Hans W. Hagen, a young instructor of German literature and an "adviser" for the book burning at the University of Greifswald, noted that "a large part of the people," accustomed to the kind of literature that had been incinerated, faced the burning of these books "helpless and surprised."[32] Stefan Zweig recalled that in 1933 and 1934, that is, until the formal proscription of his literary work in 1935, his books sold almost as well as before.[33] A few German newspapers dared to express cautious criticism. Rudolf Geck, an editor of the reputable *Frankfurter Zeitung*, wrote: "It is an error, young gentlemen, to believe that the spirit of poets and thinkers can be defeated by the burning of books."[34] But not a single university protested against this barbarity, and not a few professors gave it their blessing. The Börsenverein der deutschen Buchhändler, the trade association of German book dealers, on May 11 issued a statement in which they named twelve authors whose books had been burned—Lion Feuchtwanger, Ernst Glaeser, Arthur Holitsche, Alfred Kerr, Egon Erwin Kisch, Emil Ludwig, Heinrich Mann, Ernst Ottwalt, Theodor Plievier, Erich Maria Remarque, Kurt Tucholsky, and Arnold Zweig—who "are to be regarded as damaging Germany's reputation" and whose books are not to be sold.[35]

Abroad, on the other hand, the impact was immediate and forceful. On May 10, the day of the large book burnings, demonstrations of protest took place in dozens of American cities. Editorial opinion was nearly unanimous in condemning this attack on intellectual freedom. Well-known foreign writers like Helen Keller and Romain Rolland expressed their dismay and horror. In London, H. G. Wells proclaimed that book burnings had never yet destroyed a book. Together with other authors, Wells established the Library of Burned

Books, which opened in Paris in the spring of 1934. The library housed copies of all books burned or banned by the Nazis.[36]

Some authors whose works had been burned considered this persecution a badge of honor. The books of the writer Oskar Maria Graf, a socialist pacifist married to a Jew, had inadvertently had been left off the list of condemned books. To make it worse, his name had appeared on a "white list" of recommended authors. From self-chosen exile Graf protested against this preferential treatment. In an article headed "Burn me!," published in the *Volksstimme* of Saarbrücken on May 15, 1933, Graf wrote: "This dishonor I have not earned! On the basis of my entire life and literary work I have the right to demand that my books be consigned to the pure flame of the stake and not be put into the bloody hands and the corrupted brains of the brown murder squads." About a year later his wish was granted. His books were burned at the University of Munich and he was deprived of his German citizenship.[37] Sigmund Freud noted that there was progress after all. "During the Middle Ages they would have burned me, today they are satisfied to burn my books."[38]

In retrospect one can see that this attempt to remove Jewish influence from German intellectual life was just the beginning of far worse measures against the Jews of Europe that culminated in the Holocaust and some six million dead. The link between the burning of books and the killing of human beings had precedent. During the Middle Ages, the burning of the Talmud and other Hebrew books often preceded the extermination of Jewish "heretics."[39] In Heinrich Heine's play *Almansor*, set in Spain in the 1500s, when triumphant Christians reconquer Spain and forcibly convert Moors, a Moorish character tells of a Koran being burned in the marketplace. Another Moor then says, "That is just a prelude. Where they burn books, they will ultimately burn people as well."[40] Heine in 1821 was referring to the autos-da-fé of the Inquisition in order to draw attention to what might follow the book burning by the Burschenschaft. He could not know how prophetic his words would be.

In part because of the strongly negative reaction of the outside world, the book burning of 1933 was followed by control of German literature in more discreet ways. Indeed the word *censorship* was hardly ever used in public pronouncements that instead spoke of preventing the sale of "harmful and undesirable" books. It is characteristic of what has been called the "polycratic" nature of the Nazi regime that this control was exerted by a number of competing state and party authorities and, for a long time, in a distinctly unsystematic manner. Despite the proclaimed unity of state and party, these organizations strenuously fought with each other for turf, a struggle that sometimes enabled unwelcome authors to slip through the cracks and made it possible for them to continue to publish. Some became part of what after 1945 was called the "inner emigration." About 250 German writers—among them some of the best-known German authors such as Bertold Brecht,

Heinrich and Thomas Mann, Robert Musil, Joseph Roth, Kurt Tucholsky, Franz Werfel, Arnold and Stefan Zweig, and Carl Zuckmayer—spent the years of Nazi rule in exile.

The fame of the librarian Wolfgang Hermann, who as the author of the first list of proscribed books had made an important contribution to the book burning of 1933, was short-lived. Hermann, in sympathy with the left wing of the Nazi party led by Gregor Strasser, had applied for membership in the party in December 1931. In 1932 he had the audacity to write of Hitler's *Mein Kampf* that this autobiography represented the most important authorita-tive source for the movement. "However it contains no original and 'theo-retically' thought-out ideas." This criticism of the Führer appears to have been overlooked for a time. Hermann achieved his pinnacle of power when in March 1933 Goebbels appointed Hermann to be his "commissar" for the *Gleichschaltung* (compulsory reorganization) of the Association of German Librarians.[41] But two months later Hermann's impolitic remark was brought to public attention. A polemic against Hermann, "Eine Fehlbesetzung?," published in *Grossdeutscher Pressedienst* on May 19, 1933, cited Hermann's earlier critical appraisal of Hitler's mental acuity. The material for this article apparently had been leaked by the Kampfbund für deutsche Kultur. Rosenberg wanted to discredit Hermann and thereby prove that the critical evaluation of literature undertaken by his own organization was superior to that of the DSt. Hermann wrote to the Kampfbund on May 26, apologizing for his indiscreet remark and affirming his loyalty to Hitler, but his career in the Nazi state was over. In 1934 he was given the consolation post of director of the public library in Königsberg, though hostility against him continued. In order to clear his name, in late 1936 Hermann asked for a trial before the party court. Proceedings there dragged on for almost two years. On April 27, 1938, his trial was halted by Hitler's order. Conscripted into the army, Hermann was killed in action in 1945 amid the collapse of the Nazi regime he had helped to bring into power.[42]

PART 2

THE AGENCIES OF CONTROL

The Ministry of Public Enlightenment and Propaganda

German books had long been celebrated as the vanguard of German science and culture. But after Hitler's accession to power this was to change. For the Nazis, the realm of culture was an important weapon to shape and control the thinking of the state's subjects and to inculcate them with the National Socialist ideology. As Joseph Goebbels, the newly appointed minister for public enlightenment and propaganda, put it in October 1933, the Nazi revolution was a total revolution "that stops at nothing" and would impose its imprint on all aspects of the life of the mind.[1] In this endeavor, the printed word, and especially the book, were essential tools for educating the German people in the spirit of the new Germany.[2] The burning of "un-German" books during the year 1933 was followed by the development of a system of censorship designed to safeguard the dominance of National Socialist ideas in the realm of literature. A publication of the Ministry of Public Enlightenment and Propaganda issued in 1940 bore the propitious title "The Book a Sword of the Mind."[3] At the same time, the regime invested huge sums of money in the promotion of culture. The goal was to persuade the German population as well as the Nazis' foreign detractors that the exodus of so many artists, musicians, and writers had not created any significant deficit and that German civilization was flourishing as never before.[4]

Goebbels grew up in a Catholic family of moderate means and was educated at a Catholic school. He went on to receive a doctorate in German literature at Heidelberg University. Ian Kershaw calls him one of the most intelligent of the leading figures in the Nazi movement. His deformed right foot left him with an inferiority complex that "produced driving ambition and the need to demonstrate achievement through mental agility in a movement which derided both physical weakness and intellectuals. Not least it produced ideological fanaticism."[5] Goebbels was an early member of the Nazi party, where he became known for his oratorical gifts and his ability to stage theatrical effects such as parades and large gatherings to mobilize the masses. In 1926 Hitler made

Joseph Goebbels in Nuremberg, 1933. *Courtesy Library of Congress LC-USZ62-43629.*

Goebbels Gauleiter (leader of a party district) of Berlin, and in 1929 he became Reich Propaganda Leader of the Nazi party (NSDAP). Goebbels was elected to the Reichstag in 1928 and openly acknowledged that the Nazis would use the democratic process in order to destroy it: "We are entering the Reichstag, in order that we may arm ourselves with the weapons of democracy from its arsenal. We shall become Reichstag deputies in order that the Weimar ideology should itself help us to destroy it."[6] This highly influential and increasingly powerful individual at the time of Hitler's assumption of power in 1933 was but thirty-two years old.

As a leading Nazi veteran, Goebbels had his eyes on heading a ministry, but he had to wait until after the elections of March 5, 1933, to see his desire come to fruition. On March 13 a decree signed by President Hindenburg and Chancellor Hitler established a National Ministry for Public Enlightenment and Propaganda (Reichsministerium für Volksaufklärung und Propaganda, or RMfVP). The new ministry, led by Goebbels, was to carry out "enlightenment and propaganda among the population about the political goals of the government and the rebuilding of the German fatherland." The specific jurisdiction of the ministry, including the determination of which tasks were to be transferred to it from existing ministries, were to be made by Hitler.[7]

Obtaining the consent of the affected officials took some time. On June 30, finally, Hitler issued an ordinance that defined the powers of Goebbels' ministry. The Minister for Public Enlightenment and Propaganda was "responsible for all matters that involve the impact of the intellectual life on the nation, the strengthening of state, culture, and economy, the instruction of the public about these matters in the country and abroad, and the administration of all organizations serving these tasks." For all these enumerated powers Goebbels was to have "exclusive jurisdiction."[8] The vagueness and potentially far-reaching scope of this grant of authority probably was deliberate and was sure to sow conflict. Hitler liked to employ the tactical principle of "divide and rule" in order to prevent the creation of centers of power that could threaten his own superior position.[9] Not surprisingly, therefore, the ambiguous formulation of Goebbels' mandate led to prolonged struggles for turf between several state and party organizations, which were never conclusively resolved.

The Ministry of the Interior, previously in charge of most cultural matters, incurred the greatest loss. It had to give up the portfolios of press, radio, music, theater, movies, as well as the "struggle against trash and filth." It was the 1926 Law against Trash and Filth that now provided the Ministry of Propaganda with the legal authority to control literature. The Bureau of Literature and Publishing at first was part of the Department of Propaganda, but as of October 1, 1934, it was made into an independent Department VIII: Literature (Schrifttum). In monitoring the book trade, Department VIII operated with a relatively small staff, but it used a large number of volunteers all over the country who drew the department's attention to offending titles. It also could rely on denunciations, for "[O]fficial and private denunciations were a part of everyday life in the Third Reich."[10] Additional information came from the thirteen Ministry of Propaganda offices on the state level (Landesstellen).

Heinz Wismann, the head of the Bureau of Literature and Publishing, continued as head of the new Department VIII. Wismann, like Goebbels, had a doctorate in German literature from the University of Heidelberg. He was an ambitious man who had joined the Nazi party in 1932, and who also functioned as vice president of the National Chamber of Literature (Reichsschrifttumskammer, or RSK), another office in the Propaganda Ministry engaged in the control of literature. Under Wismann's chairmanship so-called Verbotskonferenzen (conferences on bans) took place, attended by representatives of other agencies such as the Gestapo and the Ministry of Education, but no minutes of these conferences have survived. In his public pronouncements Wismann sought to downplay the censorship functions of his department. Its main task, he stressed, was to promote "good literature," though he noted that when a book ban turned out to be necessary the state would not hesitate to "seize and eliminate" offending publications.[11]

Wismann continued as head of Department VIII until 1937, when he was forced to resign in light of a scandal. In 1935 Wismann had come into conflict with Wilhelm Baur, a Nazi party member since 1920 and the powerful manager of the official Nazi publishing house Franz Eher as well as head of the trade organization of the booksellers, the Börsenverein der deutschen Buchhändler. Baur claimed that Wismann had insulted him. While negotiating a formal apology he let it be known that until 1934 Wismann had been married to a half-Jewish woman and that he had failed to disclose this fact when he joined the Nazi party in 1932 or later when he was appointed to the Ministry of Propaganda. Moreover, Wismann's father-in-law worked for the "Jewish Springer publisher."[12] Goebbels at first tried to retain Wismann, but after the discovery of "scandalous" money matters, namely irregularities in the compensation of expenses, he had no choice but to remove the trusted administrator. Wismann resigned on October 31, 1937. His successor as head of Department VIII was Karl Heinz Hederich, the deputy chairman of a party organization also involved in the control of literature, the Parteiamtliche Prüfungskommission (PPK). Hederich had joined the NSDAP in 1922. In the early 1930s he played a leading role in the Nazi takeover of the Deutsche Studentenschaft. His degree was in engineering, but being a party member with the Blutorden (medal for participants in the Hitler-Ludendorff-Putsch of 1923) and a proven fighter for the Nazi cause, Hederich obviously was a person who deserved a responsible post in the new regime.[13]

Goebbels at first thought that this appointment would eliminate the feuding among the various authorities engaged in book censorship and cement the unity of party and state. Shortly after appointing Hederich, he admonished him to maintain good relations with Rosenberg.[14] However, Hederich turned out to be anything but a conciliator. In a speech given in Essen in October 1937, Hederich affirmed the leading role of the PPK in developing a National Socialist policy on literature.[15] This claim raised the ire of Rosenberg, who considered his organization the proper place for this ideological leadership role and asked for the dismissal of the aggressive upstart. Hederich also antagonized Max Amann, the head of the Eher publishing house as well as publisher of the *Völkischer Beobachter,* by making disparaging remarks about this leading party newspaper. Officials in the Ministry of Propaganda complained that Hederich was infiltrating the ministry with PPK personnel. Goebbels attempted to stop the campaign against Hederich. On February 4, 1938, he informed Rosenberg that he had given Hederich "a severe reprimand."[16] Matters came to a head when in August 1938 Hederich imposed a ban on two publications of the Eher house. As was to be expected, this act of interference infuriated Amann, who insisted that Hederich be removed. Once again Goebbels had to give in, and in October 1938 he dismissed Hederich, who now concentrated on his position as deputy head of the PPK.[17]

Although Goebbels had bad luck with some of his key appointees, he was able to score an important victory over his competitors when in 1935 he issued the first official list of forbidden books. In the eyes of the Nazis, authors had to conform to the National Socialist ideology, but at first there was no ready agreement how this goal was to be achieved. The confused situation until that time had attracted criticism from various quarters. On December 6, 1933, the Berlin author and publisher Wilhelm Jaspert, a member of the Nazi organization of writers and of Rosenberg's Kampfbund, had alerted the Ministry of Propaganda to the fact that since Hitler's assumption of power more than 1,000 publications had been forbidden by at least twenty-one different authorities. These book bans were being publicized in the gazettes of the criminal police and in other publications, and this unwelcome publicity about censorship had led to much criticism in the foreign press. The domestic book-buying public and publishers had become agitated and confused. Jaspert proposed that either the book bans stop entirely or that a central authority be created that could evaluate manuscripts or, as the only such office, forbid a book after it had appeared.[18]

A year later, in December 1934, as Wismann pointed out to Goebbels, nothing had changed. The banning of books was still in a sorry state. Various local and state police officials confiscated books, but no authority could issue a book ban for the entire country, and there existed no uniform standards and rules to guide such censorship. Certain books were forbidden in one state but not in others. Some of the confiscated works, Wismann noted, belonged to the staples of world literature and should never have been banned. On March 7, 1934, Goebbels had requested all state governments to issue book bans only in provisional form and to consult the RSK before making a final disposition. Unfortunately the states did not always comply with this request. The Bavarian police, for example, operated on the basis of a list that had never been submitted to the RSK. Wismann suggested that the control of books be put into the hands of the president of the RSK. The police should be largely excluded from this task or, preferably and if at all possible, be left out completely.[19]

Wismann followed up this letter with another communication to Goebbels on January 23, 1935, in which he proposed that the Ministry of Propaganda issue "a national list of forbidden and confiscated books." Police officials and various organizations had compiled lists that were completely inadequate and conflicted with each other. The resulting confusion had to be ended. Department VIII, Wismann told Goebbels, after hard work over several months and making use of the various existing lists, had compiled a comprehensive index of undesirable books. The list could not claim to be definitive, but it could of course be amended at regular intervals. The Minister of the Interior should be asked to confirm that this list be the only one considered official and binding; it should be put at the disposition of the police and other relevant authorities nationwide. Wismann noted that he had consulted widely, and that the Gestapo was "literally waiting for the appearance of this list." The Gestapo would then immediately move to purge the stocks of antiquarian books that remained the last uncleansed refuge for undesirable books.[20]

An ordinance issued by the president of the RSK on April 25, 1935, implemented Wismann's suggestions. The preamble announced that the Law against Trash and Filth of 1926 had been annulled on April 10. For about twelve months prior to this action the propaganda ministry had considered various proposals to revise the 1926 law in light of the new political situation, but it was finally decided that such a law was no longer necessary.[21] The idea that young people require a special protection, Goebbels explained in a letter to Hans Heinrich Lammers, the head of the office of the chancellor and Hitler's trusted legal adviser, presumed that adults had the right to purchase trash and filth as much as they desired. "That is a principle that the legislator in 1926 accepted as self-evident, but that is irreconcilable with the National Socialist ideology. The state today prevents the entire distribution of trash and filth literature as such." Moreover the RSK was able to handle this task far more efficiently than the inspection officers under the 1926 law.[22]

The ordinance of April 25, 1935, bore the title "Harmful and Undesirable Literature." It empowered the RSK to compile a list of books and other published materials that jeopardized National Socialist cultural policy. "The distribution of these books and materials through public libraries and the book trade of any kind (publishers, book stores, mail orders, traveling salesmen, lending libraries, etc.) is forbidden." In addition the RSK was to issue another list of books and other published materials that, while not included in the first list, were nevertheless unsuitable for young people. Such publications were not be shown in shop windows or other publicly accessible book displays, distributed by traveling salesmen, or given to young people below the age of eighteen. Individuals who violated any of these provisions justified the assumption that they lacked the necessary reliability and suitability. For minor violations they would be fined. For more severe transgressions they were to be excluded from membership in the RSK and denied the right to sell books.

Proposals for titles to be included in the lists were to be submitted to the RSK. Decisions on these proposals would be made by the president of the RSK with the concurrence of the Ministry of Propaganda. For inclusion in the second list, the consent of the minister for science, instruction, and adult education was also required. Purely scientific literature was not affected by this ordinance. However, such writings could be included in the list if the minister of education desired it or agreed to it.[23]

There remained the task of bringing the various police authorities into line, and here too Goebbels was making progress in consolidating his primary jurisdiction for banning books. In a communication to all state governments on May 11, 1935, Goebbels pointed out that with the issuance of the official list of harmful books, "large-scale book bans by the police will become dispensable." The police should be reminded that no permanent book bans are to be issued before the RSK had had the opportunity to evaluate the work in question. Disregard of this provision, issued on March 7, 1934, had led to "undesirable inconsistencies" that recalled the territorial balkanization of earlier times.[24] These instructions were repeated in a decree issued jointly by the Ministry of the Interior and the Ministry of Propaganda on September 27, 1935. The order affirmed that the ordinance of April 25 did not affect the ability of the police to confiscate and seize books. However they were to observe the circular letter of March 7, 1934, according to which book bans by the police, if they could not be postponed, were to be issued only in provisional form. The final decision had to wait until a copy of the objectionable book had been sent to the RSK and the latter had made its decision.[25] The Central Office for Combating Indecent Publications at the Berlin headquarters of the criminal police that handled outright pornography forbidden by Article 184 of the criminal code continued to function unimpeded, though in doubtful cases it now sought the advice of the RSK.[26]

And yet even this second ruling, designed to subordinate the seizure of undesirable books by the police to the supervision of the Ministry of Propaganda, did not end the practice of the police to act without such approval. On January 2, 1936, Hans Schmidt-Leonhardt, the head of the legal department of the Ministry of Propaganda, urged Goebbels to seek the help of Hitler in this matter. The Bavarian police, he wrote, was not the only police force that continued to issue improper book bans. Other police authorities too, intentionally or unintentionally, violated the applicable legal provisions. The Führer's decree of June 30, 1933, had granted the Ministry of Propaganda exclusive jurisdiction in various areas of public life, including literature, but the minister of the interior refused to honor this provision as it related to the police. The only way to solve this festering problem was to have Hitler issue a ruling to the effect that the exclusive jurisdiction of our ministry for its enumerated powers included the activities of the police.[27]

About two months later Goebbels finally obtained the desired clarification. On April 3, 1936, Lammers, the head of the office of the chancellor, reminded all ministers of the Führer's decree defining the tasks of the Ministry of Propaganda. "In order to resolve any doubts," Hitler now wanted it be known that the exclusive jurisdiction of the Ministry of Propaganda for the subject matters, enumerated in the decree of June 30, 1933, included "the actions of the police."[28] On May 7 Goebbels followed up with a letter to all state governments in which he reminded them of the authorization he had received with regard to the police. Books, he stressed, were to be confiscated and seized only if they appear on the list of undesirable books compiled by the RSK. In urgent cases Goebbels was to be contacted directly, but nothing was to be done until he personally had made his decision.[29] A day later Goebbels noted in his diary that "in order to prevent mischief the procedure regarding book bans [now] was centralized."[30] Even the notoriously independent-minded Bavarian police conceded in a memo of September 17, 1936, that the confiscation and seizure of books no longer involved the autonomous actions of the police but merely constituted legal assistance for the RSK, "which used the police for the enforcements of its bans."[31]

Even this unequivocal order apparently was not always obeyed. The Gestapo in particular continued its disregard of Goebbels' orders. On November 21, 1940, Hanns Johst, the president of the RSK, asked the *Börsenblatt* to publish an announcement on book bans reminding everyone that "only the RSK, or better the Ministry of Propaganda," was authorized to forbid books. The police was to act only "with the consent of the above authorities."[32] The same announcement was published in the December 1940 issue of the *Zeitschrift der Leihbücherei*.[33] But this too was not the end of problems. About two years later, on March 20, 1942, Wilhelm Ihde, the chief administrator of the RSK, had to confirm to Goebbels that in accordance with previous repeatedly issued ordinances he would include a book in the List of Harmful and Undesirable Books only "if the order for such a listing has been signed by the Minister personally."[34]

For a time Robert Ley's German Labor Front (DAF) appeared to become a significant competitor for Goebbels. The dissolution of the trade unions and the confiscation of their property had brought the DAF into the possession of a large number of publishers, bookstores, and printers. One of these publishing houses, Albert Langen in Munich, brought out a series of books, patterned on the highly successful Insel-Bücherei, a series of short books, which by 1939 consisted of 122 titles and had sold 2.5 million copies. By 1942 the DAF owned twenty publishers, seven printing house, two book clubs, and a paper factory. In November 1936 an official of the DAF proposed the creation of an office that would function as a censor for this mammoth empire, but, fortunately for Goebbels, nothing came of this plan. Even though he carried the title Reich Organization Leader (Reichsorganisationsleiter), the erratic and uncouth Ley was an inept administrator who lacked any kind of organizational talent. As a result Ley never became a serious rival to the adroit propaganda minister.[35]

Goebbels ran the propaganda ministry as a personal fiefdom in which subordinates had little say. During the war years he convened almost daily conferences to decide the next propaganda move, but these gatherings of heads of departments and other party dignitaries were conferences in name only. There was little or no discussion, and it was Goebbels alone who posed questions, answered them, and decided what was to be done.[36] The censorship of books was to be implemented the same way. Goebbels completed his personal domination of book bans by transferring all matters involving the supervision of the book market from the RSK to Department VIII in his ministry. The propaganda ministry appears to have discussed this scheme for the first time in November 1937.[37]

On January 12, 1938, Goebbels noted in his diary that he had been able to overcome the resistance of Wilhelm Baur, the vice president of the RSK in charge of handling memberships and exclusions in the RSK. "They all obey eventually if one acts forcefully."[38] The change was finally implemented with an ordinance that became effective on April 1, 1938.[39] To make sure that everyone got the message of who was really in charge of forbidding books, on December 16 he informed all heads of the different chambers in the Reich Chamber of Commerce: "I once again draw your attention to the fact that I have reserved *all* decisions regarding proscriptions *without exception* to myself personally."[40] Given Goebbels' other commitments and the large volume of books screened, we cannot be certain that he was able to make good on this claim of personal involvement, but it does indicate the importance that he assigned to this task.

4

The Reich Chamber of Literature

During the Weimar Republic, according to the Nazi view, the state had had a limited involvement with the cultural life of society. It concerned itself with schools, universities, and museums, but otherwise, in line with the prevailing individualism, the domain of culture was left unregulated. In the new Germany, it was now argued, all those active in creating culture had to become responsible to the nation. The state had to make sure that everyone absorbed the National Socialist ideology.[1] Just as it was self-evident that the state had the duty to protect the body of every person, so it was clear that the state also had to protect the soul of every citizen. "We have a law for combating venereal diseases," Goebbels declared, "and it is obvious that we also need a law for doing battle against spiritual and intellectual bacteria."[2] Or as Goebbels put it in a speech in 1936: "Just as a soldier cannot be allowed to hit and shoot when and how he pleases, just as a farmer cannot be permitted to sow and harvest what and where he wants it, so the writer does not have the right to put his individual life before the common good."[3] It was this view of the cultural life that had found expression in the establishment of the Ministry of Propaganda and that a little later led to the creation of the National Chamber of Literature (Reichsschrifttumskammer—RSK) within the National Chamber of Culture (Reichskulturkammer—RKK).

As Goebbels envisaged it, the new corporatist organizations were to embrace all those active in the cultural life and make them part of the state—to have them in their "Schaffen und Wirken dem Staat eingegliedert." In order to fulfill its tasks, the Ministry of Propaganda had to put under its tutelage the press, radio, literature, and the arts. These workers of the brow were to be linked in occupational associations and would not, as before, be organized as employers and employees. There was need to counter the attempt to resurrect trade union activities, a swipe at Robert Ley's German Labor Front (DAF), which threatened to intrude into the domain of the Ministry of Propaganda by establishing its own trade associations in the realm of culture.[4]

Die Reichsschrifttumskammer

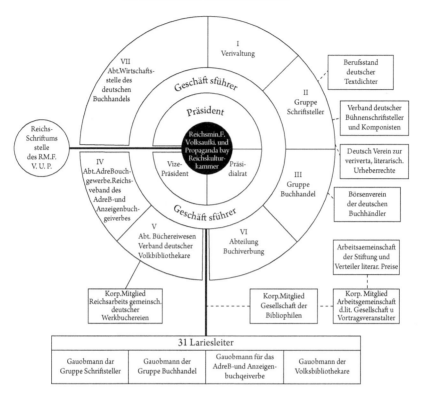

Organizational structure of the Reich Chamber of Literature. Hans Hinkel, *Handbuch der Reichskulturkammer. Berlin: Deutscher Verlag für Politik und Wissenschaft, 1937, p. 141.*

The law of September 22, 1933, establishing the RKK was signed by both Hitler and Goebbels. The Ministry of Propaganda was instructed to combine all those working in the various realms of culture into public corporations— chambers of literature, press, radio, theater, music, and fine arts. Goebbels, Reichspropagandaleiter as well as head of the Ministry of Propaganda, now also became president of the new RKK, an appointment that, it was said, would further cement "the unity of party and state."[5] Holding these three offices would enable Goebbels effectively to control all aspects of cultural life. He was empowered to issue the necessary regulations to implement this legislation.[6] In a more detailed explanation, published a few days later, the RKK was assigned to participate in the Ministry of Propaganda's mission of promoting and supervising cultural activities. "In the realm of culture it is the task of the state to combat harmful elements and to promote those that are valuable. . . . In this sense [only] cultural creativity remains personal and free."[7]

Regulations issued on November 1 obligated everyone active in creating or distributing cultural assets to be a member of the corporate body responsible for his particular occupation. Paragraph 10 provided: "Acceptance into a chamber can be denied or a member be expelled if, according to known facts, the person in question lacks the reliability and suitability for the exercise of his calling." Goebbels, as president of the RKK, appointed the presidents of individual chambers; he also could annul any decisions they made. The presidents of the chambers were authorized to impose fines up to RM 1,000 on those who practiced their profession without membership in their respective chamber or who violated orders of the chamber. The courts and the police were required to enforce these orders.[8]

The official explanation for creating this corporate structure had stressed that it "is not the intention of the National Socialist state to create a culture from above."[9] At the ceremonial opening of the RKK on October 15, 1933, Goebbels affirmed that the government did not intend to "constrict artistic and cultural development but promote it. The state will extend its protecting arm over it."[10] The chief administrator of the RKK claimed that the corporate bodies made possible an unprecedented degree of "self-administration" of the arts and literature.[11] In actual fact, just as in Fascist Italy and authoritarian Austria between 1934 and 1938, in Nazi Germany the occupationally organized chambers were a mere cloak for the control exercised by party bureaucrats. On one hand, it was specified, nobody could exercise his profession without membership in the appropriate chamber. At the same time, the chamber could refuse acceptance to or expel anyone who lacked "reliability and suitability."

Under the guise of establishing criteria of quality, the regime had found a way to establish a political test for admission to cultural creativity. These professions now required a license. In line with its mandate, the RKK and its various chambers also concerned themselves with the "economic and social problems" of their members. However, their most decisive impact undoubtedly resulted from their control functions. As one official celebrating the first five years of the RKK recalled in 1938, from the beginning of the RKK "its work was directed at eliminating from the country's cultural life all those elements that for reasons of blood or ideology did not live up to what the National Socialist German had a right to expect."[12]

On July 31, 1933, the Association for the Protection of Authors (Schutzverband deutscher Schriftsteller, or SDS), founded in 1909, became part of the Nazi-controlled National Association of German Authors (Reichsverband deutscher Schriftsteller, or RDS). Less than six months later the SDS dissolved itself, completing a process that became known as *Gleichschaltung* (compulsory reorganization).[13] Membership in the new organization, created at the behest of the Ministry of Propaganda, was open to all "authors of German blood who are politically unobjectionable." The intention was to develop the RDS into a

"compulsory organization." In the future "membership in the RDS will be decisive in deciding whether a literary work can be published."[14] After the creation
of the RSK the regime thus had two effective means of ensuring the political
loyalty of authors—both the RDS as well as the RSK screened their members
for political reliability. With only the politically trustworthy allowed to publish, and with the various other elements of the publication and distribution
of books such as publishers, editors, and book dealers made subject to similar tests, it was hardly necessary to provide for an elaborate system of book
censorship.

The decree establishing the RKK had named the RDS as a constituent section (Fachschaft) of the RSK, and soon other organizations were added—the
trade association of the German book trade (the Börsenverein der deutschen
Buchhändlers, in October 1934 replaced by the Bund Reichsdeutscher
Buchhändler—BRB), the association of German librarians, the society of
bibliophiles, and many others. Each of these organizations had been *gleichgeschaltet* (reorganized under Nazi control), and, according to the *Führerprinzip,*
was headed by a leader. Thus, for example, the Börsenverein with its close to
5,000 members was led by the twenty-nine-year-old party stalwart Wilhelm
Baur, assisted by a new slate of loyal directors. However, the fiction of self-
administering trade organizations within the RSK was soon abandoned. The
RDS dissolved itself on September 20, 1935, and the BRB on October 24,
1936. The members of these organizations now became individual members
of the RSK. Separate trade organizations, it was pointed out, were no longer
necessary. What National Socialists had always longed for was now accomplished: "the complete gathering of all those active in a certain occupation
under the supervision of party and state."[15] Wilhelm Baur now became head
of the Fachschaft Buchhandel in the RSK and was put in charge of deciding
membership applications of individual book dealers as well as the imposition
of fines and expulsions.[16]

The RSK encompassed all those involved with literature—from poets, writers of fiction, librarians, and publishers to those engaged in the commercial sale
of books. Membership in the RSK was a precondition for exercising these occupations. This requirement could be waived for individuals whose writings were
strictly scholarly or scientific as well as for those who were part-time authors
(defined as producing a maximum of twelve small publications—articles,
poems, etc. annually).[17] As of May 1941, the RSK included about 5,000
authors, 5,000 publishers, 7,000 book dealers, 10,300 employees of publishers
and the book trade, 1,500 librarians at public libraries, 3,200 traveling salesmen, etc. for a total of about 34,900 persons.[18] The mission of the RSK was "to
keep these occupations free of undesirable elements and to keep the book market clear of un-German wares."[19] By regulating the membership of the RSK,
another official acknowledged, "it becomes possible to prevent the creation of

inappropriate literature."[20] Before accepting a new member, the RSK inquired at the appropriate district party leadership (Gauleitung) and the Gestapo about the political reliability of the candidate. Book dealers had to assure themselves that none of the books they sold were in the newly created Index, the list of harmful and undesirable books. Publishers, before accepting a manuscript for publication, had the duty to make sure that the author was a member of the RSK. They also had to report any titles that they had rejected for political reasons.[21] Printers had to assure themselves that the publishers of books to be printed were RSK members.[22]

The rules about membership in the RSK were strict and unambiguous, but writers with personal connections to important personalities of the regime or able to hire good lawyers were at times able to get around them. On account of his pacifist and allegedly pornographic writings published before 1933, all the books of Erich Kästner, the author of such famous children's books as *Emil und die Detektive,* were banned. However, Goebbels appreciated Kästner's talent and issued him what was known as a *Sondergenehmigung* (special permission) to write film scripts under the pseudonym Berthold Bürger. The writings of Ernst Glaeser composed before 1933 were forbidden for similar reasons, causing the left-leaning author to emigrate in late 1933. However Glaeser gradually turned into a conservative, and in April 1939 he returned to Germany. He was also now given a *Sondergenehmigung* and was able to publish under the pseudonym Ernst Töpfer. And authors with non-Aryan kin were at times provided with these special permissions to write and publish.

The authors of scientific books were not required to be members of the RSK, and Paragraph 5 of the decree of April 25, 1935, establishing the RSK's list of harmful and undesirable books, had exempted "purely scientific literature" from inclusion in the Index unless the minister of education requested it. Hence these works could, in principle, be published and sold if they were judged to be scholarly in nature and thus presumably not accessible to the average reader. The Gestapo informed one bookstore in 1935 that while it regarded a book on "The Essence and History of the Human Race" as not suitable for propagating the National Socialist understanding of race, the book could continue to be sold because it constituted a scientific work.[23] After the author of a treatise on international law in 1938 had been convicted of treason, the publisher of the work asked the RSK whether the book could be continued to be sold. The RSK replied that the sale of the writings of traitors was not welcome but that the book could not be listed on the Index.[24] Even works written by authors who were "hostile to Germany or [were] Jews," as the RSK confirmed on January 2, 1940, were allowed to be imported for "scholars and scientific institutes."[25]

Not everyone agreed with this practice. In a letter of March 11, 1937, to Hitler's deputy Rudolf Hess, Philip Bouhler, the head of the Party Commission for the Protection of National Socialist Literature (PPK), insisted that scientific books dealing with politics should be subject to the scrutiny of the PPK because they touched on the most basic ideas of National Socialism.[26] The PPK publication *Nationalsozialistische Bibliographie*, as a declaration of purpose in 1938 reaffirmed, also evaluated "purely scientific literature."[27] Hess, on the other hand, warned against involving the party in scientific controversies of any kind. In a "confidential order" issued on November 11, 1937, he proclaimed that in speeches and publications the "mixing of political-ideological questions with technical scientific views in the future has to cease."[28] Hess's order probably was not meant as a reply to Bouhler, but it indicated Hess's reluctance to enmesh the party in science in ways that went beyond the existing controls over who could teach and do research.

Although "purely scientific literature" was supposed to be under the exclusive control of Rust's Ministry of Education, the Ministry of Propaganda used its own criteria of what kinds of books belonged to this category. As a result, many clearly scientific writings appeared in the official Index. This included the psychoanalytical works of Freud and Adler, which were said to exaggerate the instinctual life, especially the sex drive, and thus denied moral values. Also banned were the writings of Siegfried Marck, professor of sociology at the University of Breslau and the author of scholarly works in the fields of the history of philosophy and of political philosophy.[29] Marck, a member of the SPD, had emigrated to France in 1933, and this move apparently had made him a *"Schädling des Volkes"* (parasite of the people), whose writings had to be forbidden irrespective of their scholarly nature. In October 1939 the Ministry of Propaganda forbade a book on biological subjects. The work in question, the Ministry conceded, was "purely scientific," but it violated "essential elements of National Socialist biology and race."[30] The sweep of unacceptable scientific books also caught a treatise dealing with the "Pure Theory of Law" by Hans Kelsen.[31] Surely a more "purely scientific" work was hard to imagine.

According to established practice, the authors of schoolbooks were exempt from membership in the RSK because they were considered scholars of pedagogy, and therefore their writings, like those of other scientists, fell under the jurisdiction of the Ministry of Education. Until 1942 the RSK had exempted only scholars whose works were "purely scientific." As part of the simplification of administrative procedures necessitated by the shortage of manpower, the RSK announced in February 1942 that the distinction between "pure science" and "popular science" would no longer be made.[32] As Wilhelm Ihde informed Hanns Johst in November 1943, however, this new formulation had not ended disagreements as to which writings were or were not subject to control by the RSK. He therefore proposed that instead of making decisions on the basis of the *content* of a work, the RSK should let the Ministry of Education vet the writings of all *persons* subject to their jurisdiction.[33] We do not know whether Johst agreed to this change, which would have provided Rust with a welcome increase in authority. In the eyes of Martin Bormann, chief of staff of Hess and a rising power in the Nazi regime, on the other hand, Rust did not make adequate use of the powers that he already had. In October 1943 Bormann let it be known that he would urge Rust to be more vigilant about the writings of scientists who misused their scientific standing to promote the interests of the Catholic Church.[34]

At the time, publishers and authors could seek special treatment for a book on the grounds that it constituted a scientific work and therefore was entitled to protection. After the Gestapo in Berlin on May 11, 1935, had confiscated a book on Freemasonry on the grounds that it was of inferior quality and therefore "likely to cause confusion in the population," its publisher lodged a complaint with the Gestapa, the Gestapo's head office in Berlin. The book, *Hinter der Maske der Freimaurerei*, he argued, sought to help the state in its struggle against the Freemasons. "Moreover we claim the shield of science since the content of the book makes it a scientific work." Neither the Gestapo nor the RSK was impressed by these arguments. The book was put on the official Index and remained confiscated.[35]

Given the high stakes of violating the regulations of the RSK, it is not surprising that most publishers practiced self-censorship. The situation was especially acute for publishers such as Gustav Kiepenheuer, among whose authors were Brecht, Freud, Marx, Toller, Heinrich Mann, and Arnold Zweig. The list of books to be banned published by the Börsenverein in November 1933 had included sixty-four Kiepenheuer titles, about three-quarters of his total seasonal list.[36] Hence while Kiepenheuer occasionally demonstrated courage in bringing out titles that the Nazi media and the censors looked upon critically, the publisher for the most part thereafter limited himself to nonpolitical books that were unlikely to cause problems.[37] In February 1934 the Ullstein editor Otto Lachmann assured Rosenberg's Kampfbund that the publisher had carried out a "definitive purge of the inventory," and had destroyed all books that Rosenberg's watchdog organization had declared to be "objectionable." Not only he, but all of Ullstein's staff, Lachmann declared, were fully determined "to work in the spirit of today's state leadership."[38]

The same pattern of self-censorship was at work at the Insel publishing house. Insel had counted among its writers Johannes R. Becher, Leonhard Frank, Heinrich Heine, and Stefan Zweig. The publisher now withdrew any title that was likely to threaten the survival of the Insel-Verlag.[39] All together it lost twenty-nine titles of nineteen authors.[40] The Jewish publisher Schocken also practiced "voluntary self-control" and avoided politically sensitive topics such as the relationship of German Jews and the German people.[41]

The files of the RSK include numerous examples of publishers who were told "voluntarily" to withdraw certain offending books from circulation and to prevent any further distribution. In case they refused to do so, the books would be listed in the Index, "which would lead to the confiscation of all copies by the Gestapo."[42] In grievous cases the RSK could, and indeed did, expel publishers from the RSK, which amounted to the demise of the enterprise. Problems would arise at times if a book was cleared for publication, but the author was later expelled from the RSK. The publisher then incurred the expense of printing the book but got no income from it. Delays in vetting books that made it impossible to sell the item during the lucrative Christmas season also created difficulties for publishers.[43]

On November 15, 1933, Goebbels appointed the author Hans-Friedrich Blunck to be the first president of the RSK. Blunck was a prolific writer whose books dealt with Nordic and *völkische* themes, though he did not join the Nazi party until 1937. In his memoirs published after the war Blunck tried to pass himself off as unpolitical and opposed to Nazi principles, but this claim was without merit. On several occasions Blunck did try to moderate the impact of censorship, as when he argued that previous members of the Communist and Socialist parties should not automatically be barred from publishing. He also opposed the automatic exclusion of Jewish authors from the RSK. Blunck otherwise conducted himself as a loyal enforcer of Nazi policies.

In a talk to foreign journalists attending the Berlin book fair in late 1933, Blunck argued that the RKK provided a strong defense of personal liberty.[44] In an article published in March 1934 he insisted that there had to be limits to "the freedom of artistic creation," but on the whole, despite some missteps, the various groups in the RKK had more freedom than the liberal state had ever granted them.[45] The burning of books in 1933 had upset him, he asserted, but "such things happen in all revolutions."[46] On the occasion of Blunck's fiftieth birthday in 1938, both Hitler and Goebbels sent him congratulatory telegrams with appreciation of his service for the cause of German culture.[47] The same year, after Hitler had bestowed on Blunck the prestigious Goethe Medal for Art and Science, Blunck sent him a letter of thanks that began with "Mein Führer!," in which he expressed "the deep love that I have for you and your achievements." He promised to continue untiringly to educate the young Germany in the spirit of the time.[48] In August 1944 Blunck was one of only twenty-two writers considered important enough to the regime to merit exemption from compulsory labor service, part of the total mobilization ordered by Goebbels.[49]

On December 9, 1935, Blunck was relieved as president of the RSK. In a personal letter Goebbels thanked him for his successful efforts to build the RSK, gave him the title of president emeritus, and appointed him to handle the foreign relations of the RSK.[50] In his memoir, published in 1952, Blunck described this event as an "overthrow" in retaliation for one of his speeches that was seen as not sufficiently anti-Jewish,[51] but this claim too is probably false. Other leading Nazi functionaries never accepted Blunck as "one of theirs" and Blunck was left in office only because of his usefulness as a figure-head.[52] It appears that Blunck had finally become tired of his administrative job. Almost from the beginning Blunck had expressed misgivings about not having enough time for his creative work, and in the spring of 1935 he finally applied to Goebbels to be released from his onerous post. Goebbels agreed, on condition that Blunck take on the foreign relations of the RSK, and Blunck accepted this arrangement. As his successor he proposed his friend Hanns Johst, a playwright, member of Rosenberg's Kampfbund, and a high-ranking SS officer on the staff of Heinrich Himmler.

Johst carried out his duties as president of the RSK with the zeal of a Nazi ideologue. It was Johst who, in 1933, to celebrate Hitler's assumption of power, had published the play *Schlageter* about the proto-Nazi martyr Albert Leo Schlageter; this play contained the line, later often falsely attributed to Göring, "whenever I hear of culture, I release the safety-catch of my Browning" (Act 1, scene 1). At a speech given on October 25, 1936, at the opening of the "Week of the German Book" in Weimar, Johst insisted that "Germany is National Socialist, and only the National Socialist book deserves to be published." Writers who failed to embrace the National Socialist ideology were dispensable. These authors should know, however, Johst said, that the RSK would undertake "a radical, brutal, and decisive cleansing" of the foundation on which a mighty national socialist art would grow. At the same time, Johst liked to play the role of the "benevolent patriarch" who at times was willing to close an eye in order to help someone he liked. The best known of these cases of cronyism involved the poet Gottfried Benn.[53]

As his daughter put it in 2001, Johst was distinguished by a "blessed lazi-ness." With the help of an able secretary he conducted most of his business from his home in Oberallmannshausen, in Bavaria. The day-to-day affairs of the RSK were taken care of by trusted underlings, all of them proven Nazis and most of them fellow-members of the SS. Johst also liked his comfort. When he was asked to take on the presidency of the RSK, he requested that he be given a free countrywide first-class ticket on the German railroad "so that I can control my friends, the *gleichgeschalteten* book dealers, everywhere."[54] Johst enjoyed steady supply of domestic servants from Germany's concentra-tion camps. A Polish girl who failed to please him was replaced by a young Jehovah's Witness from Ravenbrück.[55] Johst adored Himmler, whom he addressed in his frequent correspondence as "Mein Reichsführer, lieber Heini Himmler" (My Reichsführer, dear Heini Himmler); the letters were signed "in old friendship and fidelity."[56] Johst kept Himmler informed of the work of the RSK. He also proved useful in allowing members of the SD, the intelligence arm of the SS, to infiltrate the RSK and thus gain a foothold in this important agency of control. One of these operatives, Herbert Menz, for a time became Johst's "right hand man."[57]

Johst spent much time at the various headquarters of Himmler,[58] and on January 1, 1943, Johst was promoted to Gruppenführer, the second-highest rank in the SS. There is no doubt that, as a high-ranking SS officer, Johst knew what was going on in the concentration camps, staffed by the SS, and he was willing to use that repressive system in order to discipline authors. After he had seen an especially offending manuscript he advised his chief administrator, Wilhelm Ihde, on August 4, 1938: "If the swine is insolent, I suggest that the SD allow this man to enjoy four weeks of concentration camp. We cannot tolerate such impudence."[59] In June 1936 the owner of a bookstore in Berlin who had sold banned books was sent to a concentration camp.[60]

The earliest list of forbidden books had been compiled by the Nazi librarian Wolfgang Hermann to guide the book burning of 1933. The first list of books issued specifically for censorship purposes, that is, to direct the removal of forbidden books from libraries or bookstores, was composed by Rosenberg's Kampfbund. The new *völkische* state, the introduction to the list stated, rejects "unhindered freedom of opinion" and claims the duty "to obliterate [*vernichten*] everything that runs counter to the basic instincts of the German people."[61] The list of banned titles included sixteen pages of works of fiction as well as seventy-seven pages of books on history, jurisprudence, pedagogy, psychology, and other humanistic disciplines. Librarians at the Deutsche Bücherei in Leipzig, since 1912 the central archive of German-language publications, which received copies of all new books and maintained a registry of all printed works (comparable to the Library of Congress in the United States), assisted in compiling these "blacklists."[62] On July 13, 1933, the Kampfbund sent the lists to the new Ministry of Propaganda with the request that Goebbels "enforce the removal of these books from the book trade and the libraries."[63] After some delay, in early November 1933 and with the consent of Wismann in the Ministry of Propaganda, the Börsenverein der deutschen Buchhändler began to send out letters to publishers ordering them not to sell certain named books that the Kampfbund had characterized as "undesirable for national and cultural reasons." The order, the letter pointed out, referred only to "sales to the *breite Masse*" (the general public); it did not prohibit the sale for proven "scientific or literary studies." The letters were sent out by registered mail and recipients were ordered to regard this notification as "strictly confidential."[64] Follow-up letters were sent out weekly with the names of additional undesirable books.[65] According to Wilhelm Jaspert, a member of the Kampfbund, by the end of February 1934 the total number of banned titles was between 1,500 and 2,000.[66]

Another list of forbidden books was compiled by the librarian Ernst Drahn, a newly minted Nazi (previously a Socialist and later a Communist), who had joined the NSDAP in May 1933.[67] In December 1933 Drahn published his list as a "guide for the *völkische* organization of the lending libraries." The thirteen-page-long list included books that were banned or forbidden by the Trash and Filth Law, as well as works "that on account of political or moral objections should be withheld from the German people, that is, should be removed from the lending libraries." Drahn singled out as especially objectionable "the products of the Jewish mentality [and] of the bourgeois-decadent subjectivism," composed by big-city literati, who falsified the true values of the people. Also to be removed were works that promoted the class struggle, Marxism, pacifism, anti-religious sentiments, a pan-European ideology, vulgar Darwinism, or the Freudian outlook. In the case of some authors of fiction, like the novelists Alfred Döblin and Heinrich Mann, Drahn urged the banning of all of their works. The list also included books by foreign authors, such as John Cleland's *Memoirs of Fanny Hill*, and the writings of Henri Barbusse.[68]

The title page of Drahn's Index noted that the list had been composed on orders of the Fachschaft (section) "Lending Libraries" in the RSK. Such sponsorship gave the list a quasi-official character. On the other hand, Drahn noted in his preface that, unlike the list issued by the Thuringian Ministry of Education on which he had relied extensively, his list "lacked official preparation." In other words, the list had an ambiguous status as being neither official nor simply a private initiative. Local police commanders and the Gestapo meanwhile were confiscating books they considered objectionable. All this created the kind of confused situation described in Wilhelm Jaspert's letter of December 6 to the Ministry of Progaganda in which he had spoken of more than a thousand publications being banned by twenty-one different authorities.[69]

During several months of 1934 Department VIII of the Ministry of Propaganda worked hard to create a more systematic system of book control, and the ordinance "Harmful and Undesirable Literature" of April 25, 1935, embodied the results of this effort. It empowered the RSK to compile a list of books and other published materials that jeopardized National Socialist cultural policy.[70] The text of the ordinance was published in the *Börsenblatt* of April 30; a news release by the Ministry of Propaganda noted that the new regulation would produce a more unified system of banning books and would prevent conflicting decisions by different police authorities.[71]

The "State Index of the Third Reich"[72] did not appear in print until the end of 1935. The work included objectionable books as of October 1935 and was 144 pages long. For 3,601 authors one or more of their works were banned, for 524 others all of their writings were forbidden. In the case of serial publications, most entries covered all volumes of the journal in question.[73] The compilation appears to have been put together by amateurs. It did not include the name of the publisher or the year of publication and had numerous errors and inconsistencies. The list was a selective compendium of earlier lists including those of Hermann Rosenberg's Kampfbund, the *Polunbi-Katalog* of obscene books, and the books banned under the Trash and Filth Law. It also relied upon the lists of books banned by the various police authorities, the Gestapo, and the SD.[74]

Three supplements totaling 30 pages appeared in 1936[75] and a completely revised edition in December 1938.[76] The second edition was 181 pages long and for the first time also included the names of twenty foreign publishers whose entire output was banned, as well as books published abroad that had been forbidden by the Reichsführer SS, Himmler. The new edition took into account the books that had been banned or removed between 1935 and 1938 and listed 4,175 individual titles and 565 authors all of whose writings were banned.[77]

Streng vertraulich!
Nur für den Dienstgebrauch!

Jahresliste 1939
des schädlichen und unerwünschten Schrifttums

Druck von Ernst Hedrich Nachf. in Leipzig

Title page of the List of Harmful and Undesirable Books for the year 1939.

I. Einzelschriften

+ **Aberrigoyen,** Iñaki de: Sieben Monate und sieben Tage in Franco-Spanien. — Luzern: Vita Nova Verl. 1939.
+ **Alexander,** Edgar: Deutsches Brevier. — Zürich: Europa Verl. (1938).

   Andermann, Friedrich: Irrtum und Wahrheit der Biologie. — Wien, Leipzig, Bern: Verl. f. Medizin 1937.
+ Die Rote **Armee** von heute. Reden auf dem 18. Parteitag der kommunistischen Partei. — Moskau: Verl. f. fremdsprach. Literatur 1939.
+ **Azpilikoeta,** de: Das baskische Problem im Urteil des Kardinals Goma und des Staatspräsidenten Aguirre. — Luzern: Vita Nova Verl. 1939.
+ **Bauer,** Hans: Warum Krieg? — Zürich, New York: Europa Verl. (1938).
+ **Behrend,** Hans: Die wahren Herren Deutschlands. — Paris: Éditions Prométhée (1939).
+ Hans **Beimler,** Symbol der Einheit. — (Barcelona [1937]: Sociedad general de publicaciones.)

   Bobrowskaja, Z. Selikson s. **Selikson**-Bobrowskaja.

   Gesegnete **Brautzeit** s. **Klehr,** Leopold [Verf.]
+ **Brown,** Sidney H.: Für das rote Kreuz in Aethiopien. — Zürich, New York: Europa Verl. 1939.
+ **Buehrer,** Jakob: Im roten Feld. Roman. — (Zürich: Büchergilde Gutenberg 1938.)
+ (**Burkhard,** William): Geheimnisse des Weltalls. — Zürich: William Burkhard 1939.

   Busch-Essen, Wilh[elm]: Was tun wir mit dem Alten Testament? — Wuppertal-Ba(rmen): Aussaat-Verl. [um 1939].

   Cahen, Fritz Max: sämtliche Schriften.

   Cartier, Raymond: Laisserons-nous démembrer la France? s. **Kerillis,** Henri de.
+ **Cohn,** Emil Bernhard: David Wolffsohn, Herzls Nachfolger. — Amsterdam: Querido Verl. 1939.
+ Nazi-Bastille **Dachau.** Schicksal u. Heldentum dt. Freiheitskämpfer. — Paris: Internat. Zentrum f. Recht u. Freiheit in Deutschland 1939.
+ **Diaz,** José: Die Lehren Spaniens für Europa und Amerika. — Paris: Éditions Prométhée (1939).
+ Das sozialistische **Dorf.** — Paris: Éditions Prométhée (1938).

   Duehring und Nietzsche. Hrsg. v. H[ans] Reinhardt. — Leipzig: Reisland 1931 = Gemeinverständl. Einführungsschriften zu Eugen Dührings reformatorischen Denkergebnissen. Folge 3.
+ **Dunstan,** Mary: Banners in Bavaria. — London, Toronto: Heinemann (1939).
+ **Dyck,** J., u. M. Schäfer: Deutsches Lesebuch für die dritte Klasse. — Engels: Dt. Staatsverl. 1939.

First page of the List of Harmful and Undesirable Books for the year 1939.

The work had been edited by professional librarians at the Deutsche Bücherei, today known as the Deutsche Nationalbibliothek. For the period between January 1939 and February 1944, the Deutsche Bücherei issued monthly updates.[78] Entries were divided into works marked "forbidden" and "secret." The former included works that had been put on the *Liste des schädlichen und unerwünschten Schrifttum,* books confiscated by the police without having been part of the *Liste,* and all new works by authors and publishers whose entire output had been forbidden. The appellation "*geheim*" was reserved for the confidential announcements of state and party authorities, militarily sensitive writings, and works so designated by the SD, Himmler's intelligence service.[79]

For the years 1939 to 1943 there also were yearly summaries of newly indexed books.[80] The Deutsche Bücherei reported a total of 5,485 banned titles for the years 1933 to 1945.[81]

All these lists were marked "Strictly Confidential! For Official Use Only!" Publishers were admonished not to tell customers that a certain book was "forbidden"; instead they were to say that the book "was no longer available."[82] It was similarly not allowed in advertising for books to include a notation that the book had been checked by the Ministry of Propaganda or the RSK before printing and had been approved for publication.[83] An official in the Ministry of Propaganda claimed that the lists had to be kept secret in order not to defame the publishers of books that had to be forbidden,[84] but such consideration would hardly have been typical of the hard-nosed Nazi bureaucracy. Another official argued that forbidden fruit had a special attraction and that the publication of a list of banned books could make the banned books more attractive.[85]

The real reasons for not making the lists public, it would appear, were, first, to prevent the kinds of attacks on the cultural policy of the Nazi state that had followed the burning of books in 1933 and to be able to deny the existence of blacklists.[86] Second, publishers and booksellers knew that certain books were forbidden, but they were kept in the dark which authors and books were actually banned. This had the effect of creating insecurity and encouraged self-censorship. Authors, publishers, and booksellers now lived under the shadow of those who had knowledge and power, the propaganda ministry and the Gestapo.[87] Repeatedly being caught publishing or selling books found by the regime to be objectionable could mean expulsion from the RSK and the loss of one's livelihood. By not making the official Index public, the regime thus had another powerful instrument for preventing undesirable literature.[88]

A publisher complained to the RSK in July 1936 that he could not have known that the writings of one Walter Bauer, printed before 1933, should not have been printed.[89] However, these kinds of complaints—filling a large file—were rejected by Nazi officials out of hand. In October 1936, during a search by the Gestapo of a bookstore in the town in Traben-Trarbach, a number of books were confiscated, and the owner was fined RM 25. "He should have known," he was told in a form letter, that the writings of Arnold Zweig, Stefan Zweig, and Jakob Wassermann "may no longer be sold in Germany today." Another bookstore in Bad Kreuznach received the same notification and fine in April 1937: "He should have known that the writings of Sigmund Freud may no longer be sold in Germany today."

In March 1937 a lending library in Neuwied requested that the fine imposed upon it be canceled because the owner had made every effort to find out what kinds of books could and could not be stocked. "There is great insecurity everywhere." In the case of some authors only some books had been banned at first and only later—something he had not been aware of—had the designation been changed to "all works." Moreover, one of the confiscated books had been not by the notorious and banned sex expert Magnus Hirschfeld but by a scribbler with the same name. This request too was turned down. A lending library in Koblenz, owned by a local consultant of the RSK, received a warning in April 1937. "The fact that the List of Harmful and Undesirable Books is not available to you and other book dealers is not a valid excuse. Especially in your case we had every reason to expect that you would know not to stock the books of Josef Delmont and Michael Zwick" (two indexed authors).[90]

In the face of numerous such complaints, Nazi officials went out of their way to justify the unavailability of the list of forbidden books and to intimidate those voicing dissatisfaction. An article published February 1937 in the semi-official monthly magazine *Der Buchhändler im Neuen Reich* argued that "it is completely superfluous to possess the List of Harmful and Undesirable Books." He whose heart is in the right place "will not be in danger of violating the laws of the National Socialist Germany." Those "who have even a modicum of decent convictions and just a bit of good will" will know what they have to do. "A healthy natural German sense speaks more reliably than any list."[91] In theory, book dealers and lending libraries could see the list of forbidden books in the RSK, the state offices of the RSK, and at the Gestapo. But after being told that only those with insufficient National Socialist conviction were in need of the list, few individuals could be expected to avail themselves of this right. The magazine also published notices of book dealers who had been warned and fined so that everyone would know what awaited wrongdoers.

A change in the policy of keeping the list of forbidden books secret came in 1940. Nazi officials apparently felt that in time of war, foreign public opinion was already strongly hostile and that negative publicity about the existence of blacklists now could be disregarded. Beginning with the February 1940 issue, the official gazette of the RSK section handling lending libraries, *Grossdeutsches Leihbüchereiblatt,* now regularly published the titles of books, arranged by publisher, that were "not to be lent or sold." The editors stated the hope "that this publication will help especially the work of the lending libraries."[92] The publication of lists of objectionable books continued until 1942. By that time, as an official in the Ministry of Propaganda indicated, the purge of the book market had been largely completed, and "book bans [had] become extremely rare."[93] Moreover the shortage of paper had become severe, and few new books were being published. Those that were had to undergo the most rigorous screening by the authority allocating paper. In other words, by 1942 there were few offending books to be announced any more.

The burning of books in 1933 had been followed by post-publication censorship; titles were banned *after* they had appeared in print. With the very large number of books being published every year—about 22,000 according to one estimate[94]—this mode of control necessarily missed some potentially offensive books, a problem that led to the growing resort to prior restraint; that is, publishers had to apply for permission to publish a certain book and offending titles were banned *before* they were printed. Some categories of books apparently were considered so important that the censors did not want to take any chances of an objectionable title slipping through the net.

Some of this pre-publication control occurred as result of self-censorship on the part of publishers, who were concerned about the financial loss suffered when a book that had been edited and printed was ordered suppressed and pulped. Editors and publishers therefore frequently consulted the RSK or the Gestapo in advance about whether a planned book would pass muster. For example, a publisher in Westfalen on January 1, 1937, sent a letter to the Gestapo in Berlin inquiring whether he could publish a series of radio lectures entitled "This Is the Soviet Paradise." Since these lectures had already been approved for radio broadcast, the publisher noted, he would assume that publication in book form would not be a problem. Still, "to be on the safe side I nevertheless want to submit this inquiry." The Gestapo as a rule did not make this kind of assessment, and in this case too they suggested that the publisher submit the manuscript to the Ministry of Propaganda. After looking at the text, that office informed the publisher that the planned work suffered from faults of style and treated certain matters unduly superficially. Hence while the work was essentially "good and worthy of recommendation," permission to print could not be granted in the present form. The publisher was advised "to revise the manuscript thoroughly."[95]

In the case of a book dealing with home remedies, which the Ministry of Health had criticized, the RSK ordered changes before a new edition could be published.[96] On May 20, 1937, a publisher sent a manuscript entitled *Völkerpsychologie* (The Psychology of Nations) to the RSK for "evaluation." The reader found the work to be "on a high scientific level" and recommended publication.[97] Another such case occurred when in September 1937 the Catholic publisher Joseph Bercker sought permission to sell the rights to a pocket encyclopedia by a deceased Jesuit author to foreign publishers. Such agreements, together with accords for the publication of foreign books in Germany, fell under *Anzeigepflicht* (obligation of prior submission), that is, they required the permission of the Ministry of Propaganda.[98] The book in question had been published first in 1919 and had been reissued in 1922 and 1933. Given the tensions between the Nazi regime and the Catholic church, the publisher apparently did not think that the authorities would allow a new edition for a German audience. When the attempt to sell the rights abroad failed, he tried to get the book republished in Germany after all. In a letter of February 2, 1938, to the RSK, Bercker acknowledged that "it goes without saying that the work will have to be brought up to date and that its content will have to satisfy the demands of the state." Despite Bercker's willingness to submit to the heavy hand of the censor, the Ministry of Propaganda informed him that a reissue of the book was forbidden and that the text of any revised edition required the permission of the PPK, a party organization also engaged in the business of censorship.[99] The RSK could be sure that the PPK would not approve such a book.

Another way in which the Ministry of Propaganda sought to avoid taking a position that was inconvenient for one reason or another was to claim "that the RSK in principle does not pass judgment upon the future plans of publishers." This is the reply the RSK sent, for example, to a publisher who in December 1937 inquired about bringing out a three-volume reprint of the collected works of Georg Christoph Lichtenberg (1742–1799), a mathematician, the first German professor of experimental physics, and also considered the father of the German aphorism. "Our letter," the publisher had written, "has the purpose of ascertaining whether [our proposal] can be sure of receiving a sympathetic consideration."[100] The refusal of the RSK to respond to this inquiry with the statement that the RSK does not "pass judgment upon the future plans of publishers" was of course a deliberate falsehood. The Ministry of Propaganda and its mouthpiece the RSK regularly "passed judgment" by imposing *Vorlagepflicht* (obligation to obtain permission to publish) upon some publishers as well as upon certain categories of books. Both *Anzeigepflicht* and *Vorlagepflicht* of course were simply different names for what in German is called *Vorzensur*, and which in English-speaking countries is known as prior restraint.

The first instance of such prior restraint appears to have taken place as early as October 1934 when the RSK asked four publishers to submit their publication plans for vetting. The issues that prompted the RSK to subject these four publishing houses to pre-publication scrutiny are not known. On March 21, 1935, the RSK informed the Ministry of Propaganda that it had decided to put seventeen additional publishers under the same restriction. These publishing houses had been asked to hand in a list of the titles they had published during the preceding half year. After checking this list it would "perhaps" be decided to impose *Vorlagepflicht*.[101] The record does not show whether the "perhaps" indeed led to prior restraint for these publishers.

On July 24, 1935, the RSK announced that the publishers of popular literature "could be asked" to submit their books to a new Advisory Office for Popular Fiction (Beratungsstelle für Unterhaltungsliteratur).[102] Using more blunt language, RSK president Wismann on April 30 explained to Goebbels that this office, operating under the supervision of the RSK, would make the "manufacturers of dirt and trash" reveal their products "*before* publishing them. In this way we can now catch everything that [previously] would have had to be eliminated after publication."[103] Contemporaries were not privy to this communication, but by 1935 everyone probably knew that in the Third Reich the word "Advisory Office" was a euphemism for censorship office, and that if something could be done, it usually was done.

On August 12, 1935, the publishing house Wilhelm Goldmann, which specialized in detective stories, was instructed from here on to inform the Advisory Office of all new books in that genre. When Goldmann applied for permission to publish German editions of English and American crime novel authors, the applications were rejected. In order to survive the publisher abandoned the field of popular literature and began to issue books in history, economics, and art.[104] The publisher Otto Weber in 1937 had come under attack by the *Schwarze Korps*, the weekly newspaper of the SS. Among other misdeeds, one of his books had included the well-known song "Ich weiss nicht was soll es bedeuten," based on an 1824 poem by the "Jew Heinrich Heine." On November 23 Weber was informed that henceforth he had to submit his entire publication program for "assessment" by the Beratungsstelle.[105]

Still another publisher, Erich Zander, who also had been put under *Vorlagepflicht,* on September 24, 1937, requested that the RSK release him from this requirement. He promised that his books would display "unmistakably clear ideological and literary quality." In their reply the RSK's Wilhelm Ihde told Zander that it had been decided to free him from *Vorlagepflicht,* but added: "I suggest that you submit future publication plans for novels voluntarily." This was not the end of his troubles. On September 20, 1938, he was reprimanded for having published a contribution by a non-Aryan writer, and in August 1940 two of his books were entered on the official Index.[106]

In addition to putting the output of selected publishers under prior restraint, the RSK also subjected certain kinds of book topics to pre-publication scrutiny. On January 1937 Hans Hinkel, in charge of the cultural activities of non-Aryans in the Ministry of Propaganda, ordered that new books on the history of literature were *anmeldepflichtig.* Literati of the Weimar Republic (called by the Nazis the *Systemzeit,* or the time of the system) and Jewish authors, he noted, had repeatedly been described in a manner more suitable for a liberal viewpoint than for a National Socialist cultural philosophy. Hence all publishers from here on had to inform Hinkel about planned new books as well as about new editions of older works of literary history "and await my assessment before starting the printing process."[107] On March 31, 1938, Hinkel imposed *Vorlagepflicht* on any publication dealing with the "Jewish question," including by Aryan authors.

As the RSK announced on August 9, 1935, books that contained pictures of German industrial firms required prior approval.[108] Effective April 1936, books on colonial issues were made subject to evaluation by the NSDAP Office for Colonial Policy (Kolonialpolitisches Amt der NSDAP).[109] On January 29, 1937, the Ministry of Propaganda let it be known that in order to prevent the "appearance of works that contradict the cultural policy of the National Socialist state," all books dealing with the dance—classical, social, and folk dancing—required approval.[110] In early 1937, Hermann Göring, Hitler's Plenipotentiary for the

Four-Year Plan, complained that many publications dealing with the plan were superficial or outright bad. Hence on March 25, 1937, the RSK announced that from here on all publications on the Four-Year Plan were subject to vetting by Bouhler's PPK. Also in 1937 the RSK made it known that books containing aerial photography needed the approval of the Ministry of Aviation.[111] In order not to provide material for Polish propaganda against Danzig, as of July 1, 1937, all articles on Danzig written for dictionaries and other reference works had to be submitted for clearance to the Ministry of Propaganda.[112] On February 4, 1938, Goebbels banned the publication of new encyclopaedias because the market was satiated and many of them "left much to be desired from a political point of view." New editions had to be submitted to Department VIII of the Ministry of Propaganda and to Bouhler's PPK. Approval would be granted only if these works were found to be "impeccable both in terms of substantive quality and political reliability."[113] And on June 10, 1938, the RSK announced that the publication of travel guides and city guides required permission.[114] The spread of prior restraint, it is evident, was far-reaching.

Himmler too was instrumental in initiating pre-publication oversight for a subject dear to him. In 1935 the Reichsführer SS had created the research institute Ahnenerbe (Ancestral Heritage) for the purpose of studying the spirit and heritage of the Nordic Indo-Germanic race. The institute aimed to legitimate SS ideological assumptions through what was billed as scientific study. Himmler had other esoteric interests, including the so-called *Welteislehre* (Glacian Cosmogony), the brainchild of the Austrian engineer Hanns Hörbiger. According to this idea, which according to Hörbiger had come to him in a vision, ice was the basic cosmic substance, and the struggle between ice and fire had created the universe. One of Hörbiger's enthusiastic followers was SS Hauptsturmführer Edmund Kiss, a member of Himmler's staff, and in 1936 Himmler agreed to the establishment of a research program for meteorology in the institute Ahnenerbe. The aim of this research was to prove the correctness of the *Welteislehre* by developing long-range weather forecasts. In an undated letter to the RSK, probably from the year 1937, the director of Ahnenerbe "confidentially" drew attention to the fact that besides Himmler, the Führer himself and other leading personalities in the Party such as Göring and von Schirach had a strong interest in the *Welteislehre*. Hence "it is imperative that all publications dealing with the *Welteislehre* be subjected to strict control in order to prevent damage and difficulties for a program of research supported by the leadership of party and state." He suggested that SS Untersturmführer Hans Robert Scultetus, the head of the bureau for meteorology in Ahnenerbe, become a reader for the RSK, and on September 13, 1937, the RSK confirmed that Scultetus from here on would be tasked with vetting all manuscripts and books on the *Welteislehre*.[115]

Individual authors could also be made subject to prior restraint. Writers who had received a special permission were required to submit their manuscripts to the RSK for vetting. The Nazi race theorist Hermann Gauch, noted for his fanatical dedication to the Nordic theory, had embarrassed the party leadership by claiming that the Italians were "half ape." On November 11, 1935, a confidential memo conveyed the information that "Dr. Hermann Gauch's writings on population policy and race are subject to prior censorship by the NSDAP Office of Racial Policy."[116] On March 25, 1937, that office sent out a reminder that all publications on the subject of race before printing had to be submitted to it "for vetting and evaluation."[117]

Artur Dinter was another well-known Nazi who later fell into disgrace. His anti-Semitic book *Die Sünde wider das Blut* (The Sin against Blood) by 1934 had sold more than 260,000 copies, but in 1928 Dinter had had the temerity to criticize Hitler over the issue of Christianity. He was expelled from the Nazi party, and in 1937 publishers were warned not to accept a manuscript on race Dinter was supposed to have completed.[118] During these years, the RSK's gazette repeatedly included announcements that the publication of books by certain named authors was "undesirable."[119] The RSK's net of prior restraint had a wide reach that included publishers, forbidden topics, and individual authors.

From the very beginning, the RSK had played a subordinate role in the control of the book market. It maintained the List of Harmful and Undesirable Books, but final decisions about individual books had always been made by Department VIII of the Ministry of Propaganda and by Goebbels personally. The files show several cases where the RSK on its own put a book considered totally unacceptable on the Index only to be overruled and having to ask the Gestapo to release the book. On February 20, 1937, the Gestapa informed local Gestapo offices that the RSK had put the *Das Buch vom persönlichen Leben* by the eccentric philosopher Hermann Alexander Graf von Keyserling on the Index and asked them to confiscate the book. Keyserling was the founder of the "School of Wisdom" in Darmstadt, which had brought together outstanding personalities like Thomas Mann and other leading literary figures. Keyserling himself was considered one of the best known intellectuals of the Weimar period, and the Ministry of Propaganda apparently was concerned about the reaction of the outside world if a book by Keyserling were banned. Moreover, Kayserling was married to Bismarck's granddaughter and was close to important government officials, such as Field Marshal Werner von Blomberg, until 1938 Reich Minister of Defense and supreme commander of the Wehrmacht. On February 24 the Gestapa learned that the Ministry of Propaganda had vetoed the listing of Keyserling's book, and on March 13 it was formally informed by the RSK that the book had been removed from the Index and should be allowed to circulate freely.[120]

At times the Ministry of Propaganda's Department VIII even acted without bothering to enter a book in the List of Harmful and Undesirable Books and advised the Gestapo directly to confiscate an offending work. From 1936 on, the RSK repeatedly had to remind the ministry that its own regulations forbade the seizure of books that were not on the list of forbidden books.[121] One such letter, dated July 5, 1943, pointed out that "even if the Minister [Goebbels] has reserved to himself decisions regarding book bans," such bans "must proceed legally" by way of listing the offending books in the Index.[122] At a time when the Nazi state had all but abandoned the rule of law, an agency of that state in 1943 insisted on "correct legal procedures," a rather amusing spectacle.

On April 1, 1938, the RSK's *de facto* status regarding book bans was made official, that is, it was now formally relieved of any decision making for forbidding books.[123] The RSK, it was announced, "functions as a subordinate agency, as a practical arm of Department VIII [Schrifttum]." It also takes over in "situations where the Ministry [of Propaganda] wishes to keep its dealing with literature out of the public eye."[124] Hereafter the RSK still handled correspondence concerning books, but it was understood that the RSK spoke in the name of the Ministry of Propaganda. In its independent work the RSK from here on limited itself for the most part to regulating and attending the economic interests of the literary professions (*berufsständische Betreuung*), continuing a function it had assumed from the beginning. For example, the RSK had developed old-age, sickness, and disability insurance for writers, and it helped elderly and needy authors.[125] It also originated and enforced a standard contract for authors. A measure that will appeal to authors today was a requirement that publishers provide authors with a temporary or final decision about submitted manuscripts within four weeks. They were allowed to delay a manuscript for a longer time only if the author had given his consent.[126] Even more than before, the RSK now became a kind of clearinghouse for disputes between authors and publishers, with the control of literature handled by other authorities and organizations.[127]

5

The Gestapo and SD

Between 1933 and 1935 various police forces engaged in the control of objectionable literature. Local police commanders continued to enforce Article 184 of the Criminal Code, which forbade the publication of obscene writings. Probably encouraged by the Nazis' well-known hostility to trash and filth, between January 30, 1933, and the end of 1933, the courts issued ninety-eight book bans (as against four in 1932).[1] A decree issued by the Prussian Minister of the Interior on May 15, 1933, broadened the jurisdiction of the German Central Office for the Control of Obscene Publications by allowing it to confiscate not only outright pornography but also publications and pictures that offended decency. Moreover the office was allowed to act on its own, without obtaining the consent of a court of law.[2] By the end of 1936 the office was able to report that as a result of enhanced enforcement the commercial trade in obscene materials had been almost completely eliminated.[3]

Books considered politically offensive were seized by the Gestapo. Until June 1936 the state branches of the Gestapo operated under the supervision of the respective ministers of the interior, though their ability to act in unison was assured by the fact that all of them were led by Heinrich Himmler, the head of the SS. (In Prussia Himmler was deputy head of the Prussian Political Police, which operated under the direct control of the Prussian prime minister, Hermann Göring.) The headquarters of the organization was the Geheime Staatspolizeiamt or Gestapa in Berlin. Himmler's leadership was recognized officially when on June 17, 1936, Hitler appointed him to the newly created position of Reichsführer SS und Chef der Deutschen Polizei (National Leader of the SS and Head of the German police). Even though Himmler was formally subordinated to Minister of the Interior Frick, subsequently issued ordinances made it clear that Himmler was authorized to act on his own with regard to all matters involving the police. This appointment has been called "the most important step in changing the police into an instrument of the Führer."[4] Combining the SS with the police gave a party organization control over a key state function and provided the SS with a powerful tool for persecuting those deemed to be enemies of the Nazi state. When Himmler assumed control of Germany's entire apparatus of repression, he was thirty-six years old; his deputy, Reinhard Heydrich, head of the Gestapa and chief of the Security Police (Gestapo and criminal police), was thirty-two.

In carrying out its control of the book market, the Gestapo relied upon two emergency decrees issued by President Hindenburg on the basis of Article 48 of the Weimar Constitution. Paragraph 7 of the decree of February 4, 1933, "for the protection of the German people" provided: "Publications the content of which threatens public security and order can be confiscated and seized by the police."[5] This sweeping provision gave the police an almost unlimited power, but there was more to come. One day after the fire in the Reichstag building, on February 28, Hindenburg promulgated another decree "for the protection of people and state," Paragraph 1 of which empowered the minister of the interior, as necessary, to limit the constitutional protections of personal liberty, freedom of opinion, and freedom of the press as well as to order searches of homes and to confiscate property. This second decree also contained heavy penalties (up to three years' imprisonment) for those who authored or distributed publications that encouraged violent acts against the government or in other ways committed the crime of treason. The emergency decree of February 28 ostensibly had been issued for the "defense against communist acts of violence that threatened the state."[6] Its use for confiscating books by Heinrich Mann and Stefan Zweig, needless to say, represented quite a stretch. Book bans had to be issued by the minister of the interior, but after Himmler became head of the German police in 1936, the right to seize books became part of the powers of the Gestapo.[7]

Searches by the Gestapo of the premises of publishers, bookstores, and lending libraries began almost immediately after the promulgation of Hindenburg's emergency decrees. On May 20, 1933, the Berlin office of the Gestapo informed the press that it had confiscated 10,000 Zentner (750 tons) of books and journals. The *Völkischer Beobachter* reported a day later that the searches had not always gone smoothly. The owners of many bookstores had hidden books in cellars, gardens, and private apartments, but the Gestapo found most of those hideouts.[8] The same Gestapo office notified their superiors in the Gestapa that on November 20 its officials had confiscated 3,411 copies of Erich Maria Remarque's book *Im Westen nichts Neues* from the Ullstein publishing house. On December 4 the Gestapa gave the green light for the destruction of the Remarque books.[9] Similar raids took place in other German cities. In Königsberg, for example, a search of sixty-three bookstores led to the confiscation of about 3,000 books.[10]

The total number of confiscated books is not known. We do have figures for Prussia, where between February 1, 1933, and October 1, 1935 (the effective date of the first RSK list of forbidden books), a total of 660 books were seized by the Gestapo on the basis of Paragraph 7 of the emergency decree of February 4, 1933.[11] In Frankfurt am Main about a thousand books were confiscated between 1933 and 1936.[12] The RSK admonished the Gestapo in 1935 that searches for forbidden books were not to damage the legitimate business of bookstores, though this consideration was not to be extended to stores that were known to stock and sell politically undesirable works.[13] The confiscation of books by the Gestapo suffered from clear direction because of the absence of a reliable list of objectionable books. To some extent, this changed with the appearance of the first official list of the RSK at the end of 1935. As Wismann, the head of Department VIII in the Ministry of Propaganda, had already informed Goebbels on January 23, 1935, the Gestapo was "literally waiting for the appearance of this list."[14]

Some of the searches that now got under way were carried out at the specific suggestion of the RSK. On March 14, 1936, the RSK informed the Gestapa that "weighty suspicions had been aroused about the publisher J. Singer in Berlin" and that a search of the premises therefore was indicated. Four days later the Gestapo Berlin was able to report that it had seized 913 forbidden books.[15] Between October 1936 and June 1937, the Gestapo, with the concurrence of the RSK, raided about 5,000 suspect publishers, bookstores, antiquarian bookshops, and a few lending libraries, and confiscated about 300,000 forbidden books. The Gestapo report on the campaign noted that more than three years after the assumption of power by the National Socialists the number of offending books was "surprisingly high." A large number of book dealers had been guided by economic considerations only and therefore had refrained from purging their stock. The report included a list of twenty-one bookstores where an especially large number of objectionable books had been found or where the conduct of the booksellers during the search had been particularly reprehensible. At a bookstore in Nürnberg almost 4,000 forbidden books had been found, among them pamphlets by Gustav Landauer, Karl Marx, and Lenin. The owner of a bookstore in Görlitz during the search had tried to hide seven banned books. The report concluded with the observation that on the whole the campaign had been successful and that from now it would be sufficient to follow up with occasional re-examinations.[16] As it turned out, this expectation was far too optimistic. In the Düsseldorf district the Gestapo conducted such re-examinations between September 8 and November 14, 1936, and found 37,040 books that had to be confiscated.[17]

An order for Prussia issued on April 25, 1934, provided that officials of the Ministry of Propaganda were to examine the confiscated books and offer them to the Prussian State Library in Berlin. Books not kept by the State Library were to be made available to other scholarly libraries in Berlin such as the library of the University of Berlin.[18] But most of the seized books were pulped.[19] Germany had a chronic shortage of paper and the large number of confiscated and subsequently pulped books undoubtedly helped alleviate the scarcity. Publishers at times would submit confirmations that this destruction had indeed taken place. One Berlin dealer in scrap paper sent a publisher an "affidavit of pulping" to certify that he had pulped 1,148 printed books and the proofs of 3,360 books.[20] The total value of the seized books must have been enormous. The publisher Rowohlt estimated his loss between 1933 and 1936 as one half million Marks.[21] It is estimated that in annexed Austria, where local and German Nazis engaged in a far more rapacious seizure of books, well over two million books were confiscated or destroyed.[22]

To minimize the damage caused by these seizures, publishers at times were allowed to sell the objectionable books abroad. One book for young people, first published in 1911 and having reached 244,000 printed copies, was indexed in 1937 because, while not hostile to the state, it was "outdated for the education of our youth today." However, since the publisher had successfully shown that he would suffer severe economic damage, he was given six months to sell any remaining copies of the book abroad.[23] Such sales, as the Ministry of Propaganda explained to the RSK in December 1936, also helped bring in much-needed foreign currency.[24] On the other hand, in the case of about 41,000 copies of the works of Emil Ludwig, the RSK refused this permission on the grounds that "this kind of literature may not be sold *in any manner*, hence also not abroad."[25] Ideology at times trumped economic interests.

From 1936 on, the Gestapo usually seized books in accordance with the official list of objectionable books, the state Index. But in some instances, the Gestapo confiscated books that turned out to be completely harmless or were classics of German literature. On November 14, 1936, the Gestapo Frankfurt am Main suggested that the historical novel *Oberst von Steuben, des grossen Königs Adjutant* by Albert Emil Brachvogel be banned because it included favorable comments by King Frederick the Great on the Freemasons. The Nazis were hostile to the Freemasons because they stood for tolerance and equality, and because the would-be totalitarian state was opposed to any organization that challenged its hold over public opinion. In a response the RSK pointed out that the book had been published in the middle of the nineteenth century by an author of considerable fame. "To put this book on the Index would be analogous to stop performing Mozart's *Magic Flute* because it favored the Freemasons." The Gestapa eventually concurred in this decision.[26]

In another similar case the Gestapo eventually prevailed, but only after again being scolded as naive and as a result of a direct appeal to Goebbels. The controversy involved a collection of letters, diary entries, and speeches by Gustav Stresemann, secretary of foreign affairs from 1924 to 1929 and considered by many the greatest master of German foreign policy since Bismarck. It was Stresemann's successful diplomacy that improved relations with the victors of World War I, lightened the load of reparations, and gained Germany's acceptance into the League of Nations. The three-volume work *Stresemann's Vermächtnis* (Stresemann's Testament), edited by Stresemann's former private secretary Henry Bernhard, had been published by Ullstein in 1932. In 1937 the book attracted the attention of the Gestapo as a work that "justified Stresemann's policies" and "therefore was completely opposed to National Socialist principles."[27] On July 19 the RSK informed the Gestapa that the request to put this book on the Index had been rejected. "A ban on historical chronicles cannot change history." This kind of historical writing by well-known opponents of National Socialism should not be banned "unless one wants an entire epoch of history to fall into oblivion." In that case future generations would never understand what a gigantic struggle Hitler and the National Socialist movement had had to fight in order to triumph over its adversaries.[28]

The Gestapo persisted in its campaign against the book. A blistering article on September 23 in *Das Schwarze Korps*, the official weekly newspaper of the SS, charged that the true testament of Stresemann was "eight million unemployed, red terror, disintegration of the economy, cultural decay, dishonesty." In order to grasp this testament in all its "outrageousness" one did not need the 2,000 pages of this work that deserved to be discarded as "garbage" rather than be offered for sale in today's Germany.[29] When this attack did not have the desired result, *Das Schwarze Korps* ran another assault on the book, and two days later the Gestapa addressed Goebbels directly. The Stresemann book, the message pointed out, was being marketed by Ullstein as a work that the RSK considered "an important historical document." The department store Wertheim in Berlin had bought a large number of copies and offered the book as a sale item. The Gestapa asked that Goebbels agree "forthwith, and preferably via telephone" to the confiscation and seizure of the Stresemann book.[30] This intervention finally brought about the desired result, and Goebbels, as requested, replied by telephone that he agreed to have the book confiscated.

The kind of judgment displayed by the Gestapo in these instances must have happened not infrequently, which may explain the angry tone the RSK adopted in a case that arose in the fall of 1936. After the Gestapo Köln had seized once again a publication not on the list of forbidden books, the president of the RSK on October 22 asked the Gestapa for "an immediate reversal of this action" and added, "I would be grateful if you would take all suitable measures that will prevent the repetition of this case under any circumstances."[31] It is possible that the Gestapo did not take kindly to this kind of rebuke, for in another such instance in June 1937 the RSK used far more restrained language. At a bookstore in Dortmund the Gestapo had seized twenty-two titles, none of which was found to be on the Index of Harmful and Undesirable Books or deserved to be put on the Index. Putting the best face on this occurrence, the RSK noted: "It must be assumed that the Gestapo in Dortmund was not sufficiently informed about harmful or undesirable literature."[32] Moreover, the RSK pointed out, it was the practice of the Gestapo to seize books that were "considered suspicious" and send them to the RSK for examination, and not a few of these were subsequently accepted into the Index of forbidden books. After this had been done, the Gestapo changed the tentative confiscation to a final one.[33]

Much of the time the Gestapo indeed followed this procedure. A local Gestapo office would seize a book deemed to be dangerous and send it to the Gestapa in Berlin, which would send the book to the RSK. The RSK then forwarded the book to Department VIII of the Ministry of Propaganda for a decision. If the book was found to be objectionable, the RSK would enter the book on the Index and instruct the Gestapo to confiscate the book. The standard notification sent to the publisher then ran: "In agreement with the Minister for Popular Enlightenment and Propaganda and on the basis of Paragraph 1 of the Reichspräsident's Ordinance for the Protection of People and State of February 28, 1933, the distribution of [title, publisher, year of publication] inside the country until further notice is forbidden." Most of the banned books would then be pulped.

In the case of books published abroad, the Ministry of Propaganda dealt with Himmler directly, especially after his appointment in 1936 as Reichsführer SS und Chef der Deutschen Polizei. The usual practice was to ask him to forbid the offending book in accordance with President Hindenburg's emergency decree of February 28, 1933. A copy of this notification would go to the RSK with the request to enter the book on the List of Harmful and Undesirable Books. The entry of such books in the Index was preceded by the symbol +, and a note at the beginning of the list explained that the Reichsführer had issued "a general ban against these books." Based on the edition of 1938, it appears that this involved about 10 percent of the listed books. In actual practice, of course, it made no difference whether a book was forbidden with or without "a general ban." In either case the book could no longer be sold or lent. Unlike the bans of domestically published books that between 1936 and 1940 were considered strictly confidential, the titles of banned books published abroad were published in the *Reichsanzeiger* (the gazette of administrative decrees) and in the *Deutsches Kriminalpolizeiblatt* (gazette of the German criminal police). In 1934 and 1935 the Ministry of the Interior issued a list of banned foreign publications, a compilation of the titles listed in the *Reichsanzeiger*.[34]

The listing of offending books published abroad was easy. But to prevent the importation of such books proved to be a major problem. In December 1935, Wilhelm Ohnesorge, the minister for postal affairs, complained to Minister of the Interior Frick that the list of forbidden foreign-published books had reached 946 items. Given the high volume of mail from abroad, it was becoming impossible to screen foreign mail for these many titles. Moreover, "precensorship was irreconcilable with an orderly and timely delivery of the mail."[35] Ohnesorge, it should be pointed out, was, like Frick, an early companion of

Hitler and his concern certainly was not to protect foreign anti-Nazi literature. Frick convened a meeting for January 14, 1936, in order to discuss "limitations of the number of [imported] banned books," but the results of this conference are not known.[36]

As a rule, private libraries, books owned by individuals in their homes, were not affected by these bans. During a search of the premises of the writer Arnold Holtz by the Gestapo Potsdam, the officials found books listed on the Index, and they asked the Gestapa in Berlin whether these books should be confiscated. They were told that unless Holtz could be charged with activities against the state or unless Holtz had sold or lent the banned books to others, the offending works could not be seized.[37] And yet this rule was not always followed. As part of an investigation of the former SPD editor Gustav Schröder, the Gestapo Elbing (Westpreussen) found in his apartment a large number of Marxist books as well as about 2,750 Marxist brochures. Some of these had been published before World War I. In its letter of inquiry about what to do with these materials, the local Gestapo office noted that Schroeder was "an old and very frail man, who should no longer be taken seriously." There also was no indication that Schroeder had lent the offending publications to others. Nevertheless the Gestapa replied that thirty-one of the listed books and all brochures should be confiscated and put at the disposal of the Reichsführer SS.[38]

In many cases local Gestapo offices were more zealous than their superiors in Berlin. On August 18, 1935, Hjalmar Schacht, president of the Reichsbank, minister of economic affairs, and a highly effective promoter of German economic recovery and rearmament, gave a speech in Königsberg in which, as an aside, he complained about "irresponsible 'heroes'" who endangered the reduction of unemployment by acts of violence against Jewish enterprises. "These people mean well, but action against the Jews must be taken legally, under the leadership of the state." The Reichsbank distributed a reprint of the speech, and several Gestapo offices thereupon inquired whether the pamphlet should be confiscated. In a reply, Werner Best, Heydrich's deputy and the Gestapo's chief legal adviser, let it be known that Schacht held the office of a cabinet minister, and that approval or disapproval of his speech therefore was "out of the question."[39]

Publishers sometimes inquired at the Gestapo whether a certain book could be published, but they were told that it was not the task of the Gestapo to evaluate manuscripts.[40] Both publishers and bookstores many times asked for the reasons that had led to the confiscation of books, but the standard reply was that no reasons need be given. A few courageous individuals even hired lawyers and sought to bring legal action against the seizures. Predictably, these efforts too usually ended in failure. When attorneys for the Greifenverlag in Rudolfstadt inquired at the Gestapo why a certain book had been confiscated, their letter was referred to the RSK, which replied that the book had been entered on the List of Harmful and Undesirable Books. "I determine that your complaint has therefore become moot."[41]

When the publisher of another confiscated book in February 1938 asked for compensation, the Gestapo termed the application "impertinent" and promised an "appropriate reply."[42] In another such case that began in June 1936, the Gestapo informed the attorneys for a publisher that there existed no legal remedies for the confiscation of books by the Gestapo. The attorneys nevertheless pressed on, and the case eventually reached the Reichsgericht, Germany's highest court. After the Gestapo had stated there that the seizure had taken place to protect "public safety and order," the Reichsgericht dismissed the complaint on February 14, 1938.[43] The Gestapo, it was now official, was above the law.

The same result was reached in the case of the retired mayor of the town of Rathenow in Brandenburg, Carl Dieckmann, who had had the nerve to demand compensation for a wrongly confiscated book. On October 26, 1937, the Gestapo had ordered the seizure of Dieckmann's book *Verwaltungsrecht: Ein Hand- und Lehrbuch,* a treatise on administrative law first published in 1922 and reissued in 1937, on the grounds that it showed "a complete lack of understanding for National Socialist ideas and demands."[44] Dieckmann complained to the RSK, which ordered an examination of the book by the Academy of German Law. This vetting apparently was largely positive, though Dieckmann was asked to make some changes. On September 20, the Ministry of Propaganda informed the Gestapa of this outcome and asked that the confiscated work be released. Meanwhile, however, both the publisher and the Gestapo had destroyed all copies of the book, an action the Gestapo said it had undertaken because it had not known of Dieckmann's appeal to the RSK.

In a registered letter of October 14 to the Gestapo Dieckmann now maintained that the Gestapo had never been justified in confiscating his book. By pulping the work, the Gestapo had "illegally caused me considerable damage. I request to learn whether the Gestapo is willing to compensate me for this damage. I shall be glad to negotiate this matter with you." The Gestapo's response to this inquiry was to make a note in the file: "Because of Dieckmann's insolent tone he will not receive a reply." After Dieckmann had waited several months for an answer that never came, on August 31, 1940, he sent a letter addressed to Himmler personally in which he expressed "his unshakeable conviction that right will eventually be done" and requested that "the damage that has been caused me be made good for in some manner." [45] Regarding the details of such compensation Dieckmann again declared his willingness to negotiate. Not unexpectedly, the case came to an end with a reply to Dieckmann that declined any kind of negotiations "because the confiscation has taken place as a measure of the Gestapo [*eine staatspolitische Massnahme*] from which there is no appeal." A subsequent letter to the minister to the interior dated September 26, 1940, has the handwritten notation "No more reply."[46]

Still another way to prevent any challenge to the actions of the Gestapo was to confiscate a book without establishing an official paper trail. This procedure was called "informal confiscation" (*formlose Beschlagnahmung*). Even though this practice ran counter to its own regulations according to which books to be banned had to be entered in the list of harmful books, both the RSK and the Ministry of Propaganda at times encouraged its use. After the Gestapo Munich had requested the listing of all books issued by the publishing house Reinhardt, the Gestapa informed the Munich office on August 11, 1937, that the RSK had found these books to be "hardly current." However, the RSK was "not opposed to informal confiscation."[47] A week later the RSK told the Gestapa that "in order not to burden the list unduly," certain books published in the years 1920, 1921, and 1922 would not be put on the Index because for some time already they were no longer being traded. However if they are encountered, they should be confiscated and seized.[48] On May 10, 1937, the Gestapa suggested that the books by the well-known American journalist H. R. Knickerbocker, published by Rowohlt in 1931, be listed on the Index. The Propaganda Ministry replied that the anti-German attitude of Knickerbocker was well known, but in order not to give him additional publicity abroad it was better not to list the books. The ministry suggested that Rowohlt be "advised" not to distribute the books or publish any new editions.[49]

At times the Gestapa made the decision to forego the listing of an objectionable book on its own without consulting either the RSK or the Ministry of Propaganda. A memo of September 19, 1935, in the files of the Gestapa observed that in view of the strained relations between National Socialism and Bolshevism, books on Stalin could under no conditions be tolerated. "Obtaining an expert evaluation from the RSK is not necessary, since the confiscation takes place for purely political reasons."[50] The Gestapo in this case may have acted on its own in part because, as the files reveal, its officers felt frustrated that their recommendations for forbidding books were frequently overruled by the RSK. A memo of October 25, 1937, noted that the RSK "in recent times with regard to various publications has taken an indefensible position opposed to that of the Gestapa and SD."[51] "Strained relations," as we see here again, existed not only between National Socialism and Bolshevism, but also between different centers of power in the Nazi state.

From the spring of 1933 on, the pages of the gazette of the German criminal police (*Deutsches Kriminalpolizeiblatt*) and the pages of the *Börsenblatt* (reprinting the announcements of the criminal police) contained long lists of books that had been seized on the basis of Paragraph 7 of the decree of February 4, 1933. Beginning with the January 25, 1934, issue, the *Zeitschrift der Leihbücherei* too published lists of *Verbotene Bücher*, and even the daily press reported on "Confiscated Books." On November 20, 1935, the *Berliner Tageblatt* informed its readers that certain books had been seized "because their content was likely to give a completely false picture of National Socialism."[52] At times, we learn, a book dealer appealed to a court to prevent the destruction of confiscated books, but in each reported case the court upheld the seizure and pulping of the offending books.[53] The publication of these announcements was ended in 1935 when its damaging impact on foreign public opinion was noticed. As we have seen in the previous chapter, the official List of Harmful and Undesirable Books, which began to be issued at the end of 1935, also was kept out of the hands of the public; numbered copies were made available only to the police, customs offices, scientific libraries, and the state offices of the RSK. Announcements of book bans were resumed in 1940 when war conditions made the reaction of the outside world irrelevant.

The work of the Gestapo was complemented by that of the Security Service (Sicherheitsdienst, or SD). It was established in 1931 as an intelligence arm of the SS, and it was led by Reinhard Heydrich. Initially a party organization, as of November 11, 1938, it was decreed to operate "on orders of the state" and its actions thus had state sanction.[54] The mandate of the SD included the gathering of intelligence about ideological enemies (*weltanschauliche Gegnerforschung*) as well as defense against opponents of the state, and it was in fulfillment of these tasks that the SD took on the control of literature. Through the use of *V-Leute* (*Vertrauensleute*, or confidential informants, said to number as many as 30,000), the SD monitored the operations of about 300 to 400 publishers who were deemed politically dangerous. This supervision was to enable appropriate agencies such as the RSK and Gestapo "to discover and prevent undesirable publication plans before they can be implemented."[55]

In early 1934 the SD established in Leipzig an Office for Literature (Schrifttumsstelle). It was located in the Deutsche Bücherei, the central archive of German-language publications that received copies of all new books. In this way the SD had a convenient overview of the book trade.[56] In April 1936 this office moved to Berlin, where it became a Hauptabteilung (a main division) of the Hauptamt SD, the command center of the Reichsführer SS. At the same time the Berlin office continued to be assisted by a liaison bureau in the Deutsche Bücherei. Relations with the Deutsche Bücherei were not always smooth. Heinrich Uhlendahl, its director, even though a member of the SA and of Rosenberg's Kampfbund, was not happy about the presence of the SD, which monopolized newly arrived books and even lost books entrusted to them.[57] In 1937 the SD suggested to Hanns Johst, president of the RSK, that he help find a new head of the Deutsche Bücherei "who is willing to cooperate with the SD,"[58] but Uhlendahl, who was exceptionally dedicated to the central book archive, was able to keep his job. In April 1940 the Deutsche Bücherei was put under the administration of the Ministry of Propaganda, a measure that probably provided the agency with additional protection.[59]

One of the key figures in establishing the SD's supervision of literature was Franz Alfred Six, later to become infamous as commander of one of the Einsatzkommandos (special task forces) that followed the advancing German armies in Russia and murdered Jews, Gypsies, and Soviet political commissars. When in 1936 Six was put in charge of the *weltanschauliche Gegnerbekämpfung* (fight against ideological enemies), he was twenty-six years old. In 1934 he had been awarded a Ph.D. in media science with a dissertation on "The Political Propaganda der NSDAP in the Struggle for Power" that has been called "more a work of propaganda than a dissertation."[60] Like other SD leaders, Six belonged to the cohort that came of age immediately after World War I. Many of these young people eventually found their way to the Nazis because most of them had been deeply influenced by the hardships of the war and the consequent defeat. These men were ruthless and strongly motivated by the ideological tenets of the extreme-right-wing organizations of the early 1920s to which many of them belonged.[61] Shortly after Himmler reorganized the German police in October 1939 by establishing the Reichssicherheitshauptamt, Six became head of Department VIII, Weltanschauliche Forschung und Auswertung (Ideological Research and Evaluation).[62]

In 1937, Six had 142 people working under his direction, all of them, including the clerical personnel, members of the SS. Through its liaison in Leipzig, Six's office supervised the *Deutsche Nationalbibliographie*, the compilation of all German-language publications issued by the Deutsche Bücherei, and decided which books were to be omitted from this reference work. Excluded as a matter of course were all works by emigrated authors as well as "Jewish literature." In addition, all "harmful and undesirable" books were kept out of this important bibliographical work. In 1949 the *Deutsche Nationalbibliographie* issued a supplement with 5,485 titles that had been blacklisted between the years 1933 and 1945.

The main task of the SD in the area of book control was to compile information about objectionable books and then apply to the Ministry of Propaganda for their ban and confiscation. Many of these applications were accompanied by expert assessments (*Gutachten*); in other cases the application merely quoted passages that were said to prove the "bad tendency" of the work in question. According to an internal memo, by 1937 the SD had submitted "several thousand book titles" for listing on the Index.[63] Occasionally, the files show, a local SD official participated in an actual raid, though that role was not to be made a matter of record. On May 15, 1937, the Gestapa issued a rebuke to the police in the town of Buchholz in Lower Saxony that had confiscated a book and in its report on this action had mentioned the name of an SD official who had taken part in the seizure. The head of the police force in the town was instructed to make sure that in the future such assistance not be recorded.[64]

The SD was considered powerful and influential because its chief, Heydrich, was Himmler's deputy, and the great majority of its applications for the listing of books were approved. However, it did not always get its way. On December 8, 1937, the Gestapa, at the behest of the SD, asked the RSK to put the novel *Die andere Seite der Welt* by Georg Korf on the Index. The book, with the subtitle "a metaphysical novel," had first been published in 1914 and in 1936 it appeared in a new edition. The application to suppress the book was supported by a *Gutachten* by the SD. On March 29, 1938, the RSK informed the Gestapa that Goebbels had refused to approve this request because "the book did not contain any attacks on the National Socialist ideology and there was therefore no reason to move against it."[65]

In many instances, and undoubtedly much to the displeasure of the Propaganda Ministry, the SD failed to follow the expected protocol and simply asked the Gestapa to ban a certain book. Publishers and authors at times tried to fight back. On May 11, 1935, the Gestapa, at the request of the SD and invoking Paragraph 7 of the emergency decree of February 4, 1933, had confiscated the book *Hinter der Maske der Freimaurerei* (Behind the Mask of the Freemasons) by one Richard Hannuschka. The book's content, the Gestapa informed the publisher Deutsche Kultur-Wacht (established by Rosenberg's Kampfbund), was "unclear" and likely "to create confusion in the population and thereby threaten public security and order."[66] The publisher thereupon lodged a complaint, arguing that the book had been brought out "in order to support the state in its struggle against the Freemasons. We also claim the protection of science, since the book represents a scientific work."[67] When this complaint remained unanswered, the author, a retired captain, asked for Hitler's help. In a letter addressed to "Mein Führer," Hannuschka suggested that the seizure of his book "probably had been carried out by overzealous officials who had been insufficiently informed about the content and purpose of the book."[68] The author sent similar letters to Göring, the prime minister of Prussia, the RSK, and several other organizations, but the proscription remained in force and the book was put on the Index.

At times the SD used the threat of confiscation to have its way with publishers. On March 4, 1937, the SD asked that the book *Der Knabe und der Tod* (The Boy and Death) by Wilhelm Vermeulen be put on the Index because it originated in "decadent circles" that had no understanding of National Socialist youth and its outlook. The RSK demurred on the grounds that the author was a veteran party member and a SA-Sturmbannführer. Moreover, the publisher's editor who had handled the book was a member of the SS, and the publisher was prepared to have the author make changes in the text. After seeing the corrected version, the SD did not consider the changes sufficient: "The fact that the author is a veteran party member and the responsible editor a member of the SA is no reason to approve the book."[69] (Actually the RSK had described the responsible editor as a member of the SS and not the SA, but there is no way of knowing whether this mistake on the part of the SD played a part in its decision.) On December 8, 1938, the Gestapa complained to the Ministry of Propaganda that the case had been dragging on for a year and a half and that the book should either be listed on the Index or the publisher should be asked to destroy it. Another year passed without any recorded decision on the part of the RSK or the Propaganda Ministry. On December 13, 1939, the Gestapo Hamburg informed the Reichssicherheitshauptamt (Reich Main Security Office or RSHA) in Berlin that on the preceding August 15 the publisher had withdrawn the book. A few days earlier, the Gestapo Hamburg wrote, the publisher had received a telephone call from the Ministry of Propaganda in which he was informed that the Gestapo demanded the withdrawal of the book. Unless the publisher complied with this demand, the SD would seize the book. An order to this effect had already been signed by Heydrich. In the face of this threat the publisher gave in and promised to recall all outstanding copies and cease distributing the book.[70]

From 1936 on the SD Hauptamt in Berlin maintained a "scientific central library of the entire corpus of politically undesirable literature." Using this source and the reports of lower-echelon SD offices, the SD provided information to the Gestapo on individuals considered opposed to the National Socialist ideology. After July 1937 the SD, as part of keeping tabs on the state of public opinion, also took on compiling information about the general condition of literature. These accounts became a regular feature of *Meldungen aus dem Reich* (Reports from the Reich) that were issued until the end of the war.[71]

Six, who had played a central role in the research on opponents (*Gegnerforschung*), eventually moved on to other assignments. Heydrich, it appears, had little appreciation for the intellectual aspects of the SD's research on enemies. Hence in order to escape the tense situation in the RSHA, in 1940 Six volunteered for the Waffen-SS, the military branch of the SS, and in 1941 he became commander of an Einsatzkommando. After the war Six was tried by a U.S. military tribunal. The court was unable to link him directly to any killing, and Six was sentenced to twenty years' imprisonment, escaping the death penalty meted out to several of his SS comrades. This sentence eventually was reduced to ten years, and in September 1952 he was released. Like several other former Nazi intelligence officials, Six was recruited for the Gehlen Organization, the forerunner of today's Bundesnachrichtendienst (Germany's foreign intelligence agency).[71] His career in the Federal Republic of Germany shows how de-Nazification and the punishment of war criminals were undermined by what were considered pressing intelligence needs in the Cold War with the Soviet Union. Six died in 1975.

6

The Party Commission for the Protection of National Socialist Literature

On April 16, 1934, Rudolf Hess, Hitler's deputy and head of the Nazi party's chancellery, announced the creation of the Party Commission for the Protection of National Socialist Literature (Parteiamtliche Prüfungskommission zum Schutze des nationalsozialistischen Schrifttums, or PPK). In recent months, the announcement noted, many books and magazines had been published dealing with the aims and leading personalities of the NSDAP. Some of these publications were authored by persons who lacked the necessary expertise, distorted important principles of the party, and left their readers with a false picture of the movement. "The NSDAP has the sovereign right and duty to make sure that the ideas of National Socialism are not falsified by unauthorized individuals and are not exploited for commercial purposes so as to mislead the general population." The new commission would have "the task of vetting all relevant books and publications." Books could be described as National Socialist only if they carry a declaration of no-objection (*Unbedenklichkeitsvermerk*) from the commission. The head of this commission was to be Reichsleiter Philipp Bouhler. "The NSDAP expects that manuscripts dealing with National Socialist problems and topics be offered first to the central publishing house of the party [Franz Eher Verlag, headed by Max Amann]."[1]

Bouhler, the head of the new party commission, in the words of Ian Kershaw was an "indefatigable and subservient" individual who had risen rapidly through the ranks of the Nazi party.[2] He had joined the NSDAP in 1922, holding membership card number 12, and by 1934 had become head of the Chancellery of the Führer, a Reichsleiter (the highest rank in the Nazi party), and an SS Obergruppenführer, the third-highest rank in that elite force. In 1939 Hitler entrusted Bouhler with organizing the euthanasia program, referred to as *Aktion T4*, the mass killing of physically or mentally disabled individuals. Bouhler's book *Napoleon: Kometenbahn eines Genius* (Napoleon: Comet-Path of a Genius), was one of Hitler's favorite bedtime readings.[3] The bespectacled Bouhler was a soft-spoken but extremely ambitious person who knew how to

Philipp Bouhler, head of the Party Commission for the Protection of National Socialist Literature. *Courtesy US Holocaust Memorial Museum/National Archives and Records Administration, College Park, Md.*

transform minor assignments into major undertakings and build up the requisite organization. Within a few years Bouhler managed to change the PPK from a small bureau dealing with party literature into a significant censorship operation.

The RSK confirmed this competence with an order of April 16, 1935, that forbade the sale of any books that the PPK had found "objectionable."[4] By 1939 the PKK employed 127 people and was able to censor books in all areas of the book market.[5] An order issued by Hess on January 6, 1936, gave the PPK the right to ask other party organizations as well as individual party members for assistance. "The fulfillment of such assignments represents important party service and must in all instances be accomplished quickly and carefully."[6] The PPK used this ordinance in order to have personnel of the RSK and individual party members serve as readers of books and issue assessments (*Gutachten*). By 1942 the number of such readers had reached 692, though 165 of these served in the military and may have done assessments only on an irregular basis.[7]

At the end of April 1934 Bouhler issued regulations for the operation of the PPK, which obligated publishers of publications that claimed to be National Socialist to submit these works to the PPK for examination. This included both already-published books as well as manuscripts of new works. The PPK examined these books, issued assessments, and was entitled to charge a fee for this vetting. Publishers who failed to comply with this order would "have to bear the consequences."[8] A second ordinance promulgated by Bouhler on April 11, 1935, noted that the PPK was entitled to prevent the publication of any work that "deals with National Socialist ideas in a way that contradicts the real intentions of the movement." Such books could be banned, though this would generally happen only in special cases.[9] We do not know the total number of books that were forbidden by the PPK, but, contrary to the PPK's own claims, such bans appear to have taken place quite regularly. An announcement by Bouhler on September 21, 1934, carried by the semi-official publication *Bücherei* listed eight books that had been forbidden, but noted that these eight were merely "a few" of all those that had been banned.[10] The files of the Gestapo also include numerous cases of such bans carried out at the request of the PPK.[11]

Some outsiders were aware that the banning of books by the PPK was the result of "a pure assertion of authority by the party" and had no basis in law. The RSK official who made this assessment welcomed the work of the PPK, but he considered it desirable that its banning of books "be shored up legally by a special law."[12] On the other hand, an official of the PPK, Karl Helmut Patutschnick, explained how the PPK, an organization of the party, was able to give orders to non-party members. The position of the party, he insisted, could not be understood from a "formalistic-legalistic" point of view or as a competence anchored in law. As a result of the National Socialist revolution, "the party gives orders to the state." As an example of "the employment of the state to realize the will of the nation, personified by the party," Patutschnick referred to Ordinance 69 of the RSK of April 16, 1935. According to this directive, "publications that have been examined by the PPK and have been found to be objectionable may not be sold by the book trade." Publishers who failed to obey the instructions of the PPK "justified the assumption that they lack the necessary suitability and reliability required by Paragraph 10 of the law of November 1, 1933, establishing the RKK." They have to expect fines and in grievous cases expulsion from the RSK.[13]

Unbeknown to the PPK official, Ordinance 69 was to have a short life. Less than a month later, after the appearance of Ordinance 70 on May 8, 1935, establishing the official Index, Ordinance 69 was declared to be "irrelevant." Book bans were to be issued "*exclusively* by the RSK or rather by the Ministry for Popular Enlightenment and Propaganda." RSK head Johst once again reminded everyone of this order in 1940 when he had it published in the widely read *Börsenblatt*.[14] It is likely that Johst found this repeat announcement to be necessary because the PPK had greatly expanded its power and had gradually come to challenge the authority of the Ministry of Propaganda.

In 1935 the PPK had set up an office in the Deutsche Bücherei in Leipzig, and in January 1936 this office began to publish a monthly reference work, the *Nationalsozialistische Bibliographie* (NSB). Delegates from the Ministries of Propaganda and Education, as well as from the Rosenberg organization, the Office for the Promotion of German Literature, were supposed to participate in the work of the NSB.[15] The publication listed writings that dealt with party ideas or issues and had been found to be acceptable. Publishers of approved publications were allowed to include in their books the notation "The NSDAP has no objection to the publication of this work. It is listed in the NS-Bibliography"; they also could make reference to this approval in their advertising. The declaration of no-objection (*Unbedenklichkeitsvermerk*) from here on was reserved for official party publications.[16]

In an announcement published on February 28, 1936, Minister of Education Bernhard Rust referred to the NSB as "an official party publication and *therefore* [italics added] a governmental publication (*behördliche Veröffentlichung*)."[17] Again we encounter here the affirmation of the unity of party and state. Or as Goebbels phrased it in 1935, looking back to the assumption of power in 1933: "National Socialist authorities from here on became authorities of the state; the laws of the revolution became the laws of the state, and the National Socialist way of thinking was taken over by the nation."[18]

Given the conviction that party and state were one and that the party had the right to give orders to the state, it is not surprising that the PPK soon arrogated to itself the right to impose book bans and use the Gestapo to enforce those bans. Karl-Heinz Hederich, deputy head of the PPK and its chief executive officer, noted in a short book published in 1937 that one of the central tasks of the PPK was the "cleansing" of National Socialist literature, which was accomplished by withholding the declaration of no-objection. In cases where books caused "confusion and corrosion" and where a mere rejection of this certification therefore was not sufficient, the PPK banned books, though this was necessary "relatively seldom." The commission also made authors or publishers change the text of books, and in grievous instances it denied publishers the right to issue National Socialist literature altogether.[19] Hederich stressed that the mandate of the PPK included not only actual National Socialist literature but also works that attacked National Socialism. Included here were publications by former political figures of the Weimar period as well as opponents in the various religious camps. Finally, the PPK had to supervise works that were entirely non-political.[20]

Hellmuth Langenbucher, the editor of the *Börsenblatt* and another leading Nazi figure involved with the book trade, explained the expansion of the PPK's jurisdiction in this way: Originally the PPK had been concerned only with

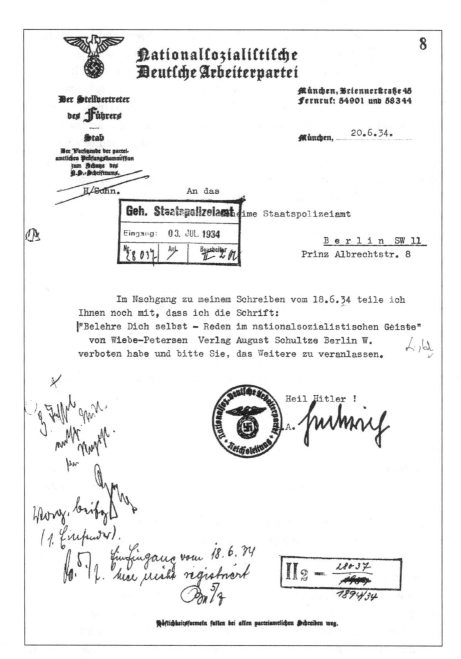

**Nationalsozialistische
Deutsche Arbeiterpartei**

Der Stellvertreter
des Führers

Stab

Der Vorsitzende der parteiamtlichen Prüfungskommission
zum Schutze des
N.S.-Schrifttums.

H/Sohn.

München, Briennerstraße 45
Fernruf: 54901 und 58344

München, 20.6.34.

An das

Geh. Staatspolizeiamt

Eingang: 03. JUL. 1934

Nr. 28 037 | Anl. | Bearbeiter II-2

Geheime Staatspolizeiamt

B e r l i n SW 11
Prinz Albrechtstr. 8

Im Nachgang zu meinem Schreiben vom 18.6.34 teile ich
Ihnen noch mit, dass ich die Schrift:
"Belehre Dich selbst – Reden im nationalsozialistischen Geiste"
von Wiebe-Petersen Verlag August Schultze Berlin W.
verboten habe und bitte Sie, das Weitere zu veranlassen.

Heil Hitler !

I.A.

II 2 — 28 037 / 189434

Höflichkeitsformeln fallen bei allen parteiamtlichen Schreiben weg.

The Party Commission for the Protection of National Socialist Literature informs the Gestapo that it has banned a book by Wiebe-Petersen on National Socialist speeches. *Courtesy Bundesarchiv Berlin-Lichterfelde* protecting National Socialist literature against distortions and falsifications. However, as the National Socialist ideology spread among all parts of the population, the work of the PPK had "to grow organically" and it had to take on an ever increasing scope of publications.[21] An end-of-year report for 1938 by the SD noted in a matter-of-fact manner that the PPK had extended its prior censorship beyond National Socialist writings to "the entire range of literature."[22]

The rivals of the PPK reached the same conclusion, but with a critical assessment of the effect of this change. The files of the Rosenberg organization, for example, are filled with letters in which Rosenberg protested the expanding reach of the PPK and charged Bouhler with disregarding the orders of Hess.[23] Robert Ley, in charge of the organization of the NSDAP (Reichsorganisationsleiter), noted in an August 1939 memo to Hess that the PPK, in addition to its original mandate, now concerned itself with books in the following fields: philosophy, political science, economics and social science, schoolbooks, history, science, folklore, defense studies, fiction, songbooks, catalogs, and calendars. Ley insisted that the ensuing overlap of jurisdictions had to be corrected.[24]

In November 1939 an official in the Ministry of Propaganda blamed the increased reach of the PPK for "the collapse of the research in the humanities." Scholars, he pointed out, stayed away from any topic that may require them to submit their work for approval to the PPK.[25] Some two years later another official, this time in Bormann's party chancellery, drew the attention of the propaganda ministry to the same unfortunate effect. The vetting of scientific writings by the PPK, he noted, often led the PPK to act as a master of scholars. As a result many of them "lose any interest in writing."[26]

This appraisal may have been unduly pessimistic, as there is no indication that humanistic scholarship indeed came to a halt or suffered a drastic decline. We know that historians, for example, together with other scholars in the humanities and the social sciences, easily adjusted to the new ideological winds and defended the restoration of German power in Europe in their writings. Their conservative leanings predisposed them to an acceptance of many elements of Nazi ideology. The shared language of nationalism was not conducive to the developments of views actively opposing the new regime.

At a meeting of historians in February 1941, Theodor Mayer called upon his colleagues to support the war effort by providing the historical justification for a new European order. Well-known figures in the profession such as Werner Conze, Karl Dietrich Erdmann, and Theodor Schieder willingly complied with this demand.[27] Their writings are characterized by hostility to the Slavs and pronounced anti-Semitism.[28] As late as December 1944, Schieder, who because of a heart condition was exempt from military service, proclaimed his willingness to participate "in the intensification of the intellectual defense" of the war.[29] The politicization of scholarship during the Third Reich, it would appear, was a result less of coercion and censorship than of the embrace of Nazi ideas by large sections of the academic profession. The notion that historians withdrew into the unpolitical domain is untenable.[30]

Some measures of control remained within the original mandate of the PPK. On September 24, 1935, Bouhler announced that the central party publishing house Eher alone had the right to publish the speeches and writings of Hitler.[31] This order was followed by a regulation of July 20, 1936, that obligated publishers who wanted to include quotations from Hitler's speeches to submit the manuscript of such works to the PPK for approval.[32] As of October 7, 1936, prior permission was also required for the publication of songs of the National Socialist movement by music publishers.[33] On June 10, 1938, Bouhler forbade any publication "dealing with the Führer" unless he personally had approved the work.[34]

The PPK also had an agreement with the High Command of the Armed Forces (OKW), which required officers to submit writings dealing with political subjects to the PPK for clearance.[35] Other such orders imposing prior censorship had little or nothing to do with National Socialist themes. An order of March 25, 1937, required that the manuscripts of all publications dealing with the Four-Year Plan be submitted to the PPK for clearance.[36] Another order, issued on August 9, 1941, with the concurrence of Himmler, mandated that the proofs of all publications dealing with the work of the police be checked by the PPK.[37]

Still more removed from the original mandate of the PPK was a rule of May 20, 1938, directing that all calendars, almanacs, and yearbooks before printing be presented to the PPK for approval.[38] Already in July 1935 Bouhler had warned the publishers of calendars that the way in which they treated the achievements of the National Socialist state was completely "inadequate and misleading."[39] An article in the NSB explained that the control of calendars was imperative because they were issued in editions of many millions and reached segments of the population that read little or nothing else. The clergy often had undue influence. A calendar for 1937 had mentioned the birthday of Muhammad but not the birthday of the Führer.[40] In the case of a calendar that the PPK found to be "a paramount example of irresponsible work," the PPK without much ado asked the Gestapo to confiscate the offending calendar. The Gestapo complied and seized copies of the calendar in various cities.[41]

The question of whether the PPK had the right to ask for the confiscation of these kinds of publications was never raised. As head of the Chancellery of the Führer, a post that gave the adroit Reichsleiter ready access to Hitler, Bouhler obviously had considerable clout. As one of its officials put it in testimony before a party court in 1942: "In contrast to state and party offices, whose competences are limited by a clearly defined set of tasks, the Chancellery of the Führer is a direct link between people and Führer, and therefore is in charge of whatever it considers appropriate."[42]

The PPK did not hesitate to take on prestigious personalities with impeccable Nazi credentials. As a reward for his faithful support of the Nazi movement, Professor Otto Koellreutter in 1933 had been given a chair in law at the University of Munich, and a little later he became a dean. He was a member of the NSDAP as well as of the Akademie für Deutsches Recht, an organization engaged in transforming German law according to Nazi principles. In 1947 a Bavarian denazification court sentenced Koellreutter, considered one of the leading theoreticians of the Führerstaat, to five years of hard labor, of which he served thirteen months. Yet in 1935 the PKK informed Koellreutter that his book on the elections of 1930 and their significance for jurisprudence had been found wanting and had to be removed from circulation. The book, the PPK charged, took a position on the Jewish question "that was unacceptable to the movement."[43] In another case the PPK ordered the Gestapo to confiscate a book because it contained "inappropriate remarks" by Friedrich Schmidt, a Nazi functionary holding the rank of Hauptbefehlshaber, the third-highest position in the party right after Gauleiter.[44] The ability of the PPK to take action against such party stalwarts demonstrates its power in the Nazi state.

Bouhler further increased the powers of the PPK through agreements with Rust, head of the Ministry of Education. According to an accord signed on July 14, 1937, a working group made up in equal parts by officials of the Ministry of Education and the PPK but chaired by Hederich, the deputy head of the PPK, was to be formed to consider questions involving scientific and educational literature.[45] As it turned out, this seemingly innocuous agreement for cooperation was used by Bouhler and Hederich to override decisions made by the Ministry of Education in matters of schoolbooks. On October 8, 1937, Hederich informed the prestigious Catholic publishing house Ferdinand Schöningh in Paderborn that a German history book published by Schöningh, *Vom Weltkrieg zum Dritten Reich: 1914–1936*, failed to describe this important part of history in a satisfactory manner. "The use of this book in its present form for the schools is therefore undesirable and must be discontinued." Hederich sent a copy of this order to the Gestapa in Berlin and requested it "to take the necessary measures."[46]

When the Gestapo office in Bielefeld acted to enforce this ban, Schöningh lodged a complaint, pointing out that the Ministry of Education on the preceding January 18 had approved the book for use in the schools. In response the Gestapa in Berlin advised the Bielefeld Gestapo that the decision of the education ministry had become void as a result of the PPK order of October 8 to Schöningh to stop issuing the book. In a communication to the Gestapa, Hederich explained that after the agreement of July 14, 1937, between the PPK and the Ministry of Education had been fully implemented, this kind of problem would not occur again. Henceforth the approval of books for school libraries would require the consent of the PPK.[47] The PPK, it would appear, had thoroughly outmaneuvered Rust, and Bouhler had achieved an important new expansion of his mandate.

Two years later Bouhler's commission was given access to the universities. On August 19, 1936, Minister of Education Rust decreed that the printing of dissertations "dealing with historical-political topics and subjects involving foreign policy" required the permission of his ministry. Dissertations that were denied approval had to be sequestered; they were declared "secret" and were accessible only by special arrangement.[48] This decree apparently did not achieve a sufficient degree of control. In an ordinance announced on October 20, 1939, Rust noted that university faculties at times approved dissertations that were "unacceptable from a National Socialist point of view." Hence he had decided that from now on the PPK was to examine dissertations before they could be printed. The PPK, Rust noted, was to vet all dissertations that took up National Socialist themes as well as dissertations that dealt with "the political, legal, humanistic, and demographic aspects of the National Socialist state"— needless to say, a rather wide range of topics. For these dissertations, the PPK could suggest changes or prevent their printing altogether.[49] In a letter to Hess, Rosenberg protested against this regulation, maintaining that it violated freedom of research,[50] a strange argument coming from a man who untiringly fought for an increase in his own censorious practice. We know of at least one instance where a student whose dissertation had been ordered sequestered was also denied his doctoral degree.[51]

One way in which the PPK achieved the "informal" suppression of a book was to bring pressure on authors "voluntarily" to withdraw manuscripts slated for publication. Karl Köster had submitted his manuscript on the production of mineral oil in Germany to the PPK for examination. On February 23, 1939, the PPK informed him that publication of this work was "undesirable since it could provide foreign nations with valuable information about Germany's economic policy in this area." He was requested to tell his publisher "that he wished to withdraw the manuscript."[52] In cases where the faults of a book were relatively minor, the PPK would make authors revise the text to make it acceptable. Such changes still did not always lead to clearance. In one instance a book was revised three times, but the PPK each time remained dissatisfied, and the book finally was ordered confiscated.[53] In cases where the author was more compliant and the book had passed muster with the PPK, the Gestapo would be informed to release the confiscated copies of the book.[54]

The Gestapo accepted, as a matter of course, the right of the PPK to ask for the enforcement of its book bans. In some cases the confiscated book would retroactively also be listed on the Index; in other instances the book was suppressed without any involvement of the RSK or the Ministry of Propaganda.[55] Indeed, we know of at least one case where a book that had been cleared for publication by the RSK was subsequently confiscated by the Gestapo on orders of the PPK. When the RSK inquired from the Gestapa why the book, the memoir of an Englishman who had served as a volunteer with Franco's air force during the Spanish civil war, had been seized, they were told that the seizure had been ordered by the PPK.[56] There is no indication that the RSK protested this high-handed action. In another case the PPK was able to overrule the action of the Gestapo that had seized a book on the grounds that it was "Marxist." In a letter of August 23, 1934, to the Gestapa the PPK inquired why this work by a veteran party member had been confiscated and urged "better cooperation with the PPK. It is necessary that the work of state and party agencies supplement each other." The Gestapa accepted the supreme authority of the PPK and informed local Gestapo offices that the book in question had been cleared.[57]

In the case of a book whose author was a Hungarian citizen and who moreover had paid for much of the cost of printing the book, the Gestapo decided that it could not carry out a request to pulp. Instead, the confiscated 707 copies of the book were put into safe storage; their ultimate fate is not recorded.[58] On occasion, especially when confiscation and pulping might cause a publisher very serious economic damage, the PPK allowed that the offending publication be sold abroad. In August 1935 the PPK informed the Catholic publisher Herder in Freiburg that the first six volumes of its encyclopedia *Der Grosse Herder,* published before 1933, were not to be sold any more. The publisher was asked to indicate how the volumes could be revised "in accordance with the present political situation." Herder apparently did not think that such a revision was possible, and it eventually was given permission to sell the remaining 2,712 complete sets abroad.[59] No such consideration was shown to publishers who were accused of having distorted the National Socialist ideology. An internal report of the SD noted that as of 1936 six publishers had been forbidden to issue any National Socialist literature.[60] The deterrent effect of these orders was enhanced by publishing them in the *Börsenblatt.*[61]

Hitler personally showed no special interest in the censorship of books, though in 1942 he ordered that the writings of the Reichsleiter, the highest ranking officers of the Nazi party, be submitted for his approval before publication.[62] In several other instances Hitler was called upon to render a decision because party officials brought the issue to him. In 1939 Georg Leibbrandt, a Russia expert in the Nazi party and in charge of its anti-Soviet and anti-Communist propaganda, submitted the proofs of a book *Adolf Hitler: Judentum und Bolschewismus* to the PPK for approval. The work represented excerpts from *Mein Kampf* as well from speeches and various other pronouncements by Hitler on the subjects of Jewry and Bolshevism. The book was to be published by Franz Eher. Bouhler decided to seek Hitler's opinion about this project and was told that the Führer "did not want his work to divided into parts and published according to various topics." On June 2, 1939, Bouhler consequently informed Eher that "the Führer has forbidden the publication of this book."[63]

NATIONALSOZIALISTISCHE ✦ DEUTSCHE ARBEITERPARTEI

PARTEI-KANZLEI

REICHSVERFÜGUNGSBLATT

München, 7. Dezember 1942	Ausgabe A	Folge 47 12

Tag   Inhalt

21. 11. 42   **Verfügung V 21/42: Herausgabe von Büchern und Schriften von führenden Parteigenossen**   137

             Die Anordnungen A 80 und A 81 42 sind im Reichsverfügungsblatt nicht erschienen

30. 11. 42   Anordnung A 82/42: Nachwuchs der Partei   138

30. 11. 42   Anordnung A 83 42: Aufnahme der NSDAP.

             Aufnahme der Angehörigen des Jahrganges 1925 in die Partei und die Über-

             weisung in die Gliederungen   139

Der Führer

Verfügung V 21/42

Ich verfüge:

Bücher und sonstige Schriften von Reichsleitern, Gauleitern, Gliederungs- und Verbandsführern sind mir vor Herausgabe vorzulegen; das gleiche gilt für Schriften anderer prominenter Parteigenossen. Auch Schriften, zu denen einer der erwähnten Parteigenossen ein Vorwort oder einen sonstigen Beitrag verfaßt hat, sind einzureichen.

Die Vorlage der Manuskripte hat über den Leiter meiner Partei-Kanzlei zu erfolgen. Vor erfolgter Genehmigung hat jede Ankündigung des Werkes in der Öffentlichkeit zu unterbleiben.

Führerhauptquartier, den 21. November 1942.

gez. Adolf Hitler.

Erscheint in Ausgabe A.

Die Anordnungen A 80 und A 81/42

sind im Reichsverfügungsblatt nicht erschienen.

137

Hitler order of November 21, 1942: Books and other publications by leading party leaders to be submitted to him for approval. *Courtesy Bundesarchiv Berlin-Lichterfelde*

In another case Hitler ruled against a new edition of a book on the sea battle at Narvik during the invasion of Norway in April 1940, which the PPK had found lacking in "National Socialist attitude." Admiral Erich Raeder, the head of the German navy, had written an introduction to the book and vigorously protested the action of the PPK. Bormann took the issue to Hitler, who sided with Bouhler and came out against reissuing the book. The PPK gave assurances that Hitler's role in the dispute would be handled with complete discretion.[64] Not surprisingly, Hitler's decisions paid no attention to the normal procedures for the control of books.[65]

In the face of growing shortages of manpower, on October 9, 1941, Hitler gave orders that party and state agencies were to take on only work essential to the successful conduct of the war.[66] But the PPK apparently was little affected by this measure. After Hess's flight to England on May 10, 1941, Bouhler, with the concurrence of Bormann, declared the PPK to be an independent office in the chancellery of the Führer (headed by Bouhler), thus sheltering it from interference.[67] During the final months of the war and under the "total mobilization" organized by Goebbels, various state and party offices were shut down or severely cut back. The PPK, it appears, continued to function more or less unimpeded.

On April 27, 1944, the *Völkischer Beobachter* congratulated the PPK on its tenth anniversary and noted the important contribution it had made in defending the National Socialist ideology.[68] When Bormann ordered the transfer of one of Bouhler's trusted co-workers to the Party chancellery in October 1944, Bouhler protested the move and insisted that only he should decide how many persons were needed to continue the work of the PPK. If the Führer wished it, he was prepared to close down his office, but as long as the PPK existed it required a certain minimum number of officials.[69] The *Nationalsozialistische Bibliographie* was still being compiled in December 1944 even though publication was no longer possible.[70] As late as February 27, 1945, the files show the submission to the PPK of a dissertation completed in the department of philosophy of the University of Leipzig.[71]

As in the case of the RSK, the very existence of an office that could issue bans in any area of book publication as well as shut down entire publishing operations undoubtedly encouraged self-censorship. Jürgen Soenke, an official of the PPK, called the system of control practiced by the PPK "preventive censorship." By leaving it up to a publisher to decide whether or not to submit a book for examination by the PPK, it "imposed on him a responsibility that for practical purposes amounted to censorship." According to Soenke, the publishers on their own often declined to publish a certain book, that is, practiced self-censorship, even though it was by no means sure that the work in question would fail to pass muster by the PPK.[72] This system was insidious but no doubt effective.

Alfred Rosenberg: Hitler's Plenipotentiary for Ideological Education

Alfred Rosenberg was a Baltic-German, hailing from an area where the name "Rosenberg" was common among both Christians and Jews. On January 24, 1934, Rosenberg became Plenipotentiary of the Führer for Monitoring the Entire Intellectual and Ideological Education of the NSDAP (Beauftragter des Führers für die Überwachung der gesamten geistigen und weltanschaulichen Erziehung der NSDAP). Hitler had appointed Rosenberg to monitor the ideological education of the Nazi party, but Rosenberg on his own enlarged this assignment, as his letterhead indicated, to "monitoring the instruction and education of the entire National Socialist movement," that is, including the party's affiliated organizations. As one of the earliest members of the Nazi party and part of Hitler's inner circle, Rosenberg had hoped to become a minister. However, even though he had attained the highest rank in the party—that of Reichsleiter—he had to settle for a post outside the government.

The new assignment was in line with Rosenberg's endeavors as head of the Kampfbund für deutsche Kultur, established in 1928 to defend German literature against its un-German enemies, and he undoubtedly hoped to achieve a major role in shaping cultural developments in the new Germany. But that was not to be. Rosenberg, known as the "philosopher" of the Nazi party, had early on impressed Hitler with his "learning." Rosenberg was the author of several books in which he gave expression to his fanatical German nationalism, his virulent anti-Bolshevism, and his doctrinaire anti-Semitism. However, by all accounts, Rosenberg lacked any kind of leadership ability, and as an intensely arrogant individual, he managed to unite practically all of the party bigwigs in their dislike of him.[1] If Hitler nevertheless appointed him to an important position, this was undoubtedly due to his strategy of creating rival and overlapping domains that sought to guarantee the Führer's own supreme leadership.[2] In the resulting struggle of competing organizations, the politically inept Rosenberg was repeatedly outmaneuvered and won few battles. He has been called a person "who wanted much and achieved little."[3]

After Hitler became chancellor in January 1933, many of those who had been active in Rosenberg's Kampfbund became bureaucrats of the new state. The Kampfbund's section dealing with books reconstituted itself in June 1933 as the Reich Office for the Promotion of German Literature (Reichsstelle zur Förderung des deutschen Schrifttums—RFdS). It was headed by Hans Hagemeyer, a veteran member of the Kampfbund. According to its title, the new office was to promote literature, and for a time it did indeed take on such tasks as helping deserving young authors to find a publisher. It also issued lists of books that every library was advised to acquire. However, as a memo of the RSK, compiled in January 1935 and discussing the work of the Reichsstelle after about nineteen months of operation, correctly noted, "the Reichsstelle is less an office for the promotion as for the examination of literature."[4]

In the eyes of Rosenberg and his men, a large part of the German book market consisted of works that "promoted pseudo-science, pseudo-religiosity, shallow fiction and youth literature, and confusing political scribble without any redeeming value." It was the task of the Reichsstelle to subject this literature to a constructive but sharp critique and persuade all those involved with the book trade to reject these kinds of works.[5] Three years later, the Reichsstelle concluded that it had made great progress. Writing in 1938, Hellmuth Langenbucher, one of the founders of the Kampfbund and in 1934 its deputy head, stated with pride that the Third Reich had succeeded in eliminating from its literature all that was "sick, un-German, and rootless."[6]

Rosenberg's appointment had made him responsible for the ideological education of the Nazi party, but his new organization quickly extended its reach to the entire corpus of German literature. In an announcement of March 25, 1934, Rosenberg let it be known that the Reichsstelle had the task of "monitoring German printed publications," functioning as the "inspection agency of the movement."[7] A circular issued on June 20, 1934, estimated that this examination included almost two thirds of the total book production in Germany.[8] This literature, in the words of Rosenberg official Bernhard Payr, had to be vetted for its educational and ideological soundness. "The implementation of this task serves to assure not only the ideological unity of the National Socialist movement but also of the entire German people."[9] The actual examination of books was done by an unpaid volunteer staff of 400 readers, who had the necessary substantive knowledge as well as ideological reliability and who were supervised by twenty editors. In 1933 the Reichsstelle issued about 2,000 assessments; the following year the number of assessments rose to 10,000.[10] The number of readers also increased steadily, and by 1941 it had reached 1,400, overseen by about fifty editors.[11] In order to prevent contact between readers and the authors of the books they were evaluating, the names of the readers were not made public. Authors were sent a summary of the readers' findings. By paying a fee, publishers were entitled to use the positive assessments in their advertising. This privilege was withdrawn in August 1939, however, and thereafter the fee entitled publishers merely to indicate that the book in question had been "positively evaluated and was recommended to the Party and its affiliated organizations."[12]

A "confidential publication" for the readers, *Lektoren-Brief*, provided instructions on how to write assessments.[13] They were to be composed in a way that made them usable as "disguised book reviews which the Reichsstelle could transmit to the press." Assessments were not to be too long, and they were to make clear whether the readers approved or rejected the book in question. "The works of ideological opponents are to be labeled as such clearly and ruthlessly. . . . The ideological opponents of National Socialism may not be felt sorry for nor be underestimated."[14]

The official publication of the Reichsstelle was the monthly *Bücherkunde*, which began to appear in 1934. In early 1944, when the scarcity of paper had become critical, the *Bücherkunde* still was able to appear in an edition of 8,000 copies.[15] The magazine ran articles about new publications and trends in German literature and the book market. According to Rosenberg official Payr, who was not a disinterested judge, the *Bücherkunde* quickly became "the leading literary journal in Germany,"[16] but even scholars writing after 1945 attest to its influence.[17] The *Bücherkunde* also included a supplement, *Gutachtenanzeiger* (Gazette of Assessments), which made known the results of the Reichsstelle's evaluation of books and manuscripts. This gazette listed approved and disapproved titles: *Positiver Gutachtenanzeiger* and *Gutachtenanzeiger—Negativ!* The positive section, in turn, was divided into "Recommended" books and manuscripts and "Conditionally recommended" books and manuscripts. Not long after these supplements had begun to appear (the exact date is not known), it was decided to discontinue these announcements. The reason probably was the same as the one that had led the RSK to keep its Index secret, that is, to be able to deny that there existed "blacklists." A notice (preserved only as a form letter without date) announced that from here on "the *Gutachtenanzeiger* may no longer be published." The gazette of recommended books and manuscripts will be sent to the appropriate organizations; the gazette of not-recommended works is to be treated as "Strictly Secret" and will be given only to a limited number of officials.[18]

From 1936 on, the RFdS issued a summary volume at the end of the year, *Jahres-Gutachtenanzeiger*, which also was marked "Strictly Confidential! For Official Use Only!" The total number of evaluated books ranged between 1,232 in 1936 and 826 in 1941. The number of negatively assessed books declined gradually—from 710 in 1936 to 229 in 1941, that is, from 58 to 28 percent. The great majority of negatively evaluated books were in the fiction category.[19] The decrease in objectionable books may have been due to the growing influence of the Rosenberg organization or to the closing of ranks in wartime when authors would have been more inclined to follow the official line. Rosenberg had built up an extensive machinery for the examination of books and manuscripts, for which he energetically sought official recognition. In a letter of November 1, 1933, to the league of Nazi teachers (N.S. Lehrerbund, or NSLB), Reichsstelle head Hagemeyer made the audacious claim that "our office is not only an organization but a *public authority* [*Behörde*], since we are an unofficial department of the Ministry for Public Enlightenment and Propaganda."[20] This assertion no doubt represented wishful thinking, but Hagemeyer's aspirations included more. In a letter of May 4, 1934, to the Ministry of the Interior he pointed out that his office could help eliminate the prevailing lack of a uniform procedure for vetting books that resulted in the states issuing conflicting book bans. "The Reichsstelle," he wrote, "already, and very frequently, has been consulted by various states with regard to the banning of questionable books. In the interest of calming the book market, it would be best if in the future only one agency were to be authorized to vet offensive literature."[21] Needless to say, the proposal to have Rosenberg become the only official examiner of books did not go anywhere.

Even more disappointing to Rosenberg was that he lacked the authority to enforce his findings—the executive power to ban books. The formulation of cultural policy, Rosenberg noted in his diary on June 5, 1934, "is now the subject of a regular tug-of-war. . . . One has hopes for *me*, but because of the *fact* that a National Socialist [Goebbels] is president of the Reichskulturkammer, it is difficult to create another party organization *without* or against it."[22] The Ministry of Propaganda under Goebbels indeed constituted a powerful rival that for a time had hoped to have the Reichsstelle under its control. Rosenberg successfully resisted this move, and in June 1934 he took the Reichsstelle into his Amt Rosenberg (Office Rosenberg and also known as Chancellory Rosenberg), where it functioned as part of the Main Bureau for Fostering Literature (Hauptstelle 'Schrifttumspflege'). As Payr, head of the Amt Rosenberg and editor-in-chief of the Reichsstelle formulated it, the tasks of the Reichsstelle "derive necessarily from the mandate for the supervision of the entire intellectual and ideological education of the NSDAP that the Reichsleiter [Rosenberg] has received from the Führer."[23]

On October 5, 1934, Rosenberg's chief of staff, Gotthard Urban, sent a circular to all Gauleiter and NS-organizations "regarding literature permitted by the party." The Reichsstelle, Urban emphasized, was the only authority to issue assessments of books to the party and its affiliated organizations. All questions regarding permitted or forbidden books were to be addressed to the Reichsstelle.[24] As if this grab of power were not enough, Rosenberg personally undertook to quarrel with Goebbels in the aggressive and disagreeable manner for which he was known. On October 12, 1934, he protested to the Ministry of

Propaganda about a list of "Six Books of the Month" and its accompanying commentary that the ministry had sent to the press. "The Reichsschrifttumsstelle [in the Ministry of Propaganda] in no way has the right to interfere in matters that concern the ideological work of the movement and on its own to recommend books to the party." Such guidance must first be approved by the Reichsstelle. "I must ask you to make sure that your ministry and its subordinated agencies do not repeat such transgressions."[25] The reaction of the Ministry of Propaganda to this letter is not known, but it is unlikely to have endeared Rosenberg to the officials of the ministry. On November 16 Goebbels noted in his diary that he had had a good talk with Hitler about "the difficulties Rosenberg is causing us."[26]

The conflict between Rosenberg and Goebbels' RSK flared up again in the spring of 1935. Hans-Friedrich Blunck, the president of the RSK, writes in his memoirs that he and his vice president Heinz Wismann had decided "to launch a major attack on Rosenberg's Reichsstelle" in order to achieve " its subordination to the RSK."[27] In an announcement dated March 12, 1935, and carried by the Börsenblatt nine days later, Wismann informed the book trade that requests for the examination of books or manuscripts had to be complied with only if they came from one of the following four authorities: the Ministry of Propaganda and its adjunct the Reichsschrifttumskammer, the Reichskulturkammer, the Parteiamtliche Prüfungskommission, and the police. No other organization had the right to interfere in the work of German publishers and the book trade.[28] Notably absent from the list of empowered authorities was the Reichsstelle. When Hagemeyer, the head of the Reichsstelle, phoned the RSK to find out the reasons for this omission, he was told that "unfortunately the Reichsstelle is not an official party organization; the announcement had mentioned only official entities." The order had become necessary because the publishing world had become greatly upset about the many demands for free copies of books, seen as the start of a process of censorship.[29]

On the same day, Rosenberg personally protested against this measure. In a letter to RSK president Blunck he stated that "no vice president of the RSK has the slightest right to decide which National Socialist organization is to be considered official or non-official." The Reichsstelle's concern with literature, he noted, was clearly related to the mandate he had received from the Führer to monitor the entire instruction and education of the Nazi party and its affiliated organizations. Rosenberg therefore urgently requested that the ordinance of March 12 be corrected and the Reichsstelle be listed as one of the authorities entitled to examine the work of publishers and the book trade. If his request were to be ignored, Rosenberg threatened, he would issue an appropriate announcement on his own.[30]

Wismann thereupon inquired from Hess whether the Reichsstelle was, as Rosenberg claimed, indeed an official party organization. He was familiar with Hess's order establishing the Parteiamtliche Prüfungskommission (PPK), but he had seen no such order for the Reichsstelle, an entity that, to the best of his knowledge, was merely a registered association.[31] Rosenberg meanwhile, not having received a reply to his protest to Wismann, decided to go public. On April 11 the *Völkischer Beobachter* ran a statement by Rosenberg in which he described the Reichsstelle as the only authority entitled to mediate between party and state in matters concerning literature. The Reichsstelle was to be regarded as "the custodian of German literature in the most comprehensive sense of that term." Walther Funk, state secretary in the Ministry of Propaganda, who forwarded this information to Hess, noted that he had checked with the Reich Chancellery and "personally with the Führer" and had learned that these claims were entirely unfounded. There existed no official order giving Rosenberg these kinds of powers. "Neither the Führer personally nor the Reich Chancellery nor any other governmental entity has even considered this matter." He asked Hess how he was to proceed.[32]

Bouhler, the head of the PPK, also entered the fray. In a statement in the *Völkischer Beobachter* of April 12, 1935, published "in order to protect the public against errors," Bouhler affirmed that "the PPK alone dealt with questions concerning National Socialist literature," and it did so independently of any other party or state office. Rosenberg's Reichsstelle was entitled to mark a National Socialist publication as "recommended" only after it had been submitted to the PPK and had received the declaration of no-objection. In order to preserve some semblance of peace, Bouhler added that his announcement did not contradict Rosenberg's statement of April 11, "but merely constituted complementary information."[33]

Seeking to bring about a resolution of the dispute, in early May Wismann met with Rosenberg. In a report on this meeting, Wismann noted that he had stood by his refusal to consider the Reichsstelle an official party organization "entitled to make requests to the German book trade." It had finally been agreed that the Main Bureau for Fostering Literature (Hauptstelle Schrifttumspflege) in Rosenberg's office, but not the Reichsstelle, be listed as entitled to deal directly with publishers. Wismann acknowledged that this arrangement did not really resolve the issue of the Reichsstelle. Nevertheless Rosenberg had had to admit that "the Reichsstelle was not an official entity of the party, but a private initiative."[34] His admission was significant.

It took several more weeks before this oral agreement could be transformed into a written document, but on July 12, 1935, Wismann was finally able to announce the end of this particular dispute. Amending his order of March 12, Wismann let it be known that the Office of the Plenipotentiary of the Führer for the Entire Intellectual and Ideological Education of the NSDAP was entitled to "submit official requests to the German book trade."[35] As it turned out, this arrangement merely papered over the basic conflict between Rosenberg on one

31

Nationalsozialistische Deutsche Arbeiterpartei

Reichsleitung

Reichsgeschäftsstelle:
München, Briennerstraße 45
Briefanschrift: München 48, Briefsach 46
Telefon-Nummern: 64901, 56364 u. 56081
Postscheckkonto München 28819

Hauptzeitung der Partei: „Völkischer Beobachter"
Geschäftsstelle der Zeitung: Thierschstraße 11
Telefon-Nummer 50647
Schriftleitung: Schellingstraße 39
Telefon-Nummer 50801   Postscheckkonto 11866

Der Beauftragte des Führers für die
gesamte geistige und weltanschauliche Erziehung der NSDAP

Berlin W 35, *11.10.35.*
Margaretenstr. 17
Fernsprecher B2 Lützow 9541
Postscheckkonto Berlin 170170

Rundschreiben Nr. 10
————————————————

An die

Herren Gauleiter der N.S.D.A.P.

Soeben ist ein Vortrag des Amtsleiters der
NS-Gemeinschaft "Kraft durch Freude", Parteigenossen Horst Dressler-Andress, unter dem Titel
"Arbeit und Kunst"im Druck erschienen. Dieser Vortrag ist in dieser Form nicht geeignet eine aufklä-
rende und erzieherische Wirkung auszuüben, er lässt
im Gegenteil , Verwirrung befürchten.

Ich untersage deshalb in meiner Eigenschaft als
Beauftragter des Führers für die gesamte geistige
und weltanschauliche Erziehung der NSDAP sowie des
Werkes "Kraft durch Freude" die Verbreitung dieses
Vortrages. Ferner bitte ich, sofort veranlassen zu
wollen, dass eine Ankündigung oder Besprechung des
Vortrages in der Presse Ihres Gaues unterbleibt.

F.d.R.:

Stabsleiter
Berlin, den 11.Oktober 1935
M.

gez. Alfred Rosenberg

Höflichkeitsformeln fallen bei allen parteiamtlichen Schreiben weg.

Rosenberg informs the Gauleiter that he has banned the publication of a lecture by
the head of *Kraft durch Freude. Courtesy Bundesarchiv Berlin-Lichterfelde*

side and Goebbels and Bouhler on the other. If anything, during the following
years this feud became even more heated and nasty.

The conflict over the Reichsstelle had ended with a decisive defeat for
Rosenberg. His elaborately built extensive apparatus for evaluating books had

been declared to be a mere "private initiative." Rosenberg was humbled, but he was not giving up on seeking to forbid publications not to his liking. Even if he could not give orders to the book trade, he felt free to take on even highly placed party functionaries. On October 11, 1935, he sent a circular to all the Gauleiter in which he described a published lecture by Horst Dressler-Andress, the head of the popular leisure organization Kraft durch Freude (Strength through Joy) as "causing confusion" and not suitable for achieving "enlightening and educational" effects. "In my capacity as Beauftragter des Führers für die gesamte geistige und weltanschauliche Erziehung der NSDAP sowie des Werkes 'Kraft durch Freude', I hereby forbid the distribution of this lecture."[36]

Even though he was not formally authorized to do so, Rosenberg used the Gestapo to achieve his ends. The files of the Gestapo contain numerous requests—some from the Amt Schrifttumspflege, others from the Reichsstelle—accompanied by assessments, to forbid certain named books. Most of the time these petitions were approved. The Gestapo would forward the request and the *Gutachten* to the RSK, then the RSK would list the work on the Index and order the Gestapo to confiscate the book. Nevertheless the RSK always had the last word, and even strongly worded demands, accompanied by hostile assessments on the part of Rosenberg's office, at times failed to be approved. In the case of a novel by Hanns Menzel, the Reichsstelle had requested "that this book be removed from the German book market" because it was both "corrosive" and included "remarks endangering the state." It also had "occasional eroticisms." Despite this clearly negative assessment, the RSK turned down the demand to suppress the novel on the grounds that this office "does not share the judgment of the Reichsstelle zur Förderung des deutschen Schrifttums."[37] Similar disagreements surfaced in connection with the work of authors like Werner Bergengruen, Hans Fallada, and Ernst Wiechert.[38] No wonder that Rosenberg increasingly came to conclude that Goebbels' judgments of books were flawed and far too lenient.

In 1941 Rosenberg invoked the needed "unity of the German people," which in times of war was "more pressing than ever," in order to remind Goebbels of his domain. On November 28, 1941, he once again asked Goebbels to make sure that books dealing with ideological, religious, or confessional questions not be approved without first obtaining the "concurrence of me, the Plenipotentiary of the Führer for Monitoring the Entire Intellectual and Ideological Education of the NSDAP."[39] By that time Rosenberg had been appointed Reich Minister for the Occupied Eastern Territories as well as head of the Einsatzstab Rosenberg (Special Task Force Rosenberg), engaged in pillaging the cultural treasures of Nazi-occupied Europe. These new assignments necessarily weakened Rosenberg's ability to devote time to his role as would-be censor. Goebbels now had even less reason than before to give in to Rosenberg's claims.

PART 3

THE PRACTICE OF CENSORSHIP

The Reasons for Banning Books

Authors had to be members of the RSK, and such membership presupposed political reliability. One would have thought that this political screening in and by itself would have made book bans a rare occurrence, but this was not the case. The men in charge of censorship, many of them with no special knowledge or training for this assignment, displayed great sensitivity to the slightest deviation from orthodoxy and exaggerated alleged threats to the Nazi ideology. The result was a huge number of book bans, especially in the first five years of Nazi rule. Pushed by several actors in different state and party offices, Nazi book censorship cast a wide net.

In his study of the banning of books in the Third Reich, Dietrich Aigner noted the large number of "delicts" on the part of a writer that could lead to his books being forbidden. As of 1939, four main groups of authors could have all their writings put on the Index:

Emigrants ("Traitors to the People")	45 percent
Marxist and Soviet authors	31 percent
"Pornographers"	10 percent
Others and not identifiable reasons	14 percent[1]

To these categories one should add authors who were banned because their writings represented "decadent literature." This group included writers whose books dealt with the ugly side of urban life or with sexual and pathological themes, or who, following an expressionist style, dwelt upon dreams and feelings. The Nazis rejected this kind of modernism in the name of "healthy popular sentiment" (*gesundes Volksempfinden*). Among such "decadent" authors were Ernst Glaeser, Maxim Gorki, Erich Kästner, Romain Rolland, Arthur Schnitzler, Upton Sinclair, and Frank Wedekind.[2] Some foreign writers were banned because they were hostile to the new Germany and engaged in active agitation against it. These included authors such as Helen Keller, Pierre van Paassen, Martha Dodd, and Sigrid Undset. A biography of Rembrandt by the Dutch writer Theun de Vries was forbidden because the author was a member of the Dutch Communist party and of the Dutch "Committee of Artists and Intellectuals Fighting the German Terror."[3] Dealers of scientific books were not allowed to supply Marxist books even to their scholarly customers. When a scientific institute had need of such a book, it had to submit an application to the RSK.[4]

Surprising as it may seem, until 1940 there existed no ordinance banning the writings of Jewish authors merely because they were Jewish or non-Aryan, though being Jewish undoubtedly represented an aggravating factor, and persons known to be non-Aryan as of May 15, 1936, were ordered excluded from the RSK. This situation had nothing to do with toleration or lack of anti-Semitic ardor but rather was the result, among other things, of the difficulties involved in discovering the "racial" origin of German authors.

During the first years of the Nazi regime, the *Börsenblatt* of the German book trade published several lists of "Schädlinge des Volkes" (Parasites of the People). These were authors who had emigrated and had subsequently been deprived of their German citizenship because "their conduct had lacked the duty of fidelity toward Reich and people" and thereby had damaged German interests. "It goes without saying," the *Börsenblatt* stressed in one of these announcements, that the works of these writers could no longer be distributed by the German book trade.[5] The use of the term *parasite* for these authors, a word generally reserved for pests that threaten agricultural crops, was symptomatic of the Nazis' willingness to consider their opponents as non-human. This attitude, in turn, made it easy for them eventually to destroy physically those they regarded as endangering the German state such as Jews, Polish intellectuals, and Soviet political commissars.

The list of literary Schädlinge included such well-known German writers as Bertolt Brecht, Lion Feuchtwanger, Leonhard Frank, Oskar Maria Graf, Konrad Heiden, Alfred Kerr, Walter Mehring, Erwin Piscator, Theodor Plievier, Ernst Toller, Kurt Tucholsky, Carl Zuckmayer, and Arnold Zweig. Also on this list were Heinrich Mann and the children of Thomas Mann, Klaus and Erika.

Because of the reputation of Thomas Mann as one of the greatest German writers, who in 1929 had received the Nobel Prize for Literature, the Nazis at first were hesitant to move against this international celebrity. But in December 1936 Thomas Mann's citizenship too was annulled, he was listed among the "parasites of the people," and his writings were put on the official Index. The Gestapo was ordered to confiscate all his books. Mann, it was charged, had participated in numerous anti-German rallies, and in an article in a leading Swiss newspaper had publicly expressed "the most serious insults against the Reich."[6] In 1940 Julius Streicher's anti-Semitic hate-sheet *Der Stürmer* inquired whether Thomas and Heinrich Mann were Jews. The RSK responded that the Mann brothers were not Jewish, but that, according to Adolf Bartel's book on Jewish authors, their mother had been a Portuguese and therefore "possibly had Jewish or Negro blood."[7]

The Reich Chamber of Literature asks the Gestapo to confiscate the writings of Thomas Mann. *Courtesy Bundesarchiv Berlin-Lichterfelde*

Even though the primary impetus for finally moving against Thomas Mann seems to have been his political activities against Nazi Germany, some of the works of authors deemed sympathetic to Thomas Mann's writings were also banned. The book of the Austrian writer Erich Heller, *Flucht aus dem zwanzigsten Jahrhundert* (Flight from the Twentieth Century), published in Vienna in 1938, was indexed because it contained approving comments for Mann's Joseph novels and followed "Mann's thinking about the intellectual future of mankind."[8] In February 1937 Thomas Mann was the driving force in establishing the Thomas Mann Fund to help needy emigrated German writers. The fund was supported by many well-known foreign authors, including W. H. Auden,

André Gide, Aldous Huxley, André Maurois, Jules Romain, Ignazio Silone, Upton Sinclair, and H. G. Wells. The announcement of this fund was said to include attacks upon the new Germany, and the RSK let it be known that the writings of authors who endorsed the fund no longer deserved to be published.[9]

In his diary, Goebbels several times defended "the need for some erotic literature." Germany, he argued, "is not a nunnery."[10] In July 1938 he decided that homosexuality was not automatically a reason for exclusion or expulsion from the RSK and the other chambers, and that henceforth he personally would make decisions in these cases.[11] And yet the practice of censorship with regard to sex was often strait-laced, not to say puritanical. Historical fiction was to avoid "scandals." The publication of a collection of letters dealing with the private life of Queen Victoria and Prince Albert was deemed "undesirable." [12] The same judgment was rendered with regard to a book about Mrs. Wallis Simpson that carried the subtitle "The story of a woman on account of whom the King of England gave up his throne." The book was held to be "sensationalist" and involved "the warming up of family stories," the kind of writing that is "not in tune with National Socialist principles."[13] Four novels were ordered confiscated because "with regard to eroticism they do not observe the necessary reserve."[14] A novel by the highly regarded Austrian author Hans von Hoffensthal was banned because its "erotic content is likely to endanger morality."[15] In February 1940 Goebbels forbade the advertising of erotic literature except for the classics *The History of My Life* by Casanova and Boccaccio's *Decameron*.[16]

In the eyes of the Nazis, a woman's highest values were marriage and motherhood, and a "healthy sexuality" was acceptable only for the purpose of procreation.[17] Hence books that ran counter to this view of women's role in society were banned. A book published in 1930 that defended birth control, abortion, and support for women who had experienced a miscarriage was forbidden in 1940.[18] Also banned was a book that described the method of natural birth control based on the woman's cycles of fecundity.[19] A calendar of conception was forbidden because it violated "healthy moral sensitivity" and was also undesirable on account of its demographic point of view, that is, it sought to limit population increase.[20] And a book with the title *The Rise of Women* was banned because it "represented the typical product of an intellectual woman" who neutralized her womanhood by taking refuge in creative literary activity. Moreover, the bibliography of the work included "more than a dozen sexual Bolsheviks (*Sexualbolschewisten*)."[21] Sex education too was unacceptable. The book *The Ideal Marriage: Its Physiology and Technique* by the Dutch gynecologist Theodor Hendrik van de Velde, published in 1926 to instant international acclaim and by 1932 reaching forty-two printings in Germany, was indexed by the Nazis.

The first nudist organization in the world was established in Germany in the late nineteenth century, and what became known as *Freikörperkultur* (literally

Reichsausschuß für Volksgesundheitsdienst
Hauptabteilung II – Gesundheitsführung
Reichsarbeitsgemeinschaft für Mutter und Kind

15

Berlin W 62
Einemstraße 11
Fernruf: B 5, 9321

An den

Herrn Präsidenten der Reichsschrifttumskammer,

B e r l i n W.8.
-.-.-.-.-.-.-.-.-
Friedrichstr. 194/199

Reichsschrifttumskammer

-9. JUL. 1937
- 2371/1.

Ihre Zeichen	Ihre Nachricht vom	Unsere Zeichen	Tag
		II.S.Dr.F/A	2. Juli 1937.

Betr. **Mina Weber "Aufstieg durch die Frau".**

Die Reichsfrauenführung, Abteilung Kultur, Erziehung
und Schulung, hat uns unter dem 7. Mai d.J. das vorgenannte
Buch mit einer abfälligen Kritik zu unserer Kenntnis und
Prüfung übersandt. Wir überreichen in der Anlage einen
Durchschlag des Ergebnisses dieser Prüfung, und unterstützen
den Antrag der Reichsfrauenführung auf Verbot dieses Buches.

Zur Begründung weisen wir darauf hin, dass das dem Buch
beigegebene Quellenverzeichnis über ein Dutzend von Autoren
aufführt, die als Sexualbolschewisten dem Verbreitungsver-
bot bereits anheimgefallen sind. Es braucht deshalb auch
nicht Wunder nehmen, dass bei diesen unsauberen Quellen das
literarische Produkt der Verfasserin für Nationalsozialisten
untragbar erscheinen muss.

Heil H i t l e r !
In Vertretung:

1 Anlage.

Höflichkeitsformeln fallen bei allen Schreiben fort.

The party organization "Mother and Child" asks the Reich Chamber of Literature
to ban a book that quotes from banned "Sexual Bolshevists." *Courtesy Bundesarchiv
Berlin-Lichterfelde*

"free body culture" or nudism) by the time of the 1920s had become a mass movement. In 1933 all nudist organizations were dissolved. As the Nazis saw it, nudism destroyed the natural modesty of women and took away men's respect for women. At the same time, all books advocating nudism were banned. Himmler was one of several Nazi leaders who disagreed with this policy, and it was in large measure due to his intervention that in 1936 the fortunes of the nudists changed for the better.[22] Nudist camps were allowed again, and the magazine *Deutsche Leibeszucht* was able to appear unhindered. The Nazis allowed the book *Mensch und Sonne* (Mankind and Sun) by Hans Surén, considered one of the best defenses of the value of nudity, to be published in 1936,[23] and by 1940 it reached its tenth printing. However, in 1941 the propaganda ministry invoked the shortage of printers, bookbinders, and paper, and nudist publications once again were denied the right to publish.[24] The champions of prudishness had won the day.

Erich Maria Remarque's *All Quiet on the Western Front,* published in 1928, sold 2.5 million copies in twenty-five languages during its first eighteen months in print, but it was banned by the Nazis on account of its realistic description of life in the trenches of World War I. Among other books that were forbidden for the same reason were the war diaries *Erlebnisse im ersten Weltkrieg* by Matthias Erzberger, a prominent Catholic politician who in 1918, as the authorized representative of the German government, had signed the armistice between Germany and the Allies, and who was assassinated by right-wing extremists in 1921. In July 1939 publishers were informed that books about the First World War in which soldiers were depicted as suffering victims rather than as fighters were undesirable.[25]

Even publications on World War I that insisted on being in tune with National Socialist ideas were often faulted. The book *Langemarck 1914: Der heldische Opfergang der deutschen Jugend* (Langemarck 1914: The Heroic Martyrdom of German Youth), by one Wilhelm Dreysse, dealt with the battle of Langemarck in October 1914, also known as the first battle of Ypres (Belgium). In this encounter, which many German writers later made into a legendary heroic episode, inexperienced infantry soldiers, some of them students, suffered severe casualties when they made futile frontal attacks on positions manned by seasoned French and British troops. The Dreysse book was criticized because it mentioned the failure of some officers and thus, "not necessarily on purpose," damaged "military preparedness." Moreover the author was said to have downgraded the futile heroic fighting at Langemarck by treating it simply as "something all-too-human." An assessment by the SD of September 14, 1939, elaborated on these mistakes and demanded that all copies of the book be confiscated. After the Gestapo Bielefeld had seized 4,500 copies of the work, the publisher pleaded for a reversal of this action on the grounds that his inability to sell these books at Christmastime would cause severe economic damage. On

December 15 the RMfVP rejected this request and approved the final confiscation of all copies.[26]

The High Command of the Army and Navy sought to prevent the publication
of works that cast a shadow on the reputation of the armed forces. Affected by
this concern were books dealing with the revolution of 1918, because the Army
was self-conscious about its failure to prevent the downfall of the monarchy.
The PPK, on the other hand, stressed the importance of these events for political education. It was essential to analyze and point out the reasons for the collapse of 1918. Only by acknowledging the failings of the then-existing regime
was it possible to understand the need for the National Socialist revolution.[27]
None of the two contending parties was able to have its point of view prevail
in all cases.

A book that advocated a united Europe was forbidden because it was said
to be written for the point of view of a "totally rootless liberalism and pacifism."[28] A work that supported the League of Nations and pan-European ideals was similarly banned as "totally utopian and of pacifist tendency."[29] The
same fate met a biography of the Austrian pacifist Bertha von Suttner, the first
woman to be awarded the Nobel Peace Prize.[30] A small book entitled *Warum
lässt Gott Kriege zu?* (Why Does God Allow Wars?) was suppressed because it
was "a Christian publication that on principle opposes all wars."[31] Books on
espionage were banned because in almost all cases of espionage the reading
of books on this subject had helped entice people to commit this crime. Books
dealing with life in the Foreign Legion were considered "undesirable," because
reading books on that subject could lure young people into leaving their country and joining the Legion.[32]

Books on religious themes received special scrutiny, for religious belief
was a competitor for the total allegiance demanded by the Nazi regime. In
the struggle for the minds of the German people, the National Socialists did
not want rivals. It was for this reason that Hitler had no use for the racialist
German church advocated by Rosenberg in his *Myth of the Twentieth Century,*
for Himmler's advocacy of a Nordic religion, or for the quasi-pagan German
Faith Movement. National Socialism, Hitler insisted, had to stay clear of all
sectarian and mystic cults.

It goes without saying that the works of Karl Kautsky and Otto Bauer, dealing with the relationship of socialism and Christianity, were forbidden. The
same fate met the writings of the religious socialists Paul Tillich, Günther
Dehn, and Paul Piechowski as well as the works of the Christian pacifists Otto
Dibelius and Leonhard Ragaz. As was to be expected, all the books of the Jesuit
Friedrich Muckermann, who had left Germany in 1934 and who carried on an
active campaign of denunciation of the Nazi regime, were indexed.[33] Equally
unacceptable were the writings of Protestant theologians such as Emil Brunner
and Karl Barth, who had voiced criticism of the Nazi regime. When the SD in

late 1937 asked for a ban of a sermon Barth had given in Basel and that had been published as a pamphlet, the RSK at first expressed doubt that forbidding a single sermon was necessary. The SD replied that Barth's writings had a strong appeal among the Confessing Church and provided "the intellectual basis for agitation hostile to the state."[34] The Index of 1938 listed all of Barth's publications. Three of Brunner's works were also indexed.

By 1937 the dissolution of monasteries, the confiscation of church property, and attacks upon denominational schools had strained relations between the Nazi state and the Catholic Church. This tension was reflected in bans of numerous books by Catholic authors, with Catholic publishers like Herder hit particularly hard.[35] Here are some examples of forbidden Catholic books:

- The translation of a biography of Father Damien, a Belgian missionary priest who for more than sixteen years ministered to the lepers on the Hawaiian island of Molokai and eventually himself died of the disease, was refused because the book was held to represent "hidden propaganda for the Catholic ideology and teaching."[36] The German-Swiss edition of the book was indexed.
- The priest of a Berlin parish sought permission to print in a private edition a history of his parish, meant only for members of the parish and not to be available in the book trade. The Ministry of Propaganda denied the request because the author affirmed the loyalty of Catholics to the Cross as especially necessary "at a time when neo-pagans attacked the thousand-year blessings of Christianity."[37]
- A book of verse that had been used in Austrian schools before the *Anschluss* of 1938 was banned because "many verses represented obvious propaganda for Catholic ideas."[38]
- A brochure on "The Family in the Lay Apostolate of Our Time" was forbidden because it equated civil marriage with cohabitation.[39]
- A book on the Catholic school system in the former German colony of East Africa was banned because it constituted "propaganda for Catholic missionary activity in the future German colonies, skillfully hidden under the cloak of a scientific work."[40]
- Two brochures addressed to boys and girls were forbidden because they advocated educational principles that lacked any kind of "political focus." Instead, the brochures "justified the interference of the Church in purely secular matters" and propagated ideas in violation "of the essential laws of the *Volk*." The publications had rejected marriage between Catholics and non-Catholics by citing the Old Testament prohibition of marriage between Jews and non-Jews. This "downgraded racial principles."[41]
- A brochure "Thoughts about Mary for Spiritual Directors" was banned because it asked the faithful "to stand up for Christ and his law."[42]

- The book *Blut und Rasse* (Blood and Race) was indexed because the title was entirely misleading. The author propagated a "Catholicism of pure blood" to be achieved by absorbing the "precious blood of Christ." This "devalued the racial principles of the National Socialist ideology" and "endangered the values of blood and soil as well as of *Volk* and race."[43]
- A novel dealing with the end of life on earth was banned because after the big catastrophe only a handful of Catholic believers were said to be left alive. This "enhancement of Catholicism was undesirable in Germany, a country with a long-standing confessional split."[44]
- A novel by a French Jesuit was banned because it celebrated the ideals of the Catholic scout movement and altogether was characterized by "blatantly unpleasant Catholic tendencies."[45]
- The brochure "The New Man" was indexed because, in addition to all kinds of objectionable content, the author had the audacity to compare the life of monks with that of the Führer: "The monk lives strictly according to the principles of the leadership principle in holy obedience, . . . in personal poverty, and like the Führer Adolf Hitler is unmarried and devoted to a great ideal."[46]
- Two books by a Catholic physician, *What a Growing Girl Has to Know* and *What a Grown-up Girl Has to Know,* were banned because they glorified the Catholic religion and included views perhaps suitable for the medieval Catholic Church but irreconcilable with the ideas of the new Germany.[47]
- The book *Der junge Gatte* (The Young Husband), published in 1930, had linked the decline of the family to the violation of "all standards and values" and had declared: "We live in bleak times." On October 2, 1940, the SD demanded that this book be forbidden because "the reader in National Socialist Germany must consider this characterization of present times as completely unjustified."[48] The book was indexed.
- The brochure *Gesegnete Brautzeit* (Blessed Engagement Period), published in 1939, was ordered banned because it "propagates the Catholic idea of matrimony and condemns religiously mixed marriages." This view "contradicts the National Socialist view of the *Volksgemeinschaft*" (the community of the *Volk*).[49]
- The writings of the Austrian theologian Johannes Ude were indexed in 1942 on the grounds that they included "pacifist ideas."[50] In 1944 Ude was arrested and condemned to death for having undermined military morale and supporting the enemy. He escaped execution when the Third Reich collapsed in the spring of 1945.

On the whole, the Nazis placed no value on the attempts of some Catholics to ingratiate themselves with the National Socialist regime. The Austrian conservative Othmar Spann had hoped that he would be able to influence the Nazi movement. Instead, he was arrested after the *Anschluss*, later put under house arrest, and in 1940 it was announced that no further writings of Spann could be published.[51] Several books by Alois Hudal, the head of the German Catholic community in Rome, were suppressed, even though the Austrian-born bishop dedicated himself to the task of "paving the way for an understanding of National Socialism from the Christian viewpoint"[52] and even defended the Nuremberg laws as a necessary measure of self-defense against the influx of foreign elements.[53] In *The Vatican and the Modern State*, a book published in 1935, Hudal had noted that the Church had been able to live with the absolutism of princes while defending its everlasting mission and freedom. It therefore would also be able to find a *modus vivendi* with regard to modern conceptions of the state derived from the teachings of Machiavelli. However, Hudal insisted, "no compromise or reconciliation are possible when a totalitarian state seeks to impose upon its citizens its own ideology as a substitute for Christianity. In such a situation, only struggle can result in clarification and decision, because it involves a battle between two worlds bound to end in victory or defeat for one or the other."[54] Needless to say, for the Nazis this affirmation of the supremacy of Christianity amounted to a declaration of war. The demand of the National Socialist state for total obedience clashed with the Catholic Church's claim for the supremacy of its spiritual teaching, and in this contest the Nazi state had the stronger hand.

The Austrian Catholic layman Wilhelm Everhard was more fortunate. His book *Bauschäden im Hause Gottes* (Structural Damage in the House of God), published in 1937, also was said to contest the state's claim for total support. However, the author maintained that the book was written "with German sensitivity" and that it denounced the "Church's misuse of temporal power" and the financial dealings of the clergy. He had expected, he wrote, that the Vatican would ban his book, not the authorities in Berlin. Moreover, he was prepared to make any changes found to be appropriate. The Ministry of Propaganda thereupon directed that the seized copies of the work be returned to the publisher and that the book be allowed to be freely sold.[55]

The regime encouraged publications that described and denounced the allegedly immoral life of monks and nuns. A favorite work was the *Der Pfaffenspiegel*, a rabble-rousing anti-clerical book by one Otto von Corwin first published in 1845, which described the history of the Catholic Church as a series of sexual and financial scandals. The Gestapo seized the book in January 1934 on the grounds that it might cause unrest among the Catholic population, but about a year later the propaganda ministry reversed the ban.[56] The *Börsenblatt* now carried large ads in which the publisher promoted the book with the argument that "in the struggle for the National Socialist ideology this work deserves the widest distribution." The ads also carried the notice: "Released by the Gestapo!"[57]

Anxious to stem the impact of this publication, pastoral letters and articles in church newspapers argued that the Protestant author Corwin had a Jewish mother and therefore (according to Nazi racist criteria now conveniently used by the Church) had been a half-Jew. When the Nazis successfully challenged the non-Aryan ancestry of Corwin, one of their favorite church-baiting authors, Catholic polemicists fell back upon the argument that Corwin's book had originally been published by a Jewish publisher, that he had been a friend of the Jews and a Freemason, and that during the Weimar Republic the *Pfaffenspiegel* had been a favorite of the Marxists. The Ministry of Propaganda thereupon banned all editions published by Free-thinker and Social Democratic publishers, but it otherwise continued to use the book to vilify the Church.[58]

When an enterprising publisher tried to cash in on the anti-Catholic agitation by publishing a memoir entitled *Escape from the Nunnery*, the book was ordered banned. According to the Gestapo Karlsruhe, the entire work, beginning with the title, represented an attempt falsely to produce a sensationalist book that would yield a large profit. The author had not "escaped" the nunnery, but had left it perfectly legally with the permission of church authorities. Serious descriptions of life in the monasteries were needed, but this book was not one of these.[59]

All through the years 1937 and 1938, the Gestapo, using President Hindenburg's Decree for the Protection of People and State, had dissolved Catholic associations. By the time war broke out in 1939, the Nazi state had succeeded in fully destroying the once-so-powerful network of Catholic organizations.[60] Many of these organizations had owned publishing houses, and in August 1940 the SD reminded the Ministry of Propaganda that the entire output of these publishers had to be put on the Index, without listing individual books.[61] On September 3, 1941 Himmler's deputy Heydrich informed the Gestapo and SD that Hitler had forbidden any measures that could damage the unity of the German people in time of war. Heydrich therefore gave orders that any "drastic action, unless in response to an imminent danger," required his consent.[62] By this time, of course, the destruction of Catholic publishing was an accomplished fact.

The beliefs of Jehovah's Witnesses, known in Germany as Ernste Bibelforscher (Serious Students of the Bible), constituted another challenge to the primacy of the National Socialist ideology. The Bibelforscher were persecuted because they refused to do military service; their writings were forbidden on account of their apocalyptic teachings. On July 18, 1941, the SD asked the propaganda ministry to ban the book *Licht auf die Endzeit* (Light on the End of Time). The work was written "entirely in the spirit of the Ernste Bibelforscher," and its prophecies "were likely to confuse simple folks." On March 1, 1941, the propaganda ministry banned the import of all publications of the Swiss Watch

Tower Bible and Tract Society. [63] The Nazis also dissolved the Anthroposophical Society and forbade most of the writings of Rudolf Steiner, the founder of what also was known as Theosophy.[64]

German Protestants, for the most part, at first welcomed the new regime. The opposition that developed was directed not at the Nazi state's political or social policies but sought to preserve the organizational independence of the church and retain control over church doctrine. The German Evangelical Church, declared the Barmen Declaration of May 1934, was not an organ of the state. The Christian commandments, the newly formed Confessing Church maintained, were not to be subordinated to National Socialist ideology. Relatively few Protestant churchmen or lay members dared to affirm these beliefs in writing, and the number of books banned for adherence to the ideas of the Confessing Church was relatively small. These were some of them:

- On November 22, 1937, the RSK ordered the indexing of a book entitled *Zur Neuordnung der Evangelischen Kirche* (On the reorganization of the Evangelical Church). The book criticized the "inroads of the temporal world into the substance of the church," and this accusation was "designed to justify the oppositional role of the Confessing Church." It represented "an incentive to disobey measures of the state."[65]
- Among the more courageous figures was the pastor of the Confessing Church, Hans Treplin, who in 1939 authored a book with the title *Um Kreuz und Altar (Concerning Cross* [Swastika] *and Altar).* He wrote: "There exists a limit to the totalitarian claims of the state, which the state for the sake of its own well-being may not transgress. That limit is called Jesus Christ. Jesus Christ is more than the state, is above the Führer and all temporal authority and greatness." On July 31, 1940, the Ministry of Propaganda ordered this book to be banned because the author had opposed "the alleged absolute totalitarian claims of the state" and thus had provided new material for the atrocity propaganda of Germany's enemies.[66] Whether the daring pastor suffered more than a ban of his book is not known.
- On June 20, 1940, the SD requested the indexing of the book *Bekenntnis zur Bibel* (Affirmation of the Bible). The author described himself as a National Socialist but the book stated that in the Kingdom of God there exist no race issues. This represented "deliberate misuse of the National Socialist ideology."[67]

Many publishers employed traveling salesmen to sell their books. On January 1, 1938, the Gestapa issued an order that forbade the sale of "religious publications" by these salesmen "even if the content of the publication itself is not objectionable."[68] Inasmuch as this ordinance was limited to religious publications and did not affect the selling of other books, it clearly represented just another attempt to create economic difficulties for religious publishers.

Given the importance of race in Nazi ideology, it is not surprising that publications dealing with the issue of race received special scrutiny and often ran into problems. In addition to the usual vetting by the Ministry of Propaganda, orthodoxy regarding racial matters was also guarded by the Rassenpolitisches Amt der NSDAP (Office of Racial Policy of the NSDAP), an agency that was supposed to deal only with party publications on race but frequently extended its reach into all writings on this subject. Thus when the RSK gave permission to a teacher to self-publish a book *Exakte Rassenkunde* (Precise Study of Race), he was advised to submit the book for clearance to the PPK or the Office of Racial Policy. The record does not show the results of this vetting, but after the book had appeared it was banned because of "numerous errors in the area of racial research that have long been refuted."[69]

An instruction published in 1941 admonished publishers not to accept manuscripts, especially fiction, that depicted marriages between Germans and members of inferior people, which "constitutes *Rassenschande*" (defilement of the race). German literature had to demonstrate "a clear affirmation of the racial doctrine of National Socialism."[70] Works regarded as favorable to the black race were banned. A book describing Catholic missionary activity in Africa was indexed because it expressed joy over the inauguration of the first black bishop. The author related how at first he had been apprehensive on account of the young priest's dark complexion. However, he soon had realized "how the spirit had left his marks on his face, to wit, decency, intelligence, self-control." This kind of writing on missionary activity was likely to have a "confusing and corrosive effect" on German readers.[71]

The same language—"causing confusion among the population regarding the subject of race"—was used in the banning of a book on the various "forms of humanity."[72] A novel published in 1931 was banned in 1939 because the hero of the story was the son of a captain serving in a German colony in Africa and a black woman. The hero's special creativity was linked to the mixture of Prussian and Negro blood—an unacceptable "glorification of racial mixing."[73] More such books apparently continued to be published. Hence in July 1943 the propaganda ministry let it be known that novels in which "relations between Germans and persons of inferior races, a relationship that constitute *Rassenschande*, are acceptable," were "definitely undesirable."[74]

Nazi "racial science" today is regarded as a pseudo-science, but the Nazis used this same label to condemn authors whom they regarded as deviating from National Socialist race doctrine. The Nazis valued exterior appearance, as when they emphasized the beauty of the Nordic race. But not every such work passed muster. A book by one Werner Altpeter published in 1934 that sought to teach people how to tell a person's character from his external characteristics was banned because it constituted "an outrageous attack on the racial teaching of National Socialism." Perhaps taking a swipe at Julius Streicher's vulgar weekly tabloid *Der Stürmer* that always showed Jews with large crooked noses, the Altpeter book was criticized for asserting that "different forms of the nose are indicative of a person's character." By stressing exterior forms, Altpeter was said to have deliberately misled his readers and to have produced a work that represented "audacious and propagandistically skillful pseudo-science."[75] Quite obviously, it was not easy to understand and teach Nazi racial science.

The practice of *Damnatio Memoriae*, the elimination of "non-persons," hails from ancient times. Several Roman emperors were made to disappear from the historical record as if they had never lived and ruled. In modern totalitarian states too, leaders who fall out of favor become non-persons—they have never existed and may no longer be mentioned. In Nazi Germany that was the fate of Ernst Röhm, one of Hitler's earliest comrades, head of the SA, and as late as December 1933 a member of the cabinet as a minister without portfolio. Röhm was one of the seventy-seven leading Nazis who were murdered during what has entered history as the "blood purge" of June 30, 1934. Earlier that year, Röhm's book *Geschichte eines Hochverräters* (The History of a Traitor) had been published by the official party publisher Franz Eher and quickly had gone through eight printings. On August 25 the Gestapa sent an urgent instruction to the Bavarian Gestapo asking it to have the Eher house withdraw all copies of the book from circulation. Five days later another message to all Gestapo offices ordered a search of public libraries in order to confiscate the book.[76]

That was just the beginning. As Hitler's earliest right-hand-man, Röhm of course was mentioned in many books dealing with the history of the Nazi party, and that history now had to be rewritten. Some of these cleansing actions took time, but they were thorough and eventually hit their mark:

- The book *Männer, Mächte und Methoden: Zwölf Jahre Kampf und Trotz, Leidenschaft und Glaube* (Men, Powers and Methods: Twelve Years Struggle and Defiance, Passion and Faith) by the well-known author Max Everwien was ordered confiscated on October 1 because "persons, disagreeably linked to the events of June 30, are described in a way likely today to threaten public order and security." The author himself was said to be in favor of this measure.[77] About a year later, the PPK informed the Gestapa that Everwien had made the necessary corrections in his book and that any copies not been destroyed should be returned to the publisher so that they could be used in the printing of the revised text.[78]
- On October 10, 1934, the PPK notified the Gestapa that the *Ehrenbuch der SA* (SA Book of Honor) could again be sold, since "the pictures of all the mutineers have been removed."[79] A similar book, *Die SA in Wort und Bild* (The SA

in Words and Pictures), which apparently could not be cleansed so easily, was forbidden.[80]

- Another history of the Nazi party, *Das Buch der NSDAP: Origin, Struggle and Aims of the NSDAP*, as it was belatedly discovered, had a preface by Röhm and was therefore banned in March 1935.[81]
- The 1933 book *Männer um Hitler* (Men around Hitler) by Edgar Schmidt-Pauli was forbidden and pulped, but a revised edition that had changed the description of "the circle around Röhm" was found to be acceptable. In May 1936 the publisher complained that Gestapo offices in Leipzig, Hamburg, and Königsberg apparently had not been informed of the revision and again confiscated the book. The pulping of the original edition had caused a damage of RM 40,000. "We kindly but urgently seek your assistance and orders for the return of the seized books."[82]
- A book of songs for the SA of Saxony was banned because it included pictures of Röhm and other former SA leaders and therefore was "likely to endanger public order and safety."[83]

Ever since the early 1920s, Ernst (Putzi) Hanfstaengl had been a great favorite of Hitler, who liked his wit, clowning, and piano playing. The well-to-do Hanfstaengl also had provided the money to purchase the newspaper *Völkischer Beobachter* for the Nazi party. In 1931 he was appointed foreign press chief of the NSDAP, but by 1937 he had come into serious conflict with Goebbels, who was envious of Hanfstaengl's close ties to Hitler. Fearing for his life, in March 1937 Hanfstaengl fled to Switzerland and eventually reached the United States. From this point on he became a non-person in Germany, and on July 26, 1937, Martin Bormann, Rudolf Hess's chief of staff, in a communication marked "Secret," asked Hederich to see to it that the name of Hanfstaengl no longer appear in any publication. The deputy head of the PPK was urged to find a way to remove Hanfstaengl's books and compositions from circulation without the public learning of this measure.[84] The files do not tell us how Hederich accomplished this task, but we know that this was the kind of assignment at which Hederich excelled.

After Hess, another close comrade and deputy of the Führer, had unexpectedly fled to England on May 10, 1941, another purging of the printed record became necessary. On June 13 Goebbels personally sent out a circular to all Gauleiter and other highly placed party leaders in which he ordered the removal of pictures of Hess from all party offices and the end of the sale of such pictures. New books were to be checked to make sure that they did not mention Hess or included his picture. The same care was to be taken with regard to calendars.[85] A slightly differently worded order to the same effect appeared in the *Vertrauliche Mitteilungen der Fachschaft Verlag* on August 9, 1941.

But what was to be done with the many official ordinances that Hess had issued? The PPK's Hederich proposed that the authors of scientific and historical works be allowed to mention Hess to the extent that this was necessary for the understanding of historical events. Hess's successor Bormann, head of the Party Chancellery and an increasingly powerful figure in the Nazi state, demurred. This way of handling the problem left it up to individual authors to decide whether Hess should be mentioned, and "this decision cannot as yet be ceded to the scientific community." Instead, Bormann ordered that in historical and other scientific works Hess's name be specified only when his signature appeared on ordinances and other measures Hess had issued in his capacity as Deputy of the Führer.[86]

Books that were non-objectionable from the point of view of any of these ideological reasons could still run into trouble if they were "irreconcilable with the views and principles prevailing in the state of today." That was the catch-all category that was used, for example, in banning books by Wassily Kandinsky, Walt Whitman, and Karl Kraus.[87] A book of verse was ordered indexed because the author, "while not untalented," had not satisfied the demands of "a responsible poetic art."[88] The writings of Rainer Maria Rilke and Manfred George were not banned, but they were among authors criticized for "deliberately standing apart" from contemporary events. Literature today, a Nazi critic wrote in 1942, must "express the pulse of the new times" and be "close to the people" (volksnahe).[89]

The control of the printed book in Nazi Germany began with the burning of books in 1933, and thereafter evolved into the banning of books after they had been published. From 1939 on the regime would increasingly resort to prior restraint. During wartime, more than ever, it was considered essential that no objectionable book escape banning.

9

Jewish Books

Nazi propaganda had long equated being Jewish with being un-German, and that included the allegedly destructive and foreign (*artfremde*) ideas that had characterized the intellectual climate of the Weimar Republic—individualism, liberalism, Marxism, pacifism, and cosmopolitanism. Hitler had argued in *Mein Kampf* that the Jews had "poisoned German culture," including literature, and had "wrecked all conceptions of beauty and dignity."[1] Another Nazi author claimed that the Jews had "cultivated shamelessness" and had "soiled German minds."[2] Moreover, Jews allegedly had dominated the German press, radio, films, music, and literature. "The people of the poets and thinkers," Goebbels declared in a speech in November 1938, "had let their culture be administered by Semites."[3] Literature was said to have been especially *verjudet* (under Jewish control)—"40 percent of all German authors had been Jews."[4] Publishers had become dependent on Jewish capital. Jews developed their decadent and corrosive version of German literature in order to attempt to subjugate the German people, a step in the Jewish conspiracy to rule the world.[5]

In point of fact, while Jews did indeed constitute a significant proportion of German avant-garde artists and writers, they were far outnumbered by "Aryans" similarly committed to new and experimental modes of artistic creation. The claim of the Nazis that Jewish publishers had lorded it over the German book market belongs to the realm of the political legend, the result of a paranoid racial anti-Semitism.[6]

It is worth noting that in 1930, a few years before the Nazis assumed power, Jews constituted less than 1 percent of Germany's population, and yet this small minority was being blamed for all the ills of a difficult time. Not every German necessarily agreed with the most extreme anti-Semitic Nazi propaganda that regarded the Jews as a deadly bacillus and the devil incarnate, but a basic attitude of seeing the Jews as a threat and subversive force was widespread.[7]

"The removal of the Jew from the cultural life of the German people," the Nazi official Rudolf Kummer recalled in 1938, "had been one of the most important immediate measures after the assumption of power."[8] With regard to Jewish books, however, the process of elimination was slow. Anxious as the Nazis were to proceed against Jewish authors, several difficulties stood in the way. The first problem was to establish who among the tens of thousands of writers actually was a Jew, not to mention the even more arduous task of ascertaining the religious (racial) background of authors of years past. An article in the *Börsenblatt* of September 3, 1936, entitled "Where Do I Find the Jew?" sought to give advice on how to identify Jewish writers. The author of the article, the propaganda ministry official Hans Richter, listed various reference works, including Adolf Bartel's *Jüdische Herkunft und Literaturwissenschaft*, published in 1925. Richter acknowledged that Bartel's book included mistakes, but he argued that this did not diminish the value of the work. This assessment was far too benevolent, for the publication of Bartel's work had led to numerous complaints and threats of lawsuits on account of errors that damaged the sale of falsely categorized books. Richter himself admitted at the end of his article that "there existed a great need for a scholarly work that was free of defects and usable."[9]

Several such undertakings soon got under way. Rosenberg's men worked for several years to create a reference work that would tackle this task, and in 1938 they produced a *Verzeichnis jüdischer Autoren* (Register of Jewish Authors) that listed some 11,000 Jewish writers. The register was marked "Strictly Confidential and for Official Use Only."[10] The subtitle called the work a "preliminary compilation" and it apparently served as the basis for a *Handbuch aller jüdischen Schriftsteller* (Handbook of Jewish Writers) that appeared in 1940 and included some 13,000 titles. It had been planned to have this handbook completed by 1941, but this aim was never achieved. The same holds true for a *Bibliographie der jüdischen Autoren in deutscher Sprache: 1901–1940* (Bibliography of Jewish Authors in the German Language), work on which began in 1941 at the Deutsche Bücherei in Leipzig on orders of the Ministry of Propaganda. The goal set for this directory was to list some 90,000 Jewish authors who should disappear from the cultural life of the country. However, by March 1944, when work was suspended because of a lack of personnel, the professional bibliographers who had undertaken this assignment had come up with only 28,000 listings.[11]

The exclusion of Jewish publishers and bookstores from the German book market ran into the problem of the very difficult economic situation of Germany, still suffering from massive unemployment. Hence while the Law for the Restoration of the Professional Civil Service of April 7, 1933, in its so-called Aryan Clause 3 had decreed the removal of Jews, the legislation enacting the RKK did not include an *Arierparagraph* (Aryan clause). At stake were tens of thousands of jobs in the publishing field and the book trade as well as the foreign currency derived from the export of books. For this reason, in late 1934 Minister of the Economy Hjalmar Schacht urged Goebbels to proceed more slowly with the process of *Entjudung* (eliminating the influence of Jews).

Goebbels replied that he had advised the various chambers to avoid economic damage as far as possible, but he insisted that in the National Socialist state the intellectual life of the nation "had priority over economic considerations." Goebbels reaffirmed this principle in a letter of June 27, 1935, to the RSK. Jews, non-Aryans, and those related to Jews were to be removed gradually; no new such members were to be accepted. As far as possible, economic assets and jobs were to be protected. [12] Dissatisfied with this response, Schacht on February 13, 1936, turned directly to Hitler, and, after once again drawing attention to the difficult conditions on the job market and the need for foreign currency, asked that his ministry be involved in all decisions that involved the closing of Jewish enterprises with significant earnings of foreign currency. On March 9 Lammers informed Schacht that the Führer had rejected this suggestion.[13] For Hitler too ideological considerations were more important that the state of the economy.

And yet the continuing high rate of unemployment soon led to the further delay of anti-Jewish measures. In a report on the state of *Entjudung* of May 27, 1935, RSK vice president Wismann noted that, in the absence of an *Arierparagraph* and in view of the constraints imposed by the difficult economic situation, anti-Jewish measures had to proceed slowly. Even though the chamber was working on finding Aryan owners for Jewish publishers, there still were about 200 such Jewish publishing houses.[14] The *Börsenblatt* at times ran ads by Jewish owners who were seeking "Aryan buyers."[15] When the Minister of the Interior in October 1935 suggested a ban of books that were meant in whole or in part for the Jewish public, the propaganda ministry replied that "for far-reaching economic considerations" this kind of ordinance was not yet possible. On January 22, 1936, the chambers were informed that on order of Goebbels and "effective immediately" all measures of *Entjudung* were to be stopped.[16]

The record does not show for how long this suspension lasted. We do know that Goebbels meanwhile proceeded with the exclusion of authors from the RSK, a measure that did not cause any appreciable economic damage. For this purpose he relied upon Paragraph 10 of the RKK law, according to which membership in a chamber could be denied "if, according to known facts, the person in question lacks the reliability and suitability for the exercise of his calling." In the eyes of Goebbels, Jews by definition lacked the appropriate "reliability and suitability" to participate in German culture, and their exclusion therefore was necessary and justified. An order issued on January 17, 1935, affirmed that as a rule non-Aryans were to be considered "unreliable and unsuitable" and that their acceptance into the chambers was to be considered only if for special reasons their reliability and suitability had been established.[17] At first this measure involved only authors who had indicated on the application form that they or their spouses were non-Aryan. However, after the enactment of the Nuremberg racial laws on September 15, 1935, the pace quickened, and soon applicants had to prove their Aryan status and that of their wives by submitting a detailed family tree reaching back at least two generations.[18] In 1934 the RSK had included 428 Jewish authors. By March 7, 1937, a total of 1,238 non-Aryan

The NSDAP Berlin informs the Reich Chamber of Literature that nothing derogatory is known about Emma Linde. Her Aryan status has also been confirmed.
Courtesy Bundesarchiv Berlin-Lichterfelde

writers had been expelled or their application for acceptance had been denied.[19] A report on the "Entjudung der Reichsschrifttumskammer" of January 26, 1937, noted twenty-eight *Sondergenehmigungen* (Special Permissions) for Jews to stay in the RSK.[20] Holders of these special permissions had to submit their writings to the RSK for approval.

On January 3, 1939, Goebbels issued a new set of guidelines regarding persons who were only partly Jewish. Half-Jews, it was decreed, could remain members of the chambers "with my specific personal permission," and quarter-Jews had to be excluded only if they had opposed the state or National Socialism or were sympathetic to Jewry. Aryans married to a Jewess were be treated like half-Jews, those married to a half-Jewish woman like quarter-Jews. Between August 1940 and April 1941 twenty-four writers were expelled from the RSK because they were three-quarter, half, or one-quarter-Jews or were married to half-Jews or full-Jews.[21] At times such partial-Jews (*Mischlinge* as they were called) were granted a *Sondergenehmigung* to practice their profession, but these were hard to come by. In 1939 the author Mario Kramer had been expelled from the RSK on account of "non-Aryan kinship and a philo-Semitic cast of mind." When he submitted an application for permission to write scientific works, the RSK, even though formally not allowed to control scientific writings, denied the request. A notice in the official gazette of the RSK announced that Kramer had been expelled from the RSK and was therefore forbidden to publish.[22] On April 26, 1939, Goebbels noted in his diary that the process of *Entjudung* was moving ahead but that there were many "borderline cases" that were difficult to decide.[23]

The development and enforcement of anti-Jewish policies was in the hands of Hans Hinkel. This dedicated Nazi had joined the NSDAP in 1920, and as a participant in the putsch of 1923 held the "Blood Medal." Since 1935, Hinkel was Special Commissioner for the Supervision of the Cultural Activities of Non-Aryans in Germany, a post that made him head of Department of II A of the Ministry of Propaganda and put him in charge of deciding the racial and political reliability of all applicants to the various chambers of the RKK (with the exception of the Reich Press Chamber).[24] At the same time Hinkel was also appointed to be one of three chief administrators of the RKK. Hinkel belonged to the SS, and all of his co-workers likewise were members of this elite force. By 1941 Hinkel had attained the rank of SS-Brigadeführer, and he belonged to Himmler's staff. In 1943 Hinkel became a Gruppenführer, the third-highest rank in the SS. When Goebbels recommended Hinkel's promotion to undersecretary in the propaganda ministry in a letter to Lammers on May 6, 1941, he praised Hinkel as capable and responsible.[25] His anti-Semitic credentials were not specifically mentioned, but they could be taken for granted. He was the right man to implement Goebbels' goal of achieving the *Entjudung* of German culture. The SS, for their part, were pleased to have in Hinkel a person who could be relied upon to "reject persons not agreeable to us."[26]

Hinkel took to his assignment as the developer and enforcer of anti-Jewish measures with determination, not to say zeal. On April 29, 1936, he addressed a circular, marked "Strictly Confidential," to the presidents of the chambers, in which they were asked to submit by May 10 alphabetical lists of chamber members who were full-Jews, three-quarter-Jews, half-Jews, and quarter-Jews as well as those married to full-Jews, three-quarter-Jews, half-Jews, and quarter-Jews. The circular included the underlined qualifier "as far as they are known until now," a recognition that existing knowledge of who was non-Aryan was not easy to come by and was necessarily incomplete. By order of Goebbels, Hinkel wrote, as of May 15, 1936, all persons belonging to the categories mentioned could no longer be members of the chambers.[27] Not surprisingly, the RSK appears to have been occupied with submitting the required lists of full and partial non-Aryans until well into the war years. The files contain the names of quarter-Jews and Aryans married to half-Jewish women sent in as late as March 22, 1943. Three cases were closed out in January 1943 because the parties had divorced. According to an order of Hinkel dated August 31, 1937, persons who divorced their Jewish spouses and "who can prove that their divorce is not just a formality, are to be treated like all other members of the chambers."[28] Among those who stood by their Jewish wives was the well-known philosopher Karl Jaspers. In the late summer of 1937 Jaspers was dismissed from his professorship at the University of Heidelberg, and from 1938 on he no longer was allowed to publish.[29]

On January 26, 1937, Hinkel submitted a progress report on "Entjudung der Reichsschrifttumskammer" to Goebbels. No Jewish authors were any longer members of the RSK, although twenty-eight such writers had been allowed to continue to write on the basis of a *Sondergenehmigung*. In the book trade and in publishing there were still 217 Jews. These enterprises were under orders to reorganize by March 31, 1937.[30] Bookstores that limited their inventory to Jewish literature (Jewish religion, philosophy, history, etc.) could apply to Hinkel for permission to function as booksellers for Jewish customers exclusively.[31] The requirement that Jewish book stores not sell books by German authors was strictly enforced. When the Jewish publisher and book dealer Schocken in 1937 included the short story "Die Judenbuche" by Annette von Droste-Hülshoff, one of the most important German authors of the nineteenth century, in a series published by Schocken, they were informed that "it is unacceptable that the book of this German poet be published by you." Schocken was ordered to remove the book from circulation within three days.[32]

In order not to lose precious jobs, Jewish publishers and bookstores were "aryanized" rather than closed down, that is, their owners were forced to sell their business to Germans. In May 1935 the Bund Reichsdeutscher Buchhändler (League of German Bookdealers, or BRB) still had 619 Jewish members, 200 of them publishers,[33] and in January 1937 there were still 268

Jewish bookstores.[34] Pressure was now brought to bear upon these Jewish owners to dispose of their property. In a few cases, as at the S. Fischer publishing house, a trusted editor (Peter Suhrkamp) took over, who did his best to carry on the traditions of this highly regarded house. In many other instances the new owners were convinced National Socialists. This is what happened at Rowohlt, a publisher that was acquired by the Deutsche Verlags-Anstalt. On February 4, 1935, an appeals court in Munich ruled that "in view of the totally different conditions now prevailing" and on account of the economic damage to be expected, German publishers were under no obligation to honor contracts with non-Aryan authors.[35]

On December 5, 1936 BRB, head Wilhelm Baur, like Hinkel a veteran Nazi, member of the SS, and holder of the Blood Medal, let it be known that publishers who had been informed of their expulsion from the RSK and who had not been aryanized or dissolved by April 1, 1937, would be closed by the police.[36] After Austria had been annexed in the *Anschluss* of March 12, 1938, some 250 Jewish bookstores and publishers were aryanized or closed. What had taken years in Germany, notes one observer, took place here within a few months "with greater harshness and less regard for international public opinion."[37] The last remaining Jewish publishers and bookstores were shut down after the *Kristallnacht* of November 9–10, 1938, a pogrom during which at least ninety-one Jews were killed and 267 synagogues and more than 7,000 Jewish businesses were burned and destroyed.

A decree of November 12, signed by Göring as Commissioner for the Four-Year Plan, ordered the "elimination of Jews from the economic life of Germany." Another order issued on December 3 made it possible to force the sale of Jewish property within a certain limited time span. On December 17 Hinkel ordered the closing of the remaining Jewish publishers and bookstores by December 31.[38] Wilhelm Baur noted with satisfaction that 474 Jewish bookstores and 186 Jewish lending libraries had disappeared, and "with them the entire Jewish and Marxist-liberal mentality had been eradicated."[39] German bookstores were told by the RSK that it was up to them whether they wanted to sell books to Jews. The RSK would support them if they refused to deal with Jewish customers, though, in view of the fact that foreigners often looked like Jews, they were warned not to rely on exterior appearance alone.[40] In 1941, both bookstores and lending libraries were ordered not to serve Jewish customers.[41] That year, too, the new Aryan owners of Jewish bookstores were reminded that the names of the previous Jewish owners had to be removed from the name of the firm.[42]

Dissolved Jewish publishers were asked to transfer their inventory of books to a new publishing house exclusively for Jews named Jüdischer Kulturbund Verlag (Jewish Cultural League Publisher), and in the major cities bookstores were designated to sell these books to Jews.[43] The import of Jewish literature required the permission of Hinkel.[44] The new Kulturbund publisher was part of a network of Jewish cultural organizations that had been allowed to organize since 1933 in order to provide work for dismissed Jewish actors and musicians. In August 1935 these local organizations had been ordered to combine in a national Reichsverband jüdischer Kulturbünde under the supervision of Hinkel.[45] Lending libraries owned by Jews were allowed to continue to operate and to become members of this network on the condition that they functioned without stores and on a mail-order basis. In this way, as Hinkel explained, it would be possible to "maintain an exact control of who is reading what."[46] The Kulturbund Verlag existed until January 1943, when, as the result of the deportations, there were not enough Jews left to justify the existence of a Jewish publisher.[47]

In order to minimize economic difficulties for the book trade, the exclusion of non-Aryan writers at first did not automatically lead to a ban of the books authored by them. However, in December 1937 publishers were instructed not to issue "new editions, let alone new works" of authors expelled from the RSK.[48] In January 1938 the publisher Reclam inquired at the RSK whether a book by a Jewish author should be removed from its Universal-Bibliothek. In 1936 he had been advised by an RSK official that the book in question should no longer be included in the collection, but the official had declined to put this information in writing. The refusal to leave a paper trail may have been due to the attempt of the Nazis during the Summer Olympics in Berlin to show moderation with regard to the Jewish question. Some two years later the battle lines had hardened again, and on May 2, 1938, the Ministry of Propaganda informed the RSK that "the continued sale of the book is undesirable."[49] Also in early 1938 the RSK and Hinkel decided that henceforth book dealers were to sell books by Jewish authors only to scientific libraries or to individuals who needed such works for their scholarly research.[50]

On the other hand, a large treatise on the chemistry of fats, one of whose editors was a Jew and which had several Jewish contributors, was allowed to appear in 1939 because the work was considered extremely valuable. In case of a ban, "the Jew Schönfeld probably would publish his work abroad, which is undesirable."[51] Scientific publishers like Springer at times avoided a conflict with the RSK by omitting the name of the Jewish editor from the title page.[52] This is what the RSK on March 19, 1939, ordered in the case of the definitive work on the drawings of Raphael that was edited by the Jewish author Oskar Fischel. "To continue the editorship by a Jew in the editing of a scholarly work today is no longer permissible."[53]

The nineteenth-century publicist and agitator Wilhelm Marr, the man who first coined the term "anti-Semitism," had considered Jewish assimilation as infiltration and a cunning attempt to achieve world domination.[54] In the eyes of Nazi censors too the most dangerous enemy were the assimilated

Jews whose Jewishness was not readily apparent and who therefore would continue to exert their nefarious influence in German culture. Until the end of 1938 the struggle against Jewish books was focused almost exclusively on the Assimilationsjudentum (assimilated Jews). The list of banned Jewish authors therefore included such writers as Vicky Baum, Emil Ludwig, Lion Feuchtwanger, Franz Kafka, Else Lasker-Schüler, Arthur Schnitzler, Kurt Tucholsky, Franz Werfel, and Arnold and Stefan Zweig.[55] The song "Stolz weht die Flagge schwarz-weiss-rot" (Proudly waves the flag black-white-red), known as the "song of the German marine," was ordered not to be included in new songbooks because it had been composed by the Jew Robert Linderer.[56] On February 12, 1937, the Ministry of Propaganda reminded the book trade that no mention was to be made anywhere of the works of Heinrich Heine.[57] The journal *Der deutsche Schriftsteller* pronounced that "Heine is not a poet, he is a Jew."[58]

However, books by Jewish authors dealing with outright Jewish themes or linked to Zionism still passed muster, though eventually these kinds of books could be published or sold only by the Jewish book trade. Thus, for example, on March 9, 1936, the Gestapa in Berlin informed the Gestapo office in Dortmund that Martin Buber's *Reden über das Judentum* (Speeches on Judaism), published by Schocken, "included no attacks on National Socialism" and therefore was not to be confiscated.[59] As of March 31, 1938, any publication dealing with the "Jewish question," including those by Aryan authors, required the permission of Hinkel.[60]

In many instances the orders banning books by Jewish authors, in addition to stating that the author was non-Aryan, also mentioned another violation as the reason for indexing the work. For example, the cover of one such book constituted "degenerate art."[61] A diary of World War I blamed Germany for the outbreak of the war and insulted Hindenburg and Ludendorff.[62] A certain author propagated a sexual psychology that "had to be strongly rejected from today's point of view."[63] Some poems had a "clearly hostile attitude toward Germany."[64] The book of a non-Aryan (converted) author, who himself was quite anti-Semitic, contained unacceptable views on sexuality.[65] Notwithstanding, a book on "Race and Blood of the Noble Family Habsburg-Lorraine," which the Race Policy Office of the NSDAP had highly recommended, was ordered banned by the Ministry of Propaganda in 1940, because the author was a Jew. The publisher was reprimanded for not having ascertained the racial purity of the author.[66]

Books considered to be *judenfreundlich* (friendly toward Jews) were regarded as just as objectionable as books by Jewish authors. A work describing the suffering of the Jews of Spain under the Inquisition was indexed because "it could lead to comparisons with the treatment of Jews since 1933" and on account of its "pro-Jewish tendency."[67] The same fate met a book describing the expulsion of more than 300,000 Spanish Jews in 1492, who, the author stated, "had to leave Spain under the most ignoble conditions, poor and despoiled."[68] Likewise banned was a book on the Dreyfus Affair because the author considered the fate of Dreyfus as typical of the many other innocent Jews "unjustly persecuted and oppressed."[69] Also considered unacceptable was a book with a positive assessment of the influence of Rahel Varnhagen's (born in 1771 as Rahel Levin) literary salon in Berlin on other authors of her time.[70]

A book on Jesus, according to which the Jews of Palestine at that time were not horse traders but peasants and craftsmen, was seen as "an attempt to save the honor of the Jews" and therefore banned.[71] Also indexed was a book with citations from the Bible, most of which referred to the Jewish people. This selection was held to "betray a pro-Jewish tendency."[72] Similarly banned was a novel with a character described as a "decent Jew." The novel expressed the view that there would be no Jewish problem if all Jews were like this decent one, but this hardly philo-Semitic remark did not save the book from being banned.[73] A biography of Gustav Mahler by his wife Alma was forbidden because "it had a pro-Semitic tendency" and described details of the married life of Richard Strauss.[74]

The onset of war in 1939, allegedly provoked by world Jewry, brought a radicalization of anti-Jewish measures, including the censorship of Jewish books. During previous years the RSK had forbidden works by individual Jews. A new version of Ordinance no. 70 dealing with the indexing of books, issued on April 15, 1940, for the first time included an outright ban on all books by non-Aryan authors. According to a new Paragraph 4, "the proscription of Paragraph 1, sect. 2 [forbidding the publication, sale, lending, or displaying of books on the list of harmful and undesirable books] also applies to works by Jews or half-Jews even if these works are not on the list of harmful and undesirable literature."[75]

Special permissions granted to certain authors (Sondergenehmigungen) were not affected by this new provision. Also new was the regulation of scientific works by Jewish authors. Standard works of German science and intellectual history—for example, an edition of the complete works of Immanuel Kant edited by a Jewish author—could be sold, but new editions required the specific consent of the Ministry of Propaganda. The same held true for collections of essays or handbooks that contained contributions by Jewish authors, for books translated by Jews, for works on social policy, as well as for books on politics even if they claimed to be strictly scholarly. Collections and handbooks edited by Jewish authors had to be submitted to the propaganda ministry for clearance by December 31, 1940. This deadline was later extended to June 30, 1941, and once more after that to June 30, 1942, probably due to the difficulty of establishing who was a Jew, let alone a half-Jew, and the shortage of personnel in wartime.[76] Works published before 1850 were not affected by these rules. Given the centrality of a virulent anti-Semitism in Nazi ideology, it is nothing short of amazing that a total ban on Jewish books did not go into effect until April 1940.

In August 1941 an official in the Ministry of Propaganda pointed out that as a result of the new policy "valuable scientific works and books of fiction are being pulped," and he suggested that such books, as for example works dealing with Asian history and fiction, instead of being destroyed, be made available to the public libraries. This proposal drew a sharp rebuff from his superior. No valuable books were being pulped, and those that were being pulped were not valuable. Scientific libraries, he insisted, undoubtedly already owned works on Oriental history by Jewish authors. For public libraries such books were "undesirable." These libraries should carry only books "that are essential for the people" (*für das Volk wesentlich*).[77]

In April 1942 Wilhelm Haegert, the head of Department VIII in the propaganda ministry, complained to Johst that the authors of scientific books still cited Jewish works, and as a result of this practice Jewish literature continued to make an unwelcome appearance. As a remedy Haegert proposed that Jewish and half-Jewish authors be cited only when they were marked with an asterisk and a footnote to indicate that the person named is a Jew.[78] The RSK submitted the draft of an appropriate decree, but the record does not indicate whether this order was ever issued. Such a decree undoubtedly would have made authors think twice before quoting a Jewish scientist, and thus would have exacerbated the politicization of German science.

The Nazi regime set out to eliminate Jewish influence from German culture, while at the same time it stressed the importance of the academic study of the Jewish problem. The fight against Jewry required not only suppression but also knowing and understanding one's enemy. In 1939 Rosenberg established in Frankfurt am Main an Institute for the Study of the Jewish Question. A year later, Walter Frank (who has been called the "self-appointed custodian of German historiography"[79]) was appointed head of a new Reich Institute for the History of the New Germany. One department of this institute concerned itself specifically with research on the Jewish Question. Since the late 1930s Rosenberg had occupied himself with plans for a Hohe Schule der NSDAP, which after the final victory was to become a university-type institution for the study of Nazi ideology. For all of these enterprises, the Einsatzstab Reichsleiter Rosenberg (Task Force Reichsleiter Rosenberg), set up in the summer of 1940, ransacked books from private and institutional libraries all over Europe. So vast was the quantity of stolen books that most of them were never catalogued. The Institute for the Study of the Jewish Question alone is estimated to have received between 1.5 million and 2.5 million volumes.[80] In a speech at the official opening of the Institute on March 26, 1941, Rosenberg declared that the victory of the German armies had made it possible to obtain solid proof for the depravity of the Jews.[81]

The Purge of Libraries

During the book burning of May 1933, trade union libraries, public libraries, and scholarly libraries such as the Magnus Hirschfeld Institute for Sex Research in Berlin had come under attack, and offending books had been seized and set afire. At the same time efforts got under way to undertake a more systematic purge of the libraries. Most of these institutions were under the jurisdiction of the ministers of education of the various Länder (states), the most important of these being Bernhard Rust, Prussian minister of science, art, and education.

Rust, by profession a high school teacher, was an early member of the Nazi party. During World War I Rust had suffered a severe head wound, and this injury is said to have affected his mental stability.[1] Bracher calls him an "incompetent alcoholic,"[2] and Broszat refers to him as "weak" and outmaneuvered by other state and party officers.[3] Whatever the merits of these assessments, Rust managed to serve as a loyal functionary of the Nazi regime. He proved his mettle when in early 1933 he purged the membership of the Prussian Academy of Writers of such liberal authors as Heinrich Mann. The performance of his ministry, run by the usual corps of reliable civil servants, appears to have been no more disorderly than that of other ministries of Hitler's polycratic regime. In 1925 Rust became Gauleiter of Hannover-Braunschweig, a post he occupied until the end of 1940.

In early February 1933 Hitler appointed Rust Prussian minister of science, art, and education. After the sovereignty of the states had been abolished on January 30, 1934, Rust became Reich Minister of Education in April. His credentials as a Nazi were impeccable, but rivals like Goebbels, Rosenberg, and Bouhler considered him unduly moderate and repeatedly fought turf battles with him. In May 1942 Goebbels asked Lammers to bring about a demarcation of competencies between the Ministry of Propaganda and Rust's Ministry of Education by convening a meeting of both parties. Rust was able to defend the exclusive jurisdictions of his ministry by citing Hitler's decree of January 25, 1942, dealing with the saving of scarce manpower in time of war. According to this order, if certain tasks could be handled by one office, it was inadmissible to have two offices deal with the same assignment.[4] Rust's use of Hitler's decree undoubtedly was self-serving, but since Hitler was busy with more important issues, the dispute between Goebbels and Rust remained unresolved. Rumors that Rust would be replaced circulated again in 1944,[5] but Rust managed to stay in his office until the collapse of the Nazi regime. He committed suicide on May 8, 1945.

As early as May 1933 the Nazi librarian Wolfgang Hermann had demanded the purging of the public libraries from corrosive *Asphaltliteratur* books about urban life that aimed to create alienation. Some books deserved to be destroyed. In the case of others, like the works of Marx and Lenin, one copy should be put into what he called the "poison cabinet."[6] It was the duty of the public libraries, another Nazi librarian declared in 1934, "to make every German into a National Socialist."[7] Still another stressed that the inventories of the public libraries had to be cleansed "in accordance with the new ideological criteria."[8] Rust, needless to say, did not have to be pressured to take on the task of making the public libraries instruments of political indoctrination. "During the time of liberalism," he declared, "the public libraries were department stores. Marxism sought to destroy all that is truly German. National Socialism has learned from both. Our public libraries are institutions of ideological education."[9] The public libraries had to work in the spirit of the National Socialist state and guide their readers to embrace the national cause. They had to be cleansed of all literature that was corrosive and opposed to the aims of the new state. To accomplish this task, on December 12, 1933, Rust ordered the establishment of the Preussische Landesstelle für volkstümliches Büchereiwesen (Prussian Office for Public Libraries).

The longtime head of the Association of German Public Librarians (Verband deutscher Volksbibliothekare, or VDV), Wilhelm Schuster, became the head of this new office. Schuster, like many other public librarians, had welcomed the Nazi revolution because it appeared to provide an opportunity to get rid of what they considered mass-produced trash, often just one notch under outright pornography. During the Weimar period these publications had abounded and had flourished despite the 1926 law against *Schund- und Schmutzliteratur*.[10] After Hitler's accession to power, Schuster did his level best to ingratiate himself and his organization with the new regime. In March 1933 Schuster joined the Nazi party (March newcomers to the Nazi cause became known as the *Märzlinge*), and in speeches and articles he called upon the librarians to welcome the new regime of national renewal. The task of the public libraries, he declared, was "Education for National Socialism."[11] Book bans were necessary because "the new German way of life is surrounded by thousands of powerful enemies."[12] A proclamation of the VDV, signed by Schuster and Wolfgang Hermann, called upon the public libraries to support the national revolution and thus provide "genuine service to state and nation." The magazine publishing the appeal called it semi-official.[13]

The new Preussische Landesstelle, established in December 1933, was to coordinate and supervise the work of the advisory authorities (Beratungsstellen) for public libraries that had existed since the turn of the century and that were now to serve as instruments of control. By December 1933, the reorganization of the twenty-four Beratungsstellen in operation in 1933 had been under way for several months. They had been put under Nazi control to become "National Socialist Beratungsstellen" and now operated in accordance with two National Socialist principles: "Total ideological penetration and absolute [centralized] leadership," also known as the *Führerprinzip*.[14]

By January 15, 1934, the public libraries were to submit to their appropriate Beratungsstelle a list of their books. Extensions of this deadline were possible when necessary. The head of the Beratungsstelle, following the guidelines of the Prussian Landesstelle, was then to decide which books had to be eliminated. *Grundlisten* (also known as "white lists") would instruct the librarians about what kind of books should be kept and acquired. New acquisitions too required the consent of the Beratungsstelle. The decrees of the Landesstelle would be published in its official gazette, *Die Bücherei*.[15] On December 1, 1933, according to a document in the files of the Ministry of Propaganda, Rust sent a list of books "that under no circumstances are to be kept in the public libraries" to the VDB and requested that this organization, by then fully under Nazi control, "confidentially" transmit this list "as *its* list" to the directors of public libraries.[16] It is likely that Rust used this subterfuge to keep the existence of government blacklists a secret or, at least, in order not to leave a paper trail. The list itself is not preserved.

In guidelines for its public libraries, issued in 1935, the Landesstelle for Saxony noted that the "political cleansing" of the public libraries was essentially complete. The directors were exhorted to concentrate on building their collections but were reminded to stay vigilant with regard to the "eradication" of unsuitable books. The Landesstelle emphasized that it would not issue blacklists. "The value of such lists ... is problematic, because in view of the large number of books involved, they can never be complete. It is essential that the directors of libraries have the correct attitude towards books and be fully aware of their responsible position in the community." After thus encouraging self-censorship, the guidelines listed several categories of book that "have no place in German libraries"—the writings of emigrants and of authors in foreign countries who were enemies of the new Germany (such as Albert Einstein, Leonhard Frank, H. G. Wells, and Romain Rolland), the literature of Marxism and Bolshevism, the works of pacifists, the liberal-democratic books that had served as propaganda for the Weimar Republic, the "decadent and corrosive literature of the asphalt literati" (such as Heinrich Mann, Arnold Zweig, and Bertolt Brecht), the books on sexual paedagogy and instruction that promote the selfish satisfaction of the individual at the expense of people and race, and the literature authored by Jewish authors irrespective of their subject matter. "Literature for Germany can be written only by Germans who have the same blood and belong to the same or related races." In addition to the books in the above categories that were completely unacceptable, librarians were told to be on the lookout for books that "misled the spiritual life of our people"—the cheap literature of entertainment that portrays life and the purpose of life in a superficial and untrue manner.[17] The librarians of the Saxon public libraries, it was apparent, had their work cut out for them.

Other Landesstellen too emphasized that the effort to maintain public libraries with the right kinds of books had to continue. In an article with the subtitle "The Cleansing after the Cleansing," the director of the Landesstelle for Westfalen argued that "the 'political' purge of the libraries has to be followed by a 'cultural' purge." There was no place for books "that promoted mere amusement without contributing to the building of the new state"—phony adventure and crime novels that offered nothing more than suspense, sentimental love stories, and other kinds of kitsch and trash.[18] The intellectual standards set by these guidelines were high, but it is doubtful that the books passing muster under these criteria were more valuable than the writings by some of the greatest names in modern German literature that had been cast aside as unsuitable for the new Germany.

Some ministers of education in the Länder meanwhile had taken their own initiative in purging the public libraries. In Bavaria, Hans Schemm, the newly appointed Kultusminister (Minister of Education and Cultural Affairs), on April 5, 1933 sent a circular to directors of the public libraries. As in the case of Prussia and other Länder engaged in cleansing their public libraries in 1933, we do not know on what lists these purges were based. The Hermann list or that of Rosenberg's Kampfbund für deutsche Kultur may have been in use.[19] Schemm declared:

> In order to prevent the contamination of the German people with Bolshevik and Marxist literature I order the following: All books and magazines in the Bavarian state and university libraries that show explicit Bolshevik, Marxist, international, pacifist or atheist tendencies as of this date may no longer be lent out.[20]

In the fall of 1933 the Thuringian Ministry of Education similarly issued guidelines for the reorganization of the inventories of the public libraries according to "*völkische* criteria." To be eliminated were "the corrosive products of the Jewish mentality," books of the decadent bourgeois subjectivist kind, works that used literature in order to propagate the class struggle, Marxism, pacifism, or anti-religious sentiments, and books in foreign languages that were not in tune with the Nordic-German sensitivity.[21]

In many cities and towns public officials and the directors of public libraries voluntarily undertook the cleansing of their inventory without waiting for official orders to do so.[22] At the time of the book burning of May 1933, most public libraries had already undergone their first purge.[23] Max Wieser, director of the municipal library Berlin-Spandau and a member of Rosenberg's Kampfbund, announced on March 25 that the task of the hour was the "uncompromising eradication of Marxist literature." Librarians who opposed the spirit of the time (*Zeitgeist*) would "lose themselves and their jobs."[24] The newly appointed head of the municipal library of Göttingen announced that from now on the library would emphasize ideological education rather than breadth of coverage. It would seek to play a role in the intellectual and spiritual renewal of the people and promote National Socialist thinking. The new director noted that the library of Göttingen actually held relatively few "politically dangerous books," a fact that spoke well for the previous administration.[25] In Breslau a new director called for the elimination of all "intellectually, socially, and religiously corrosive literature." Marxist books were to be given to the leaders of the SA and SS and other National Socialist organization to be used in their ideological training.[26] In Heidelberg the mayor of the city on April 6 forbade the lending of books by Jewish authors at the municipal libraries; the following day he extended this ban to Marxist authors.[27] The mayor of Durlach, a small town near Karlsruhe, on April 14 ordered the librarian of the municipal library to remove books "no longer suitable for a German public library."[28]

Walter Hofmann, the director of the public library of Leipzig since 1913, tried to slow down the purge of the library demanded of him by Otto Ziegler, the person in charge of books in the local party organization. On March 3, 1933, Ziegler asked for the catalog of the Leipzig public library so that the NSDAP could "examine" it, and in letters of March 16 and 17 he demanded the removal of the books by Erich Maria Remarque and Ludwig Renn as well as of all other "destructive literature." Hoffmann at first declined. "Even if I were a member of the NSDAP," he wrote Ziegler, "I could accept orders only from my professional conscience and from the authority above me, the city council." He also informed the mayor of Leipzig, Carl Goerdeler, of the pressure to which he had been subjected. Eventually, however, Hofmann had to give in. In an attempt to pacify his critics, Hofmann in 1934 let it be known that he had forsworn "the pluralism of values," but these kinds of concession were not enough to save his job. After Goerdeler resigned as mayor in the spring of 1937, Hofmann was dismissed.[29] Georg Reismüller, the director of the Bavarian State Library, was another librarian who was forced out as politically unreliable. His place was taken by Rudolf Buttmann, an *alter Kämpfer* (old fighter) and *Parteigenosse Nr. 4* (party comrade no. 4).[30]

When Joseph Gotzen, the head of the combined university and municipal library of Cologne, on April 12, 1933, was ordered to screen his inventory for

Jewish and Marxist authors, he registered his doubts about this request. He did not have the personnel to investigate the authorship of 400,000 books, not to mention the difficulty of finding out who was a Jew. Moreover, a scientific library could not do without Spinoza or the Talmud. "There exist many works by Jewish authors on the history of literature, art, and music or published by Jewish publishers that no scholarly library can do without."[31] A few other librarians also stood up for the traditional values of their profession, but German librarians for the most part became "willing assistants of the Nazi state."[32]

After Rust had become Reich Minister for Science, Education and Cultural Affairs, Hitler transferred to him from the Ministry of the Interior the area of adult education, which included the public libraries.[33] Hence as of September 1, 1935, the Prussian Landesstelle became the Reichsstelle für volkstümliches Büchereiwesen, and the other Landesstellen came under the control of the national clearinghouse. Nazi domination of these bodies was guaranteed by the use of *Personalunion* (two appointments held by the same person). For example, officials holding office in the Landesstelle often were also members of the Nazi party's Gauschulungsamt, the organization keeping watch over the cultural and educational activities of the party district. In the ministry itself many leading officials also simultaneously held important positions in party organizations such as the PPK or the Rosenberg organization. Thus Bernhard Kummer, formerly a librarian at the Bavarian State Library and now in charge of the Education Ministry's department of libraries, was also head of the Abteilung Büchereiwesen in Rosenberg's Reichsstelle zur Förderung des deutschen Schrifttums. The purpose of this office in the Rosenberg organization, established in 1935, was to "supervise and advise all German libraries."[34] Between 1935 and 1940 it issued six lists of books every public library should carry.[35] Kummer suggested that "in order to avoid difficulties," librarians should adhere to the "recommendations" of the PPK and the Rosenberg office he headed.[36]

The goal of achieving a unified policy with regard to the public libraries took time. The deadline of January 15, 1934, for turning in the list of inventories had been much too short for most libraries, and some of these lists had not been submitted even by the fall of 1935. Books that had been listed in the official Index of the RSK at times incongruously turned up on the list of recommended books issued by the Reichsstelle. When the Gestapo of Mecklenburg ran into this problem in 1936 in connection with a book on the Canadian wilderness, they informed the Reichsstelle of this discrepancy. The Reichsstelle in turn inquired from the RSK whether a listing in the Index amounted to a "ban" of the book or merely meant that the book in question "should not be recommended."[37] This question, coming at a time when the official Index had been in use for several months, leaves one wondering whether the inquiry did not so much represent genuine ignorance but was rather meant as an excuse for the bureaucratic mishap that had taken place. The Gestapa in Berlin was told by the RSK that, of course, it was the official Index that was binding. "Inasmuch as the Reichsstelle has received the main list of damaging and undesirable literature as well as later supplements," the RSK wrote, "we cannot understand how this book could have ended up in the list of books recommended for small municipal libraries." The libraries involved, the RSK added, had in the meantime removed the offending work.[38]

Given these kinds of snafus it is small wonder that Goebbels considered the performance of Rust's Ministry of Education to be lax. Back in 1933 Goebbels had hoped to have a Ministry of Culture and Popular Enlightenment, which would have consolidated his control over all aspects of cultural policy. Hitler, not wanting to let his propaganda chief become too powerful, had vetoed this idea.[39] Since then the relationship of Goebbels and Rust had been strained. "What Rust is doing," Goebbels wrote in his diary on June 14, 1936, "gradually develops into a scandal."[40] The granting of jurisdiction over the public libraries to the Ministry of Education had been a special disappointment to Goebbels. Indeed he never abandoned his claim that the public libraries should be under his control because they involved books and literature. Rust, he argued, had been given jurisdiction only over scientific books and scientific libraries. A memorandum compiled by Karl Heinl of the RSK in June 1934 maintained that putting the public libraries under the Ministry of Education because they performed an educational function was a fallacious argument. The same logic, Heinl wrote, would put the press, the radio, the theater, or even the party— all of which were providing education—under the control of the Ministry of Education. The libraries belonged in the propaganda ministry because they involved both popular enlightenment and propaganda.[41]

Goebbels was unable to make this claim stick, but, as he wrote in a letter of December 29, 1937, the resolution of this issue had merely been postponed, not abandoned.[42] The librarians, like all "workers of the brain," had to be members of the RSK, and this meant that librarians had to be not only professionally qualified but also politically reliable. Yet for the most part the RSK's jurisdiction was limited to the librarians' economic interests (berufsständische Betreuung). Control over the actual operation of the public libraries remained in the hands of Rust.

Public libraries traditionally had been financed by local communities and many of these were loath to give up their influence on library policy.[43] The mayor of Frankfurt am Main complained in December 1935 that the Reichsstelle gave orders to "my [sic] librarian of the public library" about books to be removed from the library's inventory. The Ministry of Education rejected this reproach with the argument that it was the task of the state to draw attention to mistakes and failures in building the collection, especially when ideological considerations were involved.[44] And gradually the ministry was able to assert its domination. On May 10, 1937, it issued a new decree concerning the books found unsuitable and damaging according to the RSK Index. These books until then had been merely withdrawn from circulation and kept under lock and key. The public libraries now were instructed to hand these books over to the Landesbibliotheken (state libraries) by August 1.[45]

The two largest of these were the Preussische Staatsbibliothek in Berlin and the Bayerische Staatsbibliothek in Munich. The Staatsbibliothek in Berlin appears to have ended up with the largest number of offending books because it was regularly also given books confiscated by the Gestapo. Its new head was Rudolf Kummer, "a convinced anti-Semite, a veteran National Socialist, and participant in the Hitler Putsch of 1923,"[46] and at the same time a leading official in the Ministry of Education. Duplicate copies usually were distributed to other scholarly libraries such as the Rothschild Library in Frankfurt (which in 1935 was renamed "Library for Modern Languages and Music" so as to eliminate any sense of indebtedness to the Rothschild family).[47] The rationale for keeping these books was articulated by Ministry of Education official Kummer, who stated that the successful fight against a disease required knowledge of its manifestations.[48] In other words, "Know your enemy!"

The total number of books eliminated from the public libraries for political reasons is not known. Many of the figures we have also include books that were discarded as outdated or in poor condition. We do have numbers of purged books from some locations. The public library of Leipzig until September 1935 withdrew from circulation 12,132 books, representing 10.7 percent of its total inventory. Not surprisingly, the largest category of purged books—5,186 volumes—was that of the social sciences.[49] In many other cities the percentage of purged books was far higher. In Düsseldorf between September 1933 and May 1935, 20 percent of all books in the public libraries were weeded out for political reasons, for a total of about 6,000 books.[50] In Frankfurt an der Oder, some 11,000 books out of a total of 26,000 were removed, in Kiel 11,000 out of 22,000, and in Jena 38,000 out of 50,000.[51] In Berlin some 10 to 40 percent of all books in the public libraries were withdrawn from circulation,[52] and in Vienna close to 50 percent.[53] The head of the Landesstelle for Saxony, Karl Taupitz, reported in 1937 that Saxony had purged about 50 to 80 percent of books in the public libraries because they were "hostile to state and people."[54] The bragging of the deputy director of the municipal library of Essen in October 1937 that his library had "become a National Socialist library" was true not only for Essen. Typical for such cleansed libraries, it held 120 copies of Hitler's *Mein Kampf,* but had lost practically all of the most important classics of modern German literature.[55] The National Socialist librarians had succeeded relatively quickly in thoroughly purging the public libraries of unwelcome literature.[56]

The Law for the Restoration of the Professional Civil Service of April 7, 1933, had provided for the dismissal of all non-Aryan civil servants (except Frontkämpfer who had served in combat during World War I) and of civil servants "whose prior political attitude failed to guarantee that they would at all times defend the National Socialist state without qualifications." Since both professors and administrators were civil servants, this law had a significant impact on the universities. In order to justify the dismissal of outstanding Jewish mathematicians and physicists, the Nazis began to talk about the superiority of "German mathematics" and "German physics." Politicizing both teaching and research, nationalsozialistische Wissenschaft (National Socialist science) was to overcome science that claimed to be "objective" but in fact was simply standortlos (without roots).[57] Moreover, the Nazi Führerprinzip (leadership principle) was introduced in the place of the traditional academic autonomy, seriously weakening the powerful department heads. This radical reorganization of the institutions of higher learning of course also included the university libraries. Librarians too were civil servants, and therefore only Aryans and politically reliable individuals were allowed to be or become librarians.

While Goebbels had tried to challenge the jurisdiction of Rust's Ministry of Education for the public libraries, the right of Rust to regulate and control the university libraries was beyond dispute. The supervision of these libraries was in the hands of the bureau "Scientific Libraries," part of the Education Ministry's Department 1—Wissenschaft (Science).[58] The Ministry of the Interior had an advisory committee for scientific libraries, but it met only six times and had no ascertainable influence on the running of the university libraries.[59] That these libraries would have to cease to be "unpolitical," and would have to be anchored in the ideology of the Third Reich, was taken for granted. Rosenberg official Joachim Kirchner pointed out that German academics had falsely sought a "value-free scholarship" and that this had led to the "decay of science." There had been an overproduction of books of little value. Henceforth the university libraries would serve the National Socialist idea and state. Acquisitions would be based on "völkische" criteria.[60] In a book entitled Kämpfende Wissenschaft (Fighting Science) published in 1934, Walter Frank, later to become head of the Reichsinstitut für Geschichte des neuen Deutschland (Reich Institute for the History of the New Germany), announced that "the fetters of narrow professional expertise and the guild spirit of the learned fraternity have been broken." From now on science would serve the Third Reich.[61]

Rust's first order specifically addressing offending books in the university libraries came on June 8, 1933. Writing in his capacity as Prussian Minister of Education, he instructed the Prussian university libraries not to destroy "Jewish or Marxist literature," though special attention had to be paid to the circulation of these works. They were to be lent out only to those "who could show that they needed the books for scholarly research." On September 17, 1934,

Rust, now minister of education for the entire country, sent the same instruction to all university libraries. Books that fell under the new rules included "all publications that were listed in the subject catalog under Socialism and Communism except for those who oppose Marxism and Communism." Also to be sequestered were all books in the Russian language published after 1917, as well as "all publications not suitable for general use."[62]

Additional instructions were issued on April 3, 1935. "Corrosive Jewish-Marxist literature" had to be kept "under special cloture" and only certain officials were to handle this sequestered literature, sometimes referred to as the "poison cabinet." Offending books were to be marked with a special tag. Even qualified users were not allowed to make copies. Either the library catalog could note that these books could not be lent out, or a special catalog could be set up for them.[63] A follow-up order of October 22 required the removal of cards for the offending titles from the general card catalog.[64] Instructions to sequester a particular publication were issued from time to time. Thus on November 12, 1937, the Rust ministry ordered that the British journal *Nature* be no longer available for general use because the magazine had published several articles that included "incredibly base discourse against German science and the National Socialist state."[65] Kummer, seeking to defend the sequester, stated that, contrary to the "atrocity legends" spread abroad, the corrosive literature, though hostile to the state, had not been destroyed. These books had simply been withdrawn from general circulation, and were still available to officials and researchers who needed them for their teaching and research. The scholarly libraries would preserve these books for "today and coming generations."[66]

Library directors often found it difficult to decide which books were to be sequestered. Catch-all provisions like "all publications not suitable for general use" were not very helpful. The situation improved following the issuance of the RSK Index. On March 23, 1936, Rust sent the list of "harmful and undesirable books" to the directors of university libraries. The letter was stamped "Confidential," and the list was marked "Secret." The libraries were admonished to keep the list under lock and key. The inventory of the libraries was to be checked, and books on the list were to be sequestered in accordance with earlier decrees.[67] While the directors of many university libraries regarded these rules as onerous and impossible to comply with at existing levels of personnel, the Gestapo complained that they did not go far enough. Despite precautions, there was the danger that the sequestered books "would get into the hands of unauthorized persons who would exploit them in a manner hostile to the National Socialist state." The Gestapo suggested that it would be far better if Bolshevik and other inflammatory publications were subscribed to by a special department of the Deutsche Bücherei, which could make these writings available to scholars for *bona fide* scientific work by way of interlibrary loan.[68]

The implementation of the decrees issued by the Ministry of Education varied from library to library, depending on the political outlook and courage of the director. The Ministry of Education complained on December 16, 1936, that "at some libraries books like the works of Lenin, Bucharin, Rosa Luxemburg, Karl Liebknecht, Kurt Eisner, Mühsam, etc., are still available to everybody" and urged the strict sequester of such publications.[69] Another variable was the aggressiveness of local Gestapo or SD officials who often interfered in the work of the libraries. The head of the acquisitions department of the Prussian Staatsbibliothek in Berlin later recalled that after 1936 she had to make regular visits to Gestapo headquarters at Albrechtstrasse in order to obtain approval for her foreign book orders.[70] The Gestapo of Cologne reported on July 31, 1934, that it had directed the combined university and municipal library to stop the circulation of two books that had given offense.[71] The number of sequestered books also was not uniform. At the library of the University of Marburg a special room was created to hold 3,000 forbidden books, but this facility turned out to be much too small. By January 1940 about 15,000 books had been marked as "not for circulation."[72] At the library of the University of Jena, which a local newspaper praised as an "arsenal of the swords of the German spirit," some 30,000 books were sequestered. This action was characterized as "fostering German cultural values."[73] The library of the Student Union at the Technical University of Braunschweig lost 60 percent of its collection.[74]

Some directors of university libraries, such as Josef Rest at the University of Freiburg, tried to slow down the purge of their collections. On October 11, 1936, a teacher had informed the local Gestapo that in the periodical room of the university library he had found an issue of the journal *Orient und Occident* with an article "Die biblische Botschaft und Karl Marx" that "was full of insults of the National Socialist Germany and its Führer." While Rest certified to the president of the university that he had promptly removed the offending issue, he added that it was quite impossible "to screen the about 4,000 journals the library subscribed to for open or hidden attacks against the new Germany." The same held true for newly acquired books, where it was similarly out of the question to read through all of them, especially when the title did not betray anything objectionable.[75] The director of the combined university and municipal library of Cologne had even dared to say, in 1933, that a scholarly library could not do without the books by Jewish authors.

At most universities the director of the library himself decided who was entitled to receive special permission for the reading of sequestered books. At the University of Heidelberg, professors personally known to the director were given access simply by stating that they needed a certain work for their research. Students had to bring a written authorization from their professor.[76] At the University of Graz the local SD office had to be consulted. An instruction sent to the library director on June 10, 1942, insisted that borrowers were not to be told of the involvement of the SD. The delay in issuing the permission was to be attributed to "technical reasons."[77] It is possible that this provision was part of the general tightening of book controls that began after the outbreak of war in 1939.

The librarians of Germany's public libraries had long attacked the commercial lending libraries for their "sensationalism" and their inability to prevent "trash and filth." The book burning of May 1933 and the beginning of book seizures by the Gestapo encouraged the librarians to press their offensive. Some opponents called the lending libraries "literary brothels" and hoped that they would be put under the control of the public libraries. The librarian and Rust official Franz Schriewer, in an article entitled "Fight the Lending Libraries!," argued that the spread of the lending libraries had been "scandalous." There were now between 10,000 to 18,000 such commercial enterprises that existed for profit rather than for the edification of their readers. Most of these libraries catered to the lowest human instincts and stocked primarily cheap and erotic literature in order to increase their profits. The 1926 Law against Trash and Filth had been unable to prevent this development; only 192 books or series had been banned. It was now time for the public libraries to fight back.[78]

The same argument was pressed by K. Schulz, a member of Rosenberg's Kampfbund and head of the Thuringian Office for Public Libraries. Schulz had participated in police raids and, as he stated, had thus learned at first hand how the lending libraries threatened public decency. In one library sixty pornographic novels had been found and confiscated. The author listed the titles of dime novels that dwelled on unrestrained sexuality and were unfortunately accessible to children and young people. Schulz expressed the hope that the National Socialist state would take steps against this "decay of morality."[79] Much of this vilification was overwrought. Although the lending libraries did not share the educational pretensions of public libraries, they were meeting a demand public libraries refused to satisfy.[80] This meant that they stocked the popular romances of Hedwig Courths-Mahler and the detective novels of Edgar Wallace alongside more exalted fare as well as outright trash.

Whatever the merit of the harsh criticism of the lending libraries, the RSK willingly responded to the demand to bring the lending libraries into line. The owners and employees of lending libraries had to be members of the RSK. A special Fachschaft II Leihbücherei (Section II Lending Libraries) was organized, and a new bureau, the Beratungsstelle (Überwachungsstelle) für das Leihbüchereiwesen, was established to "advise and supervise." The head of this bureau was Ludwig Hürter, though it is likely that, just as in the case of the RSK, the ultimate decision-making power was in the hands of Wismann's Abteilung VIII: Schrifttum in the Ministry of Propaganda. The acquisition of "good literature" was accomplished by the publication of *Grundlisten* (Basic Lists) in the journal of the lending libraries, *Zeitschrift der Leihbücherei*. Failure to stock these books might prompt the expulsion of the owner of the lending library from the RSK and thus the closure of the enterprise.[81] Other lists, also published in the *Zeitschrift der Leihbücherei*, targeted "un-German" and "bad" literature. The list of banned and un-German books issued by the newly minted Nazi Ernst Drahn in December 1933 was the first of such lists issued in the name of the Fachschaft for the guidance of the lending libraries.[82] Another such list was compiled by the Bavarian political police in 1934.[83] On November 28, 1934, the lending libraries were informed that on orders of the Ministry of Defense all books dealing with espionage and the Foreign Legion were to be removed from their inventory.[84]

One of the first acts of the new bureaucracy was to impose a ban on the establishment of new lending libraries. The ban was to last only six months but was subsequently extended several times. Also the lending of books was henceforth to take place only in regular stores and no longer in the lobbies of houses or by street peddlers. There followed an order requiring the libraries to submit a list of their inventory that was to be checked for "unsuitable books." Failure to comply could lead to the closing of the enterprise.[85] The due date for handing in this list had to be extended repeatedly. By August 1, 1935, a total of 3,875 lists had been handed in, of which 3,290 had been checked, but only 836 enterprises had completed the process of handing over all their offending books.[86] The purge of the lending libraries dragged on until 1938. The total number of books that were eliminated and destroyed as a result of this vetting process is not known. In Berlin alone 16,800 books had been brought in for pulping by October 29, 1934, which amounted to 1.5 percent of the 1.13 million books in the lending libraries of the capital.[87] All together, it has been estimated that between 100,000 and 200,000 books previously owned by the lending libraries were destroyed.[88]

The manner in which the cleansing of the lending libraries was carried out caused dissatisfaction. On December 1, 1934, Conrad von Heuduck, the owner of a lending library in Berlin and an official of the Fachschaft, sent a memorandum to the RSK that warned of "incredibly dangerous consequences" for the lending libraries. The author affirmed that he and his colleagues had no principled objection to the purge, but he took exception to certain important aspects of the process. Some of the books that had been found to be unacceptable were by authors who were famous figures of world literature, could not possibly damage the new state, and were not forbidden elsewhere. "Many of these books are kept in thousands of copies in private libraries, can be bought in every bookstore, and continue to be lent out by the public libraries." The order requiring the elimination of these books therefore represented a measure specifically designed to humiliate and damage the lending libraries. Even more objectionable, von Heuduck affirmed, was the requirement that the books be brought to the central collection center for their destruction. All party members were in agreement that this order represented an unacceptable encroachment upon private property not authorized by any law. If the RSK insisted on the confiscation and destruction of these books, then at the very least the affected enterprises should receive some compensation for the severe economic loss inflicted on them.[89]

Von Heuduck's complaint that the lending libraries were being held to more restrictive standards of censorship than the public libraries appears to have been justified. The list of banned books issued by the Bavarian political police in 1934, for example, in addition to 4,360 generally forbidden books, included 2,483 books banned specifically for the lending libraries.[90]

Documents in the files of the RSK show that the Überwachungsstelle did ban books for the lending libraries that were not on the official Index.[91] On October 7, 1937, the Gestapo office in Zwickau informed the Gestapa in Berlin that most of the books they had been ordered by the RSK to confiscate at a local lending library were not on the Index. Hence they inquired whether these books should be seized at other lending libraries in Zwickau as well.[92] The reply of the Gestapa is not preserved, but the inquiry itself is revealing. In an undated instruction to all Gestapo offices the Gestapa let it be known that the RSK had decided not to list Harold Nicolson's 1932 novel *Die Herren der Welt privat* (Public Faces) on the Index. "This book was unsuitable merely for lending libraries."[93] These documents confirm that the censorship of the lending libraries was indeed more rigorous than that of the book trade and the public libraries.

Not surprisingly, von Heuduck's appeal to the rule of law fell on deaf ears, and the purge of the lending libraries proceeded apace. As a result many libraries were forced to close. Ludwig Hürter, the head of the Beratungsstelle, bragged that by 1934 more than 2,000 "unhealthy enterprises" had been eliminated.[94] Between 1933 and 1938 the number of lending libraries decreased from about 7,000 to 2,000—a decline of almost two thirds.[95] Meanwhile, despite pressure and intimidation against the lending libraries, raids by the Gestapo continued to turn up "undesirable literature," especially easy-to-read novels providing entertainment and thrills that were popular with a wide readership. The RSK ordinance "Harmful and Undesirable Literature" of April 25, 1935, establishing the official state Index, was welcomed by the lending libraries as a measure "that corresponds to a long-desired wish,"[96] but the secret character of the Index deprived it of much of its utility. During the search of eighteen lending libraries in the Koblenz area at the end of 1936, more than one hundred books listed on the Index turned up at one such library. The owner pleaded that, acting in good faith, he had surrendered about 350 books and had therefore assumed to be in the clear. He had tried to see the official list but had been told that the list was secret.[97] The owner of another lending library in Koblenz, where twenty-four books had been confiscated, was told that as a responsible owner he "should have known even without seeing the list of harmful and undesirable books" that these kinds of books could no longer be lent in today's Germany. He was warned that another offense would lead to "more severe measures."[98]

Given these kinds of pressures, it is not surprising that most lending libraries complied with the demand to cleanse their inventory. RSK vice president Wismann told a meeting of Fachschaft officials on September 16, 1934, that the process of purging the libraries of "what is not worthy and offends the German people" was well under way.[99] An article in the *Zeitschrift der Leihbücherei* of September 10, 1934, counseled owners of lending libraries to follow the maxim: "Better to discard one book too many than one book too few!"[100] But not all lending libraries were willing to toe the line, and, whether for idealistic or commercial reasons, they continued to lend out the offending books. The owner of a large lending library in Berlin with more than 60,000 books recalled that, despite difficult conditions, his employees were able to provide "undesirable" books to trustworthy customers personally known to them. The entire inventory of books had the same covers, which made the search for forbidden titles difficult.[101]

The RSK had taken on the job of cleansing the lending libraries, but it did not want to destroy them. Heinz Wismann, vice president of the RSK, told a conference of librarians of lending libraries in March 1934 that together with the public libraries the lending libraries were important for the education of the people. "One would deprive oneself of a significant educational tool if, as their most intransigent opponents demanded, one were to suppress the lending libraries."[102] On March 6, 1935, Wismann announced that the RSK had formed a committee made up of three representatives each from the public and lending libraries. This committee was to seek to "overcome existing conflicts and promote mutual understanding."[103] To make sure that everyone in the profession got this message, in September of the same year the Reichsstelle für volkstümliches Büchereiwesen (in charge of the public libraries), in conjunction with the RSK, issued an order "to desist from public polemics about the nature and aims of the lending and public libraries."[104] Strange as it may seem, RSK patronage and control of the lending libraries assured the survival of these beleaguered enterprises.

Both the Protestant and Catholic churches had developed a network of libraries that, in addition to books on strictly religious topics, also included works of general interest. Many of these libraries were very popular. In Bavaria, for example, the Catholic libraries organized in the Borromäusverein attracted more readers than the public libraries, they were called public libraries, and "most important, were perceived as public libraries."[105] As of March 31, 1934, there were 4,207 Protestant libraries with 1.4 million books, and 4,880 Catholic libraries with more than 5 million books in the Reich. For a regime intent upon the total control of society, any institution not under its full domination represented a dangerous threat. The task for the new state that followed from this situation, Schuster, the head of the nazified VDV, argued, "need not be elaborated upon."[106] Hence in order to undercut the appeal of these libraries, the regime forced them to abandon the appellation "public library," ended their public subsidies, and undertook to restrict them to confessional literature.

In his decree "Noch Heute!" (Still Today!) of December 28, 1933, Prussian Minister of Education Rust had announced that libraries whose inventory was dependent entirely or in part upon non-state guidelines were not public libraries and were not allowed to call themselves such. The mode of operation and inventory of all libraries were put under the supervision of the Prussian Beratungsstelle. "The church literature of the confessional libraries is exempt from this rule."[107] All other books in the confessional libraries, however, were subject to the same regulations imposed upon the public libraries. That meant that a list of these titles had to be submitted to the Beratungsstelle, which decided what books were "unsuitable" and had to be handed in and destroyed. Enforcement of the removal of offending books was in the hands of the Gestapo. A decree issued on May 2, 1934, forbade the establishment of new confessional libraries.[108]

Many Catholic librarians at first welcomed the Nazi takeover. Johannes Braun, the head of the Borromäusverein, stated in May 1933 in a confidential memo: "It should be understood that the Borromäusverein greets the principles of the present regime in the cultural area joyfully, especially those of literature. … We rejoice in the help that we will now receive from the government in the fight against *Schund und Schmutz*." Very soon, however, it became clear that the new regime was after more than just trash. Not that the Catholic libraries had many of the books that were the target of the first wave of censorship—Marxist, Socialist, and pacifist books. As the head of the Beratungsstelle Düsseldorf confirmed in 1934: "I can be sure from my own experience that writings unsuitable on political grounds are hardly to be found in the libraries of the Borromäusverein and that, in my opinion, review will therefore be a formality."[109]

The next restriction imposed upon the Catholic libraries was an order of January 1, 1935, that limited the circulation of books to members of the Borromäusverein. Anyone seeking to borrow books from a parish library had to be a parishioner and pay the annual membership fee. This regulation hit hard the many poor and unemployed who had been allowed use of the Catholic libraries without becoming members of the society. According to a 1934 report, the libraries of the Borromäusverein had 361,465 such readers. The most damaging measure came on August 14, 1940, when the Borromäusverein was ordered to limit its lending to religious books. By January 1, 1941, the Catholic libraries had to withdraw from circulation all titles that merely entertained without addressing religious questions, such as light fiction, detective stories, and books for young adults—the very books that had done so much the build the popularity of the Catholic libraries. In lending "worldly" books, Rust argued, the Catholic libraries had exceeded their role as a charitable-religious organization. In vain did the Borromäusverein protest this order that seriously weakened the Catholic libraries.[110] Another development undermining all confessional libraries was the establishment of large numbers of new public libraries. The state of Baden, for example, in 1934 had forty-seven public libraries and 767 confessional libraries. By 1944 there were 820 public libraries.[111] The final blow to the confessional libraries came with the wartime restrictions on the use of paper.

While the weakening of the Catholic libraries took several years, the subordination of the Protestant libraries presented far fewer problems. The Deutsche Verband Evangelischer Büchereien, the umbrella organization of the Protestant libraries, was *gleichgeschaltet* in November 1934 and became the Nazi-controlled Reichsverband Evangelischer Büchereien. Without an effective national organization, the Protestant libraries had no way to resist the various decrees limiting the work of the confessional libraries.[112] Moreover, German Protestantism as a whole demonstrated less resistance to the inroads of Nazi ideology than its Catholic counterpart. Most Protestant librarians therefore more or less willingly accepted the restricted role the Nazi state allowed the confessional libraries.

11

Wartime Censorship

The onset of war on September 1, 1939, led to a discernable tightening of book controls. During the prewar years an average of about 300 writers a year had been expelled from the RSK or their applications for admission had been denied.[1] But during the month of November 1939 alone, no fewer than 211 authors were expelled or rejected. Complete figures for 1940 are not available, but during 1941 the total was 782.[2] In 1943, for the first time, clergymen were excluded as a class.[3] Moreover, new tasks arose for book censors. England and France were now enemy nations, while the Soviet Union, previously the target of vilification as the home of "corrosive cultural Bolshevism," had with the Hitler-Stalin pact become an ally.

After the invasion of the Soviet Union in 1941, this relationship changed again, and there were other twists in foreign policy that required adjustments in the control of literature. The scarcity of paper became severe and was used as a means of censorship. Light popular fiction, on the other hand, previously frowned upon as insufficiently political, was now favored because under the stress of war the population demanded easy-to-read books. On September 8 Goebbels informed his staff that new duties arising from the state of war required him to give up important matters previously handled by him personally, and he asked the heads of departments to shoulder additional responsibility.[4] Yet a year later he appears to have regretted abandoning his close involvement with what kind of books were being published. Literature, Goebbels noted in his diary on October 16, 1940, had become sterile. "But now I am taking charge and creating order."[5]

Until the onset of war in 1939, German readers had been not been cut off from foreign literature. Between 1933 and 1939, some 3.25 million books translated into German are estimated to have been sold.[6] At the same time, there had been book bans for reasons of foreign policy. In the view of the Ministry of Propaganda, the Foreign Office was overly sensitive to the complaints of foreign nations and was in the habit of asking for the suppression of books even if the impact on diplomatic relations was minimal.[7] The files indeed include numerous such bans. On May 14, 1937, the Ministry of Propaganda had let it be known that any mention of subsidies for German exports was strictly forbidden.[8]

The book *Palästina, wie es wirklich ist* (Palestine, as It Really Is) was banned on April 19, 1939, on the grounds that it included praise for the industriousness and economic proficiency of the Jews who had emigrated to Palestine and because the book denied the conflict between Jews and Arabs.[9] On November 19, 1937, the Gestapa had ordered the confiscation and pulping of a brochure by a Protestant minister who had officiated and taught in Brazil. The brochure had stated that German schools and Protestant churches in Brazil "worked in accordance with instructions from Germany" and this allegation was held to hurt Brazilian sensitivities and create a serious political burden for German culture in Brazil.[10] The books of foreigners such as Ève Curie, Romain Rolland, and Sigrid Undset had been forbidden because these authors were hostile to the new Germany and its policies, both domestic and foreign. However, a ban had never been imposed upon an author simply because he was a foreign national. This is what occurred after the beginning of the war in 1939.

On September 20, 1939, a message sent by the Reichsstelle to all public libraries asked them to check the literature about England and France and to make sure that these books did not harm Germany's "strength and endurance and the determination for victory." Offending books were to be withdrawn inconspicuously from general circulation. Anti-Soviet writings were to be lent out only with great caution. A follow-up instruction of January 16, 1940, advised a distinction between the Soviet Union and Communism, adding "that the anti-communist literature need not disappear completely from the scene."[11] In August 1940 Goebbels reminded his department that there existed no ideological affinity between National Socialism and Bolshevism and that the relationship with the Soviet Union was guided strictly by "considerations of Realpolitik."[12] This bow in the direction of maintaining an anti-communist posture was weakened again in November 1940 when Himmler ordered a ban of the entire Russian and Ukrainian exile literature.[13]

On October 15, 1939, the Ministry of Propaganda forbade all crime and adventure novels that "propagandized English institutions and character,"[14] an order obviously aimed at the highly popular crime novels of Edgar Wallace and at Scotland Yard, which was celebrated in the series. A novel for young people by the American writer Carter Dickson was banned on November 16 because it "glorified the English police."[15] Going still further, on April 18, 1940, the Ministry of Propaganda forbade the translation of any foreign fiction.[16]

Lending libraries and publishers too received new orders. On December 12, 1939, the RSK announced that all books by English and French authors had to be removed from the lending libraries. Publishers were informed on December 15 that, in view of the fact that Germany was in a state of war with England and

France, it was "unacceptable to sell and distribute German translations of the fiction of these countries," especially since this would provide them with foreign currency. These books did not have to be destroyed; it was expected that they could be traded again once the state of war had ended. Classical works by authors who were dead more than fifty years, such as Shakespeare, Milton, Dickens, Molière, and Voltaire, were exempt from this decree.[17] On September 2, 1940, the lending library ban was extended to books translated from Polish.[18]

In response to an inquiry, the Gestapa let it be known on May 22, 1940, that it had "no objections as such" to Bernard Shaw's book *The Intelligent Woman's Guide to Socialism and Capitalism,* but that the translation of this work belonged to the kind of English literature that was not to be sold for the duration of the war. Bookstores were cautioned not to transgress this order.[19] An official in the propaganda ministry warned authors not "to copy or propagate, directly or indirectly, English character, life-style or institutions."[20] On the other hand, after Marshal Pétain's government had made peace with Germany in June 1940 and had begun to collaborate with Hitler, the RSK forbade the publication and distribution of anti-French books on December 15, 1940.[21] Publishers who violated these orders received severe fines or were closed down.

Hermann Rauschning, a trusted follower of Hitler whom the Führer appointed president of the Danzig senate, by 1935 had become disillusioned with the Nazi regime and had fled to Switzerland. His books *Die Revolution des Nihilismus* (The Revolution of Nihilism) and *Gespräche mit Hitler* (Talks with Hitler) were published in Switzerland, were soon translated into French and English, and attracted a wide readership. Subsequent scholarship has shown that the alleged talks with Hitler were a hoax, but at the time the book had considerable impact. In order not to draw attention to the book, Goebbels at first gave orders that the book not be included in the state Index. But by early 1940 he had changed his mind, the book was indexed, and Switzerland was put under pressure to ban the work. On February 1940 the Swiss cabinet yielded to this demand and forbade *Gespräche mit Hitler.*[22] Nazi book censorship had successfully extended its reach beyond the borders of the Reich.

The expanding war brought about more about-faces. On June 22, 1941, Operation Barbarossa, Hitler's invasion of the Soviet Union, got under way, and the treatment of Russian literature underwent another change. Effective July 11, 1941, "in accordance with the political situation," the distribution of all books by Russian authors was banned. This prohibition was valid for current as well as for earlier Russian literature. On October 1 the order was changed to allow the sale of classical Russian literature published before 1914, but for reasons that were not made public this exemption was canceled again on October 3, 1942. In an order dated June 27, 1941, the Reichsstelle for the public libraries made it known that the display of anti-Bolshevik writings was to take place "with the emphasis dictated by the political development."[23]

Other changes in the political landscape of Europe similarly led to new instructions for the book trade. On March 14, 1939, Slovakia had become a client state of Germany, but on July 11 the RSK gave orders that "for reasons of foreign policy, it is not appropriate on maps or texts to describe Slovakia as belonging to the German Reich or dependent on it. Instead, it is recommended that Slovakia be depicted as an independent state."[24] A brochure published in 1939 that dealt with the war in the Far East was banned because it "glorified" the Chinese resistance to Japan and thus "burdened German-Japanese relations."[25]

After Germany had declared war on the United States on December 11, 1941, it was the turn of American literature to be censored. On December 22 Himmler, acting with the consent of the Ministry of Propaganda, forbade the distribution of all American publications.[26] A circular sent out by the Ministry of Education on January 7, 1942, explained that this order included all translations of North American fiction but not "clearly scientific works needed for research or teaching."[27] A list of banned authors issued by the Propaganda Ministry in 1942 included Willa Cather, F. Scott Fitzgerald, and William Faulkner.[28] Works by authors who had died before 1904 were exempt from this order, thus permitting the continued sale of the writings of Herman Melville and Stephen Crane. Some highly popular writers such as Mark Twain and Jack London were allowed even though they had died after 1904. Jews or suspected Jews were singled out for special mention.

On February 12, 1945, with Russian troops closing in on Berlin and the demise of the Thousand Year Reich apparent to all, the RSK issued an order forbidding the sale of works about Finland, Romania, and Bulgaria as well as of books by authors from these countries.[29] By that time most bookstores were no longer operating, and the German population presumably had more important things to worry about than the literature about Finland, Romania, and Bulgaria. Sheer bureaucratic inertia appears to explain the publication of this last known book ban of the Nazi regime.

Another category of books that came under the control of the wartime censor were publications that were held to be of possible aid to the enemy. From August 25, 1939, on these works were listed in the monthly updates of forbidden books issued by the Deutsche Bücherei with the designation *geheim* (secret) as well as in one of the "Strictly Confidential" gazettes of the RSK. These publications were not included in the official Index. An order dated December 15, 1939, banned books on "facilities important for the defense of the country."[30] A month later came a ban on books dealing with secret codes.[31] An instruction issued by the Ministry of the Interior on February 6, 1940, reminded everyone that "cartographic descriptions of any kind" were not to "damage the common good."[32] The vagueness of this order prompted a large publisher of maps to complain that this edict threatened "the entire private commerce in maps."[33] The

RSK agreed and noted that the insecurity caused by the order of February 6 had led to a complete stagnation in the publication and sale of maps.[34] Subsequent ordinances were more specific. For example, an instruction issued the by RSK on March 26, 1940, forbade the sale to the public of a map of the main roads of Germany with the scale of 1:800,000.[35]

Other edicts covered a wide range of forbidden topics. A regulation published on March 1 forbade the publication, sale, or lending of all books dealing with secret inks.[36] An order of May 7 pointed out that panoramic photos taken from elevated positions could be useful to the enemy in planning targets, and it therefore laid down that the use of such photos on postcards or in illustrated books required the permission of the Ministry of Aviation.[37] About a month later this requirement was extended to relief maps.[38] An order published on July 15 announced that works dealing with the operations of airborne troops were forbidden, though narrative accounts by individual fighters continued to be "desirable."[39]

Books describing the heroism of the soldier at the front appeared in large numbers, but authors were warned against "cheap exaggerations."[40] They also were ordered not to create disdain for Upper Silesians and Saxons and their dialects by including in their books wisecracks and jokes about these people.[41] The shortage of teachers was serious, the RSK informed the book trade in February 1942, in part because Jews and literati in earlier years had brought German teachers into contempt. Hence it was "urgently necessary" that publishers vet their manuscripts for "any pejorative comment" directed at teachers.[42] Writers in wartime Germany obviously did not have an easy time in navigating the obstacle course created by the censors.

The last wartime order containing a ban on a publication came on March 21, 1945, seemingly issued in completely obliviousness of the imminent collapse of the Third Reich: It restricted the distribution of maps of the scale of 1:300,000 to public authorities.[43] The inappropriate timing of this announcement, coming while Berlin was being turned into rubble, is stunning. Nazi bureaucrats were doing their duty until the very end.

On April 15, 1940, the RSK issued a new version of Order no. 70, the regulation that had established the *Liste des schädlichen und unerwünschten Schrifttum* (or what has been called the State Index of forbidden books) and had first been published in late 1935. RSK President Johst now suggested to Goebbels that a "toughening of the order" would "strengthen the inner front" and was vital for the war effort.[44] The revised Order no. 70 constituted a tightening of censorship, though the link to wartime morale was not always obvious. A new paragraph 4 banned the publication of books by Jewish or half-Jewish authors even if these works were not specifically listed in the Index. Although the original version of Order no. 70 had forbidden the distribution of listed books by libraries or bookstores, it was now ordered that listed books were not to be displayed or even stocked. Violators could face exclusion from the RSK. The Gestapo set out to enforce these provisions by staging a new wave of raids on libraries and bookstores. Between April and July 1940 the book department of the Kaufhaus des Westens department store in Berlin was searched twice and offending books were confiscated.[45]

Another new section of the ordinance of April 15 affected books for young people below the age of eighteen. The 1935 version of Order no. 70 in Paragraph 2 had mentioned the creation of a list of books that, while not included in the official Index created by Paragraph 1, were "inappropriate for young people," but until 1940 no such list had been issued. The list was now said to be ready,[46] and it was published in *Grossdeutsches Leihbüchereiblatt*, the official gazette of the lending libraries, in the *Börsenblatt* of the book trade, and in the *Völkischer Beobachter*. More publicity was held to be inappropriate so as not to make these books "interesting" and attractive.[47] An implementing regulation issued in June 1942 provided that listed books were to be made available to the Deutsche Bücherei in Leipzig, while books not needed there were to be pulped.[48] It is symptomatic for the disorderly, not to say chaotic, way in which such ordinances were devised in polycratic Nazi Germany that Hinkel, the propaganda ministry's pointman for Jewish books, was not involved in the formulation of Paragraph 4 regarding Jewish authors, and Minister of Education Rust, as he complained on August 8, 1940, saw the final text of the decree for the first time when it was published in the *Börsenblatt*.[49]

Also linked to the state of war was an order of the Ministry of Propaganda dated April 20, 1940, that created a central office for the control of technical books and textbooks (Fachbuch-Zentrallektorat). The term *technical book* was to be used in its widest sense and included not only textbooks but also books of popular science. Readers, following the guidelines of the propaganda ministry, were to make sure that textbooks were above reproach with regard to their "ideological-political content." The new office was described as an "advisory body," but it is evident that this term usually was a euphemism for an organization engaged in censorship.[50]

In earlier years Nazi organizations like the Hitler Youth, the National Socialist Teachers Assocation (NSLB), and Rosenberg's Reichsstelle zur Förderung des deutschen Schrifttums had recommended books for young people and had warned against unsuitable ones.[51] But Order no. 70 constituted an undertaking with penalties. The first list of publications "inappropriate for young people," compiled by the propaganda ministry, appeared in October 1940.[52] New editions followed in 1942 and 1943. "List 2," as it was known, included many Wild West adventure novels as well as six books by Agatha Christie. It also contained about one hundred detective stories by Edgar Wallace, filling ten pages of the seventy-seven making up the list, undoubtedly part of the endeavor to prevent the glorification of heroes with English names.

The main reason for finally issuing this list in 1940, after first announcing it five years earlier, indeed appears to have been war-related, that is, to keep young people away from exemplary foreigners, especially Englishmen. From time to time there had been expressions of concern that cheap adventure and crime literature contributed to juvenile delinquency and therefore should be suppressed,[53] but these fears had led to few bans. It is significant that in contrast to earlier practice, a list supposed to protect the morals of teens did not forbid any erotic literature at all.

The control of youth literature was part of a larger effort on the part of the regime to deal with the popularity of easy-to-read unpolitical fiction, the very kind of literature that the war-stressed German population and its soldiers craved and sought. The SD's *Meldungen aus dem Reich* (Reports from the Reich) confirm that after the outbreak of the war the demand for reading that diverted and entertained had increased substantially.[54] Light fiction, such as the more than 200 novels and short stories of Hedwig Courths-Mahler, had previously been criticized as frivolous and failing to contribute to the political education of readers.[55] While rigid ideologues like Rosenberg stuck to this negative assessment, the astute Goebbels realized that, due to the hardships of war and the resulting stress and strain, the regime had to soften its line. Literature that eased tension and distracted from the trying conditions of everyday life now had to be tolerated. To promote a good mood among the people, Goebbels noted in his diary in February 1942, is not just "important but decisive for the war effort."[56]

The trouble was that, as a result of earlier attacks on this kind of fiction and the shortage of paper, there now were not nearly enough such books available for the population at home and the soldier at the front. Germany faced a dearth of good entertaining fiction (*Unterhaltungsromane*), Wilhelm Haegert, the head of Department VIII (Schrifttum) in the Ministry of Propaganda, told a conference of the book trade in April 1940.[57] As of August 26, 1941, fifteen series of cheap fiction were no longer published.[58] The *Meldungen aus dem Reich* for July 6, 1942, told of a surplus of propaganda and war literature and a shortage of light fiction.[59] When the lending libraries of Hamburg in 1943 had succeeded in acquiring eighty new Courths-Mahler books, these titles were picked clean in next to no time.[60] Similar occurrences were reported from the public libraries. The magazine *Europäische Literatur* in 1943 published an appeal to authors to help: "Writers, do write light novels!"[61]

Like Rosenberg, Martin Bormann, ever the advocate of radical measures, also appears to have been unhappy with this downgrading of political indoctrination. Originally Hess's chief of staff, but after Hess's flight to England in 1941 head of the Party Chancellery, Bormann soon became Hitler's closest and indispensable confidant and one of the most powerful figures in both party and state. Working diligently and ruthlessly, he gradually increased his grip on all

aspects of domestic policy, and eventually he sought involvement also in the
censorship of literature. For September 30, 1944, Bormann convened a conference for several "*völkische* authors," all of whom harshly criticized the Ministry
of Propaganda for rejecting works of fiction with links to the National Socialist
ideology. A report on the meeting compiled by an official of the Amt Rosenberg
noted that the "massive attacks" on Goebbels' ministry "were of a kind that, if
taking place in a different forum, would have led straight to a concentration
camp."[62]

Shortly after this conference, the Party Chancellery asked the PPK to ban a
named book. Bouhler's office responded to this request with a protest against
the interference of the Party Chancellery in matters of book control. Today
more than ever, the PPK declared, it was imperative to avoid any duplication of
work in the Party. The PPK was the only agency in the Party empowered to deal
with questions of literature.[63] Coming at a time when the shortage of paper had
practically ended the publication of new books for the general population and
when most bookstores had been shut down, both the criticism of Goebbels'
allegedly soft line on popular fiction as well as the PPK's complaint about the
role of the Party Chancellery in matters of censorship undoubtedly represented
a tempest in a teacup without any practical consequences.

Pre-publication censorship had already taken place in peacetime. An
expansion of the resort to prior restraint began after 1939 as a result of the
increased vigilance thought to be necessary in time of war. The record of the
Amt Rosenberg includes the undated draft of a circular Rosenberg had planned
to send to all publishers. The would-be czar of the book trade assured the publishers that the National Socialist state had no intention to impose censorship.
However, the draft continued, for the duration of the war publishers might
appreciate receiving "substantive and political advice" with regard to planned
new publications that would be provided by a Beratungsstelle (Advisory Office)
at the Deutsche Bücherei in Leipzig, the central archive of German-language
publications.[64] Nothing came of this idea, which would have established a system of censorship for the entire production of books. Instead, controls were
imposed piecemeal on an ever-expanding array of book topics.

On February 1, 1940, the confidential gazette of the Fachschaft Verlag, the
department dealing with publishers in the RSK, published an order of Goebbels
that required publishers to submit publications "dealing with political questions, especially those involving foreign policy, as well as with economic and
military issues to the appropriate authorities for scrutiny in a timely manner."
The book market, Goebbels explained, now faced important new tasks. "The
closer the cooperation with the relevant agencies, the less likely is it that a new
publication jeopardizes the defense of the Reich and therefore faces the risk
of being forbidden." Implementing regulations effective April 1 informed publishers that they must send to Department VIII of the Ministry of Propaganda

detailed information about planned publications in the fields enumerated in the order of February 1, including why they thought a particular book should be published in time of war. If necessary, the ministry would consult appropriate agencies. Publishers who did not receive a notification within fourteen days could assume that the planned publication had passed muster.[65]

As could have been predicted, the fourteen-day time allowed for evaluating book plans proved impossible to keep, and on June 16 it was announced that, while the ministry would try to make decisions promptly, the original deadline was no longer operative. Another clarification drew attention to the fact that encyclopedic publications and fiction dealing with the issues listed in the order of February 1 were also *anmeldepflichtig* (requiring clearance).[66] After the *Börsenblatt* had run ads for two banned books and for several objectionable confessional books, Goebbels on June 25, 1941, required the paper in the future to submit the text of all ads to his ministry for clearance. Wilhelm Baur, the head of the Börsenverein, protested this measure as a personal slap, but it remained in force.[67] Soon additional topics came under *Vorlagepflicht* (requiring submission): books dealing with the work of the police on October 10, 1940, plans for the publication of Russian and anti-Bolshevik writings on July 11, 1941, all proposed calendars, yearbooks, guidebooks, almanacs, as well as all anthologies on September 12, and the publication of all maps on November 4. This last requirement had become necessary, it was said, by the failure of publishers promptly to keep abreast of the territorial changes under way in Europe.[68]

Seeking to stigmatize confessional publishers, the RSK on March 31, 1939, required religious publishing houses to indicate publicly their confessional purpose and whether they were ready to abandon their links to the churches.[69] On November 28, Goebbels noted in his diary that the churches were increasingly insolent, and that he would impose censorship upon the publication of the bishops' pastoral letters. About a month later he recorded that he had talked to Heydrich and that the latter had advised against this step. "He believes that he can reach the same goal in a painless manner. I am willing to go along."[70] The "painless manner" to silence unwelcome publications probably was the refusal to allocate paper, and after early 1940 the rationing of paper indeed became an ever more important means of censorship.

Germany had a chronic shortage of paper, for it produced only about one third of its needs. Campaigns against waste and the pulping of large quantities of confiscated banned books had helped, but did not solve the problem. In July 1937 the RSK gave orders that works of fiction henceforth be printed only on inferior paper containing wood, and about a year later it admonished the book trade to practice "extreme frugality."[71] The onset of war led to more stringent measures. On October 10, 1939, an office in the Ministry of Propaganda set up in 1935 to deal with the export of books, the Wirtschaftstelle des deutschen

Buchhandels, was now put in charge of the allocation of paper. At first publishers simply had to report the amount of paper they had used for a particular publication, but in April 1940 this order was changed into a requirement that publishers apply for approval of the necessary paper and bindery material for all books that were *anmeldepflichtig* under the order of February 1. These applications were handled by the Wirtschaftstelle working in close cooperation with Department VIII.[72]

After the invasion of the Soviet Union in June 1941 and the introduction of rationing for all raw materials, this procedure was extended to all publications, no matter what the subject matter. A commission, headed by Paul Hövel of the Ministry of Propaganda and made up of representatives of the Ministries of Education and Economy, as well as of the High Command of the Armed Forces (OKW); Himmler's Reichssicherheitshauptamt; the Party Chancellery; the Amt Rosenberg; and Bouhler's PPK now decided upon the allocation of paper for each individual book, whether a new title or a reprint. A positive decision, as the Ministry of Propaganda put it, depended on whether the planned publication was *kriegswichtig* (important for the war effort) and for "the struggle for survival of the German people."[73] *Vorzensur,* that is prior restraint, now had become the norm for the entire production of books.

That decisions on the allocation of paper would be guided by political considerations was taken for granted by everyone. Rudolf Erckmann, the deputy head of Department VIII in the Ministry of Propaganda and thus a key figure in the decision-making process, openly acknowledged the supreme importance of ideological criteria. It is the basic principle of National Socialist cultural policy, he told a gathering of publishers in 1941, that "politics have priority over aesthetics."[74] Books considered important for the Party could receive a "certificate of priority." For example, the PPK supported the allocation of paper for a menstruation-calendar because the work was considered important for "maintaining the propagation of the nation."[75] Publishers seen to be especially loyal also could be rewarded with such a certificate. Hence preferred treatment was granted in 1939 to a book by the publisher G. Grotesche in Berlin on the grounds that Grotesche since 1896 had not published a single novel by a Jewish author, and, forgoing translations, had brought out German authors exclusively.[76] In a further attempt to favor German authors and save paper, the Ministry of Propaganda in April 1940 banned the publication of all translated fiction.[77]

The "present extraordinarily difficult situation in the supply of paper"[78] now became the standard argument employed to refuse the allocation of paper for publications deemed undesirable. For example, the would-be author Jakob Michels had sought since 1937 to publish a book with the title Ehre, Treue, Friede (Honor, Faith, Peace) that he described as dedicated to the promotion of "harmony between state and church." The RSK had repeatedly rejected the book as "unsatisfactory" and had refused Michels's application for membership in the RSK, the precondition for being a writer and being able to publish. On July 18, 1941, in response to another petition, Michels was sent a form letter of rejection that invoked the shortage of paper and suggested the submission of another application after the end of the war.[79]

The use of the rationing of paper for purposes of censorship was convenient because it made possible what Nazi bureaucrats called "informal confiscation." For example, in September 1942 the Gestapo informed the RSK that it had seized 400 copies of a publication that the geologist Wilhelm Jäger had printed and sent to various technical universities, scientific institutes, as well as to Goebbels and Rust. The content of the work was not specified. The RSK imposed a fine of 100 RM, a sizable sum at that time. Jaeger avoided a more severe penalty since the book apparently had been printed before the restrictions on the consumption of paper had gone into effect. The RSK also accepted the suggestion of the Gestapo that it was not necessary to list the book in the Index because, without an allocation of paper, Jaeger "would not be able to continue his undesirable conduct."[80]

Meanwhile, the shortage of paper and books had turned severe. In September 1941 Head of Department VIII Haegert advised bookstores to sell books "not to those who wanted them but to those who needed them." Persons who had private book collections should resort to these for their reading, and books in stores should be reserved for "our soldiers and the men and women [working in industry] who badly needed alleviation of tension and relaxation."[81] On February 26, 1942, Goebbels noted in his diary that the situation of the book market had become "catastrophic." There simply were not enough books of any kind, and people snapped up whatever the bookstores had in stock. "A decent person can hardly buy a book."[82] At the same time Ministry of Propaganda official Paul Hövel complained that "incredible amounts of paper" were being used for political propaganda. This was going on despite the fact that the men who approved paper for this purpose knew "that nobody in Germany picked up these publications, let alone read them."[83]

Another problem was the long time it took to get a book into print, the result of the ever-growing shortage of manpower. In May 1942 Haegert complained to Goebbels that he had two staff members who had to vet 4,000 manuscripts a year. Hence an average of one and a half years passed between the examination of a manuscript, action on the application for paper, and the printing of a book.[84] By early 1943 the scarcity of personnel had become worse, and Haegert was forced to abandon altogether the vetting of manuscripts for fiction. Publishers, he noted, by now should know what it takes to produce a good book for easy reading; they would be held accountable for "inferior or objectionable titles."[85] In October 1943 Haegert introduced a new procedure according to which the application for political clearance and for the allocation for paper could be submitted at the same time.[86]

Not surprisingly, the shortage of paper encouraged corruption. In October 1941 publishers had been warned not to try to influence the just allocation of paper by making use of personal connections and "thus gain an unfair advantage over those who acted responsibly and in accordance with applicable regulations."[87] This admonition had little effect; the files reveal instances of underhanded practices not only on the part of publishers but at the very top of the bureaucracy. The representative of the RSK in Vienna on September 9, 1941, thanked Wilhelm Ihde, the chief executive officer of the RSK in Berlin, for "the comradely manner in which you have pressed the importance of the book of Pg. [Parteigenosse (party comrade)] Dr. Traugott at the Wirtschaftstelle."[88] Acting on instructions of Johst, Ihde in September 1943 was able to obtain an allocation of paper for two books by a friend of Johst.[89] Rosenberg official Hellmuth Langenbucher in July 1943 not only managed to receive paper for a book he had authored, but he urged the Wirtschaftstelle not to allocate paper for a similar book planned by another publisher.[90]

Of course, such favoritism had to remain in certain bounds, and Ihde appears to have gone beyond what was acceptable. On July 26, 1944, Johst was informed that Himmler wanted Ihde dismissed "because he had conducted himself in his official post in a manner inappropriate for a member of the SS."[91] The extent to which Ihde's influence peddling played a role in this decision is not known. There were charges that, at a time when it was almost impossible for a private individual to acquire carpets, Ihde had bought an expensive rug for his office for 672 RM and that he had purchased a parcel of land for the stately sum of 5,517.50 RM, claiming falsely that Johst had given permission for this transaction. Ihde resigned from his position in the RSK effective October 8, 1944; he was expelled from the SS on November 1.[92] During the postwar denazification proceedings it was revealed that Ihde had pressured several writers of a series of detective stories, issued under the patronage of the criminal police, to accept him as a co-author and allow him 20 percent of the royalties. The authors had had to agree to this arrangement, since otherwise they would have been conscripted for military service.[93]

Another center of pre-publication censorship operated in the High Command of the Armed Forces (OKW). In November 1934 the Ministry of Defense asked the RSK to remove from the lending libraries all books dealing with espionage and the Foreign Legion.[94] Since 1919 the military had had their own Deutsche Heeresbücherei (Library of the German Army), and after the outbreak of war in 1939 the OKW established bookstores for soldiers at the front. As the supply of paper shrank, the civilian book trade increasingly was left without paper while the military was able to commission a large number of books, a total of ten million titles during the years 1940 to 1944 and a lifeline for many publishers. The Protestant publishing house Bertelsmann, for example, which had had its problems with the censor in the prewar years, now made large profits with huge editions for the armed forces.[95] The publisher Gustav Kiepenheuer in 1933 had been near bankruptcy because so many of his authors had been banned. During the war, on the other hand, Kiepenheuer had record profits by publishing books for soldiers.[96] All this necessarily involved the armed forces in the selection and evaluation of books. Finally there was Goebbels' order of February 1940 that imposed *Vorlagepflicht* for books dealing with military issues, and this required the armed forces to decide what constituted a "military subject."[97]

The military censorship was run by the author Jürgen Eggebrecht, who previously had served as editor for several publishers. In the selection of books for the Frontbuchhandlungen (bookstores for soldiers at the front) he was assisted by a committee composed of representatives of the OKW, the Ministry of Education, the German Labor Front, the RSK, and the Börsenverein. Despite Rosenberg's protest, his organization was not invited to participate.[98] Eggebrecht had a certain independent streak, though the assertion that the military censorship "was in constant struggle and opposition to the party"[99] is undoubtedly exaggerated. It is true that some books unlikely to pass muster with the censors of the Ministry of Propaganda appeared under the auspices of the military. Thus the novel *Der grosse Tag des Leutnants Passavant* (The Big Day of Lieutenant Passavant) by the anti-Nazi Prussian aristocrat Friedrich Reck-Malleczwen was published in 1940 in a special edition of 100,000 copies. Four years later Reck-Malleczwen was arrested by the Gestapo; he died in 1945 in the concentration camp Dachau. His remarkably insightful diary *Tagebuch eines Verzweifelten* (Diary of a Man in Despair) was published posthumously and has been translated into several languages. The book *Das Vaterunser* (The Lord's Prayer) by the Catholic poet Reinhold Schneider, whose unpublished (or rather unpublishable) sonnets circulated clandestinely, appeared in a military edition in 1942.[100]

On the other hand, some books or categories of books were banned at the request of the OKW. On July 3, 1939, the RSK announced that pursuant to a demand of the OKW, the publication of books on the First World War and the experience of fighting was "undesirable." These books all too often portrayed the individual soldier as a victim of the war rather than as fighter, and therefore were likely to weaken the fighting spirit of the nation.[101] A book with the title *Christ und Soldat* (Christ and Soldier), authored by a retired major, was ordered to be listed because "it could lead readers to draw wrong conclusions with regard to the armed forces."[102] As the PPK's Bouhler complained to Hess, the OKW sought to prevent the publication of any work dealing with the revolution of 1918 because it feared criticism for not having prevented the collapse of the monarchy.[103]

In January 1942 Goebbels too harshly criticized the military censorship on the grounds that as a result of misplaced caution and envy the military censors suppressed anything that could make some generals more popular than others. Thus, for example, they had sought to forbid mentioning the fiftieth birthday of Field Marshal Rommel.[104] Much of this kind of disagreement soon became academic because of the ever-shrinking number of books that could be published. In October 1943 even the paper allocation for the previously highly favored OKW was reduced by 50 percent, supposedly because of several cases of flagrant corruption.[105] Soon the censors could close their shop because there were fewer and fewer books to be censored.

By the time war broke out in 1939, both public and university libraries had been largely cleansed of offending books. In 1940 the public libraries had been asked to remove all fiction that included "confessional elements."[106] That year, the confessional libraries had been sidelined by being limited to religious subjects. In 1940 and 1941, in response to the state of war with certain foreign nations, authors who belonged to these nationalities were banned. For the lending libraries, on the other hand, regimentation by way of new regulations continued unabated throughout the war years. Just as in the years 1933 to 1939, the lending libraries were singled out for special scrutiny and control. Paradoxically, this additional attention was the result of the increased importance of the lending libraries in time of war. They carried the kind of light fiction that diverted and entertained, and that had now become indispensable for both the war-stressed population at home and soldiers at the front. Moreover, at a time of a growing shortage of books, the lending of books was by far the most economical way of satisfying demand.

Already back in 1933 and 1934, Department VIII of the Ministry of Propaganda had begun to circulate *Grundlisten* (Basic Lists) for the lending libraries, one way of supplementing the cleansing of the libraries by way of "suggested acquisitions." More elaborate lists began to be issued in 1940. The first of the series *Das Buch ein Schwert des Geistes: Erste Grundliste für den deutschen Leihbuchhandel* (The Book a Sword of the Spirit: First Basic List for the German Lending Libraries), again compiled by the Department Schrifttum in the Ministry of Propaganda, appeared in 1940 and was followed by sequels in 1941, 1942, and 1943. The lending library, it was stated, had become *kriegswichtig* (important for the war effort). The lists were to direct the libraries "to the best German book of National Socialist significance."[107] More restrictive measures followed. The journal *Grossdeutsches Leihbüchereiblatt* in early 1940 began to publicize books that could no longer be lent.[108] In June, the lending libraries for the second time were asked to submit lists of their inventory so that it could be checked for "banned and undesirable literature."[109] A month later the RSK announced that lending libraries suspected of not being in compliance would be examined by local RSK officials. Those found to have violated the rules would be asked to attend a "lesson." Only if this did not help would penalties be imposed.[110] On September 19, the RSK let it be known that "the lending libraries must work harder at purging undesirable stock."[111]

This admonition apparently did not have the desired effect. On March 11, 1941, the lending libraries were told that henceforth violations of applicable orders would be regarded as "willful" and that in case of repeat transgressions "the profession will know how to protect itself with suitable measures."[112] What this meant became apparent in the case of a lending library in Leipzig, which on account of "continuing noncompliance with the lists of damaging and undesirable literature" had been expelled from the RSK, an action tantamount to a closing the library. Another lending library was fined 400 RM, a ruinous sum for most small enterprises.[113] A tightening of supervision followed. In April 1942 lending libraries were ordered to submit a list of their inventory twice a year so that it could be vetted for banned books. After receiving the results of this examination, lending libraries "have to expect spot checks." The libraries had to keep a catalog of all books and record the the nationality of every author.[114] Soon the Gestapo carried out these checks and reported continuing violations. In one district, thirty-eight of forty searched lending libraries still had forbidden books.[115] In practically all these cases, the owners claimed ignorance of the edicts banning or restricting these books.[116]

In contrast to books on List 1 banned for adults, books on List 2, unsuitable for young people, did not have to be destroyed. Lending libraries were merely forbidden to lend them to youth. The SD was reminded of this rule after the last recorded search of a lending library by the Gestapo that took place on April 13 and 14, 1944, in Chemnitz.[117] With the deterioration of Germany's military situation, the increasingly destructive effect of the Allied bombing campaign, and as a result of the total mobilization for war that began in July 1944, the number of lending libraries left to be raided declined sharply. In 1938 there had been about 2,000 lending libraries. By October 1944 that number had been reduced to 944, and these libraries had few books left. The collapse of normal life in the German cities also meant the end of commercial libraries.

For many different reasons, the reading of forbidden books could never be prevented completely. On May 19, 1942, the RSK noted that "because of the removal of numerous Jews from the big cities of the Reich, a large number of Marxist and Jewish books as well as many other harmful and undesirable books have come on the market, and for the most part are now held by antiquarian book dealers who acquired them in auctions." The RSK therefore gave the order that the owners of used bookstores "immediately sequester these books and send a list . . . to the Deutsche Bücherei in Leipzig." The Deutsche Bücherei was entitled to take possession of these works without compensation. Books not thereby confiscated were "to be pulped immediately"; book dealers who failed to comply with this order could expect "severe punishment."[118] The enforcement of this order apparently was less than successful and it therefore was reissued on July 5, 1944. Violators had to expect expulsion from the RSK.[119]

The edict ordering the confiscation or pulping of ideologically objectionable books was issued at a time when the dearth of any kind of reading material had become critical. The shortage of paper and the scarcity of workers available to produce and print books had reached alarming dimensions. Fewer books were being written because so many authors had been conscripted. Due to the tightening of censorship, others had been expelled from the RSK and thus put under *Berufsverbot* (forbidden to practice their profession). But worse was to come. At the end of 1942, under pressure to release workers for military service, Goebbels began to consider the closing of publishers. In 1940 there had been 3,122 publishers,[120] though that number soon began to decline as a result of the growing scarcity of paper and personnel. The first list of publishers to be closed included 1,200 publishing houses, which would have reduced the total number of publishers to about 500. However, since the large publishers producing *kriegswichtige* books for the armed forces were going to be exempt, this plan was shelved. Only relatively small family-operated houses would have been affected, and the number of workers freed for conscription would have been insignificant.[121] Some of the publishers on the list informed the RSK that they had not published for three years because they had not been allocated any paper.[122] Large-scale closings of publishers began only after Goebbels in July 1944 had been appointed by Hitler to be his Plenipotentiary for the Total War Effort.

Goebbels for some time had sought full control over the country's mobilization for total war. He achieved his ambition after the failed assassination of Hitler on July 20, 1944. Hitler now rewarded him for his presence of mind during the hours of uncertainty in Berlin, where the plotters had come close to taking over the government. As Plenipotentiary for the Total War Effort, Goebbels was thereafter empowered to give orders to all government authorities in the Reich. As he told a conference in the Reich Chancellery on July 31, it was not enough to tease out a few persons here and there. There was now need for thorough structural change that would involve closing down entire fields of activity and institutions.[123]

In line with this blueprint, as of August 1, Goebbels forbade the publication of all works of fiction. In an edict entitled "Total Mobilization of the Book Trade" issued on August 31, the owners and employees of all enterprises of the RSK—publishers, printers, and bookstores—were ordered to report for work in the armament industry. No more books could be sent through the mail, and, to make up for the losses incurred by the "terror bombing," all bookstores were to sell their fiction as well as books on politics and popular science to the public and lending libraries.[124] The official gazette of the RKK referred to these measures as in effect constituting the "temporary stillstand of all cultural activities for our people."[125] As of November 13, 1944, the "total mobilization of the book trade" had resulted in the closing of 1,269 publishers, 4,178 bookstores, and 1,015 lending libraries,[126] a cultural bloodletting of major proportions.

12

The Battle for Turf

Never in the history of Germany, it has been said, was the state organized more chaotically than during the Third Reich.[1] A country claiming to be a pillar of strength and unity in fact operated as a system of feuding fiefdoms. The overlap of offices and agencies was to considerable extent deliberate, a creation of Hitler, who believed that the person coming out on top would be the best and most efficient. The system also would prevent any one official from becoming too powerful and thus threaten his supreme leadership.

Competition between party and state was another source of conflict. In the face of the unbridled violence that characterized the early days of the Nazi regime, in July 1933 Hitler forbade unauthorized measures against individuals and laid down that party agencies were not to arrogate to themselves state functions.[2] On the other hand, the Law for Safeguarding the Unity of Party and State, enacted on December 1, 1933, declared the party to be a "public entity" whose measures the state was expected to enforce. According to party stalwarts like Rosenberg and Bouhler, this meant that the "party commands the state," but powerful Nazi functionaries holding high state positions like Propaganda Minister Goebbels never accepted this maxim. Occupying an office in both party and state was known as *Personalunion,* and at times this practice added to the disarray. Hitler's deputy Hess noted the continuing friction between party and state in a speech to party functionaries at the 1935 party congress,[3] and this confused situation continued until the downfall of the Nazi regime. Indeed, Hitler himself, in line with his reliance on bonds of personal loyalty rather than functional position, did his best to sustain the dualism of party and state that existed at everly level.[4]

In few other areas of government was the resulting disarray more extensive than in regard to the censorship of books. Goebbels, the Minister of Popular Enlightenment and Propaganda, was "responsible for all matters that involve the impact of intellectual life on the nation," and for these tasks he had "exclusive jurisdiction."[5] Rosenberg was tasked with monitoring the intellectual and ideological education of the Nazi party and Bouhler was in charge of protecting National Socialist literature.[6] There also was the power of the Gestapo to confiscate any publication that threatened public order and security, while the SD had the mandate to gather intelligence about the ideological enemies of the Nazi movement and to defend the state against its opponents. Not surprisingly, these overlapping jurisdictions resulted in constant and often heated battles for the control of book censorship.

All the rival contenders bewailed the resultant confusion, and agreed that there was need for one central authority to carry out the control of books. A memo dated September 7, 1939, prepared by the PPK, called the situation in regard to the censorship of books "completely unacceptable." The chronic tensions over the jurisdiction of other party agencies made it impossible for the PPK to carry out its assigned functions.[7] At the same time each adversary was convinced that only he (there were no women in these positions), and he alone, was the appropriate person to constitute this unified authority, and so the disorder continued unabated. "Everyone does as he pleases," an exasperated Goebbels wrote in his diary on March 2, 1943, "because nowhere has a strong authority been established."[8] Goebbels and Rosenberg did not often agree, but in 1943 they concurred that the Nazi state had reached a state of disorganization. The Führer managed to take care only of the most urgent matters, Rosenberg noted in his diary on July 20. "We have no government."[9]

Several particularly flagrant conflicts, which involved the usual mixture of squabbling over rival and overlapping jurisdictions and clashes of personality, demonstrate once again that the Nazi state, despite its claim to be governed with an iron hand from the top, in fact operated as a system of rival officeholders, totalitarian in its aspirations but polycratic in practice.

Both Rosenberg and Bouhler received their mandate from Hitler in early 1934. The conflict between these two ambitious individuals began the same year, and, with some short interludes of an uneasy truce, continued until 1944, practically until the end of the Nazi regime. On April 29 and 30, 1934 the *Völkischer Beobachter* informed its readers that Rosenberg and Bouhler had agreed on a demarcation of their respective jurisdictions, but it soon became clear that this agreement had merely papered over existing differences. By September Rosenberg found it necessary to file a protest against Bouhler's edict of September 21 that had outlined the tasks of the PPK. Some of the provisions of this edict, Rosenberg wrote Bouhler, "constitute an attack upon the Reichsstelle zur Förderung des deutschen Schrifttums and therefore against my office as Plenipotentiary of the Führer." He asked Bouhler to acknowledge that "the entire German literature, unless it is specifically characterized as National Socialist, is within the exclusive jurisdiction of my office."[10]

When Bouhler ignored this protest, Rosenberg issued a public announcement that repeated the claim that he and his Reichsstelle had "the task of vetting the *entire* German literature in regard to its ideological, political, cultural, or educational orientation."[11] Probably also from 1935 is an undated draft law composed by Rosenberg that went even further in its reach. The proposal envisaged a Reich Ministry for Ideology and Culture, to be headed by Rosenberg, that was to ensure "the unity of the cultural and ideological posture of the National Socialist state." All new legislation and appointments in these domains were to require Rosenberg's consent. The scheme would have fulfilled Rosenberg's ambition to become not only an important party functionary but also a minister of the state. Needless to say, this presumptuous plan would have clashed not only with Bouhler's PPK but, more important, would have completely undermined Goebbels' Ministry of Propaganda and its affiliated agencies, such as the RSK. It became one of several such proposals that never went anywhere and merely swelled the files of the Rosenberg organization. Rosenberg was a person who wanted much and achieved little.

When the frustrated would-be minister failed to make headway in putting Bouhler in his place, Rosenberg took his case to Hess, Hitler's deputy. Hess, assisted by his chief of staff, Bormann, often shouldered the task of restraining the battles of rival officeholders in the Nazi state.[12] In a letter to Bormann, Rosenberg noted that he had never been informed about the establishment of the PPK. Moreover, it had by now become evident that Bouhler was intent "to evaluate the entire [German] literature" and thus claim a competence that he had never been granted. Rosenberg considered this situation to be "completely unacceptable."[13] The only solution, he wrote Hess a month later, was to "move the PPK into the office of the Führer's Plenipotentiary for Monitoring the Entire Intellectual and Ideological Education of the NSDAP,"[14] or, to put it more plainly, to put the PPK under Rosenberg's control.

Not surprisingly, Hess ignored this audacious proposal, and Rosenberg was left complaining about the way Bouler was thwarting the work of his organization. In a letter of August 13, 1937, to Hess, he grumbled that most recently the PPK was claiming even the ideological control of literature. This meant, he added, that now "not a single point of the original mandate I have received from the Führer is left intact."[15] Two days later Hess made it known that the PPK would continue its work, including the publication of the reference work *Nationalsozialistische Bibliographie*. Rosenberg was given the right to see proofs of the bibliography, to raise objections, and to propose the inclusion of books.[16] But this edict failed to end the dispute. The PPK, it appears, frequently ignored the disapproval by Rosenberg's office of items in the *NS-Bibliography*.[17] In a speech given in October 1937 PPK deputy chairman Hederich affirmed the leading role of the PPK in developing a National Socialist policy for literature. Rosenberg now told Bouhler that this claim constituted another violation of existing assignments, and that he had decided to lodge his complaint directly with the Führer.[18]

The record does not indicate whether Rosenberg was able to see Hitler in order to seek redress. We do know that on November 11, 1937, Hess informed

Bouhler and Rosenberg that for the time being both were to refrain from any public pronouncements and speeches that involved the control of literature. Their subordinates were to be advised to do likewise.[19] Also preserved is a draft of a decree Rosenberg composed for Hitler in which Rosenberg was to be given a new mandate as "Plenipotentiary of the Reich and the Party for the Defense against Bolshevism and for the Safeguarding of the Unity of the National Socialist Ideology." The proposal was similar to Rosenberg's 1935 scheme that was to have made him Reich Minister for Ideology and Culture. Once again Rosenberg was to become a leading official in both state and party. Again it was provided that all legislation, regulations, and appointments issued by ministries and party authorities that involved the National Socialist ideology required Rosenberg's consent. The draft empowered Rosenberg to order all measures of the party that he considered necessary to assure the unity of the National Socialist ideology.[20]

This high-flying scheme of course fared no better than its predecessor in 1935. Lammers, head of the Reich Chancellery, informed Rosenberg on January 17, 1938, that Hitler had decided to give Rosenberg new powers, but not in the form his plenipotentiary had proposed. This formulation was designed to spare Rosenberg's feelings, for the actual decision did not give him any new meaningful authority. Rosenberg was to be informed of any planned legislation in all matters affecting the National Socialist ideology and the defense against Bolshevism. However Hitler quite explicitly ruled out the requirement that Rosenberg give his consent to such legislation. Rosenberg's draft proposal, Lammers noted, would have meant unending conflicts of jurisdiction.[21]

The year 1938 brought a further deterioration of the relations between the two adversaries. Bouhler now informed Rosenberg that the Plenipotentiary's pronouncements with regard to specific books would be ignored by the PPK.[22] Rosenberg in turn forbade his subordinates to have any direct communications with the PPK.[23] After Bouhler once again had insisted on the primacy of the PPK in matters of literature and had disparaged the work of Rosenberg's office, Rosenberg accused Bouhler of "having deliberately misrepresented the mandate I have received from the Führer." Hitler had entrusted him with "monitoring the *entire* intellectual and ideological education and indoctrination of the NSDAP and its affiliated organizations." Education of course necessarily included literature.[24] Bouhler thereupon took the dispute to Hess. In view of the fact that Hederich was both head of Department VIII in the Ministry of Propaganda as well as deputy chairman of the PPK, he pointed out, the work of controlling literature by both state and party was now concentrated in one office, that is, at the PPK. It was imperative, he concluded, that the exclusive jurisdiction of the PPK for the vetting of all publications be reaffirmed and be made binding for all agencies and organizations.[25]

Three months later Hederich was dismissed by Goebbels, and one of Bouhler's arguments for claiming the exclusive right to control book censorship had become moot. Hederich had not only made derogatory remarks about the *Völkischer Beobachter* and its publisher Max Amann, but he had had the temerity of imposing a ban on two publications of Eher, the party's official publishing house headed by Amann. Bouhler conceded that the departure of Hederich from the Ministry of Propaganda had taken place "under the most unpleasant circumstances,"[26] but otherwise he stood by his man. This prompted Amann to inject himself into the controversy. The work of the PPK, he told Bouhler, by now had developed into something that he, the responsible head of all publishing by the party, must oppose. The PPK, established at his suggestion, originally was to do no more than steer all publications that claimed to be National Socialist in character to the party publishing house. Instead, Hederich, an engineer by training and with no knowledge of literature, had converted the PPK into a censorship office for practically all books published in Germany. The PPK, Amann argued, had become "a hydrocephaly" (*Wasserkopf*) with 125 employees and challenged Rosenberg's standing as Hitler's plenipotentiary for the intellectual and ideological education of the NSDAP. The dissolution of this administrative monster of 125 persons was imperative. The work that had to be done should be taken over by the Rosenberg organization. Amann concluded that in order to defend National Socialist literature he would submit his proposal to Hess.[27]

Rosenberg too continued to press his demands. In a letter to Hess dated May 4, 1939, he insisted that the mandate he had received from the Führer be recognized not only in words but be translated into reality within the party and state. There followed a list of four "ideological areas" where, as Rosenberg claimed, he had been granted exclusive jurisdiction: Schooling and Education, Science and Research, Literature and Art, and New ideological positions, including policy toward the churches.[28]

As if these claims were not extravagant enough, Rosenberg next submitted a draft of a decree he wanted Hess to issue. Once again the politically obtuse Nazi functionary demanded Bouhler's total surrender. At the time the Nazis assumed power in 1933, the draft decree noted, the National Socialist movement had needed protection against those who falsified its ideas and exploited them for commercial purposes. In the six years of its existence the PPK had managed to do away with this *Konjunkturschrifttum* (literature of opportunism). All activities that went beyond the original mandate of the PPK were therefore now to be transferred to Rosenberg, the Plenipotentiary of the Führer for Monitoring the Entire Intellectual and Ideological Education of the NSDAP. In matters of literature, Rosenberg was to have exclusive jurisdiction, and this meant "the monitoring of the ideological posture of German literature." The *NS-Bibliographie*, previously issued by the PPK, was henceforth to appear under the auspices of Rosenberg and be published by the Central Publishing House of the NSDAP (Franz Eher, led by Amann).[29] Not surprisingly Hess never responded to this memo. By then he probably had come to regard Rosenberg as somewhat megalomaniacal. A resigned Rosenberg noted in his diary that he had asked to meet with Hess to discuss the draft decree, but that Hess let him know that "at the moment there is nothing to decide."[30]

Meanwhile, the publication of the book *Der Führer* by the Nazi poet Eberhard Wolfgang Moeller had led to another row between Rosenberg and Bouhler. Moeller was a leader of the Hitler Youth; in 1934 he had become an official in the Ministry of Propaganda dealing with theater. Goebbels greatly admired Moeller's work, and in 1935 he had bestowed on him the National Prize for Literature. In December 1938, undeterred by Moeller's prestige, Rosenberg lodged a complaint with Hitler's staff in which he criticized Moeller's treatment of the personality of the Führer as "unacceptable."[31] The complaint was forwarded to Bouhler, and the latter informed Rosenberg that in the future Hitler's adjutant did not want to receive such interventions. Moeller's book had not been evaluated by the PPK, but the author had now agreed to another editing of the manuscript. Rosenberg's criticism of the book, Bouhler noted, revealed "a prejudice against Moeller that did not do justice to the poet."[32]

Bouhler also complained to Hess that the publisher (Amann's Eher) had failed to submit the book to the PPK, even though, according to an ordinance of the Führer, the PPK was responsible for all publications dealing with the history of the movement. Bouhler asked that his office, and not Rosenberg, be entrusted with vetting Moeller's book.[33] The reply to this letter came from Hess's chief of staff Bormann. Rosenberg, Bormann wrote, had expressed his reservations about the Moeller book to the Führer in person. Hess shared Rosenberg's criticism and was convinced that the Führer, had he known of the book, would have banned it forthwith. The further editing of the book had been assigned to Rosenberg because the latter had already dealt with this matter at some length and because Amann refused to tender his books to the PPK for evaluation. Bormann conceded that Bouhler should have been given the opportunity to vet the book before it was printed. In view of the fact that by now one half million copies of the flawed book had been sold, a ban of the book was out of the question. The publisher had been told to stop the circulation of the work. "If the Führer allows a revised version, the editing will take place with the concurrence of the head of the PPK."[34]

The record from here on is incomplete. It appears that Bouhler was supposed to appear before Hitler and lay out options, including how to clear up the clashing jurisdictions of the PPK and the Rosenberg organization. However, meanwhile war had broken out, and, as Bormann informed both of the contending parties on November 1, 1939, Hess did not want to bother the Führer at this time with "such issues." Bormann added that in time of war Hess considered it "undesirable to discuss or carry out changes in matters of public policy for literature."[35] Rosenberg had meanwhile been able to see Hitler. While Hitler acknowledged that he did not understand Rosenberg's philosophical writings, he felt indebted to Rosenberg, one of his earliest followers. According to Rosenberg's diary, Hitler agreed with him that the defense of the

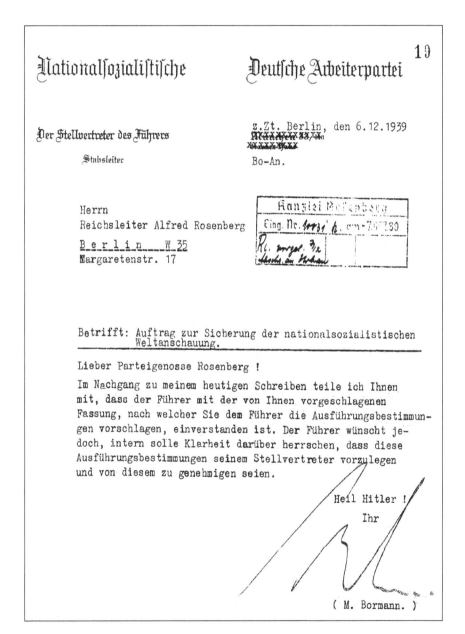

Bormann informs Rosenberg that Hitler wants Hess to confirm the regulations Rosenberg has proposed. *Courtesy Bundesarchiv Berlin-Lichterfelde*

National Socialist ideology had to be concentrated in one hand and he allowed Rosenberg to work up an appropriate decree.[36] Thus encouraged, Rosenberg on November 25 sent Hess a draft that reiterated all his long-standing claims: The unity of the National Socialist ideology and the defense of the German way of life required "that *one* person be entrusted with these tasks." Hence Hitler had appointed Rosenberg as his "Plenipotentiary for the Safeguarding of the National Socialist Ideology." Rosenberg had the right to issue the necessary orders "to party and state (including the armed forces)," and he had to be informed of all laws and ordinances that involved "intellectual and ideological instruction, science, literature, and general cultural appreciation.[37]

When Lammers received a copy of this draft, he noted that it went considerably beyond Rosenberg's 1938 proposal, which "the Führer had considered questionable."[38] Hitler himself apparently also had second thoughts about the new draft. Bormann explained to Lammers that Hitler considered Rosenberg's assignment to be strictly personal. It was not meant to give any new powers to the Rosenberg organization, and Hitler did not want any "change in existing authorities."[39] Other officeholders who had been consulted weighed in with various comments, and Rosenberg too made several alterations in the draft. Bouhler, the person most affected by the new scheme, sent his reaction directly to Hitler. The draft decree, he noted, left open two interpretations. On one hand, it could mean a continuation of the present machinery of control, in which case a clear demarcation of jurisdictions was necessary to prevent "a gradual shifting of competences to the organizational apparatus of Pg. Rosenberg." On the other hand, if the intent was indeed to move the entire control of literature to Rosenberg, "my own position as head of the PPK will become obsolete and I ask you, my Führer, to relieve me honorably from the responsibility for public policy toward literature."[40]

By the end of 1939 Hitler had had enough of a dispute that had been dragging on for several years, and he empowered Lammers to take charge of the matter. There ensued more acrimony when Rosenberg and Bouhler accused each other of falsifying documents.[41] A high-level meeting in Lammers' office on February 9, 1940, took up a revised draft for Rosenberg's appointment, but it failed to produce a decision. The listing of a book in Bouhler's *NS-Bibliographie* provided another opportunity for Rosenberg to vent his anger. The work in question, he wrote Bouhler in April 1940, had nothing to do with National Socialism. It was not part of Bouhler's mandate to evaluate a work that involved historical, scholarly, and ideological issues, a task clearly falling into Rosenberg's portfolio. He therefore asked Bouhler to desist from actions that encroached on the delegation of authority he had received from the Führer.[42]

And so the tug of war continued. Hitler was occupied with more important issues, and, as Bormann explained to Rosenberg, "the Führer as a matter of principle signs drafts only if the issue has been discussed by all the concerned parties and if everyone has given his consent to the draft."[43] Lammers, for his part, though authorized to handle the matter, seemed disinclined to act on his own with regard to these two important movement figures. Both Bouhler and Rosenberg were Reichsleiter, the highest rank in the Nazi party, and therefore directly responsible to Hitler. Bouhler not only was in charge of the PPK but also was head of the Führer's Chancellery. On May 10, 1941, Hess flew to England, and Bormann took over the position of Head of the Party Chancellery, the new name of what had been the Office of the Deputy of the Führer. In a decree of May 29, Hitler bestowed upon Bormann the title of Minister, and on April 2, 1942, Bormann was authorized to participate in the drafting of laws and decrees.[44] Within a short time Bormann had become one of the most powerful figures in the Nazi state, increasingly involving himself in domestic policy issues. When Rosenberg once again urged a clarification of the clashing domains, Bormann told him that the Führer "has reserved for himself a decision" regarding the issue.[45]

On June 22, 1941, Germany invaded the Soviet Union, and on November 17 Rosenberg was appointed Reich Minister for the Occupied Eastern Territories. He now had attained his ambition to become a minister, but this victory proved to be hollow. Actual power in the East was increasingly exercised by Himmler and his SS commanders in the field.[46] From 1940 on Rosenberg also served as head of the Einsatzstab Reichsleiter Rosenberg (Task Force Reichsleiter Rosenberg), an organization that became infamous for its theft of books and valuable works of art from Jews and other collectors all over German-occupied Europe. All this took up lots of Rosenberg's time and weakened his ability to keep abreast of the matter of book control.

As Germany's manpower situation worsened, Bormann ordered all party offices to reexamine their modes of operation in order to free more men for military service. In January 1943 this edict led to an agreement between Rosenberg and Bouhler to establish a NSDAP Office for Literature under the direction of Bouhler but operating in Rosenberg's office and with the participation of Rosenberg officials.[47] However, the implementation of this accord quickly ran into problems, and on March 8 Bouhler wrote Rosenberg that "I am unwilling to give up my decision-making power with regard to the publication or banning of publications. As until now, I reserve this power to myself."[48] At this point Hitler intervened, and in June 1943 he gave orders that the new Schrifttumsamt der NSDAP be put under Bouhler while Rosenberg was to concentrate on his important mandate to govern the eastern territories.[49] Another attempt made in September 1944 to bring about a reconciliation predictably failed.[50] As late as November 1944 Bouhler continued his work as censor of National Socialist publications when he examined a short work by Robert Ley on the Jewish question.[51] In the competition with Rosenberg, Bouhler had successfully defended his claim to have the last word in matters of books dealing with National Socialist ideology.

Even before 1933, many instructional materials used in the schools were strongly nationalistic. Hence the introduction of new schoolbooks did not seem to be a very urgent matter. Minister of Education Rust apparently shared this view, for in the first five years of the Nazi regime nothing much was done about introducing new books. In 1934 Rust established an Office for the Publication of Readers for Primary Schools (Geschäftstelle für die Herausgabe von Volkschullesebüchern), yet it was not until 1939 that the new readers had come into general use. The creation of other schoolbooks lagged. In April 1937 an article in *Das Schwarze Korps,* the organ of the SS, castigated the use of a book at a gymnasium (high school) in Remscheid because it maligned the Germanic tribes. Rust, on the defensive, wrote the Gestapa that teachers could be relied upon to correct any "false description of our ancestors." Unfortunately, new books were not yet available.[52] In July 1937, a working group made up in equal parts by officials of the Ministry of Education and the PPK had been formed to examine the state of educational literature. The head of this group was the PPK's Hederich, and he used this assignment to increase the PPK's role in the evaluation of schoolbooks.

According to Hess's order of August 15, 1937, and as Hess reminded Bouhler on July 6, 1938, Rosenberg had been granted the right to examine schoolbooks for their ideological soundness.[53] Bouhler resented this intrusion into what he regarded as his domain. In order to put his rival on the defensive he argued that publishers of schoolbooks, who had to submit their books to the Ministry of Education and the PPK, should not be asked to correct their books a third time after an examination by the Rosenberg organization. The number of books he allowed to be sent to Rosenberg therefore remained small. Rosenberg's chief of staff, Gotthard Urban, protested this situation on May 12, 1938, and announced that Rosenberg at the next opportunity would raise the issue with the Führer.[54]

In Rosenberg's office Hans Hagemeyer noted about a year later that after six years of National Socialist rule there still existed no "schoolbooks that conformed to National Socialist principles." The PPK had argued that schoolbooks were deficient because not enough personnel had been available to create a better product. In view of the fact that the Rosenberg organization had been prevented from having its input, Hagemeyer stated, this excuse constituted "a monstrous impertinence." The PPK and the Ministry of Education were out to exclude Rosenberg's office from the evaluation of schoolbooks, an action that amounted to sabotage of the mandate Rosenberg had received from the Führer.[55] In turn, Rosenberg pleaded with Hess once again to subordinate the PPK to his organization.[56]

The politically shrewd Bouhler used the unsatisfactory condition of the school books to outmaneuver both Rosenberg and Rust and add another exclusive competence to his portfolio. Hitler trusted Bouhler and used him for special assignments. Thus, in October 1939, Bouhler, together with Hitler's personal physician Karl Brandt, had been charged with organizing the euthanasia of the physically and mentally impaired, a program with the code name *Aktion T 4*. On October 2, 1940, Lammers informed Bouhler that the Führer had received numerous complaints about the outdated schoolbooks still being used for instruction. They were not in line with the National Socialist ideology and indeed were "damaging." Hence the Führer had appointed Bouhler and the PPK, in cooperation with the National Socialist Teachers Organization (NSLB), to organize "the development of schoolbooks that conformed to National Socialist demands." At the same time, Lammers added, the Führer had relieved the Minister of Education for ten years from responsibility for the selection of schoolbooks.[57]

The Plenipotentiary of the Führer for the Creation of New School Books, as Bouhler called himself, thereupon established a National Office for School and Pedagogical Literature (Reichsstelle für das Schul- und Unterrichtsschrifttum). The Führer, Bouhler explained in a circular, had given him "the sole responsibility for cleansing the school and pedagogical literature," but to assist the work of the new office he asked Rosenberg, Hess, von Schirach, Rust, the NSLB, and Ley to send a representative to a national advisory committee (Reichsausschuss).[58] Bouhler's appointment apparently took Rosenberg completely by surprise. Suspecting a trick, on December 5 he asked Bouhler to send him a copy of Hitler's order. Hederich, the deputy head of the PPK, thereupon sent Rosenberg a copy of Lammers' letter of October 2. He also mentioned that in order not to weaken Rust's authority with the school administrators, Hitler and Bouhler had decided to treat the removal of the Minister of Education from involvement with schoolbooks as confidential. Bouhler also would keep Rust informed about his actions.[59]

In April 1941 Bouhler let it be known that the planned participation of representatives of various other offices by way of the Reichsausschuss could not be realized due to the "the strain imposed on all leading party comrades by the demands of the civilian and military conduct of the war." He therefore was going to keep them informed and involved by way of an exchange of letters. He reported that Fritz Wächtler, head of the NSLB, on Bouhler's orders had supervised a fact-finding effort in order to determine the magnitude of the job ahead. Unfortunately, this effort could be carried out only in part. For example, there existed some very large libraries for teachers and pupils with up to 40,000 books each and the manpower to sift through these libraries simply did not exist. Still, Wächtler had succeeded in eliminating from the school libraries almost three-quarter million books found to be "unusable, outdated, and ideologically unacceptable." These books represented 21,431 different titles, and the Reichsstelle was now engaged in making the final determination of the suitability of each seized book. Many of the offending titles were authored by

Jews such as Heine, Theodor Herzl, and Stefan Zweig; others were by Marxists, anarchists, Freemasons, and pacifists. It was expected that the total number of confiscated books would reach one and one half million and that it would not be easy to acquire substitutes. Bouhler concluded his report with the request to treat these issues confidentially. The time for going public had not yet come.[60]

The Ministry of Education periodically issued lists of books suitable for school libraries,[61] but the situation with regard to instructional books was so disorderly that the government did not even know what books were actually used by teachers in the classroom. Hence in August 1941, Bouhler asked all publishers of schoolbooks to send to his Reichsstelle a list of the books they had provided for use in the classrooms as well as a roster of handbooks for teachers. Publishers who did not comply with this order could expect that their unreported books would be banned.[62] Bouhler also decided to reduce sharply the variety of schoolbooks. For each subject there was to be only one book to be used throughout the country. Books that failed to pass muster would be confiscated by the Gestapo. Thus, on October 31, 1941, Bouhler informed the Gestapo in Münster that the publisher Velhagen & Klasing had failed to withdraw a series of schoolbooks that the PPK had criticized for some time as both "substantively and politically inadequate." Objections to this series had been voiced as early as April 1936, but Rust at that time had failed to act. With Rust no longer involved with schoolbooks, Bouhler now was able to move ahead resolutely. As instructed, the Gestapo confiscated a total of 113,150 copies of the offending series,[63] undoubtedly a serious economic setback for the prestigious publisher.

The preserved record thereafter is incomplete. Rust is said to have reacted to his removal from the issue of schoolbooks with passive resistance, and in 1942 Bouhler and Rust are supposed to have entered into an agreement according to which Bouhler was to postpone any further changes in schoolbooks until the end of the war. This concession probably was in large measure the result of the growing shortage of paper. Bouhler also promised to deal with the various school administrators only through the Ministry of Education.[64] This agreement apparently did not work out as planned. In early 1944 Bouhler accused Rust of creating delays in the production of schoolbooks by insisting that his ministry handle the technical aspects of book production such as the allocation of paper. Bouhler expressed the hope that their cooperation would continue, but he insisted that he had to preserve his freedom of action.[65]

Bouhler's "freedom of action" meanwhile had become more and more limited as a result of the steadily worsening situation in the availability of both paper and manpower to produce books. In May 1944 Bouhler's Reichsstelle had become linked, or, probably more accurately put, subordinated, to Albert Speer's Ministry of Armaments and War Production, the authority that by then had emerged as the principal planner of Germany's war economy.[66] As late as

January 12, 1945, a meeting was convened in Bouhler's Reichsstelle that discussed the supply of maps and atlases for schools,[67] but Bouhler's activities at
that point had become an exercise in futility. The Third Reich had reached its
bloodstained end. On May 19 Bouhler committed suicide.

Within the Third Reich, books on astrology were a particular target for
some of the various censorial bodies. On February 3, 1936, RSK president
Johst established an Advisory Office for Astrological and Related Literature
(Beratungsstelle für das astrologische und verwandte Schrifttum). Publishers
of astrological, graphological, and occult writings were told that, upon request
by this office, they were obligated to submit their publications for approval.[68]
The head of this new office, Karl Friedrich Schulze, explained that astrology had
become a serious subject that could withstand any scientific critique. Physics
and chemistry had provided knowledge of the kind that the "occultists" had
propagated for a long time; hence it was necessary for the new Beratungsstelle
to separate valuable astrological writings from inferior products.[69] This was the
beginning of another censorship operation that would again involve major figures in party and state in a harsh dispute over their respective jurisdictions.

Making a distinction between "serious" and "inferior" astrology at first
seemed to present no problem. In several instances Schulze's office accepted the
negative assessment of various police authorities who asked for a ban of certain
volumes. In the case of several astrological works that based horoscopes on the
movement of the sun, Schulze concurred with the police in Erfurt that this
work was trash "that had nothing to do with serious astrology."[70] In October
1936, when the Gestapo of Munich confiscated a book that linked conception
to the position of the moon, the Beratungsstelle agreed that this work had to be
rejected, and it was put on the official Index.[71] At times Schulze's office required
changes before it would approve a certain work. A series called "Which Man?
Which Woman?" that aimed at providing advice on how to recognize a suitable
marriage partner, was found to jeopardize "the reputation of scientific astrology," and the publisher was admonished to revise the series in the light of existing "valuable cosmo-biological knowledge."[72]

Karl Heinz Hederich, from October 1937 until October 1938 the head of
Department VIII of the Ministry of Propaganda in charge of book bans, was
known as an ardent astrologer, and he protected and supported Schulze's work.
Hederich maintained that the basic teachings of astrology were supported by
science and were closely linked to the National Socialist ideology. By relying on
these insights, he said, it had been possible to predict important events during
the Party's struggle for power. Cosmic rays exerted an influence not only on
a child at the moment of conception but also on the origins and subsequent
fate of political ideas.[73] After Hederich's dismissal by the RMfVP, the Ministry
of Propaganda dissolved the Beratungsstelle in March 1939. Hederich, deputy
chairman of the PPK, thereupon transferred the Beratungsstelle to the PPK.

He took with him the astrologist Dr. Kittler who had worked in that office.[74] The result was a number of new conflicts between the Ministry of Propaganda and Bouhler's PPK.

On March 15, 1939, the Propaganda Ministry banned nine astrological calendars on the grounds that they advocated "unacceptable links" between the Four-Year-Plan and astrology.[75] Both Rosenberg and Walther Darré, the Minister of Agriculture and Reichsbauernführer (Reich Leader of Farmers), objected to the ban. All these calendars previously had received the approval of the PPK's Beratungsstelle. An assessment by Kittler had found that they represented a valuable depiction of "the consequences of cosmic tensions."[76] The publisher of one of these calendars pleaded with the RSK that the ban inflicted serious economic damage and made it impossible to plan for the future. It appeared, he wrote, that everything that had anything to do with astrology from now on would have to disappear.[77] In a letter to the Ministry of Propaganda Hederich suggested that a ban of these calendars was unjustified. His office was determined to prevent any prophecies regarding the political life of the day, leading National Socialist personalities, and the National Socialist ideology. The calendars, he insisted facetiously, included nothing but "harmless astrological speculations."[78]

The hapless Rosenberg used the opportunity to get back at his nemesis Bouhler, and he did so in his usual clumsy manner. These calendars, he wrote Goebbels, made human conduct dependent on uncontrollable constellations of the stars and therefore deprived humans of their freedom of thought and action. He had heard, he added, that his request to ban the astrological calendars had prompted Bouhler to register a defense of these publications. This made it necessary for him to point out that "Bouhler in no way is authorized to take an official position with regard to ideological issues. Any expression of opinion on his part is therefore to be regarded as a private matter without official significance. It is well known that the Führer has appointed me to be his plenipotentiary for the entire intellectual and ideological education." Rosenberg ended his letter with the request that in the future the mandate he had received from Hitler be honored. The views of persons whose competence lies in other areas, he wrote, should not be regarded as official.[79]

Goebbels was resolutely opposed to astrology, but he was not above using the occult in his propaganda. The sixteenth-century French astrologist Michel de Nostre Dame, known as Nostradamus, had included among his predictions the emergence of a powerful and large Germany, and in November 1939 Goebbels gave orders to use this prophecy in leaflets and chain letters in the French language. These copies of Nostradamus' prediction were to be handwritten or typed, to give the appearance of being an illegal leaflet, and distributed in France. In this way, Goebbels believed, the well-known French seer could be used to support the Nazi claim of building a Thousand Year Reich that would dominate in Europe.[80]

In June 1940 the Ministry of Propaganda banned all works by the leading graphologist and advocate of "scientific astrology" Ernst Issberner-Haldane.[81] A year later he was arrested, and he spent the next four years in a concentration camp. The PPK meanwhile continued to issue approvals for astrological works that the Ministry of Propaganda had banned. In November 1940 PPK official Rehm informed Hugo Koch in the Ministry of Propaganda that Hess had authorized him to decide which astrological works were to be forbidden. The Ministry of Propaganda, it appears, was sufficiently impressed by this turn of events that it offered to grant the PPK an official right to participate in book bans. In the past, they told Hederich, the PPK had hardly ever asked for the listing of a book and instead had transmitted its orders for book bans directly to publishers or the Gestapo. Hence a satisfactory cooperation had not developed. Several of Hederich's letters on various differences of opinion in the past had not been conducive to promote mutual understanding. The Ministry of Propaganda now was willing to work out a reordering of procedures that would serve the interests of both organizations.[82]

Bouhler and Hederich must have interpreted this gesture as a sign of weakness, and they pressed their advantage. In March 1941 Bouhler was received by Hitler, who was generally well disposed to the head of the Führer Chancellery. As Bormann informed Goebbels on March 14, the Führer had granted Bouhler's PPK the right to ask the Gestapo directly to confiscate already published books or to prevent the publication of new titles. The Gestapo was obligated to respond to these requests that became effective after the consent of the Ministry of Propaganda. This consent would be assumed as given if the Ministry had not issued a counteracting order within three weeks.[83] But a few days later, on April 2, Lammers sent Goebbels a correction: If Goebbels made an objection within three weeks, the Führer himself would make the final decision.[84]

Hitler's new mandate for Bouhler, it would appear, gave both contenders something to be happy about. Seen in one way, Hitler's order merely made official a practice Bouhler had followed all along. But since the Ministry of Propaganda had never reconciled itself to this infringement of its jurisdiction over book bans, Bouhler had indeed scored a victory. As Bouhler wrote Heydrich in a letter bragging about his success, the new order did not so much limit the jurisdiction of the Ministry of Propaganda as it reaffirmed "the sovereign right of the NSDAP."[85] The party, as Bouhler had long claimed, gave orders to the state. On the other hand, Bouhler's assertion regarding the supremacy of the party to some extent constituted wishful thinking. While Bouhler's requests to the Gestapo to confiscate a book previously had been carried out forthwith, they now were subject to Goebbels' veto and a final decision by Hitler. In some measure, the playing field had been leveled.

Yet Goebbels was not pleased by what had transpired. In a letter to Bouhler he expressed his displeasure at the fact that, instead of seeking to resolve existing disagreements by direct negotiations, Bouhler had chosen to seek out Hitler to gain an advantage.[86] On the same day, April 4, 1941, Goebbels reminded Lammers that Hitler in the past had insisted that issues be brought before him only after both parties had made an effort to resolve the issue in question by themselves. In the case at hand, Bouhler had never even contacted him.[87] There followed a telephone conversation between Goebbels and Lammers and a written statement expressing Goebbels' dissatisfaction with the new arrangement regarding book bans; to entrust two offices with a decision would necessarily lead to disagreements. Goebbels acknowledged that he indeed issued book bans as head of a state office [the Ministry of Propaganda], but he added that he certainly had the necessary qualifications to make these decisions in accordance with the ideological principles of the party. He therefore suggested that in the future Bouhler propose book bans but that he, Goebbels, should make final decisions. After all, he wrote, the PPK was called "Prüfungskommission" rather than "Verbotskommission" (commission for vetting rather than forbidding). In case of disagreements one could convene a meeting between the two top officials. If, as probably would happen only very seldom, no agreement could be reached, both officials should present their case to the Führer. Goebbels concluded that in view of the serious responsibilities facing Hitler at the present time every effort should be made not to bother the Führer repeatedly with the same issue.[88]

As was to be expected, Bouhler sharply disagreed with this proposal. "The right to ban [books]," he wrote Lammers, "since the establishment of the PPK in 1934 is an indispensable function of the head of the PPK and is derived from the sovereign position of the NSDAP to decide what is National Socialist." This right could not be handed over to a state agency. Such a transfer would create a situation in which the state supervised the party. He found it unacceptable for Goebbels to ask the Führer to issue orders that clearly contradicted what the Führer had already decided. Both Gestapo and SD had begun to enforce these rules. As far as astrological works were concerned, Bouhler insisted that the PPK was determined to oppose superstition, but at the same time it was intent to protect writings that "contributed to an understanding of the coherence of cosmos and universe."[89] In his diary Rosenberg called Bouhler "the main defender of the astrological jerk [Schmock] Hederich."[90]

On May 7, 1941, Bormann sent a confidential circular to the Gauleiter dealing with "Superstition, Belief in Miracles, and Astrology as Means of Propaganda against the State." No party member was to participate in these kinds of prophecies that exploited the natural gullibility of simple people. The Gauleiter were advised to strengthen the National Socialist ideology, which was based on scientific knowledge regarding race and the laws of nature.[91] This implicit rebuke of Bouhler and Hederich did not end the dispute with Goebbels, and Hitler, who could have done so, was busy with a more important matter— making final preparations for the invasion of the Soviet Union. On August 1, 1941, Lammers therefore informed both contending parties that "on account of the strain imposed upon the Führer by the war," he (Lammers) at this time could not bother Hitler with the issues they had raised. As soon as conditions allowed it, he would arrange for Bouhler and Goebbels to present their case to Hitler.[92] With the resolution of the conflict postponed, both contenders therefore continued to act as they saw fit. In November 1941 Bouhler asked Bormann to remind all party organizations not to issue publications without clearing these with the PPK.[93]

The uneasiness of the truce between Bouhler and Goebbels was revealed in early July 1944 when a conference in the Ministry of Propaganda took up a planned new edition of the *Meyers Lexikon*, a well-established encyclopedia dating back to 1840. The publisher had asked to be relieved of the obligation to submit the text to the PPK. He was prepared to work with other authorities to obtain clearance for all articles that were *zensurpflichtig* (subject to censorship). The representative of the SD voiced his strong agreement with this proposal. It was imperative to make sure that the new edition not "end up enmeshed in an endless paper and competence dispute of the various relevant authorities." The personal deputy of Hederich was the only one to disagree. The PPK, he insisted, could not give up its rights of long standing. Hederich personally was prepared to take on the supervision of the editing that had to take place. Wilhelm Haegert, the head of Department VIII in the Ministry of Propaganda and the convener of the conference, noted in his report on the meeting that he would get in touch with Hederich and then render his decision. He added that to work with Hederich, "a notorious liar," was impossible.[94] And that is how the dispute ended during the last year of the Nazi regime.

Goebbels' diary includes many brief critical comments on his rivals in the censorship of books. On June 21, 1935, Goebbels recorded "trouble with Rust over questions of jurisdiction. Constant fighting with Rosenberg." The problems with Rosenberg continued for another year. On April 4, 1936, Goebbels noted that "Rosenberg makes me angry," though some six weeks later, on May 22, he wrote that "Rosenberg retreats more and more." Goebbels' success in sidelining Rosenberg probably contributed to Rosenberg's increasing frustration. A series of meetings dealing with book bans, held in the Ministry of Propaganda, were attended by representatives of the Ministry of Education, the PPK, the RSK, and the Gestapo. Rosenberg was the only interested party not invited.[95] But this was not the end of these kinds of problems. On November 15, 1939, Goebbels complained that the "constant conflicts of jurisdiction take a toll on my nerves." A week later he noted that since the quarrel between Rosenberg and Bouhler cannot be ended from his side, he would issue orders for book censorship on his own. "I cannot wait until they resolve their fight over competence." And on November 26 Goebbels wrote that "the squabble over book censorship continues. Rosenberg and Bouhler have fallen out completely. Let the devil try to bring about peace."[96]

Rosenberg, for his part, was disdainful of Goebbels, and he insisted that he understood art and culture far better than the minister of propaganda. Rosenberg considered Goebbels as too soft with regard to Jewish, Marxist, and modern culture and literature.[97] He also was upset over Goebbels' private life. Despite his physical handicap, Goebbels was known as a successful seducer, often having several affairs at the same time. In his diary entry for February 6, 1939, Rosenberg called Goebbels "an abscess on our revolution," and he spoke of dozens of rapes of women on Goebbels' staff. In a conversation with Himmler noted in his diary, Rosenberg refers to Goebbels as "morally isolated and despised in the party."[98] The party veterans and the Gauleiter, he recorded on September 24 of the same year, "completely reject Goebbels."[99] Rosenberg may have been entitled to claim the higher moral ground with regard to the treatment of women, but it was Goebbels who proved the superior and more successful combatant in the struggle for turf.

PART 4

THE IMPACT OF CENSORSHIP

13

The Inner Emigration

Several hundred German writers left their homeland after the Nazis' rise to power in 1933. Among these emigrés were some of the best-known figures of German literature, such as Lion Feuchtwanger, Heinrich and Thomas Mann, Ernst Toller, Kurt Tucholsky, Franz Werfel, and Arnold and Stefan Zweig. Yet there was another group of authors who stayed in Germany and who, it has been said, constituted an "Inner Emigration." Some of these writers, unable to publish, wrote "for the drawer." Others concealed the true meaning of their publications by "writing between the lines" and using allegories or parables. Still others composed historical novels about tyrants or, in one form or another, manifested their principled opposition to the Nazi regime.[1]

The existence and significance of the Inner Emigration has been the subject of controversy. The unimpeachable anti-Nazi Günther Weisenborn, whose writings were banned and who in 1942 was convicted of treason, barely to escape with his life, has argued that the Inner Emigration produced "noteworthy work."[2] On the other hand, no less a personage than Thomas Mann insisted in 1945 that all books published in Germany between 1933 and 1945 should be pulped because they were "less than worthless" and "smelled of blood."[3] According to Arthur Koestler, those who chose to live while others were dying and did not feel guilty for it were "accomplices by omission."[4]

Numerous German writers did, in fact, become ardent stalwarts of the Nazi regime. The list of pro-Nazi writers includes Rudolf Ahlers, Bruno Brehm, Edwin Erich Dwinger, Hanns Johst, Erwin Guido Kolbenheyer, Georg Schmückle, Hermann Stehr, and many more. These authors were rewarded for their service to the state with literary prizes, generous honoraria, and often exemption from compulsory labor or military service, obtaining the valuable draft classification "uk" (unabkömmlich, or indispensable). An RSK memo of February 12, 1943, gave the number of writers excused from the draft as 300.[5] By having actively supported a regime of infamy, these authors share the responsibility for the horrors that took place, and it can be said, in the words of Thomas Mann, that their work indeed "smells of blood."

The new rulers were able quickly to establish and fortify their new order not only because of outright compulsion but as a result of the support of the elites of German society, including its literary class. After the collapse of the Nazi regime, it became convenient to exaggerate the repressive role of censorship and in this way to excuse the abject surrender of most writers to the new rulers.[6] Many writers had never identified themselves with the Weimar democracy and had opposed its cultural modernism. This outlook made it easy to embrace the new National Socialist creed. There were true Nazi authors, but many more were opportunists who enjoyed the patronage and benefits that had become available for those who toed the line. The exodus of so many authors had created a gap where writers of often limited ability, previously disdained by the critics, could find a place.

There is general agreement that, if anyone deserves to be regarded as a member of the Inner Emigration, it is Ricarda Huch. When the Nazis assumed power in 1933, Huch was almost seventy years old. She had studied philosophy, history, and philology at the University of Zurich, because at the time women were not yet eligible to receive degrees at a German university. She received her doctorate in 1890, one of the first women to do so at the University of Zurich. In Germany she soon became a highly regarded public intellectual, the author of significant works of history as well as of fiction and poetry. On the occasion of her sixtieth birthday in 1924, Thomas Mann had called her "the first lady not only of Germany but of Europe."

In March 1933 Huch refused to remain a member of the purged Academy of Writers and she denounced the brutality of the new regime. To a large extent, of course, this freedom to speak her mind was the result of her great international reputation. The Nazi authorities kept tabs on her activities, but she remained unmolested and her writings continued to be published.[7] In 1934 the first volume of her *Deutsche Geschichte Römisches Reich deutscher Nation* (German History: Roman Empire of the German Nation) appeared. The work stressed values like freedom and self-government, all opposed to the ideology of the day. At a time when the Nazis staged boycotts of Jewish shops and dismissed Jews from all public positions, Huch wrote: "The persecutions of the Jews during the fourteenth century stirred up whatever beastly instincts lay hidden amongst the German people and revealed the heroism of which the Jews were capable." The work was severely criticized by Rosenberg's *Nationalsozialistische Monatshefte*, in which Huch was accused of being someone who does not deserve to belong to contemporary Germany.[8]

By the time the second volume of her German history was ready, censorship had been fully implemented. She made a few changes so as not to provoke the censors, and *Das Zeitalter der Glaubensspaltung* (The Era of the Schism) appeared in 1937. The third volume, *Untergang des Römischen Reiches* (Downfall of the Roman Empire), could not be published until after the war. Several of her works written during the following years were brought out by her Swiss publisher. And yet the regime liked to brag about the famous author. For her eightieth birthday on July 18, 1944, the newspapers, including the *Völkischer Beobachter*, published tributes, there was an official Festschrift, and Hitler sent a congratulatory telegram. At the behest of Goebbels, Huch was presented with a literary prize of 30,000 RM. Subsequently she expressed deep regret that she did not have the presence of mind to reject this distinction bestowed by a regime she loathed. In one of her last letters, written three years later, she considered this failure "a stain on my honor that I cannot expunge."[9]

Werner Bergengruen too is regarded as an outstanding member of the Inner Emigration, even though he managed to publish twenty-six titles during the Nazi era. His moral integrity was exemplary,[10] though no more than Ricarda Huch and others who stayed in Nazi Germany did he manage to avoid all compromises. In October 1936 he was one of the signers of a telegram "expressing eternal fidelity" that a conference of writers in Berlin sent to Hitler.[11] This acquiescence does not call into question a positive assessment of Bergengruen's overall record, but it does show that Nazi rule set limits to personal independence and courage.

Born in 1892 in Riga, at the time part of the Russian Empire, Werner Bergengruen grew up in Lübeck. He studied theology and German literature at the University of Marburg, and, following military service during World War I, worked as an editor. Bergengruen gradually became known as a writer and translator. His first great literary success came in 1935 with his novel *Der Grosstyrann und das Gericht* (The Big Tyrant and the Tribunal). The book deals with a despotic ruler during the Renaissance, who is also a statesman and man of great intellectual sophistication and who eventually finds in his own conscience a tribunal leading him to repentance. Bergengruen began the novel in 1926 and completed it in the fall of 1934, when suddenly he realized that his book had a "terrifying actuality." And yet Bergengruen considered the attempt to draw a parallel between his autocrat and Hitler, an insult to his hero. The dangers and temptations of unlimited power, he insisted, had to be demonstrated by way of an outstanding and gifted individual and not in regard to "a criminal fool belonging to the dregs of humanity."[12]

The *Grosstyrann* found near-universal acclaim. The *Völkischer Beobachter* praised it as "the novel of a Renaissance Führer." Several newspapers printed excerpts, and it sold more than 100,000 copies. The acceptance of the book was helped by the fact that it was issued by the Hanseatische Verlagsanstalt in Hamburg, a conservative publisher that by 1935 was owned by the German Labor Front and therefore had unchallengeable Nazi credentials. Two years later Bergengruen was excluded from the RSK because he was married to Charlotte Hensel, a descendant of Fanny Mendelssohn and hence classified three-quarters Jewish. Wismann, the chief censor in the Ministry of Propaganda, the record shows, saw to it that Bergengruen received a *Sondergenehmigung* on account of his "literary distinction."[13] This was the special permission to publish that was granted to authors who, for one reason or another, could not be kept in the RSK but who were nevertheless considered valuable on account of their popularity.

In 1936 Bergengruen converted to Catholicism and moved to Munich, where he became a friend of the fellow-Catholic poet Reinhold Schneider. His books increasingly dealt with concepts such as power, justice, and conscience, and they stressed the Christian value of the inherent dignity of all men. In Bergengruen's books readers encountered uncorrupted human beings and moral standards that the Nazi regime had repudiated. Numerous letters and personal conversations, Bergengruen recalled after the war, made clear to him that a large number of his readers understood what he intended to say and felt encouraged by his reaffirmation of the eternal values. As an example of such refined perceptiveness of people living under a dictatorship, Bergengruen tells of a newspaper article he published in 1933 or 1934 that dealt with the unpleasant winter weather. The essay ended with the question, "Wann wird die Schweinerei nun endlich aufhören?" (When will this horrible mess finally end?), and these seven words quickly acquired a life of their own. They circulated widely and took on a political meaning that told those near despair that they were not alone.[14]

In the spring of 1936 Bergengruen completed a collection of poems entitled *Der ewige Kaiser* (The Eternal Emperor). Realizing that the poems could never be published in Nazi Germany, Bergengruen found an Austrian publisher, who issued the collection anonymously in 1937. A year later Austria was annexed and the Gestapo promptly confiscated the book. The publisher was put under pressure to reveal the name of the author, and Bergengruen, not wanting to harm the publisher, sent an explanatory letter to the Gestapo. He argued that the collection involved a ballad style of poetry that he had never tried before; in order not to risk the reputation he had built up with his novels he had withheld his authorship. The lie worked, helped by the fact that the Gestapo officials were not overly sophisticated. Moreover many of the poems included references to the Roman Empire of the German nation, a period of German history that had become highly popular after the *Anschluss* (annexation) of Austria.[15]

By 1940 Bergengruen's lucky breaks had come to an end. The Rosenberg organization attacked his writings, and the Ministry of Propaganda, too, felt it necessary to clip his wings. His novel *Am Himmel wie auf Erden* (In Heaven as on Earth) was not allowed to be reviewed, though it nonetheless sold 60,000 copies.[16] In June 1940 the Ministry of Propaganda inquired at the party organization of Munich about Bergengruen's politics—whether he belonged to the party or any of its affiliated organizations. The reply stated that "Bergengruen was 'not politically reliable.'" Neither he nor his wife belonged to any National Socialist organization, and even though he displayed the swastika flag when appropriate, he and his family never used the German greeting of "Heil Hitler."[17]

As a result of growing political pressure and the shortage of paper, Bergengruen now increasingly wrote for the "drawer," that is, he no longer sought to to get his work published. He frequently read at private gatherings, and his poems, copied by admirers, circulated clandestinely.[18] Together with his wife, Bergengruen is said to have distributed leaflets of the "Weisse Rose" and copies of Bishop Galen's sermons against the Nazi euthanasia program.[19] During the postwar years Bergengruen's literary achievements and his exemplary conduct during the Nazi era were widely recognized. He received an honorary doctorate from the University of Munich, and the president of the German Federal Republic inducted him into the order of Pour le Mérite, one of the highest German distinctions for extraordinary achievement.

The record of other authors who stayed in Germany is less clear-cut, and few have been as controversial as Ernst Jünger. Both Ernst Loewy and Thomas Mann have called him a "trailblazer of barbarism," a spokesman for militarism and brute force.[20] Jünger's opposition to the Nazi state, it has been said, remained caught in "esoteric allegories."[21] On the other hand, the journalist Rolf Sternberger recalled after the war that Jünger's 1939 book *Auf den Marmorklippen* (On the Marble Cliffs) was "a signal of light" that appeared unexpectedly in the darkness and fortified those prepared to fight the Nazi tyranny. The harrowing vision of the torture chamber, named "Köppelsbleek" after a street in the town of Goslar, bore such an uncanny resemblance to the Nazi concentration camps that one wonders how the book ever passed the scrutiny of the censors.[22] While Jünger was stationed in Paris he provided information about the dates of deportations to the French resistance, and thus, as the anti-Nazi author Joseph Breitbach revealed many years later (Jünger was too proud to brag about it), saved the lives of many Jews.[23] Are these different critics talking about the same man?

Jünger was born in 1895 into a wealthy family. At the age of seventeen he ran away from home and joined the French Foreign Legion. During the First World War Jünger was repeatedly wounded and received the order of Pour le Mérite for outstanding military courage. He described his experience in the trenches in his 1920 book *In Stahlgewittern* (In Storms of Steel). His political outlook was *völkisch*. In articles that appeared in nationalist publications like *Die Standarte*, Jünger polemicized against parliamentary democracy and pacifism and advocated a "militant dictatorship" led by the elite of the front generation. After the publication of another war diary, *Feuer und Blut* (Fire and Blood), Jünger in early 1926 sent a copy to Hitler, who thanked him for the "friendly dedication." Yet when Hitler a year later offered Jünger a place on the Nazi party list for the Reichstag, he declined on the grounds that he considered the writing of one verse more meritorious "than representing sixty-thousand jerks in the parliament."

The real reason for this refusal was rooted in Jünger's distrust of the masses and their vulgar instincts. From the beginning the Nazis had mobilized the populace against the old elites, the very elements on whom Jünger and other national-conservatives counted for the renewal of the German nation. Moreover, Jünger found himself at odds with some of the core elements of the Nazis' racial ideology—the link between blood and race and the myth of the Aryan lineage. We do not want to hear, he wrote, "of head forms and Aryan profiles." Blood, Jünger insisted, stood for courage, energy, and enthusiastic vigor. It could not be used to support the superiority of a race. These disagreements for a while were papered over, but they eventually brought him into conflict with the National Socialist regime.[24]

In April 1933 the Gestapo searched Jünger's apartment. Apparently, as he explained in a letter, he was being regarded as a National Bolshevik, a member of the circle of Karl O. Paetel and Ernst Niekisch known in the 1920s as the Widerstand-Kreis (Resistance Circle). These men shared the Nazis' rejection of the ideals of humanitarianism, rationalism, and other liberal values, but they were not convinced that the new regime was necessarily on the right path to realize their conception of a new autocratic Germany.[25] In many ways that was also Jünger's attitude, in part because Nazi critics had received the publication of his 1932 book *Der Arbeiter* (The Worker) less than enthusiastically. Hence, for a while Jünger preferred to play the role of the interested observer. When Jünger was chosen to be one of several new members of the German Academy of Writers in October 1933, he declined the offer. His work, he informed the Academy, did not allow him to accept academic obligations. After his negative reply had been acknowledged, Jünger in a new letter of November 18 once more affirmed his respect for the Academy. He was perfectly prepared to cooperate with the new state, even though he was angry on account of the search of his apartment. His refusal to become a member of the Academy was due solely to certain personal principles that guided his way of life.[26]

In June 1934 Jünger once again demonstrated his independence when he objected to the unauthorized publication in the *Völkische Beobachter* of excerpts from his 1929 book *Das abenteuerliche Herz* (The Adventurous Heart): "My interest does not lie to be quoted in the press as often as possible but rather in that there be no lack of clarity about the nature of my political substance."[27] At the same time Jünger did not hesitate to hold numerous readings from his works, including before National Socialist audiences. Sales of his war diaries flourished; the book *In Stahlgewittern* reached 100,000 copies. As an author, it has been said, Jünger profited from the new state.[28]

In March 1937 Niekisch and more than seventy members of the Widerstand-Kreis were arrested. Both Jünger and his younger brother Friedrich Georg had published in the circle's organ *Der Widerstand,* and they were concerned about possible repercussions. Nevertheless, Ernst Jünger traveled to Berlin to help organize the legal defense of Niekisch.[29] As it turned out, Niekisch was sentenced to a long jail term, but Jünger remained untouched, supposedly protected by influential friends in the army. Nazi critics continued to praise Jünger's writings about his World War I experience, but some saw in his more recent books nothing but nihilism.[30]

Auf den Marmorklippen appeared in 1939, causing a great stir. The first 10,000 copies were sold quickly, and the armed forces printed several new editions because the publisher's request for additional paper had been refused. The book's torture chamber provided a nightmarish picture of what was known to go on in the concentration camps. These are the cellars, Jünger wrote, on top of which the great castles of tyranny are built and where the torturers enjoy their gruesome work of ravishing human dignity and human freedom. The censors, it has been suggested, could not ban this book without admitting at the same time that the horrors of the novel were indeed describing the hell of the camps.[31] Jünger's widow Liselotte Jünger later indicated that Hitler apparently appreciated and protected the author of *Stahlgewittern* and the recipient of a medal for his distinguished service in World War I.[32]

The Nazi press gave the novel the silent treatment, and from here on Jünger's work received enhanced scrutiny. The same year Jünger was conscripted. When his diary about the 1940 campaign against France, *Gärten und Strassen* (Gardens and Streets), was published in 1942, the censors forbade reviews of it.[33] Meanwhile, Jünger's erstwhile comrades from the 1920s, many of whom now occupied important positions in the army, saw to it that their friend was posted to the staff of the military commander of France in Paris.[34] Jünger was in Paris from 1941 to 1944, and it was in Paris that for the first time he saw three Jewish girls wearing the yellow star. In his essay "Über Nationalismus und Judenfrage" (On Nationalism and the Jewish Question), published in 1930, Jünger had taken the position that the Jews could not assimilate and therefore had the choice of ceasing to be Jews or leaving Germany.[35] But as he witnessed the roundup of Jews by the French police in July 1942, his reaction was personal and emotional: "Parents were separated from their children, and wailing was heard in the streets. I must never forget that I am surrounded by unfortunates, suffering most grievously. Otherwise what kind of a human being or officer would I be."[36]

It was also in 1942 that Jünger learned of camps where thousands of Jews were exterminated like vermin. "I am seized with loathing for the uniforms, the shoulder straps, the medals, the weapons, the glamour of which I have loved so much," he wrote in his diary. "The old chivalry is dead, the wars are led by technicians." After the October 1943 bombing of Hannover, which devastated the city, Jünger stated that he was not surprised. This, he said, is what we had to expect after burning churches in Russia and synagogues in Germany and incarcerating individuals in concentration camps without a sentence by a court of law. In his book *Der Friede: Ein Wort an die Jugend Europas, ein Wort an die Jugend der Welt* (Peace: A Word for the Youth of Europe and the World), completed in 1943 and published six years later, Jünger proposed the creation of a federal Europe governed by Christian values. If ever the country were to experience a new arrogance, it could be cured by thinking of "the multitudes who like beasts for slaughter were driven to graves and crematoria, where their executioners were waiting. There they were stripped of the rags that they wore and were slaughtered naked like sheep that had been shorn."[37]

And yet Jünger refused to participate in the planned assassination of Hitler. The military conspirators tried to convince him otherwise, but he insisted that resistance had to be limited to morally unobjectionable means. He also felt that the killing of the tyrant would only remove the shoots from branches that later would sprout all the stronger. Moreover, a successful assassination could create a new "stab in the back" legend. The plotters apparently considered Jünger as one of theirs, and, after the expected favorable outcome, intended to give him an important post.[38] On the other hand, it has been suggested, it may be that the conspirators did not fully trust him. Apart from his loyalty to the army, Jünger always conducted himself as an outsider and observer and therefore hesitated to commit himself to this obviously dangerous cause.[39] After the failure of the uprising Jünger was investigated by Roland Freisler's dreaded Volksgerichtshof (People's Court) for having made defeatist remarks during his tenure in Paris and for his book *Die Marmorklippen*. This proceeding was stopped only because of a personal phone call from Hitler to Freisler.[40]

Where does all this leave Jünger? Critics have pointed out that between 1933 and 1945 there appeared not only works that confirm Jünger's reputation as an opponent of the Nazi regime but also new editions of his most militant writings from the 1920s in which he glorified force and war.[41] During the Second World War, Jünger criticized the German generals for abandoning the chivalry of old but there is no indication that he ever condemned Hitler's wars of aggression as a deliberate misdeed.[42] Does Jünger's strengthening of the home front by his diaries of the First World War outweigh the boost in morale he provided to opponents of the regime by his book *Auf den Marmorklippen*? The answer to this question is not obvious.

The well-known writer Ernst Wiechert is another ambiguous figure. Thomas Mann called Wiechert the most "unbearable" figure of the Inner Emigration,[43] and Zuckmayer praised him as "one of the best and most courageous writers who stayed in Germany."[44] Neither appraisal is quite accurate. Wiechert, like many good people of his generation, thought that he could maintain his personal integrity by a complete withdrawal from anything political. He believed that in addition to being a fellow-traveler of the regime or being active in the resistance there was a third way—that of inwardness, of taking refuge in one's own spiritual life.[45] That was the theme of his 1939 novel *Das einfache Leben* (The Simple Life), which became a best-seller.

Wiechert was born in 1887 in East Prussia. He became a teacher and published his first novel in 1911. After military service in the First World War, Wiechert resumed his profession of teaching. His political outlook was conservative and *völkisch,* indistinguishable from that of the radical right: There was the same glorification of blood and soil and of struggle and war, the need for a cultural renewal, and a return to the Germanic traditions. The dust jacket of his 1924 novel *Der Totenwolf* (The Werewolf) carried a swastika, and when the publisher inquired whether Wiechert would agree to the publication of an excerpt in a newspaper, Wiechert replied in the affirmative on condition that the newspaper was not Jewish.[46]

In a letter of April 24, 1922, Wiechert called democracy "the basic root of all evil."[47]At the same time his elitist view of the role of the writer prevented him from joining any party. Wiechert strove for solitude and a quiet life, and this soon brought him into conflict with a regime that emphasized mass meetings, marches, and regimentation.[48] In an article published in the *Börsenblatt* in December 1933, Wiechert noted that it was convenient to cleanse literature by way of blacklists, "but that which is convenient is rarely the right thing." In a hopeful mood he added: "The state will know that confidence is better than orders."[49]

Wiechert's novels remained within the framework of what was acceptable. They described the simple life of the peasant and praised the German forest and the solitary East Prussian landscape. The semi-official *Die Bücherei* praised his autobiographical work *Wälder und Menschen: Eine Jugend* (Forests and Men: A Youth) as "belonging in every public library."[50] His books sold well, and he was able to stop teaching and concentrate on his writing. On April 16, 1935, on invitation of the NS-cultural organization of Munich, Wiechert addressed an assembly of students in the Auditorium Maximum of the university. This was his second appearance before the students of Munich, and his remarks reflected his growing dissatisfaction with what the regime regarded as cultural renewal. His theme was "The Writer and His Time." Current criticism, Wiecher argued, emphasized political rather than artistic criteria. Yet it was the task of the writer to guard the eternal values, to elevate truth, justice, and freedom and make man better and purer. It was essential for a people to know how to distinguish between *Recht und Unrecht* (Justice and Injustice). Wiechert ended his talk with an admonishment to the young people "not to remain silent when your conscience tells you to speak up."[51]

Wiechert's criticism of the cultural policy of the new regime was a small part of a long lecture, rich in the lyrical language characteristic of all of his writings. And yet the ideological watchdogs of the movement did not miss it. The

Völkischer Beobachter of April 18 voiced strong dissatisfaction, and an undated and unsigned report on the speech argued that it was a mistake to give individuals like Wiechert a public platform. A large number of Catholic students had attended the address and had greeted his "pessimistic utterances" with great applause.[52] The speech was not allowed to be printed, but it circulated clandestinely in typescript. Wiechert's relations with the Nazi state now deteriorated. He was not invited to a conference of writers on the Great War held in Berlin in October 1936, and the Rosenberg organization called him "ideologically and politically unreliable."[53]

A public reading in November 1937 of his short story "Der weisse Büffel oder von der grossen Gerechtigkeit" (The White Buffalo or the Greatness of Justice), which represented a not-so-hidden denunciation of the brutal power politics of the regime, was halted by the police in Cologne. Those who heard him understood that the torture, *Sippenhaft* (families sharing the responsibility for crimes against the state committed by one of its members), and the deification of the murderous ruler Murduk in India were allusions to what was going on right around them.[54] The publisher Langen-Müller refused to publish the story. The Rosenberg official Langenbucher called Wiechert's writings preoccupied with the "inner I" and "lacking in a clear commitment to a joyful will to live."[55]

Two actions that Wiechert took in 1938 precipitated a crisis and landed him a short stay in a concentration camp. In February the Lutheran pastor Martin Niemöller, active in defending the independence of the German Protestant church, had been sent to the concentration camp Sachsenhausen. Wiechert thereupon informed the authorities that he would no longer make his contributions to the state's Winter Assistance Program and other welfare agencies. Instead, he would send the money to the wife and the eight children of the incarcerated Niemöller, and he would continue to do so until Niemöller was set free. In his speech to the Reichstag after the annexation of Austria Hitler had justified the *Anschluss* with the statement, "Right must prevail and also must extend to Germans." Wiechert insisted that this principle had to be applied to Niemöller as well.[56] The second reason for his arrest supposedly was his failure to vote in the plebiscite of April 10 following the *Anschluss*. In his memoirs, published after the war, Wiechert described this act as motivated by political conviction. However it appears that he did not vote because on the day in question he was hunting with a friend in the Black Forest.[57] Be that as it may, in the early morning of May 6 three Gestapo officials appeared at Wiechert's home, searched the house, and took Wiechert into custody.

For seven weeks Wiechert was held at the Munich jail, where he was interrogated. During this time he managed to keep a diary written on small pieces of paper in tiny letters. After the war it was published as *Häftling Nr. 7188: Tagebuchaufzeichnungen und Briefe* (Prisoner no. 7188: Diary Entries and Letters). On July 4 Wiechert was taken to the Buchenwald concentration camp.

He described his stay there in *Der Totenwald* (Forest of the Dead).[58] Wiechert's health was precarious, and on August 26 he was freed and taken to Berlin. There Goebbels personally admonished Wiechert to cease his opposition to the regime; otherwise he would be sent back to the concentration camp and kept there until he perished. Weichert wrote to his wife that he also gave a written assurance of compliance, but the text of that declaration is not preserved. The 1938 year-end report of the SD, the intelligence arm of the SS, noted that Wiechert, "since 1933 constantly in opposition, was forcibly brought to his senses."[59] On August 30, 1938, Wiechert was back at his home.[60]

Wiechert's incarceration had led to his expulsion from the RSK. But after Wiechert had given assurances of future good behavior, his exclusion was revoked and his books could again be sold. At the same time, Wiechert was ordered to submit all new writings to the RSK for approval.[61] At a press conference held on September 2, 1938, the RSK announced that Wiechert had been "pardoned conditionally" but that his writings were not to receive too much publicity. He was to be tolerated but not promoted.[62] And yet Wiechert's book *Das einfache Leben,* published in 1939, was a great success, and within three years it had sold 260,000 copies. The hero of this work, a retired navy officer, leaves the big city and decides to live a solitary life in the sparsely settled East Prussia. The book's advocacy of a retreat into a pure inwardness corresponded to the course of conduct Wiechert himself had decided to pursue. It also appealed to many Germans, giving them the illusion of having retained their moral integrity in the midst of so much that was evil. For its part, as the war created ever harsher conditions of life, the Ministry of Propaganda liked this kind of writing that created an imaginary realm of stability and happiness. This sphere existed only on paper, but it nevertheless provided refuge and solace.[63]

Rosenberg's people were less than happy with the pardon Wiechert had received from Goebbels. Many of his writings, they insisted, had too much of what is "negative and unpleasant." The public libraries were advised to choose carefully which of Wiechert's books they would acquire.[64] In 1941, Wiechert recalled in his memoirs, he was invited to the Hauptamt Rosenberg and told that his books lacked *Lebensfreude* (Zest for life).[65] The same year, the first volume of his novel *Die Jerominkinder* (The Jeromin Children) was rejected by the censorship of the Ministry of Propaganda, and his 1931 book *Jedermann* (Everyman), probably considered quasi-pacifistic, was withdrawn from circulation. Wiechert's other writings continued to be sold.

Wiechert now rejected all invitations for public appearances and lived a withdrawn life in his home. In June 1943 Hans Frank, the governor-general of Poland, invited Wiechert to give a reading in Krakow. Wiechert declined. "Every hardly grown-up journalist has the right to vilify me and my writings," he wrote Frank, but no paper was available for his books, and he did not know how he would pay his bills. Not so long ago, Wiechert added, he had been led in chains through the main railway station of Munich, and this only because he had "dared to follow his conscience." He was not bitter, but on the other hand he could not forget this event either. He therefore had decided to remain silent as if dead and to live a quiet life "amidst plants, animals, and books."[66]

After the end of the war, Wiechert defended his decision to remain in Germany. Critics argued that Wiechert never repudiated the national-conservative, not to say pro-Nazi, ideas he held during the Weimar Republic. His disapproval of the Nazi regime, it was said, was rooted not in a repudiation of the Nazi ideology—the leadership principle, opposition to democracy, and so forth—but rather involved a denunciation of National Socialist practice, a practice that had abandoned and falsified what he regarded as the positive values of National Socialism.[67] For his part, Wiechert was critical of the way postwar Germany was coming to terms with its Nazi past. In 1948 he moved to Switzerland, where he died in 1950.

Gottfried Benn, it has been said, has written "the most beautiful German poems of the twentieth century,"[68] and yet his high repute as a poet is tarnished by the ardor with which he supported the Nazi regime in 1933 and 1934. Born in 1886, the son of a Lutheran minister, Benn studied theology and later medicine. After receiving his medical degree he worked on cruise ships, and during the First World War he served in the German army's medical corps. At war's end he opened a practice for venereal and skin diseases in Berlin. Benn's first collection of poetry was published in 1912. It was marked by a pronounced existentialist pessimism.

In March 1933, Benn played a leading role in the purge of the Academy of Writers, a section of the Prussian Academy of the Arts. This endorsement of the Nazi state is all the more remarkable considering that as late as December 1932 Benn had urged his fellow members to take a position against the attempted politicization of the Academy of Writers. The creative spirit of the German nation, he had insisted, should not be subordinated to specific political norms or views. It required freedom and openness as advocated by Herder and Schiller, and this wide space, Benn affirmed, "is *our* Third Reich."[69]

The purge of the Academy of Writers was precipitated by a call for the formation of an anti-Fascist front that Academy members Heinrich Mann and Käthe Kollwitz had signed in early 1933. This prompted Prussian Minister of Education Rust to threaten the dissolution of the Academy unless the two political activists were expelled. Both Mann and Kollwitz thereupon resigned, but this did not end the crisis. At a meeting of the Prussian Academy of the Arts held on February 15, 1933, some members defended Mann and Kollwitz with the argument that they had merely exercised their constitutionally guaranteed right of freedom of speech. Benn, on the other hand—in order, as he said, to prevent a dissolution of the Academy—at the next meeting proposed a declaration of loyalty that obligated members "to forgo public political activities against the government and to participate loyally in whatever cultural tasks the Academy, according to its constitution, would assume in the light of the new historical situation."[70] This declaration was adopted by six members, including Benn; twenty-seven others were absent. It marked the transformation of the independent Academy of Writers into an organ for the implementation of the cultural policies of the new government.[71]

Alfred Döblin, Ricarda Huch, Alfons Paquet, and Thomas Mann refused to sign the declaration of loyalty and resigned from the Academy. Huch's letter of resignation of April 9 was forceful: "The national cast of mind prescribed by the present government does not constitute my sense of being German. Centralization, coercion, brutal methods, defamation of those who think differently, bragging self-praise I consider un-German and disastrous."[72] Ten other members, among them Leonhard Frank, Alfred Mombert, Fritz von Unruh, Jakob Wassermann, and Franz Werfel, were excluded on orders of Rust. In their place twenty-two writers considered politically reliable were inducted into the Academy. They included Hans Friedrich Blunck, Hans Grimm, Hanns Johst, Erwin Guido Kolbenheyer, Wilhelm Schäfer, and Emil Strauss. The Academy was renamed the German Academy of Writers, and Benn became its vice president.[73]

On April 24 the German radio broadcast a speech by Benn entitled "The New State and the Intellectuals." In a letter sent on the same day to his friend Carl Werckshagen, Benn explained that he wanted to stress the importance of "adopting a positive posture toward the new state.... All must protect the state, our lives and existence depend on it." In his speech Benn argued that the current political movement was simply history and therefore neither good nor bad. It was a historical necessity. The new "total state," marking the end of the liberal mentality, had the duty to "oversee" freedom of thought, freedom of the press, and academic freedom.[74] Little did Benn expect that his own work soon would run afoul of the very controls he had advocated in 1933.

From exile, Klaus Mann reproached Benn for siding with a regime of infamy that the civilized world rejected unanimously. "He who in this hour conducts himself equivocally will no longer belong to us today and forever."[75] In a "Reply to the Literary Emigrants," broadcast on May 19 and reprinted the next day in the *Deutsche Allgemeine Zeitung,* Benn defended his acceptance of the Nazi state. Only those who had experienced the events of the last few months, Benn insisted, could understand what had transpired in Germany. Only they would have learned the true meaning of *Volk* and the concept of the "national." It was not so much a question of the form of government but "a new vision of the birth of man" and of the white race, "probably one of the most magnificent manifestations of the world spirit."[76] In a personal letter to Klaus Mann, Benn added that he had declared his support for the new state because "it is my people who are paving the way here." His spiritual and economic existence, his language, his life, and his human relations were at stake. He could not abandon all that.[77]

On October 26, 1933, following Germany's withdrawal from the League of Nations, eighty-eight writers signed a "Vow of Most Faithful Allegiance" (*Gelöbnis treuester Gefolgschaft*) to Hitler. The declaration was organized by the Prussian Academy of the Arts. "In this serious moment," it affirmed the signers' loyal obedience to the Reich Chancellor. Among the Führer's "faithful followers" were, as one would expect, the "usual suspects" such as Hans Friedrich Blunck and Hanns Johst, but also Gottfried Benn.[78] Some two months later Benn made his most far-reaching concession to the Nazi ideology when he endorsed the censorship of books. Literature, he conceded, needed a certain latitude for experimentation. At the same time, "it appears to me to be self-evident, that no book should be allowed to be published in Germany that brings the new state into contempt." Foreigners should not believe the hateful outbursts of the emigré literature that was doomed to die out. We here in Germany represent "the voice of German history."[79] In March 1934 Benn once again expressed his admiration for the "new Reich," for the building of which "the Führer, whom we all admire, has summoned also the writers."[80] When a newspaper suggested that Benn probably was Jewish because the name "ben" was the Hebrew word for son, Benn published an elaborate denial. After drawing attention to the old roots of his name in the Franconian dialect and in Old High German, Benn affirmed that he was "thoroughly Aryan" (*urarisch*), had pure blood, and would have nothing to do with "this [Jewish] race." The writer Carl Zuckmayer, who reported this incident after the war, called Benn's apologia "very distressing."[81]

The bloody events of June 30, known as the "night of the long knives," during which Hitler ordered the killing of some of his closest followers, had demonstrated that all who opposed the Führer were in danger of losing their heads. There were at least eighty-five known victims, but some estimates put the total number killed at between 150 and 200. The butchery marked a high point in the substitution of violence and summary justice for legal norms,[82] and it appears to have had a powerful and sobering effect on Benn. He lost his romantic illusions about the Nazi regime and ceased being its "useful idiot."[83] In a letter of July 24, 1934, to his friend F. W. Oelz, Benn speaks of a "tragedy for which there are no words. Another German dream has come to an end." Several months later he decided to return to the Army medical corps. This would enable him, he tells Oelz, to abandon all of his obligations, including the Academy; "the R. W. [Reichswehr, or German army] is the aristocratic form of emigration."[84]

Benn regarded his return to army medical service as a way of escaping from an impossible political situation, and in his correspondence he felt free to express his disillusionment. In a letter of April 4, 1937, to his friend Elinor

Büller, Benn argued that whatever today passes the censor is "filth" and "whatever does not lead directly to the concentration camp is foolish." The Nazis, for their part, were not done with him. As Benn explained in a 1935 letter, he was increasingly being caught between two fronts: "Abroad I am being mocked as a Nazi and racist, while the Nazis regard me an un-German, formalistic, and intellectual."[85] The *Schwarze Korps*, the organ of the SS, was at the head of the hounds, and other Nazi papers followed suit in denouncing Benn as a "repulsive lyricist." When a compilation of *Selected Poems 1911–1936* was published in the summer of 1936, the PPK in a letter to the Gestapo condemned Benn's poetry as being rife with "cynicism and pathological self-abuse" and likely to damage the aims of National Socialism.[86] Benn expected to be expelled from the army, but when the Gestapa inquired at the RSK about the steps to be taken, it was informed that both Johst and the Ministry of Propaganda had decided not to do anything.[87]

When a book appeared in 1937 that called for the silencing of the *Kulturbolschewist* (cultural Bolshevist) Benn, the beleaguered poet turned to Johst, the head of the RSK, for help. The new charges, he wrote, were completely unjustified. The poems that the PPK had objected to had been removed from the 1936 edition and new poems had been inserted in their place. Altogether, Benn insisted, he was conducting himself "in an exemplary manner." He was doing his duty in the army, did not appear in public, and wrote practically nothing.[88] Johst, who liked to play the role of the "benevolent patriarch," wrote Benn that he condemned the new assaults which he regarded as "outdated and anachronistic."[89] In a formal testimonial, Johst confirmed that Benn from the beginning had supported the new state, and he expressed his thanks "for the pugnacious effort Dr. Benn has made on behalf of German culture in the tenor of the Third Reich."[90] Himmler too called the attacks on Benn "unnecessary and foolish" and ordered his subordinates not to become involved in the matter.[91]

What happened next demonstrated who really pulled the strings in the RSK and the Ministry of Propaganda. On March 18, 1938, Benn was informed in a form letter signed by the RSK's chief executive officer Ihde that, on account of his deficient political suitability, he had been expelled from the RSK. "As a result of this decision you lose the right further to exercise any profession within the jurisdiction of the Reichsschrifttumskammer."[92] Benn's expulsion had taken place without the involvement of Johst, who, as usual, spent more time in his home in Bavaria than in Berlin working on the dull day-to-day affairs of the RSK. In a letter to Himmler, Johst noted that this "sudden action" by Goebbels, as he had learned, had taken place at the behest of Göring. Both Goebbels and Göring most likely had been misinformed. Probably piqued for having been excluded, Johst asked Himmler to help in reversing Benn's expulsion.[93]

Himmler's response to this request is not preserved, but, whatever Himmler may or may not have done, Benn's expulsion from the RSK remained in force.

Posted to a garrison in eastern Germany, he wrote poetry and essays that remained unpublished until after the war. The occupation authorities at first banned his writings, but he soon became once again well known and esteemed. Benn helped along his rehabilitation by insisting that he had lived from his practice as a physician and had ignored politics. The government in 1933 had been legal, and there was therefore no reason to oppose it.[94] Benn also omitted from the reissue of earlier publications passages that were likely to put him in a bad light.[95] He asked his friend Oelz to advise him which sections should be left out "in the light of the changed political conditions.... Whoever wants it can use these old things against me and find there poison for his arrows." As was to be expected, such critics, who insisted on giving Benn his due both in terms of his achievements as a poet and his infatuation with the early Nazi regime, soon emerged. Ernst Loewy's appraisal can count as a widely shared assessment: "Benn was a brilliant essayist and a distinguished poet; in politics he was a man of pitiful blindness."[96]

A similar assessment is appropriate for Gerhart Hauptmann, regarded as the most prominent German dramatist of the early twentieth century and well known all over the literary world. By 1947 Thomas Mann had distanced himself from his sweeping condemnation of German literature during the Nazi era. In a conversation with his brother Viktor he acknowledged that if a German writer or artist was not well enough known to be able to make a living outside the country, he should not be blamed for having stayed in Germany. However, Mann added, if an author had world fame, his "remaining and creating in Germany served the propagation of evil. Even love of one's native country (*Heimatliebe*) cannot serve to excuse such conduct." This judgment certainly fits a writer like Hauptmann who considered the option of emigration but ultimately rejected it, supposedly with the admission that he was a coward.[97] To his close friend Erich Ebermeyer, Hauptmann said in February 1934 that he was a German writer and would not leave Germany just because a government that he did not like and that did not approve of him had come to power.[98] For his decision to stay and continue to publish in Nazi Germany, Hauptmann has been roundly criticized and has even been called the "Quisling of the Inner Emigration."[99]

Gerhart Hauptmann was never a Nazi author like Kolbenheyer or Stehr. His writings composed after 1933 do not show any concession to the Nazi ideology. He was neither a Nazi nor an anti-Nazi, but that was enough to earn him criticism from ideologues like Rosenberg, for whom any failure actively to endorse National Socialism was a sign of subversion. Moreover, at the beginning of World War I Hauptmann had been a pacifist, and subsequently he had strongly identified himself with the Weimar Republic. There had been attempts to nominate Hauptmann as a candidate for the office of president. And yet Hauptmann was too well known all over Europe, and his prestige as a German writer too great for him to be excluded from Germany's cultural life. In 1912 the Silesian author had been awarded the Nobel Prize in Literature in recognition of his outstanding achievements in dramatic art. Hence, with the exception of *The Weavers*, a naturalistic drama based on the 1844 revolt of the Silesian weavers against the abuses of the Industrial Revolution, his plays continued to be performed, often in the presence of high Nazi officials. For Goebbels Hauptmann became a useful *Aushängeschild* (advertisement) to prove that, contrary to the claims of the emigrants, German culture was alive and well in Nazi Germany. For his part, Hauptmann happily accepted whatever praise and honors the regime bestowed upon him.

Hitler declared October 15, 1933, to be a "Day of German Art," and he expressed the wish that a new play by Hauptmann, *The Golden Harp,* receive its first performance on that day in Munich. By coincidence, on October 14 Hitler announced Germany's exit from the League of Nations, a decision that the German people were asked to vote on in a plebiscite on November 12. Hauptmann participated in the campaign for an affirmative vote by signing a declaration that was published under the headline "I say 'Yes'" in the *Berliner Tageblatt* of November 11. Leaving the "so-called League of Nations," Hauptmann stated, was a necessary step "taken by our leading statesman" in order to achieve a just peace in Europe.[100] A few days later, Hauptmann was one of the invited guests at the opening ceremony for the German Chamber of Culture that took place with the participation of Hitler and other high Nazi functionaries.

Other foreign policy initiatives of Hitler also drew Hauptmann's support. On March 7, 1936, Hitler announced that, in contravention of the Treaty of Versailles, German troops had entered the demilitarized Rhineland, and he scheduled another referendum for March 29 in which the German people were asked to approve this action. In an article headlined "Gerhart Hauptmann zum 29. März: Ein Bekenntnis zu Führer und Volk" (Gerhart Hauptmann on March 29: An Affirmation of Loyalty to Führer and People) published in the *Berliner Tageblatt* of March 27, Hauptmann expressed his regret that he could not vote in the plebiscite from his villa in Rapallo. However, he wanted it known that "in this world historical moment I share the determined will of Führer and people."[101]

In the annexation of Austria in 1938 Hauptmann saw "a historical necessity" carried out by a son of Germany's Austria "whose iron will was chosen by the powers behind the stars to realize their verdict."[102] After the partition of Poland between Germany and the Soviet Union in 1939, Hauptmann expressed regret about the spirit of "merciless nationalism" that appeared to be at work all over the world, but the victory over France in the *Blitzkrieg* of 1940 made him forget this lament. In his diary entry for June 28 Hauptmann noted that Germany now ruled over Europe, an amazing development brought about "by the unique, superhuman will of Hitler."[103] At the invasion of Russia in 1941 Hauptmann composed a "Greeting to the Front" that was broadcast by Radio Breslau.

Hauptmann was opposed to all anti-Semitism, and his son Klaus was married to a Jewish woman. He had many Jewish friends, to whom he remained loyal. He attended the funeral of his longtime publisher Samuel Fischer in October 1934, and he even published an obituary in the *Neue Rundschau*, for which he was harshly criticized. He also helped some of those who were being persecuted on racial or political grounds.[104] But Hauptmann failed to understand the seriousness of the situation faced by Germany's Jews. In a conversation with his friend the writer Erich Ebermeyer in Rapallo in February 1934, Hauptmann belittled the growing discrimination against Jews with the saying "A few Eastern Jews—my God, that is not so important!" With great disappointment Ebermeyer noted in his diary that Hauptmann had forgotten the dozens of Jewish friends who were being held in concentration camps or who had been forced into exile.[105] Increasingly, it would appear, Hauptmann did let his vocabulary be influenced by the kind of anti-Jewish stereotypes rampant in Hitler's Germany, and he expressed his antipathy to individual Jews in anti-Semitic clichés.[106] After the break with his friend the critic Alfred Kehr, Hauptmann vilified him as a "Ghetto-Jew."[107] Gradually he moved away from the German-Jewish symbiosis that had been so fruitful for German culture and began to characterize the Jew as someone foreign. Following the establishment of a German Academy in New York in 1936, Hauptmann denounced the emigrants who had taken this step with the argument that "it is impossible to call a selected group of Jews a German Academy. This would mean that the German *Geist* (mentality) is Jewish."[108]

Following the violent events of *Kristallnacht* in November 1938, Hauptmann wrote in his diary: "This cannot go on, this is too stupid." Upon seeing a well-dressed Jewish man with a large yellow star and the word *Jude* on his chest, Hauptmann noted: "Have we Germans reached the point to see this without shame?" Hauptmann's papers reveal that he knew of the mass murders taking place in 1941 after the invasion of the Soviet Union. A letter written to him by the professional soldier Erhard von Mutius, dated November 17, 1941, described a massacre of Jewish men, women, and children by Ukrainians with German soldiers standing around and looking on.[109] Yet at no time did Hauptmann give expression to his opposition to the persecution of the Jews, a deportment he shared with most of his kinsmen.

The ambivalent attitude of the Nazi bureaucracy toward Hauptmann can be seen in the prolonged discussion of how to take notice of his eightieth birthday on November 15, 1942. Rosenberg, forever the rigid ideologue, would have preferred to ignore Hauptmann's birthday. At the very least he did not want the Nazi party to be involved in any celebration for Hauptmann because, as he put it, "he is not one of us."[110] Goebbels for his part felt that the birthday of the famous dramatist could not be overlooked. After he had invited Hauptmann to a dinner party in his home on June 10, 1942, he recorded in his diary the favorable impression the venerable poet had made on him. "He [Hauptmann] supports the war with a warm heart and with almost youthful enthusiasm." One should therefore now make an attempt "to gain his full support for the National Socialist regime. This will not be difficult, for he belongs to us internally—he is an upright patriot and close to his people." In this respect, Goebbels added, he was the exact opposite of the brothers Mann, "about whom he [Hauptmann] expressed the most disparaging views."[111] Yet for various reasons, not all of them related to Hauptmann's own attitudes, the attempt of Goebbels to win Hauptmann for the Third Reich must be regarded as unsuccessful.[112]

Goebbels agreed with Rosenberg that there was no need to describe Hauptmann as an exponent of the National Socialist ideology or to discuss his worldview.[113] After Bormann had informed the Minister of Propaganda that the tributes for Hauptmann should be "kept to a bearable scale,"[114] Goebbels took steps to keep the planned celebrations from being too extravagant. When the Gauleiter of Silesia, Karl Hanke, proud of the "great son of Silesia," proposed to rename the municipal theater of Breslau "Gerhart Hauptmann Theater," Goebbels opposed this honor as "excessive."[115] Hanke and von Schirach, head of the Hitler Youth and Gauleiter of Vienna, wanted the main celebration to take place in Vienna because Breslau was regarded as too "provincial," but Goebbels rejected this suggestion as well.[116] Breslau was to stage five of Hauptmann's plays, other cities only one.[117] When it was discovered that the anti-Semitic literary historian Adolf Bartels shared his birthday with Hauptmann, the press was advised to stress Bartel's achievements. In contrast to the *Judenfreund* (friend of Jews) Hauptmann, Bartels had a "clear ideological position." The more Bartels was celebrated, the Ministry of Propaganda assumed, the less place remained for Hauptmann.[118] To make sure that everything went as planned, Goebbels gave orders that all press coverage of Hauptmann celebrations be submitted to him personally for approval.[119]

As Goebbels had ordered, the main celebration of Hauptmann's eightieth birthday took place in Breslau from November 10 to 15. There were speeches by Hanke and von Schirach. Hitler sent a congratulatory telegram as well as a precious vase as a birthday present. In an improvised reply in which he thanked everyone, Hauptmann called Hitler the *Sternenschicksalsträger des Deutschtums* (One Sent by the Stars to Realize the Destiny of Germany).[120] Thanks to the efforts of Hanke and von Schirach, the celebration of Hauptmann's birthday turned out to be more extensive than Goebbels had wanted. After the conclusion of the formal ceremonies in Breslau, von Schirach escorted Hauptmann in a special train to Vienna. There Hauptmann was taken to the Palais Pallavicini, a mansion reserved for state visitors, and von Schirach accompanied Hauptmann to the performances of Hauptmann plays at various theaters. The high point of the festivities was a gala performance at the Vienna Opera attended also by Richard Strauss.[121]

Among Hauptmann's friends was Hans Frank, the governor-general of Poland, known for his brutalities toward both Poles and Jews, who would later be hanged as a war criminal. In January 1944 Frank spent four days at Hauptmann's castle-like House Wiesenstein in the Silesian village of Agnetendorf (Jagniatkow), and Hauptmann recorded in his diary his admiration for this well-educated man, anxious to improve his extensive knowledge, and with "deep human dispositions."[122] By 1942 Frank had his problems with the SS leadership in Poland, who were eroding his authority as well as with the party leadership over his advocacy of constitutional rule. At his postwar trial at Nuremberg, Frank confessed his guilt.[123] Still, to see in the man who has entered history as the "hangman of Poland" a humanist desirous of further education required quite a stretch. Another visitor in 1944 was Josef Pfistner, the Nazi stalwart and deputy mayor of Prague during the German occupation, who was hanged in Prague in September 1945. Pfistner noted in his diary that Hauptmann had repeatedly expressed his "admiration and deep respect" for Hitler and his iron will.[124]

Hauptmann lived to see the end of the Third Reich. When the Communist writer Johannes R. Becher, with the concurrence of the Soviet military authorities, invited Hauptmann to join the "cultural renewal" of Germany, Hauptmann gladly accepted. By this step Hauptmann, for the third time after 1918 and 1933, put himself at the disposal of a new political regime. Hauptmann died on June 6, 1946, before his cooperation with the Communist regime in East Germany could be put to the test.

The harshest denunciation of Hauptmann's quiescence in the face of the barbarities of the Nazi regime came from his good friend the theater critic Alfred Kerr in 1934. Hauptmann, the poet of altruism, had not only cowered but fawned, Kerr wrote. Inhuman events had taken place before his eyes. "His closest friends became victims. He remained silent." Given Hauptmann's great prestige, he could have dealt a huge blow to the murderers who hunted down those whose only guilt was their birth. "The great altruist remained silent."[125] This surrender, Kerr added later, was caused in part by Hauptmann's need for money—lots of money. He maintained three full-time residences and also had to provide support for his son, who never earned enough.[126]

Others have been less condemnatory. When the Nazis came to power in 1933, Hauptmann was seventy years old. All his life he had regarded the highest authority of the state as appointed by providence or at least sanctioned by historical necessity. Could one expect Hauptmann to give up the political fatalism of a lifetime at this ripe age? Add to that Hauptmann's love of the German fatherland and a certain political naiveté, and the surrender of

Hauptmann becomes understandable though not necessarily more admirable.[127] Hauptmann's passivity, it has been said, was typical of the defenselessness of the German educated classes when confronted with the onslaught of National Socialism.[128] All critics agree that the regime derived propagandistic benefit from the Nobel laureate Hauptmann, who continued to live and publish in Nazi Germany.[129]

The fate of the writer Jochen Klepper is probably one of the most tragic in an era not lacking in personal misfortunes and calamities.[130] Born in Upper Silesia in 1903, the son of a Protestant minister, Klepper studied theology and then worked as an editor of the Association of Protestant Media in Breslau. In 1929 he joined the Social Democratic Party (SPD) and became active in the League of Religious Socialists. When in 1931 Klepper was offered the job of a producer at the German Radio, he canceled his membership in both organizations and moved to Berlin. But after the Nazis' assumption of power, he lost this position because of having belonged to the SPD and having a Jewish wife.[131] The same year Klepper had his first literary success with the novel *Kahn der fröhlichen Leute* (Boating with Merry People).

On his application for acceptance into the RSK, the necessary condition for being a writer, Klepper had listed his wife as "freethinker," a designation that was appropriate for many assimilated German Jews. For the Gestapo, on the other hand, applying the usual racial criteria, Klepper's wife was a *Volljüdin* (full-blooded Jew), and in a letter to the RSK it argued that the acceptance of an author who was married to such a person was "not defensible."[132]

The Gestapo's position was in line with customary practice, and on March 25, 1937, Klepper was excluded from the RSK. Supported by his publisher, Klepper filed a grievance and asked for a *Sondergenehmigung* (special permission). Meanwhile Klepper's new novel *Der Vater: Ein Roman des Soldatenkönigs* (The Father: A Novel of the Soldier-King) had been published. The book received numerous favorable reviews and sold well, especially in Prussia. Even the *Völkischer Beobachter* liked the novel. A notice from the RSK to the book trade at first had argued that it is inappropriate "for a man who is married to a Jewess with three [sic] full-blooded Jewish daughters to write about the father of Frederick the Great."[133] However the favorable reception of *Der Vater* helped Klepper's case, and on September 2 his application for a special permit to publish was approved.

Klepper now had to submit all his manuscripts for approval before printing.[134] Three works Klepper handed in during the second half of 1937 remained stuck with the censor; a collection of poems passed muster.[135] In a personal meeting at the Ministry of Propaganda he was told to keep his "psychology of solitariness" out of his writings and to minimize their "Catholic tendency,"[136] a strange reproach in view of Klepper's strong identification with Protestantism. In a letter to his friend Reinhold Schneider, written on January 15, 1938, he

The NSDAP Berlin informs the Reich Chamber of Literature that it cannot vouch for the political reliability of Jochen Klepper because he is married to a Jewess. *Courtesy Bundesarchiv Berlin-Lichterfelde*

related that the official had been especially critical of his "spiritual poems" because they reflected "a servile submission" to Christ. At stake, he added, was something that is "central to my work."[137]

To obtain the necessary clearance, Klepper had to write numerous letters, most of which he signed "Heil Hitler." The use of this greeting is said to have caused him considerable soul-searching, but he felt that it was necessary if he wanted to protect his ability to publish.[138] His attitude to the Nazi state at first had not been altogether negative. He had liked the rejection of *Asphaltliteratur*, books dealing with life in the big cities and stressing loneliness and alienation, as well as the repudiation of communism. On the other hand, he was increasingly put off by the regime's persecution of the churches and its anti-Semitism. Both policies attacked a key element of his personal identity. Klepper was a deeply religious person, and his marriage to a Jew necessarily made him reject the Nazis' crude anti-Semitism.[139] He now began to worry that he would be pressured to divorce his wife. To add to his concerns, he was advised by the RSK in July 1939 to forgo public appearances such as lectures and readings.[140]

The tightening of paper rationing that began with the outbreak of war especially affected works that the regime considered "undesirable." From 1940 on that included most of Klepper's writings, and despite strong demand by 1941 his books were completely out of print. On December 5, 1940, Klepper was conscripted for military service, but less than a year later, on October 8, 1941, he was discharged "dishonorably" because of his Jewish wife. Shortly before the war, Klepper's oldest stepdaughter had been able to emigrate, but repeated strenuous efforts to obtain such a permit also for his younger daughter were unsuccessful. Fearful that his wife and daughter would be deported, Keppler, his wife, and his daughter Renate committed suicide on December 11, 1942.

Unperturbed, the bureaucratic apparatus continued to handle the "Klepper case." On December 22 his file was marked *"Erledigt"* (Done); it also carried the handwritten reminder to "cancel the *Sondergenehmigung*." Klepper's sister Hildegard Klepper was informed on January 12, 1943, that if she intended to publish any writings of her deceased brother, she would have to obtain the permission of the RSK.[141]

After the collapse of the Third Reich, many writers asserted that they had been part of the Inner Emigration and thus in opposition to the Nazi regime. These claims were helped by the fact that few writers did not at one time or another run afoul of criticism amid the sweeping scope of Nazi censorship. These attacks could be cited after 1945 as proof of having been among the "persecuted" or at least to have been considered an undesirable author. But not everyone who was attacked by Rosenberg was therefore an opponent of Nazism. In order to be considered part of the Inner Emigration, a writer in some manner had to manifest an oppositional attitude.[142] Not everyone who wrote non-Nazi books wrote thereby anti-Nazi books. Remaining silent and unpolitical was not enough. Those who withdrew into their inner self and cultivated their private garden should not be regarded as members of the Inner Emigration.

The flight into *Innerlichkeit* (introspection) was escape and not an act of opposition.[143] A good case in point is Hermann Hesse, who from his secure haven in Switzerland asserted his political neutrality and concentrated on his literary work. For the failure to link his work to the "life and fate of his people," Hesse was criticized in 1937 by a Nazi publication.[144] Thomas Mann and other emigré writers, for their part, found fault with Hesse's endeavour to "promote peace between the warring factions" in German literature. To remain neutral in the defense of Western civilization against Nazi barbarism could not be considered a moral position.[145] For many Germans the flight into the private realm represented an attempt to block out the information about the horrors committed by the regime and to silence their conscience.[146]

The writer and poet Hans Carossa has claimed that he was able to maintain "his complete inner independence."[147] In 1933 he refused membership in the Prussian Academy of Writers, and in a letter to the wife of his publisher the same year he affirmed: "Whatever the new state will do, I will preserve my small, intellectual realm free and unattached, and I am convinced that in this way I can best serve the German people."[148] But this cautious attitude soon gave way to an increasing cooperation with the new rulers. Carossa accepted many prizes, he was an "honorary guest" at the Nuremberg party rally of 1938, and on the occasion of Hitler's birthday in 1939 he contributed a poem in which he expressed his "best wishes [Segenswunsch] for the work of the Führer."[149] On November 20, 1938, after the Anschluss of Austria and the annexation of the Sudetenland in Czechoslovakia, Carossa gave a speech at the Rosenberg organization in which he praised the Führer "whose deeds this year have brought about an enormous enlargement of the Lebensraum [living space] of the German Volksgemeinschaft [people's community]."[150] At a time when a skilled worker was earning 112 RM and Hitler's favorite architect Albert Speer 1,500 RM a month, Carossa's income from his books and readings was more than 35,000 RM.[151]

Carossa intervened with Goebbels seeking to obtain the release from a concentration camp of the German-Jewish poet Alfred Mombert, and he tried to help other writers who had run into trouble. Most of these interventions proved unsuccessful, but even if they had been crowned with success, it is unlikely that these acts of solidarity would have made up for the support Carossa provided for the Nazi regime. Carossa enjoyed widespread respect among the educated classes, and his continued publication during the Nazi era undoubtedly helped convince many in the intellectual elite that the Nazis appreciated culture and established values. Carossa, whether he liked it or not, became a valuable tool of Nazi propaganda.[152] In August 1944 Carossa was one of twenty-two writers who, on account of their prominence and usefulness as eminent figures of German literature, were exempted from compulsory labor, part of the total mobilization ordered by Goebbels.[153] Looking back upon these days, in 1962 Carossa acknowledged that his attempt to concentrate on his creative work and ignore the political events around him had been a mistake. The attempt to retreat into Innerlichkeit had been an error.[154]

Erich Kästner is another important German writer who stayed in Germany. On account of his pacifist and allegedly pornographic poems published before 1933, Kästner was denounced as a Kulturbolschewist, and all his writings, including his immensely popular books for children like Emil und die Detektive, were forbidden. It is indicative of the disorder prevailing in the cultural controls of the Nazi regime that the film *Emil und die Detektive* was still shown in 1936 and 1937. For a short time in 1941 several of Kästner's plays were again performed on German stages.[155] Yet the fact that Kästner was a banned author does not make him a member of the Inner Emigration. Goebbels considered Kästner a talented writer and agreed to give him a special permission to write for the German film production company UFA under the pseudonym Berthold Bürger.[156] In order to gain foreign currency, Kästner also was allowed to have books published abroad, and films based on these books were licensed to foreign companies. In January 1943 his *Sondergenehmigung* was withdrawn, supposedly on orders of Hitler.[157] Kästner could thereafter no longer work as an author, but he probably did not suffer hardship on that account. His work for UFA is said to have earned him 115,000 RM, enough to live on for several years.[158] Hans Fallada, the author of *Kleiner Mann, was nun?* (Little Man, What Now?), was another writer who benefited from the availability of film script work.[159]

Another example of a writer who unfairly claimed membership in the Inner Emigration is Erich Ebermayer. Six of his books written before 1933 were indeed banned, but during the Nazi era Ebermayer managed to make a good living as a screenwriter and to publish two books. One of these books was *Kampf um Deutschland: Ein Lesebuch für die deutsche Jugend* (The Struggle for Germany: A Reader for German Youth) that was published in 1938 by Franz Eher, the official publishing house of the NSDAP. Ebermayer's book *Napoleon: Kometenbahn eines Genius* (Napoleon: The Cometary Path of a Genius), published in 1941, is said to have been favorite bedtime reading of Hitler.[160]

Ebermayer was regarded as a homosexual, and was often criticized by the Rosenberg organization. But Ebermayer had the good fortune of being a cousin of Philip Bouhler, one of Hitler's trusted confidants, who protected him. Ebermayer reciprocated by calling the high-ranking SS officer, later in charge of the euthanasia program, "a thoroughly decent, good-natured, indeed noble human being."[161] Not only did Ebermayer not suffer any harm, but he was invited by people like Viktor Lutze, the head of the SA, to a garden party in June 1939 where Ebermayer danced with the wife of Hermann Göring. Before accepting an invitation for dinner at Bouhler's house he noted in his diary that he had hesitated "whether one should sit at a table with the ruling clique when one rejects the regime and the dictator ... and considers all that a disaster for Germany." But he quickly overcame his doubts with the argument that "one cannot write the chronicle of these days without using every opportunity to get to know those who today are powerful."[162] In October 1941 he complained to Johst about never having been invited to the meetings of writers in Weimar: "In view of my achievements and position in German literature, this appears to be not in order." He added that Bouhler also shared this reaction and signed the letter "with the most cordial greetings and steady devotion, Heil Hitler."[163] Ebermayer, whatever his alleged anti-Nazi views, was primarily an opportunist. To consider him a member of the Inner Emigration does not seem appropriate.

The official gazette of the RSK mentions several cases of writers who were condemned to death for treason and whose writings were therefore forbidden.[164] Under the Nazi regime even a critical utterance about the food supply could lead to a conviction for treason, and the number of individuals thus executed was in the tens of thousands. For most of these victims of the Nazis' criminal system of justice no detailed information is available, and this holds true also for the writers among them. The Protestant theologian Dietrich Bonhoeffer was hanged in April 1945 for his role in the failed plot against Hitler of July 20, 1944. From 1941 on he had been forbidden to publish. But for practically all other condemned writers we do not know whether their treasonable activities had any connection to their political attitude and their writings.

A writer's opposition to the Nazi regime could make itself visible in many different ways, and the Inner Emigration therefore was not a homogeneous group. Much depended on an author's circumstances and his personal courage. Ricarda Huch's refusal to be a member of the nazified Academy of Writers and her public statement explaining this decision made it unequivocally clear where she stood politically. Bergengruen and Jünger provided assistance to those who actively resisted the regime. Wiechert publicized his reasons for supporting the family of the courageous pastor Niemöller and paid for this with a stay in a concentration camp. On the other hand, while Jochen Klepper's fate, which eventually drove him and his family into suicide, was tragic, he probably does not thereby become part of the Inner Emigration. Neither in his writings nor in any public act did he ever express any principled objection to the Nazi regime, and there is reason to think that, in the absence of a threat to his non-Aryan wife, he would have made his peace with it. Benn was expelled from the RSK, but he never doubted the legality of Nazi rule and conducted himself accordingly.

The Catholic poet Elizabeth Langgässer, who in 1936 had been excluded from the RSK on account of her Jewish father, noted in 1947 that numerous writers now claim to have hid the true meaning of their work. They had done this so successfully, she went on to say, that Goebbels and his servants in the Ministry of Propaganda never noticed their opposition to the regime. As a result their books continued to be published and read. That of course raises the question whether the readers of these books were more perceptive than the allegedly stupid Goebbels and his fellow-censors.[165] In other words, could authors be considered to have been members of the Inner Emigration, if their rejection of the Nazi ideology was so subtle and well hidden as not to be noticed by any of their readers, whether friend or foe?

As we have seen earlier, there were writers during the Nazi era who used Aesopian language with the intent to communicate a political message. Bergengruen's *Der Grosstyrann und das Gericht* and Jünger's *Auf den Marmorklippen* are cases in point. Another example is Rudolf Pechel's magazine *Deutsche Rundschau,* which managed to be published until 1942. In a retrospective of 1961 Pechel acknowledged that some of the journal's articles did not adhere to the anti-Nazi outlook of the *Deutsche Rundschau,*[166] but he leaves it unclear whether these failures were the result of ideological missteps or concessions to protect the journal from its enemies. For example, the lead article in the April 1938 issue celebrated the *Anschluss* of Austria, accomplished by the Third Reich and its Führer, as a step to a general European peace.[167] However it is a matter of record that the *Deutsche Rundschau* was able to publish carefully camouflaged articles that conveyed criticism of the Nazi regime. For example, in September 1937 a book review of *Die Verlorenen* (The Lost) by Iwan Solonewitsch appeared under the title *"Siberien"* (Siberia). The author had spent time in various Soviet penal camps and eventually had managed to reach the West. The review recounted Solonewitsch's description of Stalin's tyranny and included the following comment: "From Peisistratus to Napoleon and Stalin, the same events repeat themselves in history. With the advance of technology, only the methods become more refined and accentuated." Even though the statement in itself was unexceptionable, its political potential was right below the surface. By adding the name of Hitler to those of Peisistratus, Napoleon, and Stalin, the reader had a perfect description of Nazi terror.[168] Eventually Pechel's luck ran out with an article on Germany's news coverage that was read as an implied criticism of Goebbels. Pechel and his wife were arrested and ended up in a concentration camp. They survived to tell the tale.[169]

The *Neue Rundschau,* under the editorship of Peter Suhrkamp (publisher of the aryanized S. Fischer publishing house), was another serial publication that was able to hide its non-conformist intentions. It continued to note the birthdays of emigrated writers; "forgetting" to take cognizance of Hitler's birthday in 1939 almost led to its demise. On April 13, 1944, Suhrkamp, accused of high treason, was arrested and sent to the Oranienburg concentration camp. He outlasted the ordeal, and in October 1945 Suhrkamp received the first publishing license issued in the defeated Germany by the British Military Government.[170]

The quandary of the Inner Emigration writers was that if their rejection of the Nazi dictatorship was too obvious, it would lead to the banning of the book in question. On the other hand, if their political message was too covert, it might not be noticed. In some instances, as in the case of Jochen Klepper's novel *Der Vater,* a book might defend the values of humanism and decency, but the author was not explicit enough and the book therefore drew the praise of the Nazi media. Bergengruen's *Der Grosstyrann und das Gericht* was lauded by the *Völkischer Beobachter.*[171] Moreover, the very fact that these writers continued to be active as authors had undesirable consequences. It is undisputed that even the best of the best, as Sebastian Haffner put it, "played a small part in Goebbels' orchestra."[172] That their works could be published and sold, helped to prove "to observers in Germany and abroad that National Socialism itself was equally respectable and cultured and operated as a counter-weight to the horror stories about the new Germany's intellectual and cultural barbarity."[173] The more prestigious these writers were, the more beneficial to the Nazis was their staying in Germany. Whether they liked or not, all of them functioned as an *Aushängeschild* (advertisement) for a regime of infamy.

It might be argued that this unintended role of shoring up Nazi rule was counterbalanced by the good the writers of the Inner Emigration did through the encouragement they provided to readers badly in need of moral sustenance. Many individuals who lived through the era of the Third Reich and who are of impeccable political integrity, have spoken of the comfort and solace they derived from certain books, written by authors like Bergengruen and Jünger. But in the final analysis we do not know how many readers did indeed understand what these writers wanted to say "between the lines," whether their readership comprehended the allegorical language or simply enjoyed the work as an unpolitical good book.[174]

All this leaves us with a dilemma: If we do not know the impact of the books written by the members of the Inner Emigration, we are unable to draw a balance sheet between their salutary and harmful roles in the Nazi era. Both of these roles are well established, but we cannot tell which of the two was more important. We are left with the rather unsatisfactory prosaic conclusion that the Inner Emigration, like so much in human life, was a force for good as well as for bad.

14

Conclusion

The Nazi revolution claimed to be a movement for radical change in all spheres of life, and that necessarily included the realm of culture. In his speech to the Reichstag on March 23, 1933, Hitler promised to work for a thoroughgoing moral renewal, and art and literature would be used in this endeavor. Blood and race were to become sources of artistic creativity. In place of the anarchic individualism that had prevailed during the Weimar Republic, it was expected that in the new Germany those active in the sphere of culture would subordinate their individual lives to the good of the nation. Just as the state as a matter of course protected the citizens' bodies, the government was held to have the duty to guard their souls against cultural bacilli in the form of corrosive literature and to make sure that everyone absorbed the National Socialist ideology. Hence the need to safeguard the political reliability of writers and to control their publications. Several hundred German writers and scholars, who were unwilling to give up their intellectual freedom, left their homeland, and among these emigrés were some of the best-known figures of German literature such as Heinrich and Thomas Mann and Arnold and Stefan Zweig. The result was an irreplaceable loss for German culture.

The control of books at first consisted of post-publication censorship. Given the high cost of misjudging the designs of the censors and bringing out an objectionable book, it is not surprising that publishers engaged in extensive self-censorship. After 1939, as a result of the increased vigilance thought to be necessary in time of war, the censors increasingly resorted to prior restraint. This meant that entire categories of books became subject to what was known as *Anmeldepflicht* (duty to submit books for vetting). From June 1941 on publishers had to apply for approval of the necessary paper and binding material for each book they planned to publish, thus making the allocation of paper an instrument of censorship for the entire production of books.

The censorship of books as well as decisions on who would be allowed to be a writer were in the hands of politically reliable state and party officials, many of whom had no special education, training, or competence for this work.

Karl-Heinz Hederich, the deputy head of the PPK, for example, had a degree in engineering. For these men (there were no women in these positions), the safe mode of operation was to follow the maxim: "Better to forbid one book too many than one book too few." If we add to this the claim for the total domination of the world of ideas inherent in the Nazi ideology, we can begin to understand why censorship during the Nazi era encompassed such a large segment of German book production. By 1938, 4,175 book titles had been banned, and in the case of 564 authors all of their writings had been forbidden. According to a tabulation undertaken by the Deutsche Bücherei in Leipzig in 1949, a total of 5,485 book titles were banned between 1933 and 1945.

The range of offending subjects was wide. Objectionable categories included alleged moral corruption, Marxist or pacifist tendencies, damaging the martial spirit and morale of the German people, propagating Catholic or other confessional ideas, being a Jew, and finally the catch-all designation of "failure to live up to what was to be expected in the new Germany." Scientific works were supposed to be free of censorship (unless the minister of education requested it), but the RSK felt free to disregard this provision, and not a few works of historical scholarship were put on the state Index. After six years of Nazi rule, an official in the Ministry of Propaganda noted that scholars stayed away from topics that required them to submit their work to the censors, and he blamed the aggressive censorship of the PPK in particular for the collapse of research in the humanities. Until the onset of war in 1939, an average of about 300 writers a year were expelled from the RSK or their applications for admission were denied, thus preventing them from exercising their chosen profession, and these exclusions continued apace until the collapse of the regime. Some publishers lost more than half of their book titles to the censor. Rohwohlt experienced the loss of 70 of its 130 titles. Gustav Kiepenheuer forfeited almost three-quarters of its total production.

And yet, as many students of Nazi society have noted, there was some "space for art and culture."[1] This space was the result of the limited effectiveness of the Nazi state, which claimed to be a well-oiled super state, total in its reach, but actually consisted of rival state and party agencies feuding with each other. Hitler could have ordered a clearer demarcation of competencies, but such orders were never issued. The creation of overlapping authorities was quite deliberate and aimed at preventing any challenge to his superior leadership. There is general agreement that never in the history of Germany was the state organized more chaotically than during the Third Reich. It was totalitarian in its aspirations but polycratic in practice, and this condition was particularly egregious in regard to the control of books.

Because censorship was exercised by several competing authorities, conflicting assessments of books were a frequent occurrence. None of the rival bureaucracies was able to achieve a monopoly of control. The marginalization of Jews and the suppression of outright opposition to the regime were the low-est common denominator, but beyond that there existed no uniform standard to govern censorship. This situation resulted in gaps that enterprising and cou-rageous individuals could benefit from or exploit. A report issued by Hellmuth Langenbucher in the Rosenberg office, issued in 1941, acknowledged the sur-vival of a "literary clique," the members of which produce writings without the requisite "proximity to the people of our time." Listed among this cabal were such authors as Stefan Andres, Werner Bergengruen, and Horst Lange.[2] The work of Ernst Jünger and Ernst Wiechert also drew criticism, but apart from occasional difficulties they were able to keep publishing. Goebbels was known to be a bit more tolerant of independent styles of writing then Rosenberg and Bouhler. The writings of Hans Fallada, the author of *Kleiner Mann was nun?*, were frequently attacked as corrosive by Rosenberg's men, but Fallada was able to continue writing his realistic novels because Goebbels liked them. Wiechert's novel *Das einfache Leben* apparently was able to see the light of day for the same reason.

The purge of the public libraries was effective, but that of bookstores and commercial lending libraries somewhat less so. The repeated admonitions in the confidential gazette of the RSK and other official journals to observe the regulations about banned books show that some owners and librarians suc-ceeded in evading the total control the censors were seeking to impose. After the collapse of the Nazi regime many writers invoked the severity of censorship as an excuse for their own subservience. But this represents special pleading. No author, it should be remembered, was forced to write anything he did not want to write. Every author could escape a dilemma of conscience by giving up his privileged status and becoming a common laborer or soldier. Finally, as Oda Schaefer, the wife of the stigmatized Horst Lange, insisted in her memoir, even under the harsh conditions of Nazi rule there existed a sphere of circumscribed space that a resolute person could use to create literature with a hidden politi-cal message.[3]

The number of such brave individuals was small, though their writings are said to have provided many readers with moral sustenance. It was comfort-ing, many witnesses confirm, to read books that displayed uncorrupted human beings and moral standards that the regime had repudiated. Unfortunately, for every Werner Bergengruen and Ricarda Huch there were numerous other German writers who made their peace with the Nazi regime. Most of the many hundreds of authors who were expelled from the RSK were excluded not because they were anti-Nazi but because their writings failed to meet the often ill-defined standards of political orthodoxy set by the censors. The purge and reorganization of the professional organizations for writers, book dealers, and librarians could be carried out in such a short period and with no discernible opposition because the large majority of the members of these organizations were predisposed to take a benevolent view of the National Socialist cause. Disappointed by the politics and culture of the Weimar Republic, they welcomed what presented itself as a national and cultural revolution, and they participated in this apparent renewal gladly and often with enthusiasm. When the dream of a new Germany began to fail and the brutal downside of Nazi rule became apparent, a widespread reaction was to close one's eyes and retreat into *Innerlichkeit* (introspection).

After the end of the Third Reich, some honest individuals acknowledged the failure of the country's cultural elite to prevent the barbarities that had taken place. The librarians of the public libraries, one of their ranks acknowledged in 1947, committed "intellectual suicide" and failed to uphold the ethics of their profession.[4] On the other hand, many writers at that point claimed to have been part of the Inner Emigration and passed quietly over their opportunism and acquiescence. The more prestigious these authors were, the more beneficial it was to the Nazi regime for them to remain in Germany, for their presence helped prove to observers at home and abroad that National Socialism was respectable and cultured. Whether they liked it or not, all of them functioned as an *Aushängeschild* (advertising) for an evil regime. The point here is not to castigate these writers for their failure to resist. Few human beings are heroes willing to stand up for abstract ideals if their life or livelihood is at stake. Few of us have been put to the test that Nazi rule imposed upon Germany's intellectuals. And yet it must also be acknowledged that certain cultural attitudes, like excessive respect for authority and equating that which is legal with what is moral, were especially pronounced in Germany. Hence it is not enough to invoke the general weakness of human nature. Certain additional and specifically German factors help explain the widespread support for the Nazi regime and the weakness of the opposition to the horrors that occurred.

The end of the Third Reich did not mean the end of book censorship in Germany. All the victorious Allies carefully monitored the emerging book market and banned writings seen to be in sympathy with the defeated Nazi regime and its ideology. The East German communist regime eagerly revived the idea of literature subordinated to politics. The constitution of the German Democratic Republic (GDR) supposedly guaranteed freedom of expression, and the office of the censor carried the innocent name "Head Administration for Publishing and the Book Trade" (*Hauptverwaltung Verlage und Buchhandel*). In fact, censorship for the most part was tight and effective, drawing strength from the self-censorship practiced by authors and the editors of publishing houses, and, when necessary, being enforced by the Stasi, the secret police. The censors were sophisticated authors, scholars, and critics, all of them loyal members of the Communist Party (formally called Socialist Unity Party of Germany) and committed to *Parteilichkeit* (Party-ness), a GDR superlative indicating adherence to the Party line.[5]

In the American zone of occupation, prepublication censorship forbade books that criticized any Allied government or propagated National Socialist or anti-democratic ideas.[6] On the basis of Allied Control Authority no. 4, "Confiscation of Literature and Material of a Nazi and Militarist Nature," issued on May 13, 1946, thousands of books and textbooks were seized and destroyed. Some of the banned works apparently were quite harmless, and *Time* magazine called it a revival of Nazi methods.[7] According to the Basic Law (*Grundgesetz*) of the Federal Republic of Germany, seeking to learn from the failings of the Weimar Republic, there is no freedom of expression for false statements of fact that threaten the stability of German society. Under a law enacted in 1994, there have been 315 convictions for Holocaust denial, and, in most of these cases the state has confiscated and destroyed the offending books or pamphlets.[8] Outlawing Holocaust denial is a limited measure aimed at right-wing extremists and cannot be compared to the systems of censorship practiced by the totalitarian regimes of the twentieth century. Nevertheless, the practice must be considered foreign to our conception of individual freedom. It is strikingly different from the near-absolute protection of freedom of expression under the First Amendment of the U.S. Constitution.

Today, some seventy years after the defeat of Nazi Germany, a new generation has taken charge in the reunited Germany. This truly new Germany has come to terms with its Nazi past in an exemplary manner. It is hard to imagine that today's Germans would be taken in by the rousing demagogic oratory of a Hitler or Goebbels in the way an earlier generation was enticed. If anything, the people of the Federal Republic of Germany today incline toward pacifism rather than militant nationalism, to philo-Semitism rather than anti-Semitism. It may take some time before Germany will have fully overcome the trauma of Nazi rule and be prepared to resume its place as a normal and responsible member of the world community.

ABBREVIATIONS AND GLOSSARY

Asphaltliteratur	term used by the Nazis to denigrate literature that dealt with life in the big cities, with undue emphasis on loneliness and alienation
BA	Bundesarchiv
Bbl.	*Börsenblatt für den deutschen Buchhandel*
BDC	Berlin Document Center
Beratungsstelle	advisory office, usually a euphemism for an office exercising censorship
Berufsverbot	order forbidding the practice of one's profession
Blutorden	Blood Medal (the medal bestowed upon the participants in the unsuccessful Nazi putsch in Munich on November 9, 1923)
BRB	Bund Reichdeutscher Buchhändler (League of German Book Dealers)
col.	column
DAF	Deutsche Arbeitsfront (German Labor Front)
DSt	Deutsche Studentenschaft (German Student Organization)
Entjudung	eliminating the influence of Jews
Fachbuch	technical book
Fachschaft	section
Fr.	frame
Gauleitung	leadership of a NSDAP Gau (party district)
Gestapa	Geheimes Staatspolizeiamt (Head Office of the Secret State Police)
Gestapo	Geheime Staatspolizei (Secret State Police)
Gleichschaltung	compulsory reorganization to bring institutions or organizations under Nazi control

Grundliste	basic list of recommended books, also known as "White List"
Gutachten	expert assessment
HJ	Hitlerjugend (Hitler Youth)
Kampfbund	Kampfbund für deutsche Kultur (Fighting League for German Culture)
Lektor	reader or editor
Lektorat	editorial office
n.p.	no pagination
NSB	Nationalsozialistische Bibliographie
NSDAP	Nationalsozialistische deutsche Arbeiter Partei (National Socialist German Workers Party)
NSDStB	Nationalsozialistischer deutscher Studentenbund (National Socialist League of German Students)
NSLB	Nationalsozialistischer Lehrerbund (National Socialist League of Teachers)
OKW	Oberkommando der Wehrmacht (High Command of the Armed Forces)
par.	paragraph
Pg.	Parteigenosse (Party comrade)
PPK	Parteiamtliche Prüfungskommission zum Schutze des nationalsozialistischen Schrifttums (Official Party Commission for the Protection of German Literature)
RDS	Reichsverband deutscher Schriftsteller (German Association of Authors)
Reichsleiter	the highest-ranking Nazi party official
Reichsstelle für ...	Reich (National) Office for ...
RFdS	Reichsstelle zur Förderung des deutschen Schrifttums (Reich Office for the Promotion of German Literature)
RGBl.	*Reichsgesetzblatt* (German Law Gazette)
RKK	Reichskulturkammer (German Chamber of Culture)
RMfE	Reichsministerium für Wissenschaft, Erziehung, und Volksbildung (German Ministry of Science and Education)
RMfVP	Reichsministerium für Volksaufklärung und Propaganda (German Ministry of Popular Enlightenment and Propaganda)
RMI	Reichsministerium des Innern (German Ministry of the Interior)
RSHA	Reichssicherheitshauptamt (German Main Security Office)
RSK	Reichsschrifttumskammer (Reich Chamber of Literature)

SA	Sturm Abteilung (lit., Storm Detachment, the paramilitary organization of the Nazi party)
Schrifttum	literature
Schrifttumsamt	Office of Literature
SD	Sicherheitsdienst (lit., Security Service, the intelligence service of the Reichsführer-SS)
SDS	Schutzverband deutscher Schriftsteller (Association for the Protection of German Authors)
Sondergenehmigung	special permission
SPD	Sozialdemokratische Partei Deutschlands (German Social Democratic Party)
SS	Schutzstaffel (lit., Shield Squadron, the Nazi party's elite force)
Überwachungsstelle	Supervisory Office
VDB	Verein deutscher Bibliothekare (Organization of German Librarians)
VDV	Verband deutscher Volksbibliothekare (Association of German Public Librarians)
Völkische	militant nationalists
Volksgemeinschaft	Community of the *Volk* (People)
Wirtschaftsstelle	Economic Office

NOTES

Chapter 1

1. RGBl. 1919, no. 152, pp. 1383–1418.
2. Klaus Petersen, *Zensur in der Weimarer Republik*, p. 182.
3. Jan-Pieter Barbian, *Literaturpolitik im "Dritten Reich": Institutionen, Kompetenzen, Betätigungsfelder*, p. 51.
4. Ibid., p. 280.
5. Dietrich Aigner, "Die Indizierung 'schädlichen und unerwünschten' Schrifttums im Dritten Reich," *Archiv für Geschichte des Buchwesens* 11 (1971): col. 948.
6. RGBl. I 1926, p. 505. Cf. Detlev Peukert, "Der Schund- und Schmutzkampf als 'Sozialpolitik der Seele,' Eine Vorgeschichte der Bücherverbrennung," in *"Das war ein Vorspiel nur…" Bücherverbrennung Deutschland 1933*, ed. Hermann Haartmann, pp. 52–53; Aigner, "Indizierung," p. 948–49.
7. The term *völkisch* derives from the word *Volk* (people) but has connotations of militant nationalism, racism, and anti-Semitism.
8. Alfred Rosenberg, "Aufruf," *Der Weltkampf* 5 (1928): 210–12.
9. Goebbels' blacklist included the Jewish theater critic Alfred Kerr. See his *Die Welt im Licht*, ed. Friedrich Luft, p. 386.
10. Wilhelm Frick, "Thüringische Bilanz," *Nationalsozialistisches Jahrbuch* 6 (1932): 212.
11. Dieter Breuer, *Geschichte der literarischen Zensur in Deutschland*, pp. 231–32; Barbian, *Literaturpolitk im "Dritten Reich,"* pp. 65–70.
12. RGBl. I p. 91.
13. Martin Broszat, *The Hitler State: The Foundation and Development of the Internal Structure of the Third Reich*, trans. John W. Hiden, p. 12.

Chapter 2

1. Hans Buchheim et al., eds., *Anatomie des SS-Staates*, vol. 2, pp. 20–22.
2. RGBl. 1933 I, p. 141.
3. Gerd Rühle, ed., *Das Dritte Reich: Dokumentarische Darstellung des Aufbaus der Nation*, vol. 1: 1933, p. 68.
4. Julius H. Schoeps and Werner Tress, *Orte der Bücherverbrennungen in Deutschland 1933*, pp. 15–19; Gerhard Sauder, ed., *Die Bücherverbrennung: Zum 10. Mai 1933* (Munich, 1986), p. 106; Fridolin Dressler, "Die Bayerische Staatsbibliothek im Dritten Reich," in *Beiträge zur Geschichte der Bayerischen Staatsbibliothek*, ed. Rupert Hacker, p. 293.
5. BA, NS 38/2416, p. 3; Friedmann Berger et al., eds., *In jenen Tagen—Schriftsteller zwischen Reichstagsbrand und Bücherverbrennung: Eine Dokumentation*, p. 267.
6. Berger et al., eds., *In jenen Tagen*, pp. 267–69.
7. Schoeps and Tress, *Orte der Bücherverbrennungen*, pp. 193–94.

8. Gertrud Kannengiesser, *Die Bibliothek der Technischen Hochschule Braunschweig wie ich sie erlebt habe 1928–1962*, p. 28.

9. Sauder, ed., *Bücherverbrennung*, p. 162.

10. Aigner, "*Indizierung*," col. 940.

11. BA, NS 38/2416, p. 26.

12. BA, NS 38/2416, p. 4. See also Volker Weidermann, *Das Buch der verbrannten Bücher*, p. 16.

13. BA, NS 38/2416, pp. 7, 16–25. On April 26 Alfred Hugenberg's paper *Nachtausgabe* published a list of thirty-four books that deserved "to be burned." The blacklist for fiction is also reproduced in Weidermann, *Das Buch der verbrannten Bücher*, pp. 246–53, and on the official web site of the city of Berlin, http://www.berlin.de/rubrik/hauptstadt/verbannte_buecher/schwarze_liste.php.

14. "Zersetzende Schriften auf den Scheiterhaufen," *Deutsche Allgemeine Zeitung*, April 26, 1933, quoted in Sauder, ed., *Bücherverbrennung*, p. 114.

15. "Die Entfernung des undeutschen Schrifttums aus den öffentlichen und privaten Leihbüchereien," *Zeitschrifte der Leihbücherei*, special edition May 5, 1933, BA, NS 38/2416, p. 67.

16. BA, NS 38/2416, p. 44.

17. BA, NS 38/2416, I, pp. 46, 48.

18. Schoeps and Tress, *Orte der Bücherverbrennungen*, pp. 115–18.

19. For the full text of the nine pronouncements and the speech of Goebbels see Joseph Wulf, *Literatur und Dichtung im Dritten Reich: Eine Dokumentation*, pp. 49–51.

20. Sauder, ed., *Die Bücherverbrennung*, p. 250.

21. Erika Elschenbroich et al., eds., *Wissenschaft und Kunst im Exil—Vorgeschichte, Durchführung und Folgen der Bücherverbrennung: Eine Dokumentation*, pp. 95–96.

22. Michael Kuhn, ed., *Verbrannte Bücher: Verzeichnis der Bücher, die 1933 aus dem Bestand der TH Braunschweig aussortiert und zum grössten Teil vernichtet wurden*, pp. 1–2.

23. Stephan Füssel, "Wider den undeutschen Geist: Bücherverbrennung und Bibilliotheks-lenkung im Nationalsozialismus," in *Göttingen unterm Hakenkreuz*, ed. by Jens-Uwe Brinkmann and Hans-Georg Schmeling, pp. 98–99.

24. Reports on the book burnings in Cologne, Hamburg, Munich, Nuremberg, and Würzburg as described by local newspapers can be found in Wulf, *Literatur und Dichtung im Dritten Reich*.

25. Sauder, ed., *Die Bücherverbrennung*, p. 79.

26. Schoeps and Tress, *Orte der Bücherverbrennungen*, pp. 21–23.

27. Ibid., pp. 127, 699.

28. Alois Klotzbücher, "Städtische Bibliotheken im Ruhrgebiet während des National-sozialismus," in *Bibliotheken während des Nationalsozialismus*, ed. by Peter Vodosek and Manfred Komorowski, vol. 2, p. 57.

29. They are listed in Schoeps and Tress, *Orte der Bücherverbrennungen*, pp. 5–6.

30. Joachim Kirchner, "Schrifttum und wissenschaftliche Bibliotheken im nationalsozialis-tischen Deutschland," *Zentralblatt für Bibliothekswesen* 50 (1933): 514–15.

31. Werner Schlegel, *Dichter auf dem Scheiterhaufen*, pp. 50–52, cited by Jan Pieter Barbian, *Die vollendete Ohnmacht: Schriftsteller, Verleger und Buchhändler im NS-Staat: Ausgewählte Aufsätze*, p. 61.

32. Hans W. Hagen, *Deutsche Dichtung in der Entscheidung der Gegenwart*, p. 11.

33. Klaus Schöffling, ed., *Dort wo man Bücher verbrennt: Stimmen der Betroffenen*, p. 144.

34. Rudolf Geck, "Scheiterhaufen," *Frankfurter Zeitung*, May 20, 1933, quoted in Horst Denkler and Eberhard Lämmer, "*Das war ein Vorspiel nur …: Berliner Colloquium zur Literaturpolitik im Dritten Reich*, p. 202.

35. *Börsenblatt für den deutschen Buchhandel* (hereafter Bbl.) vol. 100, no. 110 (May 13, 1933), p. 1.

36. Molly Guptill Manning, *When Books Went to War: The Stories That Helped Us Win World War II*, p. 5.

37. The text of Graf's protest is reproduced in Schöffling, ed., *Dort wo man Bücher verbrennt*, pp. 661–62.

38. Quoted in Reiner Wild et al., eds., *Dennoch leben sie: Verfemte Bücher, verfolgte Autorinnen und Autoren—Zu den Auswirkungen nationalsozialistischer Literaturpolitik*, p. 113.

39. Philip Friedman, *Roads to Extinction: Essays on the Holocaust*, p. 88.

40. In the German original: "Das war ein Vorspiel nur, dort wo man Bücher verbrennt, verbrennt man auch am Ende Menschen."

41. Adolf von Morzé, "Verlust des Bildungsreiches: Volksbibliothekare im Nationalsozialismus," *Buch und Bibliothek* 39 (1987): 113.

42. Weidermann, *Buch der verbrannten Bücher*, pp. 17–19; Gerndt Kunze, *Hermann Stresau und Max Wieser: Zum Beispiel bibliothekarischen Zeitgeistes während der Nazidiktatur*, pp. 49–52.

Chapter 3

1. Speech at the opening of the Reich Chamber of Culture, October 15, 1933, cited in *Der nationalsozialistische Staat*, edited by Walther Gehl, p. 139.

2. Karl Heinz Hederich, "Parteiamtliche Prüfungskommission und Buch," *Die Welt des Buches: 1938*: 208.

3. Reichsministerium für Volksaufklärung und Propaganda, *Das Buch ein Schwert des Geistes: Erste Grundliste für den deutschen Leihbuchhandel.* New editions appeared in 1941 and 1943.

4. Jan-Pieter Barbian, "Die Beherrschung der Musen: Kulturpolitik im 'Dritten Reich'," in *Hitler's Künstler: Die Kultur im Dienste des Nationalsozialismus*, edited by Hans Sarkowicz, pp. 68–72.

5. Ian Kershaw, *Hitler 1889–1936: Hubris*, p. 271.

6. Quoted in Robert S. Wistrich, *Who's Who in Nazi Germany*, p. 98.

7. RGBl. 1933 I, p. 104. The text is reproduced in Wilhelm Ihde, ed., *Handbuch der Reichsschrifttumskammer*, p. 1.

8. *Verordnung über die Aufgaben des Reichsministeriums für Volksaufklärung und Propaganda*, June 30, 1933, in RGBl. 1933 I, p. 449; Ihde, ed., *Handbuch der Reichsschrifttumskammer*, pp. 1–2.

9. Cf. Peter Diehl-Thiele, *Partei und Staat im Dritten Reich*, 2nd rev. edition, p. 7.

10. Volker Dahm, "The Limits of Literary Life in the Third Reich," in *Flight of Fantasy: New Perspectives on Inner Emigration in German Literature 1933–1945*, edited by Neil H. Donahue and Doris Kirchner, p. 172.

11. Heinz Wismann, "Schrifttumsförderung," *Der deutsche Schriftsteller* 1 (1936): 121.

12. BA (formerly BDC), Baur to Hinkel, August 30, 1935, RK B6, fr. 2808. This film also contains other relevant letters.

13. Cf. Jan-Pieter Barbian, *Literaturpolitik im NS-Staat: Von der "Gleichschaltung" bis zum Ruin*, p. 89.

14. Elke Fröhlich, ed., *Die Tagebücher von Joseph Goebbels*, part I, vol. 4, p. 324.

15. Karl-Heinz Hederich, *Nationalsozialismus und Buch.*

16. BA, NS 8/171, p. 57.

17. Barbian, *Literaturpolitik im NS-Staat*, pp. 89–92.

18. BA, R 56 V/158, pp. 4–5.

19. Head of Department VIII to Goebbels, December 17, 1934, BA, R 56 V/158, pp. 23–24.

20. BA, R 56 V/158, pp. 26–29.

21. See the discussion in BA, R 2/4921, pp. 6–19.

22. BA, R 3001/21507, pp. 24–26.

23. BA, R 3001/21507, pp. 31–32. The ordinance is reprinted in all editions of the *Liste des schädlichen und unerwünschten Schrifttums.*

24. BA, R 43II/479, p. 76.

25. BA, R 3001/21507, p. 42.

26. See, e.g., BA, R 56 V/1086, n.p.

27. BA, R 43 II/1150, pp. 9–12.

28. BA 43 II/1150, p. 21.

29. BA, R 2/4750, pp. 36–37.

30. Fröhlich. ed., *Die Tagebücher von Joseph Goebbels*, Part I, vol. 3/II, p. 77.
31. Cited by Hans-Dieter Graf, "Nationalsozialistische Schrifttumspolitik: Goebbels' Weg zur Oberaufsicht über die Presse- und Buchverbotswesen im Dritten Reich," *Buchhandelsgeschichte* 33 (1991): B118, n. 58.
32. BA, R 56 V/67, p. 19.
33. "Mitteilung der Reichsschrifttumskammer (Buchverbote)," *Zeitschrift der Leihbücherei*, vol. 9, no. 23 (December 10, 1940): 1.
34. BA, R 56 V/352, n.p.
35. Barbian, *Literaturpolitk im NS-Staat*, pp. 56–66. See also Wistrich, *Who's Who in Nazi Germany*, p. 190.
36. Willi A. Boelcke, ed. *"Wollt Ihr den totalen Krieg?" Die geheimen Goebbels-Konferenzen 1939–1943*, p. 7.
37. Department VIII memo of November 22, 1937, BA, R 55/166, p. 339.
38. Fröhlich. ed., *Die Tagebücher von Joseph Goebbels*, Part I, vol. 5, p. 93.
39. Announcement no. 127, in Ihde, ed., *Handbuch der Reichsschrifttumskammer*, p. 44.
40. BA, R 56 V/158, p. 22.

Chapter 4

1. Karl Friedrich Schrieber, *Die Reichkulturkammer: Organisation und Ziele der deutschen Kulturpolitik*, p. 14.
2. Hugo Koch, "Die Bekämpfung des schädlichen und unerwünschten Schrifttums," *Jahrbuch des Grossdeutschen Leihbuchhandels* 1941, p. 149.
3. Goebbels in Weimar on October 25, 1936, cited in Barbian, *Literaturpolitik im NS-Staat*, p. 324.
4. "Grundgedanken für die Errichtung einer Reichkulturkammer." BA, R 2/4870, pp. 4–7.
5. Helmut Erler, *Das rechtliche Wesen der Reichskulturkammer*, p. 67.
6. RGBl. 1933 I, p. 661, reprinted in Ihde, *Handbuch der Reichsschrifttumskammer*, p. 5.
7. "Amtliche Begründung zum Reichskulturkammergesetz," in ibid., pp. 6–7.
8. RGBl. 1933 I, p. 797, reprinted in Ihde, *Handbuch der Reichsschrifttumskammer*, pp. 8–12.
9. "Amtliche Begründung zum Reichskulturkammergesetz," in ibid., p. 7.
10. Quoted in Walter Gehl, ed., *Der nationalsozialistische Staat*, p. 139.
11. Gunther Haupt, *Was erwarten wir von der kommenden Dichtung?* p. 6.
12. H.T., "Fünf Jahre Reichskulturkammergesetz," *Börsenblatt für den deutschen Buchhandel*, Bbl. 105 (1938): 733.
13. BA, R 56 V/73, p. 19.
14. Reichsverband deutscher Schriftsteller, "Rundschreiben 1/33, July 22, 1933," *Der Schriftsteller* 21 (1933): 93–97.
15. "Die Eingliederung in die Reichsschrifttumskammer," *Buchhändler im neuen Reich* 2 (1937): 28.
16. "Mitteilung an alle buchhändlerischen Mitglieder der Reichsschrifttumskammer," BA, R 58/1106, p. 49.
17. Ordinance no. 88, April 1, 1937, Ihde, *Handbuch der Reichsschrifttumskammer*, p. 249.
18. Paul Hövel, *Wesen und Aufbau der Schrifttumsarbeit in Deutschland*, p. 10. Figures for June 15, 1942, can be found at BA, R 56 V/51, p. 168. By that time the total number of RSK members had been reduced to 29,996, with the largest decline among authors.
19. Hans Hinkel, ed., *Handbuch der Reichskulturkammer*, p. 136.
20. [A] Klüber, "Die Organisation der Schrifttumüberwachung," *Bbl.* 101 (1934): 769.
21. *Vertrauliche Mitteilungen der Fachschaft Verlag*, no. 24 (July 6, 1937), p. 8.
22. This requirement was republished in *Vertrauliche Mitteilungen der Fachschaft Verlag*, no. 57 (November 8, 1940): 1. According to Barbian, *Literaturpolitk im NS-Staat*, p. 239, the announcement was aimed at catching confessional publications.
23. Gestapa to Buchhandlung Gsellius, July 16, 1935, BA, R 58/901, p. 68.
24. RSK letter of February 22, 1938, RK B 124, p. 356.
25. BA, R 56 V/96, p. 125.

26. BA, NS 8/178, p. 93.

27. "Zur Eleitung," *Nationalsozialistische Bibliographie*, no. 2 (1938), p. 1.

28. BA, NS 6/227, pp. 32–33.

29. Lemberg, *Verboten und nicht verbrannt*, vol. 2, p. 36.

30. RMfVP to RSK, October 21, 1939, BA, R 56 V/215, file 1, n.p.

31. RMfVP to RSK, September 15, 1939, BA, R 56V/216, file 5, n.p.

32. Revised order no. 88, February 15, 1942, Ihde, *Handbuch der Reichsschrifttumskammer*, p. 249.

33. Ihde to Johst, November 1943, BA, R 56 V/26, p. 5.

34. Ihde to Johst, October 22, 1943, BA, R 56 V/26, p. 20.

35. The lengthy proceedings, which included an appeal to Hitler, can be found in BA, R 58/907, pp. 88–145.

36. Sabine Röttig, "'. . . bleiben Sie wie bisher in Dichters Landen und nähren Sie sich redlich:' Der Gustav Kiepenheuer Verlag 1933–1949," *Archiv für Geschichte des Buchwesens* 58 (2004): 18.

37. Cornelia Caroline Funke, "*Im Verleger verkörpert sich das Gesicht seiner Zeit: Unternehmungsführung und Programmgestaltung im Gustav Kiepenheuer Verlag 1909 bis 1944*, p. 220.

38. Lachmann to KfDK, February 21, 1934, BA, R 55/684, p. 10.

39. Heinz Sarkowski and Wolfgang Jeske, *Der Insel Verlag 1899–1999: Die Geschichte des Verlags*, p. 305.

40. Barbian, *Literaturpolitik im NS-Staat*, p. 413.

41. Volker Dahm, *Das jüdische Buch im Dritten Reich*, p. 371.

42. See, e.g., RSK to Höfling, October 11, 1937, BA, R 56 V/217, file 1, n.p.

43. Curt Zschäpe to Johst, March 30, 1938, BA, R 56 V/19, p. 14.

44. Bbl. 100 (December 7, 1933): 949.

45. "Einiges über die Reichsschrifttumskammer," Bbl. 101 (March 13, 1934): 225–26.

46. Hans-Friedrich Blunck, *Unwegsame Zeiten: Lebensbericht*, vol. 1, p. 186.

47. *Zeitschrift der Leihbücherei*, vol 7, no. 17 (September 10, 1938), pp. 6–9.

48. Cited in Ka-Uwe Scholz, "Chamälon oder die vielen Gesichter des Hans-Friedrich Blunck," in *Dann waren die Sieger da: Studien zur literarischen Kultur in Hamburg*, edited by Ludwig Fischer et al., p. 142.

49. "Liste der vom Arbeitseinsatz freizustellenden Autoren," August 24, 1944, BA, R 56 V/152, p. 132.

50. BA, R 55/21894, p. 12.

51. Blunck, *Unwegsame Zeiten*, p. 346.

52. Volker Dahm, "Künstler als Funktionäre: Das Propagandaministerium und die Reichskulturkammer," in *Hitler's Künstler: Die Kultur im Dienste des Nationalsozialismus*, edited by Hans Sarkowicz, p. 90.

53. Rolf Düsterberg, *Hanns Johst—"Der Barde der SS: Karriere eines deutschen Dichters*, pp. 249, 276.

54. Düsterberg, *Hanns Johst*, pp. 248, 227, 221.

55. Peter Fritzsche, *Life and Death in Nazi Germany*, p. 164.

56. BA (former BDC), Johst file, e.g., PK B8, fr. 1838.

57. Barbian, *Literaturpolitik im "Dritten Reich,"* pp. 266–67.

58. See, e.g., the entries in BA, R 56 V/26.

59. Cited by Düsterberg, *Hanns Johst*, p. 291.

60. Barbian, *Literaturpolitik im NS-Staat*, pp. 298–99.

61. KfdK, Reichsleitung, "Grundsätzliche Vorbemerkungen," BA, R 56 V/70, p. 4.

62. Otto Seifert, *Die grosse Säuberung des Schrifttums: Der Börsenverein der deutschen Buchhändler zu Leipzig 1933 bis 1945*, p. 20.

63. BA, R 56 V/70, p. 2. The same file also includes the actual lists.

64. For examples see BA, R 55/684, p. 29; R 58/913, p. 19.

65. See, e.g., *Börsenverein to Wismann*, January 20, 1934, ibid., p. 26.

66. Jaspert to "Zentralstelle für geistigen Aktivismus," February 28, 1934, BA, R 56 V/158, p. 6.

67. Cf. Peter Göhle, "Ernst Drahn," in *Bewahren—Verbreiten—Aufklären: Archivare, Bibliothekare und Sammler der deutschsprachigen Arbeiterbewegung*, edited by Günter Benser and Michael Schneider, pp. 58–63.

68. Ernst Drahn, *Verbotene und undeutsche Bücher* (Berlin, 1933).

69. BA, R 56 V/158, pp. 4–5.

70. BA, R 3001/1507, pp. 35–36. See also chap. 3, p. 24.

71. "Zwei Schwarze Listen," *Berliner Tageblatt*, no. 229 (May 5, 1935).

72. Dietrich Aigner, "Die Indizierung 'schädlichen und unerwünschten' Schrifttums im Dritten Reich," *Archiv für Geschichte des Buchwesens* 11 (1971): col. 974.

73. Reichsschrifttumskammer, *Liste 1 des schädlichen und underwünschten Schrifttums* (Berlin, 1935). The work was called *Liste 1* because it was authorized by Paragraph 1 of the ordinance of April 25. A second list of books unsuitable for young people, authorized by Paragraph 2, did not appear until 1940.

74. Aigner, "Die Indizierung 'schädlichen und unerwünschten' Schrifttums," cols. 975–77.

75. They are reprinted in BA, R 2/4921, pp. 96–109.

76. *Liste des schädlichen und unerwünschten Schrifttums, Stand vom 31. Dezember 1938* (Leipzig, 1938).

77. The count for both the 1935 and the 1938 edition was undertaken by Aigner, "Die Indizierung 'schädlichen und unerwünschten' Schrifttums," col. 984.

78. See also Deutsche Bücherei, *Liste der in der Deutschen Bücherei unter Verschluss gestellten Druckschriften*.

79. Barbian, *Literaturpolitik im NS-Staat*, pp. 259–60.

80. The yearly lists for the years 1939–1941 are reprinted in *Liste des schädlichen und unerwünschten Schrifttums: Stand vom 31. Dezember 1938 und Jahreslisten 1939–1941* published by the Topos Verlag in Vaduz, Liechtenstein.

81. Deutsche Bücherei, *Verzeichnis der Schriften, die 1933 bis 1945 nicht angezeigt werden durften*, p. 4.

82. RSK to Verlag H. Fikentscher, December 12, 1937, BA, R 56 V/232, p. 25.

83. "Keine Werbung mit Prüfungsvermerken," *Vertrauliche Mitteilungen der Fachschaft Verlag der Gruppe Buchhandel in der Reichsschrifttumskammer*, no. 24 (July 6, 1937), p. 7.

84. Koch, "Die Bekämpfung des schädlichen und unerwünschten Schrifttums," p. 146.

85. RSK to RMfVP, July 15, 1940, BA, R e6 V/67, pp. 297–98.

86. See the undated memo of the RSK, Referat Wismann, BA, R 56 V/158, p. 14.

87. Aigner, "Die Indizierung 'schädlichen und unerwünschten' Schrifttums," col. 947.

88. Gabriela Fleige, "Die Reichsschrifttumskammer als Zensurinstrument im Dritten Reich," *Dokumentation, Fachbibliothek, Werkbücherei* 30 (1982): 117; Graf, "Nationalsozialistische Schrifttumspolitik," p. B114.

89. BA (formerly BDC), RK B6, fr. 1798.

90. BA, R 56 V/223, file 1, n.p.

91. "Verbotenes und unerwünschtes Schrifttum," *Der Buchhändler im neuen Reich* 2 (1937): 41.

92. "Bücher, deren Ausleihe und Verkauf einzustellen ist!" *Grossdeutsches Leihbüchereiblatt* 2 (1940): 49–50.

93. Hövel, *Wesen und Aufbau der Schrifttumsarbeit*, p. 13.

94. Hans Ferdinand Schulz, *Das Schicksal der Bücher und der Buchhandel: System einer Vertriebskunde des Buches*, pp. 11–12.

95. BA, R 58/966, pp. 17–21.

96. RMfVP to RSK, July 4, 1938, BA, R 56 V/69, p. 143.

97. BA, R 56 V/239, pp. 1, 8.

98. "Erwerb ausländischer und Verkauf deutscher Verlagsrechte," *Vertrauliche Mitteilungen der Fachschaft Verlag*, no. 35 (June 18, 1938): 1.

99. BA, R 56 V/698, n.p.

100. RSK to Alster Verlag, December 22, 1937, BA, R 56 V/582, n.p.

101. BA, R 55/682, pp. 14–15,

102. *Zeitschrift der Leihbücherei*, vol. 4, no. 16 (August 25, 1935): 10.

103. BA, R 56 V/158, pp. 11-2.

104. Barbian, *Literaturpolitik im NS-Staat,* pp. 242–44.
105. BA, R 56 V/521, p. 7.
106. BA, R 56 V/537, n.p.
107. BA, R 56 V/96, p. 243.
108. *Vertrauliche Mitteilungen der Fachschaft Verlag,* no. 3 (August 9, 1935): 1.
109. *Vertrauliche Mitteilungen der Fachschaft Verlag,* no. 10 (April 21, 1936): 3.
110. BA, R 56 V/96, p. 246.
111. *Vertrauliche Mitteilungen der Fachschaft Verlag,* no. 21 (April 13, 1937): 3.
112. RMfVP to RSK, July 1, 1937, BA, R 56 V/96, p. 150.
113. BA, R 56 V/96, p. 129.
114. *Vertrauliche Mitteilungen der Fachschaft Verlag,* no. 36 (July 26, 1938): 1.
115. BA, NS 21/1945, n.p.
116. BA, R 58/904, p. 103.
117. BA, NS/240, p. 37.
118. BA, R 56 V/96, p. 248.
119. For examples see BA 56 V/95.
120. BA, R 58/914, pp. 87–102. See also Glenn R. Cuomo, "The Diaries of Joseph Goebbels as a Source for the Understanding of National Socialist Cultural Policies," in *National Socialist Cultural Policy,* ed. by Glenn R. Cuomo, pp. 205–06.
121. See, e.g., BA, R 56 V/417, RSK to Goebbels, November 20, 1937, n.p. The first such complaint is dated May 11, 1936, five days after Goebbels had issued the regulation that required listing before confiscation; the last one I have seen is contained in a letter of July 27, 1943 (BA, R 56 V/67, p. 14).
122. BA, R 56 V/67, p. 17.
123. *Amtliche Bekanntmachung Nr. 127,* in Ihde, ed., *Handbuch der Reichsschrifttumskammer,* p. 44.
124. "Organisationsplan und Etat der Reichsschrifttumsstelle," {May, 1938}, BA, R 55/686, p. 89.
125. Scott W. Hoerle, *Hans-Friedrich Blunck: Poet and Nazi Collaborator 1888–1961,* p. 134.
126. This regulation, first promulgated in 1934, apparently was not sufficiently observed and it was therefore reissued on April 1937. See *Vertrauliche Mitteilungen der Fachschaft Verlag,* no. 21 (April 13, 1937): 4
127. Barbian, *Die vollendete Ohnmacht,* p. 28.

Chapter 5

1. Aigner, "Die Indizierung 'schädlichen und unerwünschten Schrifttums'," col. 948, n. 65.
2. Wilhelm Zeck, "Die Bekämpfung unerwünschten Schrifttums im nationalsozialistischen Staat," *Deutsche Verwaltung* 11 (1936): 349.
3. "Jahresbericht," BA, R 3001/21508, pp. 22–23.
4. Hans Buchheim et al., *Anatomie des SS-Staates,* vol. 1, p. 55.
5. RGBl. I 1933, p. 36. The ordinance is reprinted in BA, R 56 V/67, pp. 144–48.
6. RGBl. I 1933, pp. 83–85, relevant parts reprinted in BA, R 56 V/67, pp. 148–51.
7. Aigner, "Die Indizierung 'schädlichen und unerwünschten Schrifttums'," col. 952.
8. Schoeps and Tress, *Orte der Bücherverbrennungen,* p. 126.
9. BA, R 58/933, pp. 198–99.
10. Gestapa to RSK, August 5, 1937, BA, R 56V/67, p. 310.
11. Aigner, "Die Indizierung 'schädlichen und unerwünschten Schrifttums'," col. 954.
12. Chief of Police Frankfurt/M to RSK, January 25, 1938, BA, R 56 V/1122, n.p.
13. Gestapa order of March 12, 1936, quoted in Graf, "Nationalsozialistische Schrifttumspolitik," p. B113.
14. BA, R 56 V/158, p. 28.
15. BA, R 58/1023, pp. 207–09.
16. "Gesamtbericht über die vom Oktober 1936 bis Juni 1937 erfolgte Durchsuchung buchhändlerischer Betriebe nach schädlichem und unerwünschtem Schrifttum," BA, R 56 V/67, pp. 310–15.

17. Seifert, *Die grosse Säuberung des Schrifttums*, p. 81.
18. Prussian Ministry of Finance to RfVP, April 25, 1934, BA R 56 V/158, p. 10. See also Alexander Greguletz, "Die Preussische Staatsbibliothek in den ersten Jahren des National-sozialismus (1933–1936)," in Vodosek and Komorowski, eds., *Bibliotheken während des Nationalsozialismus*, vol. II, pp. 243–44.
19. Gestapo Düsseldorf to Gestapa Berlin, February 15, 1937, BA R 56 V/223, file 2, n.p.
20. Albert Strutz to Ludwig Fritzsche, October 3, 1938, BA, R 58/933, p. 115.
21. Barbian, *Literaturpolitik im NS-Staat*, p. 408.
22. Seifert, *Die grosse Säuberung des Schrifttums*, p. 181.
23. RSK to Advent Verlag, June 17, 1937, BA, R 58/914, p. 117.
24. RMfVP to RSK, December 1936, BA, R 56 V/381, n.p.
25. RSK to publisher H. Fikentscher, October 21, 1937, BA, R 56 V/232, p. 20.
26. The correspondence can be found in BA, R 58/895, pp. 66–67, 75–76.
27. Chef des Sicherheitshauptamtes to Gestapa, March 9, 1937, BA, R 58/969, p. 132.
28. BA, R 58/969, pp. 142–43.
29. BA, R 58/969, p. 148.
30. Gestapa to Goebbels, December 18, 1937, ibid., pp. 156–57.
31. BA, R 58/972, p. 203.
32. Memo of April 6, 1937, BA, R 56 V/947, n.p.
33. Memo of April 30, 1937, ibid.
34. *Verzeichnis der für das Reichsgebiet verbotenen ausländischen Druckschriften nach dem Stande vom 1. April 1934* (also as of January 1, 1935).
35. BA, R 3001/21507, pp. 1–5.
36. BA, R 3001/21507, p. 6.
37. Gestapa Berlin to Gestapo Potsdam, July 22, 1937, BA, R 58/769, p. 54.
38. Gestapa Berlin to Gestapo Elbing, May 14, 1937, BA, R 58/769, p. 142.
39. Gestapa to Stapo Bielefeld, September 13, 1935, BA, R 58/964, p. 129.
40. See, e.g., the inquiry of March 26, 1936, BA, R 58/1022, p. 32.
41. RSK to Greifenverlag, January 18, 1937, BA, R 58/839, p. 118.
42. Gestapo to RSK, February 21, 1938, BA, R 58/890, p. 74.
43. BA, R 58/895, pp. 29–49.
44. BA, R 58/900, p. 9.
45. BA, R 58/900, pp. 42, 48, 50.
46. Reichsführer SS to Dieckmann, September 19, 1940, BA, R 58/900, pp. 52–53.
47. BA, R 58/1023, p. 284.
48. RSK to Gestapa, August 18, 1937, BA, R 58/890, p. 158.
49. RMfVP to RSK, May 13 and June 21, 1937, BA, R 56V/379, pp. 9, 14.
50. BA, R 58/918, p. 85.
51. BA, R 58/896, p. 66.
52. BA, R 58/1023, p. 24.
53. See, e.g., *Deutsches Kriminalpolizeiblatt* no. 1510 (March 25, 1933) and *Zeitschrift der Leihbücherei* 3 (1934): 16.
54. Buchheim et al., *Anatomie des SS-Staates*, vol. 1, p. 74.
55. Reichsführer SS, *Leitheft Nr. 5: Verlagswesen* (Berlin, 1937), p. 34, reproduced in BA, R 56 V/1107. See also Barbian, *Literaturpolitik im NS-Staat*, p. 149.
56. The letterhead of this organization read *Arbeitsstelle für Schrifttumsbearbeitung beim Sicherheitshauptamt des Reichsführers SS*.
57. Seifert, *Die grosse Säuberung des Schrifttums*, p. 79.
58. Menz to Johst, April 3, 1937, BA, R 56 V/27, p. 156.
59. R 4901/463, p. 220.
60. Werner Schroeder, "'. . . eine Fundgrube der Schrifttumsinformation: Die Leipziger 'Arbeitsstelle für Schrifttumsbearbeitung beim Sicherheitshauptamt (SD)' und die 'SD Verbindungsstelle an der Deutschen Bücherei',"" in *"Arisierung" in Leipzig: Annäherung an ein lang verdrängtes Kapitel der Stadtgeschichte der Jahre 1933 bis 1945*, ed. by Monika Gibas), p. 125.

61. Saul Friedländer, *Nazi Germany and the Jews*, vol. 1, p. 198.

62. Buchheim et al., *Anatomie des SS-Staates*, vol. 1, p. 77; Regina Urban and Ralph Herpolsheimer, "Franz Alfred Six (geb. 1909)," in *Zeitungswissenschaftler im Dritten Reich: Sieben biographische Studien*, ed. by Arnulf Kutsch, p. 172. See also Lutz Hachmeister, *Der Gegnerforscher: Die Karriere des SS-Führers Franz Alfred Six*.

63. Reichsführer SS, *Leitheft Nr. 30: Schrifttumswesen und Schrifttumspolitik*, p. 52, reproduced in BA, R 56 V/1106, p. 52.

64. Memo of May 15, 1937, BA, R 58/914, p. 230.

65. BA, R 58/915, pp. 90, 95.

66. BA, R 58/907, p. 91.

67. Verlag Deutsche Kultur-Wacht to Gestapa, May 14, 1935, ibid., p. 97.

68. Hannuschka to Hitler, May 27, 1935, ibid., p. 114.

69. Chef des Sicherheitshauptamtes to RSK, December 10, 1937, BA 58/972, p. 107.

70. BA 58/972., p. 129.

71. Hachmeister, *Der Gegnerforscher*, pp. 201, 216.

Chapter 6

1. NDSAP, Partei-Kanzlei, *Verfügungen/Anordnungen/Bekanntmachungen*, vol. 1, pp. 467–68. The ordinance was also announced in the Bbl. no. 92 (April 21, 1934), p. 367.

2. Kershaw, *Hitler*, p. 300.

3. Wistrich, *Who's Who in Nazi Germany*, p. 26.

4. BA, R 56 V/158, p. 21.

5. Barbian, *Literaturpolitk im NS-Staat*, p. 268.

6. NDSAP, Partei-Kanzlei, *Verfügungen/Anordnungen/Bekanntmachungen*, vol. 1, p. 469.

7. Karsten Jedlitschka, "Die Parteiamtliche Prüfungskommission zum Schutze des Nationalsozialistischen Schrifttum: Zensurfelder und Arbeitsweise am Beispiel des Münchner Lektors Ulrich Crämer," *Archiv für Geschichte des Buchwesens* 62 (2008): 216.

8. NDSAP, Partei-Kanzlei, *Verfügungen*, pp. 468–69. The implementing regulations of April 16, 1934, were also published in *Zeitschrift der Leihbücherei*, vol. 3, no. 9 (May 10, 1934): 5.

9. NDSAP, Partei-Kanzlei, *Verfügungen/Anordnungen/Bekanntmachungen*, vol. 1, p. 15. The ordinance can also be found in *Bbl.* vol. 102, no. 90 (April, 16, 1935): 307.

10. "Die Arbeit der Prüfungskommission zum Schutze des NS-Schrifttums," *Die Bücherei* 1 (1934): 534.

11. Beginning with BA, R 58/890, the files of the RSHA include detailed reports on "Überprüfung und Verbote von Büchern."

12. Unsigned RSK memo of January 9, 1935, BA, R 56 V/65, p. 48.

13. Karl Helmut Patutschnick, "Die rechtliche Stellung der Parteiamtlichen Prüfungs-kommission zum Schutze des NS-Schrifttums," *Deutsches Recht* 5 (1935): 445. The text of the RSK ordinance of April 16, 1935, can be found in BA, R 56 V/158, p. 21. It is reprinted in *Bbl* 105 (1938): 831.

14. *Bbl.* no. 277 (November 26, 1940). The announcemet is reprinted in Ihde, *Handbuch der Reichsschrifttumskammer*, p. 76

15. *Nationalsozialistische Bibliographie*, vol. 1, no. 1 (1936), p. 1.

16. Jürgen Soenke, *Studien über zeitgenössische Zensursysteme*. Soenke was an official of the PPK and this book was his Ph.D. dissertation. An example of a book that had been refused the right to include the NSB approval can be found in BA, R 56 V/7, p. 40.

17. *Die Bücherei* 3 (1936): 237.

18. Joseph Goebbels, *Wesen und Gestalt des Nationalsozialismus*, p. 10.

19. See, e.g., order of November 22, 1935, to Est Verlag, Düsseldorf, BA, R 56 V/65, p. 28.

20. Karl-Heinz Hederich, *Die Parteiamtliche Prüfungskommission zum Schutze des NS-Schrifttum, ihre Aufgaben und ihre Stellung in Partei und Staat* 7, pp. 6–12.

21. Hellmuth Landgenbucher, "Deutsches Schrifttum 1937—politisch gesehen," *National-sozialistische Bibliographie*, no. 2 (February 1938), supplement 3, p. i.

22. "Jahresbericht 1938 des Sicherheitshauptamtes," vol. 2, BA, R 58/1095, p. 135.

23. See, e.g, Rosenberg to Bouhler, December 21, 1937, BA, NS 8/208, p. 75.
24. BA, NS 6/215, n.p.
25. Schlecht memo, November 1939, BA, R 56 V/17, p. 34
26. Witt to Tiesler, November 25, 1941, BA, NS 18/33, n.p.
27. Edgar Wolfram, *Geschichte als Waffe: Vom Kaiserreich bis zur Wiedervereinigung*, p. 49.
28. Hans-Ulrich Wehler, "Nationalsozialismus und Historiker," in *Deutsche Historiker im Nationalsozialismus*, edited by Winfried Schulze and Otto Gerhard Oexle, pp. 310–11.
29. Götz Aly, "Theodor Schieder, Werner Conze oder die Vorstufe Winfried Schulze and Oexle, p. 170.
30. Karen Schönwälder, *Historiker und Politik: Geschichtswissenschaft im Nationalsozialismus*, p. 276.
31. BA, R 56 V/65, p. 26.
32. BA, R 56 V/65, p. 34.
33. BA, R 56 V/65, p. 37.
34. *Vertrauliche Mitteilungen der Fachschaft Verlag*, no. 35 (June 18, 1938), p. 1.
35. PPK to staff of Hess, July 20, 1938, BA, NS 11/5, p. 28.
36. *Vertrauliche Mitteilungen der Fachschaft Verlag*, no. 21 (April 13, 1937), p. 3.
37. Ihde, *Handbuch der Reichsschrifttumskammer*, p. 188.
38. *Der deutsche Schriftsteller* 3 (1938): 135.
39. BA, R 56 V/65, p. 23.
40. Heinz Finke, "Die Kalenderliteratur im Rahmen des deutschen Schrifttums," *Nationalsozialistische Bibliographie*, no. 3 (March 1937), supplement, pp. i–iv.
41. BA, R 58/914, pp. 205–07
42. Cited by Jeremy Naokes, "Philip Bouhler und die Kanzlei des Führers der NSDAP: Beispiel einer Sonderverwaltung im Dritten Reich," in *Führererwaltung contra Menschenführung im Staat Hitler: Studien zum politischen administrativen System,* edited by Dieter Rebentisch and Karl Teppe, p. 208.
43. PPK to Koellreutter, March 29, 1935, BA, NS 11/23, p. 95.
44. Hederich to Gestapa, November 18, 1941, BA, NS 11/22, n.p.
45. "Politische Ausrichtung des wissenschaftlichen Schrifttums," BA, R 56 V/65, pp. 40–41.
46. BA, R 58/965, pp. 222–23.
47. BA, R 58/965, pp. 227, 228.
48. Sören Flachowsky, *Die Bibliothek der Berliner Universität während der Zeit des Nationalsozialismus*, pp. 138–39.
49. BA, NS 11/20, pp. 23–24; NS 8/209, p. 112.
50. Rosenberg to Hess, November 11, 1939, BA, NS 8/182, p. 67.
51. Joachim-Felix Leonhard, "Vom lebendigen zum deutschen Geist: Aussonderung und Separierung von Büchern in Heidelberger Bibliotheken unter dem Nationalsozialismus," in *Bücherverbrennung: Zensur, Verbot, Vernichtung unter dem Nationalsozialismus in Heidelberg*, edited by Joachim-Felix Leonhard, p. 119.
52. BA, NS 11/23, p. 124.
53. PPK to Gestapa, February 5, 1937, BA, R58/898, p. 33.
54. See, e.g., PPK to Gestapa Berlin, March 10, 1936, BA, R 58/968, p. 11.
55. See. e.g., NS 11/38, p. 167.
56. Gestapa to RSK, August 25, 1938, BA, R 56 V/69, p. 13.
57. PPK to Gestapa, August 23, 1934, BA, R 58/767, pp. 48, 45.
58. BA, R 58/972, pp. 133–36.
59. BA, R 58/909, pp. 112–16.
60. BA, R 58/1106, p. 60.
61. See, e.g., the order of November 22, 1935, published in the Bbl. 102 (November 28, 1935): 1013.
62. Order of November 21, 1942, BA, NS 18/233, n.p.
63. BA, NS 11/23, p. 77.
64. Undated PPK memo, BA, NS 11/21a, n.p.
65. Barbian, *Literaturpolitk im "Dritten Reich,"* p. 542.

66. Bormann circular, BA, NS 6/335, p. 109.
67. Bouhler to Ley, May 29, 1941, BA, NS 11/9, n.p.
68. Reprinted in BA, NS 8/249, p. 29.
69. Hederich to party chancellery, October 23, 1944, BA, NS 11/38, p. 124.
70. Hederich letter, December 7, 1944, BA, NS 11/38, p. 195.
71. BA, ibid., p. 151.
72. Soenke, *Studien über zeitgenössische Zensursysteme*, p. 73.

Chapter 7

1. Cf. Kershaw, *Hitler 1889–1936*, p. 225; Wistrich, *Who's Who in Nazi Germany*, pp. 255–56.
2. Cf. Ernst Piper, *Alfred Rosenberg: Hitlers Chefideologe*, p. 324.
3. Piper, *Alfred Rosenberg*, p. 273.
4. "Betrifft Reichsschrifttumsstelle," January 9, 1935, BA, R 56 V/65, p. 46.
5. *Bücherkunde*, "Vorbemerkung zur II. Folge [1935], BA, NS 8/153, p. 170.
6. Hellmuth Langenbucher, *Die Welt des Buches: Eine Kunde vom Buch*, p. 21.
7. "Rückfragen und Anordnungen der Reichsstelle zur Förderung des deutschen Schrifttums," *Zeitschrift der Leihbüchereien*, vol. 3, no. 6 (March 25, 1934), p. 8.
8. "Rundschreiben nr. 24," BA, NS 12/77, n.p.
9. Bernhard Payr, "Aufgaben des Amtes Schrifttumspflege," in *Die Welt des Buches*, edited by Hellmuth Langenbucher, p. 204.
10. Gerd Rühle, ed., *Das Dritte Reich: Dokumentarische Darstellung des Aufbaus der Nation*, vol. 2, p. 180.
11. Bernhard Payr, *Das Amt Schrifttumspflege: Seine Entwicklungsgeschichte und seine Organisation*, p. 11.
12. Payr, *Amt Schrifttumspflege*, pp. 20–21.
13. The *Lektoren-Brief* at first was distributed in typed form. From the middle of 1938 until July 1944 it appeared in print.
14. "Dienstanweisung für die Lektoren Nr. 1," BA, NS 12/77, n.p.
15. Barbian, *Literaturpolitik im "Dritten Reich"*, p. 287.
16. Payr, "Aufgaben des Amtes Schrifttumspflege," p. 205.
17. See, e.g., Engelbrecht Boese, *Das öffentliche Bibiliothekswesen im Dritten Reich*, p. 175.
18. BA, NS 12/77, n.p.
19. Herbert P. Rothfeder, "Amt Schrifttumspflege: A Study in Literary Control," *German Studies Review* 4 (1981): 68.
20. BA, NS 12/77, n.p.
21. BA, R 58/971, p. 86.
22. *Das Politische Tagebuch Alfred Rosenbergs aus den Jahren 1934/35 und 1939/41*, ed. by Hans-Günther Seraphim, p. 26.
23. Bernhard Payr, "Aufgaben des Amtes Schrifttumspflege," in *Die Welt des Buches*, p. 204. See also Barbian, *Literaturpolitik im NS-Staat*, pp. 84–85, 151–53.
24. BA, NS 12/77, n.p.
25. BA, NS 8/171, pp. 35–36.
26. Goebbels, *Die Tagebücher*, Part I, vol. 3/I, p. 137.
27. Blunck, *Unwegsame Zeiten*, vol. 1, pp. 238–39.
28. BA, R 56 V/65, p. 49.
29. Hagemeyer memo, March 23, 1935, BA, R 56 V/65, p. 59.
30. Rosenberg to RSK, March 23, 1935, BA, R 56 V/65, pp. 56–57.
31. Wismann to Hess, March 26, 1935, BA, R 56 V/65, p. 61.
32. Funk to Hess, April 11, 1935, BA, R 56 V/65, pp. 65–66.
33. "Die Arbeit der Prüfungskommission zum Schutze des N.S.-Schrifttums," BA, R 56 V/65, p. 68.
34. Wismann to Funk, May 6, 1935, BA, R 56 V/65, p. 72.
35. "Die Reichsschrifttumskammer gibt bekannt," BA, R 56 V/65, p. 81.

36. "Circular nr. 10," BA, NS 8/128, p. 31. The announcement was also printed in *Vertrauliche Mitteilungen der Fachschaft Verlag*, no. 8 (January 13, 1936), p. 5.
37. RSK to Gestapa, June 27, 1936, BA, R 58/918, p. 179.
38. Barbian, *Literaturpolitik im "Dritten Reich"*, p. 289
39. BA, NS 8/172, pp. 118–19.

Chapter 8

1. Aigner, *Die Indizierung*, col. 987.
2. Cf. Margret Lemberg, *Verboten und nicht verbrannt*, vol. II, pp. 213–16.
3. RSK to Gestapa, August 29, 1938, BA, R 56 V/69, p. 41.
4. RSK to Reichsführer SS, September 15, 1939, BA, R 56 V/217, file 7, n.p.
5. "Schädlinge des Volkes," *Bbl.*, vol. 103, no. 285 (August 12, 1936): 1073.
6. *Bbl.*, vol. 103, no. 285 (August 12, 1936): 1073.
7. RSK to *Der Stürmer*, September 27, 1940, BA (formerly BDC), RK B124, n.p.
8. RMfVP to RSK, August 8, 1939, BA, R 56 V/217, file 1, n.p.
9. *Vertrauliche Mitteilungen der Fachschaft Verlag*, no. 23 (May 27, 1937), p. 3.
10. See, e.g., *Die Tagebücher*, Part I, vol. 3/I, p. 229, and vol. 3/II, p. 226.
11. Memo of Hans Hinkel, July 30, 1938, BA, R 58/984, p. 73.
12. RSK to Gruppe Buchhandel, March 3, 1941, BA, R 56 V/96, pp. 53, 184.
13. BA, R 56 V/412, n.p.
14. RSK to chief of police Munich, October 11, 1935, BA, R 58/839, p. 79.
15. RSK to chief of police Munich, April 22, 1936, BA, R 56 V/217, file 1, n.p.
16. Ihde, *Handbuch der Reichsschrifttumskammer*, p. 189.
17. Lydia Marhoff, "Von der 'Kameradschaftsehe' zur 'gesunden' Sexualität," in *Banalität mit Stil: Zur Widersprüchlichkeit der Literaturpolitik im Nationalsozialismus*, ed. by Walter Delabar et al., p. 182.
18. RMfVP to RSK, February 19, 1940, BA, R 56 V/220, file 4, n.p.
19. RMfVP to RSK, June 20, 1939, BA, R 56 V/222, file 12, n.p.
20. Gestapo Düsseldorf to Gestapa Berlin, June 25, 1937, BA, R 58/921, p. 11.
21. Reichsarbeitsgemeinschaft für Mutter und Kind to RSK, July 2, 1937, BA, R 56 V/801, p. 15.
22. Cf. John Alexander Williams, *Hiking, Nudism and Conservation: 1900–1940*.
23. BA, R 58/969, p. 195.
24. RMfVP to Deutsche Leibeszucht, May 29, 1941, BA, R 56 V/827, n.p.
25. *Vertrauliche Mitteilungen der Fachschaft Verlag*, no. 42 (July 18, 1939): 1.
26. The prolonged tug-of-war over this book, which I have described more briefly above, can be followed in BA, R 58/900, pp. 199–238.
27. PPK to Hess, February 2, 1939, BA, NS 11/23. n.p.
28. Gestapa to RSK, November 10, 1937, BA, R 56 V/479, n.p.
29. RMfVP to RSK, June 13, 1939, BA, R 56 V/215, file 2, n.p.
30. RMfVP to RSK, January 25, 1938, BA, R 56 V/69, p. 91.
31. RMfVP to RSK, November 30, 1939, R 56 V/217, file 6, n.p.
32. Such orders were imposed first in late 1934 and hereafter were repeatedly republished. See, e.g., *Vertrauliche Mitteilungen der Fachschaft Verlag*, no. 31 (January 31, 1938): 1.
33. RMfVP to RSK, November 6, 1939, BA, R 56 V/219, file 1, n.p.
34. SD to RSK, January 31, 1938, BA, R 56 V/855, n.p.
35. Cf. Albert Maria Weiss and Engebert Krebs, *Im Dienst am Buch*.
36. "Gutachten" by Günther Gablenz, BA, R 56 V/423, p. 16.
37. RMfVP to RSK, January 19, 1939, BA, R 56 V/406, n.p.
38. RMfVP to RSK, August 15, 1940, BA, R 56 V/221, file 8, n.p.
39. RMfVP to RSK, March 27, 1939, BA, R 56 V/221, file 8, n.p.
40. RMfVP to RSK, May 30, 1941, BA, R 56 V/221, file 8, n.p.
41. RMfVP to publisher Steffen, September 6, 1940, R e6 V/221, file 9, n.p.
42. RMfVP to RSK, June 26, 1939, BA, R 56 V/219, file 1, n.p.

43. SD to RMfVP, August 28, 1941, BA, R 56 V/219, file 1, n.p.
44. RMfVP to RSK, November 29, 1939, BA, R 56 V/219, file 4, n.p.
45. RMfVP to RSK, October 17, 1941, BA, R 56 V/217, file 1, n.p.
46. SD to RMfVP, May 7, 1941, BA, R 56 V/217, file 7, n.p.
47. SD to RMfVP, March 23, 1941, BA, R 56 V/216, file 3, n.p.
48. BA, R 56 V/218, file 3, n.p.
49. BA, R 56 V/218, file 3, n.p.
50. BA, R 56 V/222, file 11, n.p.
51. Ihde, *Handbuch der Reischsschrifttumskammer*, p. 133.
52. Alois Hudal, *Die Grundlagen des Nationalsozialismus: Eine ideengeschichtliche Untersuchung von katholischer Warte*, p. 13.
53. For a further discussion of Hudal's ideas see Guenter Lewy, *The Catholic Church and Nazi Germany*, pp 165, 281.
54. Cited in undated "Gutachten," BA, R 56 V/856, n.p.
55. The correspondence regarding this case can be found in BA, R 56 V/278.
56. Gestapo Berlin to Gestapa, March 15, 1935, BA, R 58/898, p. 58.
57. Reprinted in BA, R 58/898, pp. 61 and 71.
58. For a further discussion see Lewy, *The Catholic Church and Nazi Germany*, pp. 278–79.
59. RSK to Gestapa, March 16, 1937, BA, R 58/971, p. 23.
60. See Lewy, *The Catholic Church and Nazi Germany*, pp. 131–32.
61. SD to RMfVP, August 31, 1940, BA, R 56 V/222, file 12, n.p.
62. BA, R 58/268, p. 36.
63. BA, R 56 V/222, file 13, n.p.
64. RMfVP to RSK, December 21, 1938, BA, R 56 V/874, n.p.
65. BA, R 56 V519, n.p.
66. BA, R 56 V/222, file 10, n.p.
67. BA, R 56 V/216, file 3, n.p.
68. BA, R 56 V/275, p. 25.
69. RSK to P. Jügelt, July 16, 1935, BA, R 56 V/457, n.p.; RMfVP to RSK, July 19, 1937, ibid.
70. "Mischehen. Behandlung von—im deutschen Schrifttum," Ihde, *Handbuch der Reichs-schrifttumskammer*, p. 186.
71. SD to RMfVP, November 20, 1940, BA, R 56 V/219, file 4, n.p.
72. RSK to Gestapa, September 23, 1935, BA, R 58/933, p. 239.
73. RMfVP to RSK, March 30, 1939, BA, R 56 V/218, file 3, n.p.
74. RSK, *Vertrauliche Mitteilungen der Fachschaft Verlag*, no. 71 (July, 10, 1943): 1.
75. Rasse- und Siedlungs-Hauptamt der SS to Gestapa, September 16, 1936, BA, R 58/890, pp. 78–79, 83.
76. BA, R 58/935, pp. 8, 10.
77. RSK to Gestapa, October 1, 1934, BA, R 58/902, p. 96.
78. Hederich (PPK) to Gestapa, September 5, 1935, BA, R 58/902, p. 101.
79. BA, R 58/901, p. 30.
80. "Verbotene Druckschriften," *Zeitschrift der Leihbücherei*, vol. 3, no. 20 (October 25, 1934), p. 20.
81. RMfVP to Gestapa, March 4, 1935, BA, R 58/767, p. 73.
82. Verlag für Kulturpolitik to Gestapo Berlin, May 5, 1935, BA, R 58/965, p. 171.
83. RMI to police commanders, June 26, 1936, BA, R 58/935, p. 34
84. BA, NS 11/19, n.p.
85. BA, R 43 II/479, p. 42.
86. Bormann to Hederich, August 14, 1941, NS 11/19, n.p.
87. RSK to chief of police Dresden and Gestapa, November 14, 1935, BA, R 58/914, pp. 3–4.
88. RSK to Bavarian Political Police, October 15, 1935, BA, R 58/893, p. 21.
89. Emil Reuter, "Dichtung als Lebensmacht: Wozu brauchen wir noch eine Dichtung?" *Der deutsche Schriftsteller* 7 (1942): 135.

Chapter 9

1. Adolf Hitler, *Mein Kampf*, p. 358.

2. Wilhelm Stapel, *Die literarische Vorherrschaft der Juden in Deutschland: 1918 bis 1933*, pp. 25–26.

3. Quoted by Dahm, *Das jüdische Buch*, p. 18.

4. "Ein Jahr Reichsschrifttumskammer," *Bbl.*, vol. 101 (December 13, 1934), p. 1086.

5. Johannes Alt, "Grundlagen und Voraussetzungen der wissenschaftlichen Bearbeitung der deutschsprachigen jüdischen Literatur," *Forschungen zur Judenfrage* 1 (1937): 48, quoted in *NS-Literaturtheorie: Eine Dokumentation*, p. 48.

6. Dahm, *Das jüdische Buch*, p. 25.

7. Alon Confino, *A World without Jews: The Nazi Imagination from Persecution to Genocide*, p. 87.

8. Quoted in Michael Labach, "Der Verein Deutscher Volksbibliothekare während des Nationalsozialismus," in *Bibliotheken während des Nationalsozialismus*, edited by Vodosek and Komorowski, p. 152.

9. Hans Richter, "Wo finde ich den Juden?" *Bbl.*, vol. 103, no. 205 (September 3, 1936): 762–63.

10. Amt Schrifttumspflege, *Verzeichnis jüdischer Autoren*.

11. Ottmar Jung, "Der literarische Judenstern: Die Indizierung der 'jüdisschen Rechtsliteratur' im nationalsozialistischen Deutschland," *Vierteljahrshefte für Zeitgeschichte* 54 (2006): 51–53.

12. Goebbels to Schacht, December 13, 1934, BA, R 56 V/102, pp. 222, 209.

13. Dahm, *Das jüdische Buch*, p. 71.

14. BA, R 56 V/102, p. 212. This report can also be found in R 56 V/194.

15. See, e.g., *Bbl.* 101 (December 11, 1934): 1085.

16. RMfVP to RMI, November 21, 1935, BA, R 56 V/102, pp. 193, 186.

17. BA, R 56 V/102, p. 221.

18. Dahm, *Das jüdische Buch*, p. 52.

19. Barbian, *Literaturpolitik im NS-Staat*, pp. 197–99.

20. BA, R 56 V/102, p. 145.

21. BA, R 56 I/29, cited by Dahm, *Das jüdische Buch*, pp. 157, 201.

22. RMfVP to RSK, November 4, 1939. BA, R 56 V/95, p. 4.

23. Goebbels, *Tagebücher*, Part I, vol. 6, p. 328.

24. RMfVP to RSK, June 15, 1938, BA, R 56 V/57, p. 56.

25. BA, R 55/24066, p. 8.

26. BA, R 58/984, p. 73.

27. BA, R 56 V/102, p. 154.

28. BA, R 56 V/51, pp. 149, 155, 124.

29. Wilhelmine Dreschner, *Erinnerungen an Karl Jaspers in Heidelberg*, pp. 27–29.

30. BA, R 56 V/51, p. 145.

31. "Regelung der Frage jüdischer Buchverkäufer und Buchverleger im Reichsgebiet," March 30, 1937, BA, R 56 V/102, p. 46. A list of Jewish publishers who had been approved for the sale of Jewish literature was published in the *Vertrauliche Mitteilungen der Fachschaft Verlag*, no. 24 (July 6, 1937): 5–6.

32. BA, R 58/1023, p. 196.

33. BA, R 56 V/194, pp. 5–8.

34. Barbian, *Literaturpolitik im NS-Staat*, p. 220.

35. BA, R 56 V/102, p. 220.

36. Barbian, *Literaturpolitik im NS-Staat*, p. 225.

37. Otto Seifert, *Die grosse Säuberung des Schrifttums: Der Börsenverein der deutschen Buchhändler zu Leipzig 1933 bis 1945*, p. 182.

38. Dahm, *Das jüdische Buch*, pp. 146–49.

39. Cited by Seifert, *Die grosse Säuberung des Schrifttums*, p. 145.

40. RSK to Gerhard Mochau, November 19, 1938, BA, R 56 V/189, p. 15.

41. Seifert, *Die grosse Säuberung des Schrifttums*, p. 234.

42. Ihde, *Handbuch der Reichsschrifttumskammer,* p. 275.
43. Seifert, *Die grosse Säuberung des Schrifttums,* p. 151.
44. Hinkel to the Jewish book trade, September 24, 1937, BA, R 56 V/102, p. 17
45. Seifert, *Die grosse Säuberung des Schrifttums,* pp. 54–56.
46. Hinkel to Reichsverband der Jüdischen Kulturbünde, December 13, 1935, BA, R 56 V/102, p. 191.
47. Seifert, *Die grosse Säuberung des Schrifttums,* pp. 154–55.
48. *Vertrauliche Mitteilungen der Fachschaft Verlag,* no. 30 (December 13, 1937): 1.
49. BA, R 56 V/639, n.p.
50. Hinkel to RSK, February 8, 1938, BA, R 56 V/554, p. 10.
51. RSK to RMfVP, August 25, 1939, BA, R 56 V/818, n.p.
52. Heinz Sarkowski, *Springer Verlag: History of a Scientific Publishing House,* trans. by Gerald Graham, Part I, p. 336.
53. BA, R 56 V/217, file 7, n.p.
54. See his pamphlet *Der Sieg des Judentums über das Germanenthum vom nicht-confessionellen Standpunkt.*
55. Aigner, "Indizierung 'schädlichen und unerwünschten Schrifttums'," cols. 1028–29.
56. RSK to Gruppe Buchhandel, May 31, 1940, BA, R 56 V/96, p. 75.
57. BA, R 56 V/96, p. 221.
58. "Das Leben des Juden Heinrich Heine," *Der deutsche Schriftsteller* 5 (1940): 79.
59. BA, R 58/897, p. 40.
60. BA, R 56 V/102, p. 15.
61. Ba, R 56 V/219, file 1, p. 1.
62. SD to RMfVP, October 10, 1939, ibid, file 4, n.p.
63. RMfVP to RSK, January 23, 1940, BA, R 56 V//221, n.p.
64. Gestapa to RSK, October 21, 1937, BA, R 56 V/410, n.p.
65. Gestapa to RSK, October 15, 1937, BA, R 56 V/391, p. 1.
66. RMfVP to PPK, January 29, 1940, BA, NS 11/23a, n.p.
67. SD to RSK, December 20, 1937, BA, R 56 V/375, p. 3.
68. Boberach, *Meldungen aus dem Reich,* vol. 12, p. 4653.
69. RSK to Gestapa, May 15, 1936, BA, R 58/921, p. 91.
70. RMfVP to RSK, March 17, 1939, BA, R 56 V/217, file 1, n.p.
71. RMfVP to RSK, June 22, 1939, BA, R 56 V/220, file 4, n.p.
72. RMfVP to RSK, June 1, 1940, BA, R 56 V/222, file 13, n.p.
73. RMfVP to RSK, May 31, 1939, BA, R 56 V/221, file 8, n.p.
74. Reichsführer SS to Goebbels, June 11, 1940, BA, R 56 V/219, file 1, n.p.
75. Ihde, *Handbuch der Reichsschrifttumskammer,* p. 75.
76. "Erläuterungen der Reichsschrifttumskammer zur Amtlichen Bekanntmachung no. 70 of April 15, 1940," Ihde, *Handbuch der Reichsschrifttumskammer,* pp. 78, 76–79.
77. Hooffacker to Ihde, August 11, 1941, and Bischoff to Ihde, August 18, 1941, BA, R 56 V/67, pp. 212–13.
78. Haegert to Johst, April 23, 1942, BA, R 56 V/67, p. 209.
79. Wistrich, *Who's Who in Nazi Germany,* p. 80.
80. Patricia Kennedy Grimstead, "Roads to Ratibor: Library and Archival Plunder by the Einsatzstab Rosenberg," *Holocaust and Genocide Studies* 19 (2005): 407–08.
81. Peter M. Manasse, *Verschleppte Archive und Bibliotheken: Die Tätigkeit des Einsatzstabes Rosenberg während des Zweiten Weltkrieges,* trans. by Georg A. Pippig, p. 28.

Chapter 10

1. Wistrich, *Who's Who in Nazi Germany,* p. 262.
2. Karl Dietrich Bracher, *The German Dictatorship: The Origins, Structure, and Effects of National Socialism,* translated by Jean Steinberg, p. 261.

3. Broszat, *The Hitler State*, p. 246. Another scholar speaking of Rust's "weak personality" is Alan D. Beyerchen in his *Scientists under Hitler: Politics and the Physics Community in the Third Reich*, p. 57.

4. Rust to Goebbels, May 5, 1942, BA, NS 18/1298, p. 3.

5. See the correspondence in BA, R 43 II/1153a, pp. 7–14.

6. Wolfgang Hermann, "Prinzipielles zur Säuberung der öffentlichen Büchereien," *Bbl.* 100 (1933): 356.

7. Fritz Prinzhorn, *Die Aufgaben der Bibliotheken im nationalsozialistischen Deutschland*, p. 9.

8. Peter Langendorf, "Die neuen Massstäbe bei der Buchauswahl in der politisch-historischen Literatur," *Die Bücherei* 1 (1934): 279.

9. Rust in 1935 at the opening of the Dietrich Eckhart library in Berlin, cited in *Die Bücherei* 5 (1938): 320.

10. This point is correctly stressed by Margaret F. Stieg, *Public Libraries in Nazi Germany*, p. 82.

11. Wilhelm Schuster, "Bücherei und Nationalsozialismus," *Die Bücherei* 1 (1934): 2.

12. Wilhelm Schuster, "Die Volksbücherei im neuen Reich," ibid., p. 346.

13. "Erklärung und Aufruf des Verbandes Deutscher Volksbibliothekare," *Bücherei und Bildungspflege* 13 (1933): 97–98. The two authors signed their name followed by "N.S.D.A.P."

14. Richard Kock, "Die Neuordnung der Beratungsstellen," *Bücherei und Bildungspflege* 1 (1934): 18.

15. Bernhard Rust, "Noch heute!," *Bücherei und Bildungspflege* 1 (1934), pp. 11–12. See also Stieg, *Public Libraries in Nazi Germany*, pp. 60–61.

16. BA, R 55/684, p. 8.

17. "Richtlinien für die Bestandprüfung in den Volksbüchereien Sachsens," *Die Bücherei* 2 (1935): 279–80.

18. Rudolf Angermann, "Aus der Fachschaft—für die Fachschaft: Säuberung nach der Säuberung," *Die Bücherei* 2 (1935): 281–82.

19. Boese, *Das öffentliche Bibliothekswesen im Dritten Reich*, pp. 228–29.

20. Quoted in Schoeps and Tress, eds., *Orte der Bücherverbrennungen*, p. 19.

21. Jutta Sywottek, "Die Gleichschaltung der deutschen Volksbüchereien: 1933 bis 1937," *Archiv für Geschichte des Buchwesens* 24 (1983): 441.

22. Barbian, *Literaturpolitik im NS-Staat*, p. 433.

23. Boese, *Das öffentliche Bibliothekswesen im Dritten Reich*, p. 226.

24. "Aufruf," *Bücherei und Bildungspflege* 13 (1933): 99.

25. Stephan Füssel, *Die Geschichte der Volksbibliothek Göttingen: 80 Jahre Stadtbibliothek*, p. 64.

26. BA, R 56 V/137, no date, n.p. The file also includes a list of books to be removed.

27. Leonhard, "Vom lebendigen zum deutschen Geist," p. 102.

28. Stieg, *Public Libraries in Nazi Germany*, p. 91.

29. Günther Röska, "Walter Hofmann und der Nationalsozialismus: Auseinandersetzungen um das Leipziger Volksbüchereiwesen," *Buchhandelsgeschichte* (2000/4), B172–75.

30. Fridolin Dressler, "Die Bayerische Staatsbibliothek im Dritten Reich," in *Beiträge zur Geschichte der Bayerischen Staatsbibliothek*, p. 295.

31. Hans-Gerd Happel, "Die Universitäts- und Stadtbibliothek Köln im Dritten Reich," in *Die Universitätsbibliotheken Heidelberg, Jena und Köln unter dem Nationalsozialismu*, edited by Ingo Toussant, p. 304.

32. Barbian, *Literaturpolitik im NS-Staat*, p. 433.

33. RGBl. 1 (1934), p. 100, reprinted in part in Sebastian Graeb-Könneker, *Literatur im Dritten Reich: Dokumente und Texte*, pp. 47–48.

34. This is how a RSK memo of March 12, 1935, characterized the new office. Cf. BA, R 56 V/166, p. 20.

35. Lemberg, *Verboten und nicht verbrannt*, vol. 2, p. 154, n. 252.

36. Bernhard Kummer, "Nationalsozialismus und Volksbüchereiwesen," *Die Bücherei* 2 (1935): 324.

37. Reichsstelle für volkstümliches Büchereiwesen to RSK, September 7, 1936, R 56 V/293, n.p.

38. RSK to Gestapa, September 22, 1936, BA, R 56 V/293, n.p.

39. Barbian, *Literaturpolitik im NS-Staat*, p. 127.

40. Goebbels, *Die Tagebücher*, Part I, vol. 3/II, p. 115.

41. BA, R 56 V/137. The document is reproduced in Sywottek, "Die Gleichschaltung der deutschen Volksbüchereien," col. 514–20.

42. BA, R 56 V/137, p. 281.

43. Cf. Engelbrecht Boese, *Das öffentliche Bibliothekswesen im Dritten Reich*, p. 156.

44. Sywottek, "Die Gleichschaltung der deutschen Volksbüchereien," cols. 445–46.

45. The decree is reprinted in Friedrich Andrae, ed., *Volksbücherei und Nationalsozialismus: Materialien zur Theorie und Politik des öffentlichen Büchereiwesens in Deutschland 1933–1945*, pp. 181–82.

46. Christian Oesterfeld. Introduction to Klaus G. Saur and Martin Hollender, eds., *Selbstbehauptung, Anpassung, Gleichschaltung, Verstrickung: Die preussische Staatsbibliothek und das deutsche Bibliothekswesen 1933–1945*, p. 19.

47. Jochen Stollberg, *Die Rothschild'sche Bibliothek in Frankfurt am Main*, p. 82. See also Sören Flachowsky, *Die Bibliothek der Berliner Universität während der Zeit des Nationalsozialismus*, pp. 91–92.

48. Barbian, *Literaturpolitk im NS-Staat*, p. 448.

49. Engelbrecht Boese, "Die Säuberung der Leipziger Bücherhallen 1933–1936," *Buch und Bibliothek* 35 (1983): 294–95.

50. Walter Rischer, *Die nationalsozialistische Kulturpolitk in Düsseldorf 1933–1945*, pp. 22, 27.

51. Boese, *Das öffentliche Bibliothekswesen im Dritten Reich*, p. 236.

52. Barbian, *Literaturpolitik im NS-Staat*, pp. 347–48.

53. Alfred Pfoser, "Die Leipziger Radikalkur in Wien: Die Wiener Städtische Büchereien im Nationalsozialismus," in *Bibliotheken während des Nationalsozialismus*, edited by Vodosek and Komorowski, vol. 2, p. 94. See also Herbert Exenberger, "Die Arbeiterbüchereien der Stadt Wien nach dem März 1938," in *Wien 1938*, edited by the Verein für Geschichte der Stadt Wien, pp. 237–47.

54. Karl Taupitz, "Der Aufbau des Büchereiwesens in Sachsen seit der nationalsozialistischen Revolution," *Die Bücherei* 4 (1937): 251.

55. Alois Klotzbücher, "Städtische Bibliotheken im Ruhrgebiet während des Nationalsozialismus," in *Bibliotheken während des Nationalsozialismus*, edited by Vodosek and Komorowski, vol. 2, pp. 63–64.

56. Barbian, *Literaturpolitik im NS-Staat*, p. 348.

57. Peter Lundgreen, ed., *Wissenschaft im Dritten Reich*, pp. 10–13.

58. Otto Graf von Rantzau, *Das Reichsministerium für Wissenschaft, Erziehung und Volksbildung*, p. 5.

59. Manfred Komorowski, "Die Tagungsprotokolle des Reichsbeirat für Bibliotheksangelegenheiten (1937–1943)," *Bibliothek: Forschung und Praxis* 16 (1992): 66–67.

60. Kirchner, "Schrifttum und wissenschaftliche Bibliotheken," pp. 514–25.

61. Walter Frank, *Kämpfende Wissenschaft*, p. 29.

62. Cited in Lemberg, *Verboten und nicht verbrannt*, vol. 2, p. 26, vol. 1, pp. 33–34.

63. Hans Peter des Coudres, "Das verbotene Schrifttum und die wissenschaftlichen Bibliotheken," *Zentralblatt für Bibliothekswesen* 52 (1935): 466–69.

64. Ingo Toussaint, *Die Universitätsbibliothek Freiburg im Dritten Reich*, 2nd rev. ed., p. 173.

65. Lemberg, *Verboten und nicht verbrannt*, vol. 1, pp. 38–39.

66. Rudolf Kummer, "Das wissenschaftliche Bibliothekswesen im nationalsozialistischen Deutschland," *Zentralblatt für Bibliothekswesen* 55 (1938): 405–07.

67. The full text of this decree is reprinted in Lemberg, *Verboten und nicht verbrannt*, vol. 1, p. 42.

68. Gestapo memo of July 1, 1936, cited by Alexander Greguletz, "Die Preussische Staatsbibliothek in den ersten Jahren des Nationalsozialismus," in *Bibliotheken während des Nationalsozialismus*, edited by Vodosek and Komorowski, vol. 1, pp. 361–62.

69. Cited by Flachowsky, *Die Bibliothek der Berliner Universität während der Zeit des Nationalsozialismus*, p. 136.

70. Pamela Spence Richards, "Die technisch-wissenschaftlichen Bibliotheken während des Nationalsozialismus," in *Bibliotheken während des Nationalsozialismus*, edited by Vodosek and Komorowski, vol. 1, p. 530.

71. BA, R 58/767, p. 22.

72. Lemberg, *Verboten und nicht verbrannt*, vol. 1, pp. 156–57.

73. Lothar Bohmüller, "Die Universitätsbibliothek Jena in den Jahren von 1933 bis 1945," in *Bibliotheken während des Nationalsozialismus*, edited by Vodosek and Komorowski, vol. 1, p. 362.

74. Michael Kuhn, ed., *Verbrannte Bücher: Verzeichnis der Bücher, die 1933 aus dem Bestand der TH Braunschweig aussortiert und zum grössten Teil vernichtet wurden*, p. 17.

75. Toussaint, *Die Universitätsbibliothek Freiburg im Dritten Reich*, pp. 184–85.

76. Leonhard, "Vom lebendigen zum deutschen Geist," p. 348; Hildegard Müller, "Die Universitätsbibliothek Heidelberg im Dritten Reich," in *Bibliotheken während des Nationalsozialismus*, edited by Vodosek and Komorowski, vol. 1, p. 355.

77. SD Graz to University Library Graz, June 10, 1942, in Manfred Hirschegger and Werner Schlacher, *Verbotene Bücher 1938: Österreichische Autoren in nationalsozialistischen Zensurlisten: Eine Auswahl der UB Graz*, p. 556.

78. Franz Schriewer, "Kampf den Leihbüchereien!" *Bücherei und Bildungswesen* 13 (1933): 100–113.

79. K. Schulz, "Schundkomplex und Leihbüchereien," *Bücherei und Bildungswesen* 13 (1933): 297–305.

80. Stieg, *Public Libraries in Nazi Germany*, p. 171.

81. Raimund Kast, "Die Leihbibliotheken im Nationalsozialismus," in *Bibliotheken während des Nationalsozialismus*, edited by Vodosek and Komorowski, vol. 1, p. 523.

82. Raimund Kast, "Der deutsche Leihbuchhandel und seine Organisation im 20. Jahrhundert," *Archiv für Geschichte des Buchwesens* 36 (1991): 241–46. Between January 1934 and January 1938 Hürter published six articles about the work of the Beratungs- und Überwachungsstelle published in the *Zeitschrift der Leihbücherei*.

83. "Verzeichnis der polizeilich beschlagnahmten und eingezogenen sowie der für Leihbüchereien verbotenen Druckschriften," cited in Dahm, *Das jüdische Buch im Dritten Reich*, p. 163, n. 17.

84. Überwachungsstelle der Fachschaft Leihbücherei to RMfVP, BA, R 55/682, p. 92.

85. Karl-Friedrich Schrieber et al., *Das Recht der Reichskulturkammer ... und ihrer Einzelkammern*, vol. 2, p. 29.

86. "Übersicht über den Fortgang der Reinigungsaktionen," BA, R 55/682, p. 33.

87. Reichsbuchamt to RMfVP, October 30, 1934, BA, R 55/682, p. 55.

88. The larger number is given by Kast, ibid., p. 250; the smaller is by Bernd Arnim and Friedrich Knilli, *Gewerbliche Leihbüchereien: Berichte, Analyse und Interviews* p. 25.

89. "Denkschrift," BA, R 55/682, pp. 85–90.

90. Kast, "Der deutsche Leihbuchhandel," p. 241.

91. See, e.g., RSK to Überwachungsstelle, October 13, 1936, BA, R 56 V/1246, p. 10.

92. BA, R 58/769, p. 167.

93. BA, R 58/839, p. 104.

94. Seifert, *Die grosse Säuberung des Schrifttums*, p. 77.

95. Kast, "Der deutsche Leihbuchhandel," p. 273.

96. "Ganz wichtige Bestimmung der Reichsschrifttumskammer," *Zeitschrift der Leihbücherei*, vol. 4, no. 15 (August 10, 1935): 16.

97. RSK memo of May 11, 1937, BA, R 56 V/223, file 1, n.p.

98. RSK memo of March 8, 1937, ibid., n.p.

99. *Zeitschrift der Leihbücherei*, vol. 3, no. 19 (October 10, 1934): 6.

100. "Durch Schund- und Schmutzschriften verführt...," *Zeitschrift der Leihbücherei*, vol. 3, no. 13 (September 10, 1934): 12.

101. Hans Benecke, *Buchhandlung in Berlin: Erinnerungen an eine schwere Zeit*, p. 101.

102. Boese, *Das öffentliche Bibliothekswesen im Dritten Reich*, p. 184.

103. *Zeitschrift der Leihbücherei*, vol. 3, no. 5 (March 3, 1934): 2.

104. Boese, *Das öffentliche Bibliothekswesen im Dritten Reich*, p. 185.

105. Stieg, *Public Libraries in Nazi Germany*, p. 199.

106. Wilhelm Schuster, "Der Stand des deutschen öffentlichen Büchereiwesens," *Die Bücherei* 2 (1935): 250.

107. Rust, "Noch heute!," p. 12.

108. Christine Razum, "Der Deutsche Verband Evangelischer Büchereien (DVEB)," in *Bibliotheken während des Nationalsozialismus*, edited by Vodosek and Komorowski, vol. 1, pp. 502–03.

109. Cited by Stieg, *Public Libraries in Nazi Germany*, pp. 196–97, 202.

110. Stieg, *Public Libraries in Nazi Germany*, pp. 203–204.

111. Boese, *Das öffentliche Bibliothekswesen im Dritten Reich*, p. 311.

112. Razum, "Der Deutsche Verband Evangelischer Büchereien," pp. 502–06.

Chapter 11

1. The lists of expelled or rejected authors for the years 1934 to 1941 can be found at BA, R 56 V/79.

2. This number is the total of monthly figures given in *Der deutsche Schriftsteller*, vol. 6 (1941).

3. The new policy is mentioned in BA, R 56 V/7, p. 100.

4. *Nachrichtenblatt des Reichsministeriums für Volksaufklärung und Propaganda*, no. 18 (September 8, 1939): 101.

5. Goebbels, *Die Tagebücher*, Part I, vol. 8, p. 379.

6. Hans Dieter Schäfer, *Das gespaltene Bewusstsein: Vom Dritten Reich bis zu den langen fünfziger Jahren)*, p. 340.

7. Report on a conference on June 11, 1936, BA, R 58/923, p. 62

8. BA, R 56 V/96, p. 180.

9. BA, R 56 V/217, file 6, n.p.

10. BA, R 56 V/518, p. 1.

11. Cited by Andrae, ed., *Volksbücherei und Nationalsozialismus*, pp. 184, 186.

12. Boelcke, ed., *"Wollt Ihr den totalen Krieg?"*, p. 88.

13. BA, R 56 V/222, file 11, n.p.

14. Boberach, ed., *Meldungen aus dem Reich*, vol. 3, p. 583.

15. BA, R 56 V/216, file 4, n.p.

16. BA, R 56 V/96, p. 102.

17. RSK to Gestapo, December 12, 1939, BA, R 56 V/61, p. 132.

18. Ihde, *Handbuch der Reichsschrifttumskammer*, pp. 199, 202.

19. BA, R 58/918, p. 141.

20. Sebastian Losch, "Klare Haltung," *Grossdeutsches Leihbüchereiblatt* 1 (1939): 209.

21. Ihde, *Handbuch der Reichsschrifttumskammer*, p. 183.

22. Boelcke, ed., *"Wollt Ihr den totalen Krieg?"*, p. 34.

23. Cited in Andrae, ed., *Volksbücherei und Nationalsozialismus*, pp. 186–87

24. BA, R 56 V/95, p. 37.

25. RMfVP to RSK, February 21, 1940, BA, R 56 V/217, file 1, n.p.

26. BA, R 56 V/222, n.p.

27. Cited in Andrae, ed., *Volksbücherei und Nationalsozialismus*, p. 190.

28. RMfVP, *Verzeichnis englischer und nordamerikanischer Schriftsteller*. This publication listed 1,800 such authors.

29. *Vertrauliche Mitteilungen für die Fachschaft Handel*, no. 261 (February, 12. 1945), p. 1.

30. *Vertrauliche Mitteilungen für die Fachschaft Handel*, no. 45 (December 15, 1939), p. 1.

31. RSK memo, January 23, 1940, BA, R 56 V/96, p. 116.

32. Ihde, *Handbuch der Reichsschrifttumskammer*, pp. 171–72.

33. Continental Caoutchouc Compagnie to RSK, March 1, 1940, BA, R 56 V/68, p. 194.

34. RSK to Frick, March 28, 1940, BA, R 56 V/68, p. 187.

35. BA, R 56 V/68, p. 191.

36. *Vertrauliche Mitteilungen für die Fachschaft Verlag*, no. 48 (March 1, 1940): 1.
37. RSK memo, May 7, 1940, BA, R 56 V/96, p. 82.
38. RSK memo June 24, 1940, BA, R 56 V/96, p. 67.
39. *Vertrauliche Mitteilungen für die Fachschaft Verlag*, no. 54 (July, 15, 1940): 1.
40. NSDAP, Partei-Kanzlei, *Verfügungen/Anordnungen/Bekanntgebungen*, July 14, 1942, vol. 1 (1943): 474.
41. "Veröffentlichungen in oberschlesischer Mundart," May 2, 1940, "Sächsische Mundart in Buchveröffentlichungen," January 12, 1941; Ihde, *Handbuch der Reichsschrifttumskammer*, p. 188.
42. RSK memo of February 21, 1942, BA, R 56 V/96, p. 30.
43. BA, R 56 V/68, p. 67.
44. Johst to Goebbels, March 7, 1940, BA, R 56 V/67, p. 125.
45. Memo of July 24, 1940, BA, R 56 V/221, file 9, n.p.
46. RSK, *Jahresliste 1940 des schädlichen und unerwünschten Schrifttums*, p. 3. It is reprinted in Ihde, *Handbuch der Reichsschrifttumskammer*, pp. 75–76, together with *"Erläuterungen"* on pp. 76–79.
47. Memo by RMfVP official K. H. Bischoff, May 18, 1940, BA, R 56 V/67, p. 90.
48. Johst order of June 10, 1942, *Der deutsche Schriftsteller* 7 (1942): 81.
49. BA, R 56 V/67, p. 50
50. RMfVP, *Arbeitsrichtlinien für den Fachbuch-Lektor*, pp. 5–7.
51. See BA, NS 12/77, passim.
52. RMfVP, Abt. Schrifttum, *Liste der für Jugendliche und Büchereien ungeeigneten Druckschriften, Stand* as of October 15.
53. See, e.g., Reichsleitung der NSDAP to RMfVP, July 26, 1940, BA, R 56 V/67, p. 61.
54. Boberach, ed., *Meldungen aus dem Reich*, vol. 4, April 3, 1940, p. 950; vol. 5 September 16, 1940, p. 1576. See also Florian Triebel, "Die 'Meldungen aus dem Reich' as buchhan-delsgeschichtliche Quellen," *Archiv für Geschichte des Buchwesens* 58 (2004): 200.
55. Cf. Kark Robert Popp, "Das gute Jugendbuch," *Bbl.* 102 (May 7, 1935), p. 359.
56. February 27, 1942, Goebbels, *Die Tagebücher*, part II, vol. 3, pp. 382–83.
57. Wilhelm Haegert, "Schrifttum und Buchhandlung im Kriege," *Bbl.* 107 (April 23, 1940): 150.
58. NSDAP, Partei-Kanzlei, *Verfügungen/Anordnungen/Bekanntgebungen*, August 26, 1941, vol. 1 (1943): 475.
59. BA, R 58/173, p. 150
60. Christian Adam, *Lesen unter Hitler: Autoren, Bestseller, Leser im Dritten Reich*, p. 200.
61. Quoted in Ine van Linthout, "'Dichter, schreibt Unterhaltungsromane!': Der Stellenwert der Unterhaltungsliteratur im 'Dritten Reich'," in *Im Pausenraum des 'Dritten Reiches': Zur Populärliteratur im nationalsozialistischen Deutschland*, edited by Carsten Würmann and Ansgar Warner, p. 122.
62. BA, NS 8/249, p. 85.
63. PPK to Reichskanzlei, October 24, 1944, BA, NS 11/38, n.p.
64. BA, NS 8/171, p. 8.
65. "Prüfung von Schrifttum," reprinted in Ihde, *Handbuch der Reichsschrifttumskammer*, p. 137.
66. Ihde, *Handbuch der Reichsschrifttumskammer*, pp. 138–39.
67. Baur to Hinkel, July 5, 1941, BA, R 55/889, pp. 4–7.
68. Ihde, *Handbuch der Reichsschrifttumskammer*, pp. 188, 202–03, 148.
69. Boberach, ed., *Meldungen aus dem Reich*, vol. 2, p. 290.
70. Goebbels, *Die Tagebücher*, part I, vol. 7, pp. 213, 258.
71. *Vertrauliche Mitteilungen für die Fachschaft Verlag*, no. 24 (July 6, 1937): 7; no. 34 (May 11, 1938): 5.
72. Barbian, *Literaturpolitik im NS-Staat*, pp. 274–78.
73. Rudolf Erckmann, "Probleme und Aufgaben unseres Schrifttums," *Die Bücherei* 8 (1941): 311.
74. Rudolf Erckmann, "Probleme und Aufgaben unseres Schrifttums," *Die Bücherei* 8 (1941): 311.

75. Hederich to RMfVP, November 9, 1944, BA, NS 11/38, n.p.

76. BA, R 56 V/217, n.p.

77. RSK to Gruppe Buchhandel, April 18, 1940, BA, R 56 V/96, p. 102.

78. *Vertrauliche Mitteilungen für die Fachschaft Verlag*, no. 121 (October 1, 1941): 2.

79. The correspondence in the case can be found in BA, R 56 V/439.

80. BA, R 58/912, n.p.

81. Ihde, *Handbuch der Reichsschrifttumskammer,* p. 222.

82. Goebbels, *Die Tagebücher*, Part II, vol. 3, p. 376.

83. Cited in Barbian, *Literaturpolitik im NS-Staat*, pp. 278–79.

84. Ibid., pp. 94, 279.

85. *Vertrauliche Mitteilungen für die Fachschaft Verlag*, no. 338 (January 15, 1943): 1.

86. *Vertrauliche Mitteilungen für die Fachschaft Verlag*, no. 473 (October 25, 1943): 1.

87. *Vertrauliche Mitteilungen für die Fachschaft Verlag*, no. 138 (October 1, 1941): 5.

88. BA, R 56 V/61, p. 98.

89. Ihde to Max Jungmickel, Septmber 24, 1943, R 56 V/26, p. 31.

90. BA (formerly BDC), BK B110, July 27, 1943, p. 154.

91. BA, R 9361 V/6735 (formerly BDC), fr. 2652.

92. BA, SSO/124A (formerly BDC), p. 98

93. BA, R 9361 V/6735 (formerly BDC), fr. 2674.

94. RSK to RMfVP, November 28, 1934, BA, R 55/682, p. 92.

95. Barbian, *Literaturpolitik im NS-Staat,* p. 487; Saul Friedländer et al., *Bertelsmann im Dritten Reich,* p. 443.

96. Cornelia Caroline Funke, *"Im Verleger verkörpert sich das Gesicht seiner Zeit": Unternehmungsführung und Programmgestaltung im Gustav Kiepenheuer Verlag 1909 bis 1944,* p. 207.

97. Barbian, *Literaturpolitik im NS-Staat*, pp. 186–92.

98. *Bbl.* no. 242 (October 17, 1939): 100; NS 8/247, pp. 98–99.

99. Oda Schaefer, *Auch wenn du träumst gehen die Uhren: Lebenserinnerungen,* p. 286.

100. Hans-Eugen Bühler, *Der Frontbuchhandel 1939–1945: Organisationen, Kompetenzen, Verlage, Bücher,* p. 28.

101. BA, R 56 V/95, p. 42.

102. RMfVP to RSK, February 21, 1940, BA, R 56 V/217, file 1, n.p.

103. See the correspondence in NS 11/73, pp. 2–10.

104. Boelcke, ed., *"Wollt Ihr den totalen Krieg?",* pp. 209–10.

105. RSK to Wilhelm Baur, October 11, 1943, BA, R 56 V/43, p. 57.

106. Cf. *Liste des für die Volksbüchereien ungeeigneten erzählenden Schrifttum mit konfessionellem Einschlag,* discussed in Boese, *Das öffentliche Bibliothekswesen im Dritten Reich,* p. 231.

107. Cited in Adam, *Lesen unter Hitler,* p. 33.

108. "Bücher, deren Ausleihe und Verkauf einzustellen ist!" *Grossdeutsches Leihbüchereiblatt* 2 (1940): 49–50.

109. Ihde, *Handbuch der Reichsschrifttumskammer,* p. 232.

110. RSK memo, July 7, 1940, BA, R 56 V/67, p. 292.

111. BA, 56 V/67, p. 282.

112. Ihde, *Handbuch der Reichsschrifttumskammer,* p. 234.

113. *Zeitschrift der Leihbücherei,* vol. 10, no. 9 (May 10, 1941): 2.

114. RSK to Gruppe Buchhandel, April 16, 1942, BA, R 56 V/67, p. 276.

115. "Haben Sie wirklich Ihre Leihbücherei von ungeeignetem Schrifttum gesäubert?" *Grossdeutsches Leihbüchereiblatt* 4 (1942): 268

116. RSK memo of November 17, 1942, BA, R 56 V/67, p. 267.

117. RSK to SD, April 19, 1944, BA, R 56 V/67, p. 250.

118. BA, R 56 V/67, p. 205.

119. BA, R 56 V/67, p. 4.

120. Dietrich Strothmann, *Nationalsozialistische Literaturpolitik: Ein Beitrag zur Publizistik im Dritten Reich,* 4th edition, p. 116.

121. Ihde memo of January 1943, BA, R 56 V/26, pp. 135–38.

122. BA, R 56 V/110, pp. 49, 50–51, 228.

123. BA, PK D 83 (formerly BDC), fr. 1618
124. BA, R 56 V/152, p. 98.
125. *Die Reichkulturkammer*, vol. 2, no. 8/9 (August/September 1944): 121.
126. BA, R 56 V/152, p. 20.

Chapter 12

1. Reinhard Bollmus, *Das Amt Rosenberg und seine Gegner: Studien zum Machtkampf im nationalsozialistischen Herrschaftssystem*, p. 239.
2. Hess memo, BA, NS 6/215, p. 2.
3. Publicized by Bormann, October 12, 1935, BA, NS/221, p. 22.
4. Ian Kershaw, *Hitler, the Germans, and the Final Solution*, p. 32.
5. Hitler's decree of June 30, 1933, in Ihde, *Handbuch der Reichsschrifttumskammer*, pp. 1–2.
6. His appointment and the creation of the PPK occurred on April 16, 1934.
7. BA, NS 11/6, n.p.
8. Quoted in Diehl-Thiele, *Partei und Staat im Dritten Reich*, p. 244.
9. *Alfred Rosenberg's Diary*, www.ushmm.org/information/exhibitions, p. 731.
10. Rosenberg to Buhler, September 25, 1934, BA, NS 8/208, pp. 179–80.
11. "Bekanntmachung," April 8, 1935, ibid., p.155.
12. Peter Diehl-Thiele, *Partei und Staat im Dritten Reich*, 2nd rev. ed., p. 209.
13. Rosenberg to Bormann, January 31, 1936, BA, NS 8/178, pp. 293–96.
14. Rosenberg to Hess, February 18, 1936, BA, NS 8/178, p. 283.
15. BA, NS 8/178, p. 63.
16. Hess memo of August 15, 1937, BA, NS 8/208, p. 104.
17. Hagemeyer to PPK, August 16, 1938, BA, NS 8/246, p. 249.
18. Rosenberg to Buhler, October 28, 1937, BA, NS 8/183, p. 122.
19. Hess memo of November 11, 1937, BA, NS 8/208, p. 92.
20. "Erlass über den Geschäftsbereich des Generalbeauftragten des Deutschen Reiches und der N.S.D.A.P. zur Abwehr des Weltbolschewismus und zur Sicherung der Einheit der nationalsozialistischen Weltanschauung und das Zusammenwirken des Generalbeauftragten mit den obersten Reichsbehörden und Parteidienststellen," n.d., BA, NS 8/168, pp. 170–73.
21. BA, R 43 II/1200, p. 5.
22. Bouhler to Rosenberg, November 4, 1938, BA, NS 8/208, p. 23.
23. Hagemeyer memo, December 9, 1938, BA, NS 8/246, p. 284.
24. Rosenberg to Buhler, February 7, 1938, BA, NS 8//208, p. 66.
25. PPK to Hess, July 20. 1938, BA, NS 11/5, p. 30.
26. Bouhler to Rosenberg, October 24, 1938, BA, NS 8/208, p. 24,
27. Amann to Bouhler, December 10, 1938, BA, NS 11/9, n.p.
28. Rosenberg to Hess, May 4, 1939, BA, NS 8/181, p. 83.
29. Rosenberg to Hess, June 30, 1939, BA, NS 8/181, pp. 2–3.
30. Seraphim, ed., *Das politische Tagebuch Alfred Rosenbergs*, entry for September 24, 1939, p. 79.
31. Rosenberg to Adjuntantur des *Führers*, December 15, 1938, BA, NS 11/23a, n.p.
32. Bouhler to Rosenberg, January 18, 1939, BA, NS 11/23a, n.p.
33. Bouhler to Hess, March 9, 1939, BA, NS 11/23a, n.p.
34. Bormann to Bouhler, March 14, 1939, BA, NS 11/23a, n.p.
35. Bormann to Bouhler, March 14, 1939, BA, NS 11/23a, n.p.
36. Seraphim, ed., *Das politische Tagebuch Alfred Rosenbergs*, entry for November 1, 1939, p. 87.
37. "Entwurf," BA, NS 8/182, pp. 26–27
38. Lammers memo, November 20, 1939, BA, R 43 II/1200, p. 19
39. Bormann to Lammers, November 24, 1939, BA, R 43 II/1200, p. 23.
40. Bouhler to Hitler, December 13, 1939, BA, R 43 II/1200, pp. 109–10.
41. See BA, NS 8/183, pp. 38–39, 114–21.
42. Rosenberg to Buhler, April 8, 1940, BA, NS 8/209, pp. 91–92.

43. Bormann to Rosenberg, April 25, 1941, BA, NS 8/185, p. 109.

44. NSDAP, Partei-Kanzlei, *Verfügungen-Anordnungen-Bekanntmachungen*, vol. 1 (1943), p. 5.

45. Bormann to Rosenberg, June 11, 1941, BA, NS 8/185, p. 32.

46. Barbian, *Literaturpolitik im "Dritten Reich,"* p. 297.

47. "Vereinbarung," January 28, 1943, BA, NS 8/209, p. 38.

48. BA, NS 8/209, p. 35.

49. BA, NS 8/188, p. 2, cited by Barbian, *Literaturpolitik im NS-Staat*, p. 161.

50. PPK memo of September 8, 1944, BA, NS 11/38, pp. 1–2.

51. Bouhler to Bormann, November 4, 1944, BA, NS 11/38, p. 135.

52. BA, R 58/899, pp. 197–200.

53. BA, NS 8/182, p. 269.

54. Urban to PPK, BA, NS 8/208, p. 57.

55. Hagemeyer to Rosenberg, March 23, 1939, BA, NS 8/247, p. 21.

56. Rosenberg to Hess, October 12, 1939, BA, NS 8/182, p. 100.

57. BA, NS 15/107, n.p.

58. Bouhler to Rosenberg, November 28, 1940, BA, NS 8/209, pp. 84–86.

59. Hederich to Rosenberg, December 24, 1940, BA, NS 15/107, n.p.

60. "An die Mitglieder des Reichsausschusses für das Schul- und Unterrichtsschrifttum," April 1941, BA, NS 8/209, pp. 59–80.

61. See, e.g., "Ergänzungsliste zur Grundliste für Schülerbüchereien an Volksschulen," *Die Bücherei* 8 (1941): 290–94.

62. "Anordnung der Meldepflicht für Schul- und Unterrichtsschrifttum," *Vertrauliche Mitteilungen für die Fachschaft Verlag*, no. 101 (August 9, 1941), p. 1.

63. Ibid., p. 53.

64. Rolf Eilers, *Die nationalsozialistische Schulpolitik: Eine Studie zur Funktion der Erziehung im totalitären Staat*, pp. 30, 115.

65. Bouhler to Rust, January 28, 1944, BA, NS 11/38, pp. 235–37.

66. BA (formerly BDC), memo of May 18, 1944, PK E44, p. 436.

67. RMI to RMfVP, March 5, 1945, BA, R 56 V/68, p. 68.

68. Beratungsstelle für das astrologische und verwandte Schrifttum," *Der deutsche Schriftsteller* 1 (1936): 37.

69. [Karl Friedrich] Schulze, "Das astrologische und okkulte Schrifttum im neuen Deutschland," *Der deutsche Schriftsteller* 1 (1936), p. 40.

70. "Stellungnahme," n.d., BA, R 56 V/407.

71. "Gutachten!" October 5, 1936, BA, R 56 V/435, n.p.

72. Beratungsstelle to Verlag der Freunde, September 14, 1937, BA, R 56 V/266, p. 7.

73. Erckmann memo of May 21, 1941, BA, NS 8/209, p. 18.

74. This chronology is based on a memo of May 20, 1941, by Hugo Koch, the RMfVP official who had initiated the closing down of the Beratungsstelle, BA, R 43 II/479a, p. 111.

75. BA, R 56 V/68, p. 53.

76. Kittler "Gutachten," August 3, 1938, BA, R 43 II/479a, p. 116.

77. Uranus Verlag to RSK, March 23, 1939, BA, R 56 V/68, p. 39.

78. Hederich to RMfVP, October 14, 1939, BA, R 43 II/479a, pp. 119–20.

79. Rosenberg to Goebbels, November 29, 1939, BA, NS 8/209, pp. 25–26.

80. Willi Boelcke, ed., *"Wollt Ihr den totalen Krieg?" Die geheimen Goebbels-Konferenzen 1939–1943*, p. 25.

81. *Vertrauliche Mitteilungen für die Fachschaft Verlag*, no. 53 (June 8, 1940): 1.

82. Rudolf Erckmann to Hederich, January 31, 1941, BA, R 43 II/479a, pp. 81–82.

83. Bormann to Goebbels, March 14, 1941, BA, R 43 II/479a, p. 62

84. BA, R 43 II/479a, p. 69.

85. Bouhler to Heydrich, March 20, 1941, BA, R 43 II/479a, p. 67.

86. Goebbels to Bouhler, April 4, 1941, BA, R 43 II/479a, pp. 85–88.

87. Goebbels to Lammers, April 4, 1941, BA, R 43 II/479a, pp. 74–75.

88. Goebbels to Lammers, April 8, 1941, BA, R 43 II/479a, pp. 78–80.

89. Bouhler to Lammers, July 18, 1941, BA, R 43 II/479a, pp. 98–107.

90. *Alfred Rosenberg's Diary,* May 14, 1941, www.ushmm.org/information/exhibitions, p. 559.
91. BA, NS 8/185, pp. 81–82.
92. BA, R 43 II/479a, pp. 108–09.
93. Bouhler to Bormann, November 22, 1941, BA, NS 11/22, n.p.
94. "Bericht über eine Sitzung ... am 5. July, 1944," BA, NS 8/249, pp. 60–61.
95. The first of these meetings took place on June 11, 1936. See BA, R 58/923, p. 60.
96. Goebbels, *Die Tagebücher,* Part I, vol. 7, pp. 195, 207, 211.
97. Bollmus, *Das Amt Rosenberg,* p. 61.
98. Seraphim, ed., *Das politische Tagebuch Alfred Rosenbergs,* pp. 64, 65.
99. Seraphim, ed., *Das politische Tagebuch Alfred Rosenbergs,* p. 78.

Chapter 13

1. Ralf Schnell, *Literarische Innere Emigration: 1933–1945,* p. 123.
2. Günther Weisenborn, *Der lautlose Aufstand: Bericht über die Widerstandsbewegung des deutschen Volkes 1933–1945,* p. 219.
3. Thomas Mann, "Warum ich nicht nach Deutschland zurückkehre," *Essays,* edited by Hermann Kurzke and Stephan Stachorski, vol. 6, p. 37. See also Thomas Mann et al., *Ein Streitgespräch über die äussere und innere Emigration.*
4. Quoted in Fritz J. Raddatz, *Die Nachgeborenen: Leseerfahrungen mit zeitgenössischer Literatur,* p. 16.
5. BA, R 56 V/26, p. 122.
6. Hans Dieter Schäfer, *Das gespaltene Bewusstsein: Vom Dritten Reich bis zu den fünfziger Jahren,* pp. 9, 335.
7. Edda Ziegler, *Verboten—verfemt—vertrieben: Schriftstellerinnen im Widerstand gegen den Nationalsozialismus,* pp. 299–300.
8. Quoted in Barbara Bronnen, *Flieger mit gestutzten Flügeln: Die letzten Jahre der Ricarda Huch 1933–1947,* pp. 30–32.
9. Bronnen, *Flieger mit gestutzten Flügeln,* pp. 76–77.
10. Albert J. Hofstetter, *Werner Bergengruen im Dritten Reich,* p. 94.
11. Hans Sarkowicz and Alf Mentzer, *Literatur in Nazi Deutschland: Ein biografisches Lexikon,* p. 31.
12. Werner Bergengruen, *Schreibtischerinnerungen* p. 180.
13. BA (formerly BDC), PK B90, n.p.
14. Bergengruen, *Schreibtischerinnerungen,* pp. 208, 200–201.
15. Bergengruen describes the affair in Bergengruen et al., eds., *Schriftstellerexistenz in der Diktatur: Aufzeichnungen und Reflexionen zur Politik, Geschichte und Kultur 1940-1963,* pp. 70–76.
16. Bergengruen, *Schreibtischerinnerungen,* p. 195.
17. BA (formerly BDC), PK B9, pp. 704, 694.
18. Bergengruen, *Schriftstellerexistenz in der Diktatur,* p. 170.
19. Grimm, "Im Dickicht der inneren Emigration," p. 412.
20. Loewy, *Literatur unter dem Hakenkreuz,* pp. 323, 326; Thomas Mann to Agnes E. Mayer, December 14, 1945, quoted in Heimo Schwilk, *Ernst Jünger, ein Jahrhundertleben: Die Biographie,* p. 433.
21. "Im Dickicht der inneren Emigration," pp. 416–17.
22. Adam, *Lesen unter Hitler,* p. 305.
23. Schwilk, *Ernst Jünger,* p. 385.
24. Schwilk, *Ernst Jünger,* pp. 289, 311, 295.
25. See on this Abraham Ascher and Guenter Lewy, "National Bolshevism in Weimar Germany: Alliance of Political Extremes against Democracy," *Social Research* 23 (1956): 475–78.
26. The text of this correspondence can be found in Wulf, *Literatur und Dichtung im Dritten Reich,* pp. 37–39. Wulf's work has been criticized because at times he fails to note omissions in the material reproduced.

27. Quoted in Peter Trawny, *Die Autorität des Zeugen: Ernst Jüngers politisches Werk*, p. 62.
28. Schwilk, *Ernst Jünger*, p. 360.
29. Schwilk, *Ernst Jünger* pp. 367–68.
30. Graeb-Könneker, *Literatur im Dritten Reich*, p. 341.
31. Schwilk, *Ernst Jünger*, p. 377.
32. Barbian, *Literaturpolitik im "Dritten Reich"*, p. 544.
33. NSDAP, Propagandaleitung, *Kulturpolitische Informationen*, April 18, 1942, p. 2.
34. Peter de Mendelssohn, *Der Geist in der Despotie: Versuche über die moralischen Möglichkeiten des Intellektuellen in der totalitären Gesellschaft,* p. 182.
35. Trawny, *Die Autorität des Zeugen*, p. 147.
36. Quoted in Schwilk, *Ernst Jünger*, p. 385.
37. Quoted in Schwilk, *Ernst Jünger*, p. 389.
38. Schwilk, *Ernst Jünger*, p. 403.
39. Allan Mitchell, *The Devil's Captain: Ernst Jünger in Nazi Paris, 1941–1944*, pp. 54, 60.
40. Heidrun Ehrke-Rotermund and Erwin Rotermund, *Zwischenreiche und Gegenwelten: Texte und Vorstudien zur "Verdeckten Schreibweise" im "Dritten Reich"*, p. 328.
41. Loewy, *Literatur unter dem Hakenkreuz*, p. 323.
42. Mendelssohn, *Der Geist in der Despotie*, p. 220. A similar position is taken by Hannes Heer, *Vom Verschwinden der Täter: Der Vernichtungskrieg fand statt, aber keiner war dabei*, chap. 4: "Das Schweigen des Hauptmanns Jünger."
43. Quoted in Ernst Klee, *Das Kulturlexikon zum Dritten Reich: Wer war was vor und nach 1945*, p. 662.
44. Zuckmayer, *Geheimreport*, p. 23.
45. Quoted in Sarkowicz and Mentzer, *Literatur in Nazi Deutschland*, p. 352.
46. Jörg Hattwig, *Das Dritte Reich im Werk Ernst Wiecherts: Geschichtsdenken, Selbstverständnis und literarische Praxis*, p. 13.
47. *Das Dritte Reich im Werk Ernst Wiecherts*, pp. 28, 32.
48. Guido Reiner, ed., *Ernst Wiechert im Dritten Reich: Eine Dokumentation*, p. 97.
49. Ernst Wiechert, "Die Aufgaben des deutschen Buchhandels im nationalsozialistischen Staat: Hat der Buchhandel versagt?" *Bbl.* vol. 100 (December 19, 1933): 980.
50. *Die Bücherei* 3 (1936): 665.
51. The full text can be found in BA (formerly BDC), PK B230, pp. 652–72.
52. "Bericht," BA (formerly BDC), PK B230, p. 646.
53. Reiner, ed., *Ernst Wiechert im Dritten Reich*, pp. 70–73.
54. Reinhold Grimm, "Im Dickicht der inneren Emigration," in *Die deutsche Literatur im Dritten Reich: Themen, Traditionen, Wirkungen*, edited by Horst Denkler and Karl Prümm, p. 414.
55. Hellmuth Langenbucher, *Volkhafte Dichtung der Zeit*, 3rd rev. ed., pp. 205–08.
56. The text of Wiechert's letter is not preserved. We know about its content from a communication between the Gestapo Munich and Düsseldorf of July 18, 1938, reprinted in Graeb-Könneker, *Literatur im Dritten Reich*, pp. 94–95.
57. Reiner, ed., *Ernst Wiechert im Dritten Reich*, p. 103; Hattwig, *Das Dritte Reich im Werk Ernst Wiecherts*, p. 109.
58. Wiechert completed this work in 1939 and buried the manuscript in his garden. *Sämtliche Werke*, vol. 9, pp. 197–336.
59. "Jahreslagebericht 1938," BA, R 58/1095, p. 137.
60. Reiner, ed., *Ernst Wiechert im Dritten Reich*, p. 114; Hattwig, *Das Dritte Reich im Werk Ernst Wiecherts*, p. 115.
61. Haegert memo of January 13, 1940, BA, R 1501/5645, p. 97.
62. Reiner, ed., *Ernst Wiechert im Dritten Reich*, p. 124
63. Sarkowicz and Mentzer, *Literatur in Nazi Deutschland*, p. 31. Hattwig, *Das Dritte Reich im Werk Ernst Wiecherts*, p. 161.
64. J. Peters, "Das Werk Ernst Wiecherts," *Die Bücherei* 7 (1940): 28.
65. Wiechert, *Jahre und Zeiten: Erinnerungen*, in *Sämtliche Werke*, vol. 9, p. 699.
66. Wiechert to Frank, June 19, 1943, quoted in Reiner, ed., *Ernst Wiechert im Dritten Reich*, p. 184.

67. Hattwig, *Das Dritte Reich im Werk Ernst Wiecherts*, p. 242.
68. Fritz Joachim Raddatz, *Gottfried Benn: Ein Leben—niederer Wahn. Eine Biographie* (Berlin, 2011), p. 65.
69. Quoted in Inge Jens, *Dichter zwischen rechts und links: Die Geschichte der Sektion für Dichtkunst der Preussischen Akademie der Künste dargestellt nach den Dokumenten* , p. 288.
70. Excerpts from the minutes are reprinted in Graeb-Könneker, ed., *Literatur im Dritten Reich*, pp. 27–31, 32.
71. Jens, *Dichter zwischen rechts und links,* p. 191.
72. Quoted in Jens, *Dichter zwischen rechts und links*, p. 202.
73. Breuer, *Geschichte der literarischen Zensur*, p. 235.
74. Gottfried Benn, "Der neue Staat und die Intellektuellen," *Sämtliche Werke*, vol. 4, pp. 503, 15–18.
75. Letter of May 9, 1933, quoted in Joachim Dyck, *Der Zeitzeuge: Gottfried Benn 1929–1949*, p. 105.
76. "Antwort an die literarischen Emigranten," *Sämtliche Werke*, vol. 4, pp. 24–32.
77. Benn, *Doppelleben: Zwei Selbstdarstellungen*, p. 89.
78. Schöffling, ed., *Dort wo man Bücher verbrennt*, p. 206. The full list of names can also be found under the Wikipedia entry for "Gelöbnis treuester Gefolgschaft."
79. "Die Aufgaben des deutschen Buchhandels im nationalsozialistischen Staat," *Bbl.* no. 292 (December 16, 1933): 973–74; reprinted in *Sämtliche Werke*, vol. 4, pp. 95–96.
80. *Berliner Lokal-Anzeiger*, March 30, 1934, quoted in Raddatz, *Gottfried Benn*, p. 127.
81. Carl Zuckmayer, *Geheimreport*, edited by Gunther Nickel and Johann Schrön, pp. 76–77.
82. Kershaw, *Hitler*, p. 517.
83. Jörg Magenau, *Gottfried Benn* (Berlin, 2010), p. 35
84. Quoted in Graeb-Könneker, ed., *Literatur im Dritten Reich*, pp. 98–99.
85. "Briefe," edited by Marguerite Valerie Schlüter, vol. 5, pp. 201–02, 69.
86. PPK to Gestapa, August 4, 1936, BA, R 58/893, p. 29.
87. Gestapa memo of August 21, 1936, BA, R 58/893, p. 32.
88. Benn to Johst, July 23, 1937, BA (formerly BDC), PK B8, p. 1864.
89. Johst to Benn, August 2, 1937, BA (formerly BDC), PK B8, p. 1872.
90. Quoted in Raddatz, *Gottfried Benn*, p. 166.
91. Himmler to Willrich (the author of the 1937 book attacking Benn), September 12, 1937. BA (formery BDC), R 9361 V/4027, p. 1848.
92. The letter is reprinted in Graeb-Könneker, *Literatur im Dritten Reich*, pp. 102–03.
93. Johst to Himmler, March 29, 1938, BA (formerly BDC), PK B8, n.p.; reprinted in Graeb-Könneker, *Literatur im Dritten Reich*, pp. 103–04.
94. Benn, *Doppelleben*, pp. 78–79.
95. Quoted in Christiane Deussen, *Erinnerung als Rechtfertigung, Autobiographien nach 1945: Gottfried Benn, Hans Carossa, Arnold Bronnen*, p. 45.
96. Ernst Loewy, *Literatur unter dem Hakenkreuz: Das Dritte Reich und seine Dichtung—eine Dokumentation*, p. 321.
97. Cited in Eberhard Hilscher, *Gerhart Hauptmann: Leben und Werk*, pp. 403, 409.
98. Erich Ebermeyer, *Denn heute gehört uns Deutschland. .:.Persönliches und politisches Tagebuch von der Machtergreifung bis zum 31. Dezember 1935*, p. 263.
99. K. S. Guthke in *Schweizer Monatshefte*, no. 10 (981): 787, quoted in Eberhard Hilscher, *Gerhart Hauptmann: Leben und Werk*, p. 403.
100. Cited by Jan-Pieter Barbian, "'Fehlbesetzung': Zur Rolle von Gerhard Hauptmann im 'Dritten Reich'," *Bbl.* vol 17, no. 101 (December 17, 1996): B 154.
101. Cited in Hans Sarkowicz, ed., *Hitlers Künstler: Die Kultur im Dienste des Nationalsozialismus*, p. 186
102. *Berliner Tageblatt*, April 2, 1938, cited by Peter Sprengel, *Der Dichter stand auf hoher Küste: Gerhart Hauptmann im Dritten Reich*, p. 356, n. 9.
103. Cited by Sprengel, *Der Dichter stand auf hoher Küste*, p. 282.
104. Barbian, "'Fehlbesetzung'," B 156.
105. Ebermeyer, *Denn heute gehört uns Deutschland*, p. 264.

106. Hans von Brescius, *Gerhart Hauptmann: Zeitgeschehen und Bewusstsein in unbekannten Selbstzeugnissen,* p. 319.

107. Hilscher, *Gerhart Hauptmann,* p. 415.

108. Sprengel, *Der Dichter stand auf hoher Küste,* p. 74.

109. Sprengel, *Der Dichter stand auf hoher Küste,* pp. 302–03.

110. Rosenberg to Goebbels, July 2, 1942, BA, NS 8/172, p. 78.

111. Cited in Sprengel, *Der Dichter stand auf hoher Küste,* p. 308.

112. Cf. also Siegfried Hoefert, "Gerhart Hauptmann and Goebbels: Zur Situation des schlesischen Schriftstellers im Dritten Reich," *Michigan Germanic Studies* 20 (1994): 148

113. Goebbels memo of July 10, 1942, cited in Wolfgang Leppmann, *Gerhart Hauptmanns Leben, Werk und Zeit,* p. 368.

114. RMfVP memo of September 17, 1942, BA, R 55/20,235, p. 169.

115. RMfVP memo of June 29, 1942, BA, R 55/20,235, p. 109.

116. Reiner Schlösser (Reichsdramaturg) memo of April 11, 1942, BA, R 55/20,235, p. 85.

117. RMfVP memo of September 22, 1942, BA, R 55/20,235, p. 166.

118. Schlösser to Naumann, September 25, 1942, BA, R 55,235, p. 172.

119. RMfVP memo of July 22, 1942, BA, R 55/20,235, p. 148.

120. Sprengel, *Der Dichter stand auf hoher Küste,* p. 311.

121. Leppmann, *Gerhart Hauptmanns Leben,* p. 369.

122. Sprengel, *Der Dichter stand auf hoher Küste,* p. 323.

123. Wistrich, *Who's Who in Nazi Germany,* pp. 78–79.

124. Sprengel, *Der Dichter stand auf hoher Küste,* pp. 323, 320–21.

125. Alfred Kerr, "Gerhart Hauptmanns Schande," in *Exil: Literarische und politische Texte aus dem deutschen Exil 1933–1945,* edited by Ernst Loewy, p. 219.

126. Alfred Kerr, *Die Welt im Licht,* edited by Friedrich Luft, p. 290.

127. Leppmann, *Gerhart Hauptmanns Leben,* pp. 360–61.

128. Hilscher, *Gerhart Hauptmann,* p. 422.

129. Sprengel, *Der Dichter stand auf hoher Küste,* p. 336.

130. For a sensitive biography see Martin Johannes Wecht, *Jochen Klepper: Ein christlicher Schriftsteller im jüdischen Schicksal.*

131. Ernst G. Riemschneider, *Der Fall Klepper: Eine Dokumentation,* pp. 10–15.

132. Gestapo Berlin to RSK, June 18, 1937, BA (formerly BDC), RK B98, pp. 56 and 58.

133. RSK to Gruppe Buchhandel, April 13, 1937, BA (formerly BDC), RK B98, p. 78.

134. BA (formerly BDC), RK B98, p. 18.

135. RMfVP to Klepper, April 30, 1938, BA (formerly BDC), RK B98, p. 250.

136. Memo of December 30, 1937, BA (formerly BDC), RK B98, p. 84.

137. Jochen Klepper, *Briefwechsel 1925–1942,* edited by Ernst G. Riemschneider, p. 95.

138. Hellmut Seier, "Kollaboration und oppositionelle Momente der inneren Emigration Jochen Kleppers," *Jahrbuch für die Geschichte Mittel- und Ostdeutschland* 8 (1959): 343–44.

139. Barbian, *Die vollendete Ohnmacht,* p. 209.

140. Jochen Klepper, *Unter dem Schatten deiner Flügel: Aus den Tagebüchern der Jahre 1932–1942,* edited by Hildegard Klepper, p. 782.

141. Barbian, *Die vollendete Ohnmacht,* p. 225.

142. Grimm, "Im Dickicht der inneren Emigration," p. 411.

143. Franz Schonauer, *Deutsche Literatur im Dritten Reich: Versuch einer Darstellung in polemisch-didaktischer Absicht,* p. 127.

144. "Hermann Hesse und der deutsche Buchhandel," *Der Buchhändler im neuen Reich* 2 (1937): 93.

145. Egon Schwarz, "Hermann Hesse und der Nationalsozialismus," in *Hermann Hesse: Politische und wirkungsgeschichtliche Aspekte,* edited by Sigrid Bauschinger and Albert Reh, p. 67.

146. David Bankier, *The Germans and the Final Solution: Public Opinion under Nazism.* See also Peter Longerich *"Davon haben wir nichts gewusst!" Die Deutschen und die Judenverfolgung.*

147. Letter to Roger de Campagnolle, December 22, 1941, quoted in Ehrke-Rotermund, *Zwischenreiche und Gegenwelte,* p. 232.

148. Quoted in Deussen, *Erinnerung als Rechtfertigung,* p. 131.
149. Henning Falkenstein, *Hans Carossa,* p. 24.
150. Quoted in Deussen, *Erinnerung als Rechtfertigung,* p. 104.
151. Rolf Düsterberg, *Dichter für das "Dritte Reich",* p. 253. In 1941 Carossa earned 47,578 RM, BA (formerly Berlin Document Center), PK B 25, p. 1696.
152. Eberhard Lämmert, "Beherrschte Prosa: Praktische Lizenzen in Deutschland zwischen 1933 und 1945," *Neue Rundschau* 86 (1975): 405.
153. BA, R 56 V/152, p. 132.
154. Hans Carossa, "Ungleiche Welten," *Sämtliche Werke,* p. 643.
155. Markus Wallenborn, "Schreibtisch im Freigehege: Der Schriftsteller Erick Kästner im 'Dritten Reich'," in *Im Pausenraum des "Dritten Reiches,"* edited by Würmann and Warner, p. 219.
156. Barbian, *Die vollendete Ohnmacht,* pp. 171–72.
157. Sven Hanuschek, *Keiner blickt dir hinter das Gesicht: Das Leben Erich Kästners,* p. 297.
158. Franz Josef Görtz and Hans Sarkowicz, *Erich Kästner: Eine Biographie,* p. 239.
159. See Jerry Williams, *More Lives than One: A Biography of Hans Fallada*; Anja Susan Hübner, "Erfolgsautor mit allem drumm und dran: Der Fall Fallada," in *Im Pausenraum des "Dritten Reiches,"* edited by Würmann and Warner, pp. 197–213.
160. Wistrich, *Who's Who in Nazi Germany,* p. 26.
161. "*. . . und morgen die ganze Welt: Erinnerungen an Deutschland's dunkle Zeit,* entry for December 4, 1937, p. 210.
162. Entry for February 18, 1939, ibid., p. 349.
163. Ebermayer to Johst, October 30, 1941, BA, R 56 V/1, p. 72.
164. See, e.g., RSK memo of September 14, 1943, BA, R 56 V/96, p. 1.
165. Elizabeth Langgässer, "Schriftsteller unter der Hitler Diktatur," *Ost und West* 1 (1947): 40.
166. Rudolf Pechel, *Deutsche Rundschau: Acht Jahrzehnte deutsches Geistesleben,* p. 457.
167. Eugen Diesel, "An Österreich!", *Deutsche Rundschau,* April 1938, pp. 1–2.
168. Helmut Mörchen, "Gegenaufklärung und Unterwerfung: Tendenzen der Essayistik im Dritten Reich," in Denkler and Prümm, eds., *Die deutsche Literatur im Dritten Reich,* p. 236. See also Karl-Wofgang Mirbt, "Theorie und Technik des Camouflage: 'Die 'Deutsche Rundschau' im Dritten Reich als Beispiel publizistischer Opposition unter totalitärer Gewalt," *Publizistik* 9 (1964), 3–16.
169. Rudolf Pechel, *Zwischen den Zeilen: Der Kampf einer Zeitschrift für Freiheit und Recht: 1932–1942 Aufsätze,* pp. 338–41.
170. Falk Schwarz, "Die gelenkte Literatur: Die 'Neue Rundschau' im Konflikt mit den Kontrollstellen des NS-Staates und der nationalsozialistischen 'Bewegung'," in *Die deutsche Literatur im Dritten Reich,* edited by Denkler and Prümm, pp. 72–79.
171. Erhard Schütz, "Ein Geruch von Blut und Schande," *Juni: Ein Magazin für Literatur und Politik,* no. 24 (1996): 140.
172. Sebastian Haffner, *Von Bismarck zu Hitler: Ein Rückblick* p. 270.
173. J. M. Ritchie, *German Literature under National Socialism,* p. 118.
174. Lämmert, "Beherrschte Prosa," pp. 410–11.

Conclusion

1. Volker Dahm, "The Limits on Literary Life in the Third Reich," in *Flight of Fantasy,* edited by Donahue and Kirchner, p. 173.
2. "Jahresbericht 1940 des Hauptlektorates 'Schöngeistiges Schrifttum'," *Lektorenbrief* 4 (1941): 4, 7, quoted in Graeb-Könneker, *Literatur im Dritten Reich,* p. 385.
3. Schaefer, *Auch wenn du träumst,* p. 9.

4. Lotte Bergtel Schleif, "Möglichkeiten volksbibliothekarischer Arbeit unter dem Nationalsozialismus," *Der Volksbibliothekar* 1 (1947): 196, 206.

5. Robert Darnton, *Censors at Work: How States Shaped Literature*, pp. 148, 168, 231.

6. Felix Reichmann, "The First Year of American Publications Control in Germany," *Publishers' Weekly*, November 14, 1946, p. 2811.

7. "Read No Evil," *Time*, May 27, 1946. The Deutsche Bücherei in May 1946 listed 15,000 banned books for all of Germany. See Wolfgang Benz, ed., *Deutschland unter allierter Besatzung 1945–1949/55*, p. 135. Other sources speak of 30,000 books.

8. Guenter Lewy, *Outlawing Genocide Denial: The Dilemmas of Official Historical Truth*, chap. 2.

BIBLIOGRAPHY

Archival Sources

BUNDESARCHIV BERLIN-LICHTERFELDE:

NS 6 Partei-Kanzlei der NSDAP
NS 8 Kanzlei Rosenberg
NS 11 Parteiamtliche Prüfungskommission zum Schutze des nationalsozialistischen Schrifttums
NS 15 Der Beauftragte des Führers für die Überwachung der gesamten geistigen und weltan-schaulichen Schulung und Erziehung der NSDAP
NS 18 Reichspropagandaleitung der NSDAP
NS 21 Ahnenerbe
NS 38 Nationalsozialistischer Studentenbund
R 2 Reichsfinanzministerium
R 43/II Reichskanzlei
R 55 Reichsministerium für Volksaufklärung und Propaganda
R 56 V Reichsschrifttumskammer
R 58 Reichssicherheitshauptamt
R 78 Reichsrundfunkgesellschaft
R 181 Prüfstelle für Schund- und Schmutzliteratur
R 3001 Reichsministerium der Justiz
R 4901 Reichsministerium für Wissenschaft, Erziehung, und Volksbildung
BDC Files of former Berlin Document Center
NSD NS Drucksachen

Printed Sources

Abb, Gustav. "Ansprache." *Zentralblatt für Bibliothekswesen* 56 (1939): 514–16.

Abele, Bernd. "1933–1938: Der Verlag Bruno Cassirer im Nationalsozialismus." *Buchhandelsge-schichte* (Beilage zum *Börsenblatt für den deutschen Buchhandel*, no. 25, March 27, 1990), B 1–B 18.

Adam, Christian. *Lesen unter Hitler: Autoren, Bestseller, Leser im Dritten Reich*. Berlin: Galiani, 2010.

Aigner, Dietrich. "Die Indizierung 'schädlichen und unerwünschten Schrifttums' im Dritten Reich." *Archiv für Geschichte des Buchwesens* 11 (1971): 933–1034.

Aley, Peter. *Jugendliteratur im Dritten Reich: Dokumente und Kommentare*. Gütersloh: C. Bertelsmann, 1967.

Alt, Johannes. "Grundlagen und Voraussetzungen der wissenschaftlichen Bearbeitung der deutschsprachigen jüdischen Literatur." *Forschungen zur Judenfrage* 1 (1937): 141–49.

Andersch, Alfred. *The Cherries of Freedom.* Translated by Michael Hulse. New Milford, Conn.: Toby Press, 2004.

Andrae, Friedrich, ed. *Volksbücherei und Nationalsozialismus: Materialien zur Theorie und Politik des öffentlichen Büchereiwesens in Deutschland 1933–1945.* Wiesbaden: Otto Harrassowitz, 1970.

———. "Des Teufels Bücherei: Zum Standort der deutschen Volksbücherei im nationalsozialistischen Propagandaapparat." In *Bibliothek '76 International,* edited by Karlheinz Wallraf. Bremen: Stadtbibliothek, 1976.

Angermann, Rudolf. "Aus der Fachschaft—für die Fachschaft: 'Säuberung nach der Säuberung,' Eine dringende Aufgabe." *Die Bücherei* 2 (1935): 281–83.

"Anordnung der Reichsschrifttumskammer über schädliches und unerwünschtes Schrifttum." *Deutsche Wissenschaft, Erziehung und Volksbildung* 1 (1935): 205–06.

Arnim, Bernd, and Friedrich Knilli. *Gewerbliche Leihbüchereien: Berichte, Analysen und Interviews.* Gütersloh: C. Bertelsmann, 1966.

Aspetsberger, Friedrich. *Arnold Bronnen: Biographie.* Vienna: Böhlau, 1995.

Azegami, Taiji. *Die Jugendschriften-Warte.* Frankfurt am Main: Peter Lang, 1996.

Baets, Antoon de. "Defamation Cases against Historians." *History and Theory* 41 (2002): 346–66.

Bänziger, Hans. *Werner Bergengruen: Weg und Werk.* Bern: Francke, 1968.

Baranowski, Shelley. *Strength through Joy: Consumerism and Mass Tourism in the Third Reich.* Cambridge: Cambridge University Press, 2004.

Barbian, Jan-Pieter. "Die Beherrschung der Musen: Kulturpolitik im 'Dritten Reich'." In *Hitlers Künstler: Die Kultur im Dienste des Nationalsozialismus,* edited by Hans Sarkowicz, pp. 40–74. Frankfurt am Main: Insel, 2004.

———. "'Fehlbesetzung': Zur Rolle von Gerhart Hauptmann im 'Dritten Reich'." *Börsenblatt für den deutschen Buchhandel,* no. 101 (December 17, 1996): B 153–B 169.

———. *Literaturpolitik im "Dritten Reich": Institutionen, Kompetenzen, Betätigungsfelder.* Munich: Deutscher Taschenbuchverlag, 1995.

———. *Literaturpolitik im NS-Staat: Von der "Gleichschaltung" bis zum Ruin.* Frankfurt am Main: Fischer Taschenbuchverlag, 2010.

———. *The Politics of Literature in Nazi Germany: Books in the Media Dictatorship.* Translated by Kate Sturge. New York: Bloomsbury, 2013.

———. *Die vollendete Ohnmacht: Schriftsteller, Verleger und Buchhändler im NS-Staat. Ausgewählte Aufsätze.* Essen: Klartext, 2008.

Bartels, Adolf. "Verschwundene Juden." *Der Buchhändler im Neuen Reich* 3 (1938): 12–13.

Baur, Karl. *Wenn ich so zurückdenke ... Für die Freunde aus sieben Jahrzehnten.* Munich: Privatdruck, 1968.

Baur, Wilhelm. *Das Buch ein Schwert des Geistes: Erste Grundliste für den deutschen Leihbuchhandel.* Leipzig: Börsenverein der deutschen Buchhändler, 1940.

———. "Organisation und Aufgaben des deutschen Buchhandels im nationalsozialistischen Staat." *Der Buchhändler im Neuen Reich* 2 (1937): 26–32.

Bauschinger, Sigrid, and Albert Reh, eds. *Hermann Hesse: Politische und wirkungsgeschichtliche Aspekte.* Berlin: Francke, 1986.

Benecke, Hans. *Buchhandlung in Breslau: Erinnerungen an eine schwere Zeit.* Frankfurt am Main: Fischer, 1995.

Benn, Gottfried. "Antwort an die literarische Emigration." In *Sämtliche Werke,* vol. 4, pp. 24–32. Stuttgart: Klett-Cotta, 1989.

———. "Die Aufgaben des deutschen Buchhandels im nationalsozialistischen Staat." *Sämtliche Werke,* vol. 4, pp. 93–96. Stuttgart: Klett-Cotta, 1989.

———. *Briefe,* edited by Marguerite Valerie Schlüter. Stuttgart: Klett-Cotta, 1992.

———. *Doppelleben: Zwei Selbstdarstellungen.* Wiesbaden: Limes, 1950.

———. "Der neue Staat und die Intellektuellen." In *Sämtliche Werke,* vol. 4, pp. 12–20. Stuttgart: Klett-Cotta, 1989.

———. "Züchtung." In *Sämtliche Werke,* vol. 4, pp. 33–40.

Benz, Wolfgang. *Deutschland unter alliierter Besatzung 1945–1949/55.* Berlin: Akademie Verlag, 1999.

Bergengruen, Werner. *Schreibtischerinnerungen.* Munich: Nymphenburger Verlagsbuchhandlung, 1961.

Bergengruen, Werner, et al., eds. *Schriftstellerexistenz in der Diktatur: Aufzeichnungen und Reflexionen zur Politik und Kultur 1940–1963.* Munich: R. Oldenbourg, 2005.

Berger, Friedemann, et al., eds. *In jenen Tagen: Schriftsteller zwischen Reichstagsbrand und Bücherverbrennung: Eine Dokumentation.* Leipzig: Gustav Kiepenheuer, 1983.

Berglund, Gisela. *Der Kampf um den Leser im Dritten Reich.* Worms: Georg Heintz, 1980.

Bergmann, Katja. "Werner Bergengruen und die Innere Emigration: Ein topologischer Fall." In *Schriftsteller und Widerstand: Facetten und Probleme der "Inneren Emigration."* Edited by Frank-Lothar Kroll and Rüdiger von Voss, pp. 319–51. Göttingen: Wallstein, 2012.

Bergtel-Schleif, Lotte. "Möglichkeiten volksbibliothekarischer Arbeit unter dem Nationalsozialismus." *Der Volksbibliothekar* 1 (1947): 193–207.

Bermann-Fischer, Gottfried. *Bedroht—bewahrt: Weg eines Verlegers.* Frankfurt am Main: S. Fischer, 1967.

Beyer, Hans. "Schrifttum, das wir ablehnen." *Die Bücherei* 1 (1934): 255–59.

Beyerchen, Alan D. *Scientists under Hitler: Politics and the Physics Community in the Third Reich.* New Haven, Conn.: Yale University Press, 1977.

Bluhm, Lothar. *Das Tagebuch zum Dritten Reich: Zeugnisse der Inneren Emigration von Jochen Klepper bis Ernst Jünger.* Bonn: Bouvier, 1991.

Blunck, Hans-Friedrich. "Einiges über die Reichsschrifttumskammer." *Börsenblatt für den deutschen Buchhandel.* No. 61 (March 13, 1934): 225–27.

———. *Unwegsame Zeiten: Lebensbericht.* Mannheim: Kessler, 1952.

Boberach, Heinz, ed. *Meldungen aus dem Reich 1938–1945: Die geheimen Lageberichte des Sicherheitsdienstes der SS.* Herrsching: Pawlak, 1984.

Boelcke, Willi A., ed. *"Wollt Ihr den totalen Krieg?" Die geheimen Goebbels-Konferenzen 1939–1943.* Stuttgart: Deutsche Verlagsanstalt, 1967.

Boese, Engelbrecht. *Das öffentliche Bibliothekswesen im Dritten Reich.* 2nd rev. ed. Bad Honnef: Bock und Herrchen, 1987.

———. "Die Säuberung der Leipziger Bücherhallen 1933–1936." *Buch und Bibliothek* 35 (1983): 283–96.

Bohmüller, Lothar. "Aus dem Tagebuch des Direktors der Universitätsbibliothek Jena 1933–1944." *Zentralblatt für Bibliothekswesen* 99 (1985): 178–83, 100 (1986): 148–54.

———. "Der Salman Schocken Verlag Berlin und die Universitätsbibliothek Jena 1937–1938." In *Bibliotheken während des Nationalsozialismus.* vol. 1, pp. 359–67. Wiesbaden: Harrassowitz, 1989.

Bollmus, Reinhard. *Das Amt Rosenberg und seine Gegner: Studien zum Machtkampf im nationalsozialistischen Herrschaftssystem.* Stuttgart: Deutsche Verlagsanstalt, 1970.

Bracher, Karl Dietrich. *The German Dictatorship: The Origins, Structure and Effects of National Socialism.* Translated by Jean Steinberg. New York: Praeger, 1970.

Braun, Michael. *Stefan Andres: Leben und Werk.* Bonn: Bouvier, 1997.

Brenner, Hildegard. *Die Kunstpolitik des Nationalsozialismus.* Reinbek bei Hamburg: Rowohlt, 1963.

Brescius, Hans von. *Gerhart Hauptmann: Zeitgeschehen und Bewusstsein in unbekannten Selbstzeugnissen.* Bonn: Bouvier, 1976.

Breuer, Dieter. *Geschichte der literarischen Zensur in Deutschland.* Heidelberg: Quelle und Meyer, 1982.

Brockmann, Stephen. "Innere Emigration: The Term and Its Origins in Postwar Debates." In *Flight of Fantasy: New Perspectives on Inner Emigration in German Literature 1933–1945.* Edited by Neil H. Donahue and Doris Kirchner, pp. 11–26. New York: Berghahn, 2003.

Bronnen, Arnold. *Arnold Bronnen gibt zu Protokoll: Beiträge zur Geschichte des modernen Schrittsteller.* Kronberg im Taunus: Athenäum, 1978.

Bronnen, Barbara. *Flieger mit gestutzten Flügeln: Die letzten Jahre der Ricarda Huch 1933–1947.* Zürich: Arche, 2007.

Broszat, Martin. *The Hitler State: The Foundation and Development of the Internal Structure of the Third Reich.* Translated by John W. Hiden. London: Longmans, 1981.

Buchheim, Hans, et al. *Anatomie des SS-Staates.* vol. 1. Olten: Walter, 1965.

Bühler, Hans-Eugen. *Der Frontbuchhandel 1939–1945: Organisationen, Kompetenzen, Verlage, Bücher.* Frankfurt am Main: Buchhändler-Vereinigung, 2002.

Bühler, Hans-Eugen, and Klaus Kirbach. "Die Wehrmachtsausgaben deutscher Verläge von 1939–1945." *Archiv für Geschichte des Buchwesens* 50 (1998): 251–90.

Buttmann, Rudolf. "Nationalsozialistische Bibliothekspolitik." *Börsenblatt für den deutschen Buchhandel.* No. 49 (February 27, 1936): 181–83.

Caemmerer, Christiane, and Walter Delabare. *Dichtung im Dritten Reich? Zur Literatur in Deutschland 1933–1945.* Obladen: Westdeutscher Verlag, 1996.

Carossa, Hans. *Tagebücher 1925–1935.* Frankfurt am Main: Insel, 1993.

———. "Ungleiche Welten." In *Sämtliche Werke,* vol. 2. Frankfurt am Main: Insel, 1962.

Chatelier, Hildegard. "Ernst Wiechert im Urteil der deutschen Zeitschriftenpresse 1933–1945: Ein Beitrag zur nationalsozialistischen Literatur- und Pressepolitik." *Recherches Germaniques* 3 (1973): 153–95.

Confino, Alon. *A World without Jews: The Nazi Imagination from Persecution to Genocide.* New Haven, Conn.: Yale University Press, 2014.

Corino, Karl. *Intellektuelle im Bann des Nationalsozialismus.* Hamburg: Hoffmann und Campe, 1980.

Cuomo, Glenn R. "Hannst Johst und die Reichsschrifttumskammer: Ihr Einfluss auf die staatliche Situation des Schriftstellers im Dritten Reich." In *Leid der Worte: Panorama des literarischen Nationalsozialismus.* Edited by Jörg Thunecke, pp. 108–32. Bonn: Bouvier, 1987.

———. *National Socialist Cultural Policy.* New York: St. Martin's Press, 1995.

Dahm, Volker. "Anfänge und Ideologie der Reichskulturkammer." *Vierteljahrshefte für Zeitgeschichte* 34 (1986): 53–84.

———. "Ein Kampf um Familienerbe und Lebenswerk: Otto Wilhelm Klemm und die Reichsschrifttumskammer, 1937–1939." *Buchhandelsgeschichte* ((Beilage zum *Börsenblatt für den deutschen Buchhandel,* no. 25 (1997)), B 152–B 159.

———. *Das jüdische Buch im Dritten Reich.* Munich: Beck, 1993.

———. "Künstler als Funktionäre: Das Propagandaministerium und die Reichskulturkammer." In *Hitlers Künstler: Die Kultur im Dienste des Nationalsozialismus.* Edited by Hans Sarkowicz, pp. 75–109. Frankfurt am Main: Insel, 2004.

———. "The Limits on Literary Life in the Third Reich." In *Flight of Fantasy: New Perspectives on Inner Emigration in German Literature 1933–1945.* Edited by Neil H. Donahue and Doris Kirchner, pp. 168–75. New York: Berghahn, 2003.

———. "Die nationalsozialistische Schrifttumspolitik nach dem 10. Mai 1933." In *10. Mai 1933: Bücherverbrennung und die Folgen.* Edited by Ulrich Walberer, pp. 36–83. Frankfurt am Main: Fischer, 1983.

Darnton, Robert. *Censors at Work: How States Shaped Literature.* New York: W. W. Norton, 2014.

Delabar, Walter, et al., eds. *Banalität und Stil: Zur Widersprüchlichkeit der Literaturpolitk im Nationalsozialismus.* Bern: Peter Lang, 1999.

———. "NS-Literatur ohne Nationalsozialismus? Thesen zu einem Ausstaltungsphänomen in der Unterhalltungsliteratur des 'Dritten Reiches'." In *Im Pausenraum des "Dritten Reiches": Zur Populärkultur im nationalsozialistischen Deutschland.* Edited by Carsten Würmann and Ansgar Warner, pp. 161–80. Bern: Peter Lang, 2008.

Denk, Friedrich. *Die Zensur der Nachgeborenen: Zur regimekritischen Literatur im Dritten Reich.* Weilheim in Oberbayern: Den, 1996.

Denkler, Horst. "Katz und Maus: Oppositionelle Schreibtischstrategien im 'Dritten Reich'." In *Geist und Macht.* Edited by Marek Zybura, pp. 27–38. Dresden: Thelem, 2002.

Denkler, Horst, and Eberhard Lämmer, eds. *"Das war ein Vorspiel nur . . ." Berliner Colloquien zur Literaturpolitik im Dritten Reich.* Berlin: Akademie der Künste, 1985.

Denkler, Horst, and Karl Prümm, eds. *Die deutsche Literatur im Dritten Reich: Themen, Traditionen, Wirkungen.* Stuttgart: Philipp Reclam, 1976.

Des Coudres, Hans Peter. "Das verbotene Schrifttum und die wissenschaftlichen Bibliotheken." *Zentralblatt für Bibliothekswesen* 52 (1935): 459–71.

Deussen, Christine. *Erinnerung als Rechtfertigung: Autobiographien nach 1945. Gottfried Benn, Hans Carossa, Arnold Brunnen.* Tübingen: Stauffenburg, 1987.

Deutsche Bücherei, Leipzig. *Verzeichnis der Schriften, die 1933–1945 nicht angezeigt werden durften.* Leipzig: Verlag des Börsenvereins der Deutschen Buchhändler, 1949.

Diehl-Thiele, Peter. *Partei und Staat im Dritten Reich.* 2nd rev. ed. Munich: C. H. Beck, 1971.

Diere, Horst. "Das Reichsministerium für Wissenschaft, Erziehung und Volksbildung." *Jahrbuch für Erziehungs- und Schulgeschichte* 22 (1982): 107–20.

Donahue, Neil, and Doris Kirchner, eds. *Flight of Fantasy: New Perspectives on Inner Emigration in German Literature 1933–1945.* New York: Berghahn, 2003.

Drahn, Ernst. *Verbotene und undeutsche Bücher: Ein Führer zur völkischen Gestaltung der deutschen Leihbüchereien.* Berlin: Als Manuskript gedruckt für Leihbüchereien, 1933.

———. "Von Index und Zensur." *Der Buch und Zeitschriftenhandel* 47 (1926): 2–4, 21–22, 49–50.

Dreschner, Wilhelmine. *Erinnerungen an Karl Jaspers in Heidelberg.* Meisenheim: Anton Hain, 1975.

Dressler, Fridolin. "Die Bayerische Staatsbibliothek im Dritten Reich." In *Beiträge zur Geschichte der Bayerischen Staatsbibliothek.* Edited by Rupert Hacker, pp. 285–308. Munich: K. G. Saur, 2000.

Dürr, Dietmar. *Das Amt Rosenberg in der nationalsozialistischen Literaturpolitik.* Magisterarbeit, Bonn University, 1994.

Düsterberg, Rolf. *Dichter für das "Dritte Reich."* 2 vols. Bielefeld: Aistesis, 2011.

———. *Hanns Johst: "Der Barde der SS": Karrieren eines deutschen Dichters.* Paderborn: Ferdinand Schöningh, 2004.

Dyck, Joachim. *Der Zeitzeuge: Gottfried Benn 1929–1949.* Göttingen: Wallstein, 2006.

Ebermayer, Erich. *Denn heute gehört uns Deutschland ... Persönliches und politisches Tagebuch. Von der Machtergreifung bis zum 31. Dezember 1935.* Hamburg: Paul Zsolnay, 1959.

Ehrke-Rotermund, Heidrun and Erwin Rotermund, eds. *Zwischenreiche und Gegenwelten: Texte und Vorstudien zur "Verdeckten Schreibweise" im "Dritten Reich."* Munich: Wilhelm Fink, 1999.

Eilers, Rolf. *Die nationalsozialistische Schulpolitik: Eine Studie zur Funktion der Erziehung im totalitärem Staat.* Köln-Opladen: Westdeutscher Verlag, 1963.

Elschenbroich, Erika, et al., eds. *Wissenschaft und Kunst im Exil: Vorgeschichte, Durchführung und Folgen des Bücherverbrennung. Eine Dokumentation.* Osnabrück: Wurf, 1984.

Endlich, Stefanie. *"Vernichtung," "Giftschrank," "Zeifelhafte Fälle": Vorgeschichte und Folgen der Bücherverbrennung für jüdische Autoren, Verleger, Buchhändler und Bibliotheken.* Berlin: Hentrich und Hentrich, 2007.

"Die Entjudung des deutschen Kulturlebens." *Börsenblatt für den deutschen Buchhandel.* no. 76 (March 31, 1938): 262–63.

Erckmann, Rudolf. "Probleme und Aufgaben unseres Schrifttums." *Die Bücherei* 8 (1941): 308–16.

Erler, Helmut. *Das rechtliche Wesen der Reichskulturkammer.* Dresden: M. Dittert, 1937.

Exenberger, Herbert. "Die Arbeiterbüchereien der Stadt Wien nach dem März 1938." In *Wien 1938,* pp. 237–47. Vienna: Verein für Geschichte der Stadt Wien, 1978.

———. "Bibliotheken in Österreich 1933–1945. In *Die verbrannten Bücher: 10.5.1933.* Edited by Alfred Pfoser and Friedrich Stadler, pp. 10–15. Vienna: Institut für Wissenschaft und Kunst, 1983.

Falkenstein, Henning. *Hans Carossa.* Berlin: Colloquium, 1983.

Fallada, Hans. *In meinem fremden Land: Gefängnistagebuch 1944.* Edited by Jenny Williams and Sabine Lange. Berlin: Aufbau, 2009.

Faustmann, Uwe Julius. *Die Reichskulturkammer: Aufbau, Funktion und rechtliche Grundlagen einer Körperschaft des öffentlichen Rechts im nationalsozialistischen Regime.* Aachen: Shaker, 1995.

Finke, Heinz. "Die Kalenderliteratur im Rahmen des deutschen Schrifttums." *Nationalsozialistische Bibliographie (NSB)* no. 3, Beiheft (March 1937): i–iv.

Flachowsky, Sören. *Die Bibliothek der Berliner Universität während der Zeit des Nationalsozialismus.* Berlin: Logos, 2000.

Fleige, Gabriela. "Die Reichsschrifttumskammer als Zensurinstrument im Dritten Reich." *Dokumentation, Fachbibliothek, Werkbücherei (DFW)* 30 (1982): 113–24.

Flessau, Kurt-Ingo. *Schule der Diktatur: Lehrpläne und Schulbücher des Nationalsozialismus.* Frankfurt am Main: Ehrenwirth, 1977.

Frank, Walter. *Kämpfende Wissenschaft.* Hamburg: Hanseatische Verlagsanstalt, 1934.

Franke, Hans. "Über Hans Fallada." *Grossdeutsches Leihbücherblatt* 3 (1941): 145–46.

Frick, Wilhelm. "Thüringerische Bilanz." *Nationalsozialistisches Jahrbuch* 6 (1932): 211–16.

Friedländer, Saul. *Bertelsmann im Dritten Reich.* Munich: C. Bertelsmann, 2002.

———. *Nazi Germany and the Jews.* Vol. 1: *The Years of Persecution.* New York: Harper Collins, 1997.

Friedman, Philip. *Roads to Extinction: Essays on the Holocaust.* New York: Jewish Publication Society, 1980.

Friedrich, Thomas, ed. *Vorspiel: Die Bücherverbrennung am 10. Mai 1933. Verlauf, Folgen, Nachwirkungen: Eine Dokumentation.* Berlin: LitPol, 1983.

Funke, Cornelia Caroline. "Im Verleger verkörpert sich das Gesicht seiner Zeit": *Unternehmungsführung und Programmgestaltung im Gustav Kiepenheuer Verlag.* Wiesbaden: Harrassowitz, 1999.

Füssel, Stephan. *Die Geschichte der Voksbibliothek Göttingen: 80 Jahre Stadtbibliothek.* Göttingen: Göttinger Hochschulschriften-Verlag, 1977.

———. "Wider den undeutschen Geist: Bücherverbrennung und Bibliothekslenkung im Nationalsozialismus." *In Göttingen unter dem Hakenkreuz.* Edited by Jens-Uwe Brinkmann and Hans-Georg Schmeling, pp. 95–104. Göttingen: Kulturdezernat Göttingen, 1983.

Gentz, Günther, ed. *Das Recht der Reichsschrifttumskammer.* Leipzig: Verlag des Börsenverein der deutschen Buchhändler, 1936.

Geyer-Ryan, Helga. *Popular Literatur in the Third Reich: Observations on the "Groschenroman".* Translated by Kiernan Ryan. Birmingham: Center for Contemporary Cultural Studies, n.d.

Gibas, Monika. *"Arisierung" in Leipzig: Annäherung an ein lang verdrängtes Kapitel der Stadtgeschichte der Jahre 1933 bis 1945.* Leipzig: Leipziger Universitätsverlag, 2007.

Gieselbusch, Hermann et al. *100 Jahre Rowohlt: Eine Illustrierte Chronik.* Reinbek bei Hamburg: Rowohlt, 2008.

Gilmann, Sander L. *NS-Literaturpolitik: Eine Dokumentation.* Frankfurt am Main: Athenäum, 1971.

Glaser, Hermann. *Wie Hitler den deutschen Geist zerstörte: Kulturpolitk im Dritten Reich.* Hamburg: Ellert und Richter, 2005.

Goebbels, Joseph. *Die Tagebücher von Joseph Göbbels.* Edited by Elke Fröhlich. Munich: K. G. Saur, 1993–2005.

———. *Wesen und Gestalt des Nationalsozialismus.* Berlin: Junker und Dünnhaupt, 1935.

Göhle, Peter. "Ernst Drahn." In *Bewahren—Verbreiten—Aufklären: Archivare, Bibliothekare und Sammler der deutschsprachigen Arbeiterbewegung,* pp. 58–63. Bonn: Friedrich Ebert Stiftung, 2009.

Görtz, Franz Josef, and Hans Sarkowicz, *Erick Kästmer: Eine Biographie.* Munich: Piper, 1998.

Graeb-Könneker, Sebastian. *Literatur im Dritten Reich: Dokumente und Texte.* Stuttgart: Reclam, 2001.

Graf, Hans-Dieter. "Die Adventspredigten des Kardinals Michael von Faulhaber: Ein Beitrag zur Geschichte der katholischen Publizistik und Schrifttumspolitik im Dritten Reich." *Gutenberg-Jahrbuch 1990,* pp. 256–83.

———. "Nationalsozialistische Schrifttumspolitk: Goebbels' Weg zur Oberaufsicht über die Presse- und Buchverbotswesen im Dritten Reich." *Buchhandelsgeschichte* 33 (1991): B 111–B 118.

———. "Der Trierer Buchdrucker Josef Herzig und das Schicksal seiner Druckerei im Dritten Reich." *Gutenberg-Jahrbuch 1989,* pp. 249–88.

Greguletz, Alexander. "Die Preussische Staatbibliothek in den ersten Jahren des Nationalsozialismus: 1933–1936." In *Bibliotheken während des Nationalsozialismus*. Edited by Peter Vodosek and Manfred Komorowski, vol. 2, pp. 243–71. Wiesbaden: Harrassowitz, 1992.

Greve, Ludwig. *Gottfried Benn: 1886–1956*. Marbach: Deutsche Schillergesellschaft, 1986.

Grimm, Reinhold. "Im Dickicht der inneren Emigration." In *Die deutsche Literatur im Dritten Reich: Themen, Traditionen, Wirkungen*. Edited by Horst Denkler and Karl Prümm, pp. 406–26. Stuttgart: Philipp Reclam, 1976.

Grimsted, Patricia Kennedy. "Road to Ratibor: Library and Archival Plunder by the Einsatzstab Rosenberg." *Holocaust and Genocide Studies* 19 (2005): 390–458.

Grosser, Johannes Franz Gottlieb. *Die grosse Kontroverse: Ein Briefwechsel um Deutschland*. Hamburg: Nagel, 1963.

Haarmann, Hermann et al., eds. *"Das was ein Vorspiel nur . ."*: *Bücherverbrennung in Deutschland 1933: Voraussetzungen und Folgen*. Berlin: Medusa, 1983.

Hachmeister, Lutz. *Die Gegenforscher: Die Karriere des SS-Führers Franz Alfred Six*. Munich: C. H. Beck, 1998.

Haefs, Wilhelm. "Waldemar Bonsels im 'Dritten Reich': Opportunist, Sympathisant, Nationalsozialist?" In *Waldemar Bonsels: Karrierestrategien eines Erfolgsschriftstellers*. Edited by Sven Hanuschek, pp. 197–227. Wiesbaden: Harrassowitz, 2012.

Haffner, Sebastian. *Von Bismarck zu Hitler: Ein Rückblick*. Munich: Kindler, 1987.

Hagemeyer, Hans. "Vom Wesen des deutschen Schrifttums." *Jugendschriften-Warte* 40 (1935): 65–73.

Hagen, Hans W. *Deutsche Dichtung in der Entscheidung der Gegenwart*. Dortmund: Volkschaft, 1938.

Hall, Murray G., and Herbert Ohrlinger. *Der Paul Zsolnay Verlag 1924–1999: Dokumente und Zeugnisse*. Vienna: P. Zsolnay, 1999.

Häntzschel, Hiltrud. " 'Ist Gilgi eine von uns?' Irmagard Keuns Zickzackkurs durch die NS-Zensurbarrieren." In *Dennoch leben sie. Verfemte Bücher, verfolgte Autorinnen und Autoren: Zu den Auswirkungen nationalsozialistischer Literaturpolitik*. Edited by Reiner Wild et al., pp. 183–92. Munich: Edition Text und Kritik, 2003.

———. *Irmgard Keun*. Reinbek bei Hamburg: Rowohlt, 2001.

Hanuschek, Sven. *Keiner blickt dir hinter das Gesicht: Das Leben Erich Kästners*. Munich: Carl Hauser, 1999.

Happel, Hans-Gerd. "Die Universitäts- und Stadtbibliothek Köln im Dritten Reich." In *Die Universitätsbibliotheken Heidelberg, Jena und Köln unter dem Nationalsozialismus*. Edited by Ingo Toussaint, pp. 289–328. Munich: K. G. Saur, 1989.

———. *Das wissenschaftliche Bibliothekswesen im Nationalsozialismus: Unter besonderer Berücksichtigung der Universitätsbibliotheken*. Munich: K. G. Saur, 1989.

Harnack, Axel von. "Bibliotheken im 'Dritten Reich': Kulturpolitische Erinnerungen an die Berliner Staatsbibliothek." *Neue deutsche Hefte* 3 (1956–57): 123–32.

Hart, Franz Theodor. *Alfred Rosenberg: Der Mann und sein Werk*. Munich: J. F. Lehmanns, 1939.

Harth, Dietrich. "Literatur unterm NS-Diktat." In *Bücherverbrennungen: Zensur, Verbot, Vernichtung unter dem Nationalsozialismus in Heidelberg*. Edited by Joachim-Felix Leonhard, pp. 85–99. Heidelberg: Heidelberger Verlag, 1983.

Hase, Martin von. *Verzeichnis der im Jahre 1933 eingezogenen und beschlagnahmten politischen Schriften und Zeitschriften*. Leipzig: Börsenverein der deutschen Buchhändler, 1934.

Hattwig, Jörg. *Das Dritte Reich im Werk Ernst Wiecherts: Geschichtsdenken, Selbstverständnis und literarische Praxis*. Frankfurt am Main: Peter Lang, 1984.

Haupt, Gunther. "Ein offenes Wort!" *Börsenblatt für den deutschen Buchhandel*, no. 290 (December 14, 1933): 967–68.

———. *Was erwarten wir von der kommenden Dichtung?* Tübingen: Rainer Wunderlich, 1934.

Hederich, Karl-Heinz. *Nationalsozialismus und Buch*. Mainz: Hanns Marxen, 1937.

———. "Parteiamtliche Prüfungskommission und Buch." in *Die Welt des Buches*. Edted by Hellmuth Langenbucher, pp. 208–11. Ebenhausen bei Munich: Wilhelm Langewiesche-Brandt, 1938.

————. "Die Parteiamtliche Prüfungskommission zum Schutze des NS-Schrifttums." In *Der nationalsozialistische Staat*. Edited by Walther Gehl, pp. 138–51. Breslau: Ferdinand Hirt, 1933.

————. *Die Parteiamtliche Prüfungskommission zum Schutze des NS-Schrifttums, ihre Aufgabe und ihre Stellung in Partei und Staat*. Breslau: Ferdinand Hirt, 1937.

Heidtmann, Horst. "Von der 'Schmutz und Schund'-Bekämpfung zur Ausmerzung von Büchern." in *Bibliotheken während des Nationalsozialismus*. Edited by Peter Vodosek and Manfred Komorowski, vol. 1, pp. 389–99. Wiesbaden: Harrassowitz, 1989.

Heiligenstaedt, Fritz. "Zur Überwachung des Bestandaufbaus durch die Beratungsstellen." *Die Bücherei* 2 (1935): 211–15.

Hermand, Jost, and Wigand Lange. *"Wollt ihr Thomas Mann wiederhaben?" Deutschland und die Emigranten*. Hamburg: Europäische Verlagsanstalt. 1999.

Hermann, Wolfgang. "Prinzipielles zur Säuberung der öffentlichen Büchereien." *Börsenblatt für den deutschen Buchhandel*, no. 100 (May 16, 1933): 356–58.

————. "Was ist Asphaltliteratur?" *Volksbücherei und Volksbildung* 13 (1933/34): 16–21.

Heyde, Konrad. "Die Staatliche Volksbüchereistelle am Beispiel Freiburg im Breisgau." In *Bibliotheken während des Nationalsozialismus*. Edited by Peter Vodosek and Manfred Komorowski, vol. 1, pp. 113–61. Wiesbaden: Harrassowitz, 1989.

Hill, Leonides. "The Nazi Attack on 'Un-German' Literature 1933–1945." In *The Holocaust and the Book: Destruction and Preservation*. Edited by Jonathan Rose, pp. 9–46. Amherst, Mass.: University of Massachusetts Press, 2001.

Hillebrand, Bruno. *Gottfried Benn*. Darmstadt: Wissenschaftliche Buchgesellschaft, 1979.

Hilscher, Eberhard. *Gerhart Hauptmann: Leben und Werk*. Berlin: Athenäum, 1988.

Hinkel, Hans, ed. *Handbuch der Reichskulturkammer*. Berlin: Deutscher Verlag für Politik und Wissenschaft, 1937.

Hintermeier, Mara, and Fritz J. Raddatz, eds. *Rowohlt-Almanach 1908–1962*. Reinbek bei Hamburg: Rowohlt, 1962.

Hippler, Fritz. *Die Verstrickung: Einstellungen und Rückblenden*. Düsseldorf: Mehr Wissen, 1981.

Hirschegger, Manfred, and Werner Schlacher. *Verbotene Bücher 1938: Österreichische Autoren in nationalsozialistischen Zensurlisten—Eine Auswahl aus den Beständen der UB Graz*. Graz: Universitätsbibliothek Graz, 1988.

Hitler, Adolf. *Mein Kampf*. Munich: Franz Eher, 1938.

Hoefert, Siegfried. "Gerhart Hauptmann und Goebbels: Zur Situation des schlesischen Schriftstellers im Dritten Reich." *Michigan Germanic Studies* 20 (1994): 138–51.

Hoerle, W. Scott. *Hans Friedrich Blunck: Poet and Nazi Collaborrator 1888–1961*. Frankfurt am Main: Peter Lang, 2003.

Hofstetter, Albert J. *Werner Bergengruen im Dritten Reich*. Luzern: W. Blätten Erben, 1968.

Hoffmeister, Barbara. *S. Fischer, der Verleger*. Frankfurt am Main: S. Fischer, 2009.

Hoiss, Barbara, ed. *Donau Verzweigt: Schreiben unter und nach dem Nationalsozialismus. Franz Tumler und Arnolt Bronnen*. Linz: Stifter-Haus, 2008.

Hopster, Norbert, et al., eds. *Literaturlenkung im Dritten Reich: Eine Bibliographie*. 2 vols. Hildesheim: Georg Olms, 1993–94.

Hövel, Paul. *Wesen und Aufbau der Schrifttumsarbeit in Deutschland*. Essen: Essener Verlagsanstalt, 1942.

Hübner, Anja Susan. "Erfolgsautor mit allem Drum und Dran: Der Fall Fallada." in *Im Pausenraum des "Dritten Reiches": Zur Populärkultur im nationalsozialistischen Deutschland*. Edited by Carsten Würmann and Ansgar Warner, pp. 197–213. Bern: Peter Lang, 2008.

Hürter, Ludwig. "Die Arbeit der Beratungsstelle (Überwachungsstelle für das Leihbüchereiwesen." *Zeitschrift der Leihbücherei*, vol. 5, no. 1 (January 25, 1936): 1.

————. "Kampf den Leihbüchereien! Ausklang." *Zeitschrift der Leihbücherei*, vol. 3, no. 2 (January 25, 1934): 14–15.

————. "Der nationalsozialistische Leihbüchereigedanke." *Zeitschrift der Leihbücherei*, vol. 7, no. 2 (January 25, 1938): 2–3.

————. "Neuer Angriff gegen die Leihbüchereien: Unsere Antwort." *Zeitschrift der Leihbücherei*, vol. 3, no. 14 (July 25, 1934): 2–4 and no. 15 (August 10, 1934): 4–7.

———. "Die Säuberung der Leihbüchereien." *Zeitschrift der Leihbücherei*, vol. 4, no. 15 (August 10, 1935): 2–3.

———. "Zur ersten Tagung unserer Fachschaft." *Zeitschrift der Leihbücherei*, vol. 3, no. 5 (March 10, 1934): 7–8.

Ihde, Wilhelm. *Handbuch der Reichsschrifttumskammer.* Leipzig: Verlag des Börsenverein der deutschen Buchhändler, 1942.

———. "Das Kapital Vertrauen." *Grossdeutsches Leihbüchereiblatt* 4 (1942): 346–47.

———. *Das Recht der Reichkulturkammer.* Berlin: Walter de Gruyter, 1943.

Jedlitschka, Karsten. "Die Parteiamtliche Prüfungskommission zum Schutze des national-sozialistischen Schrifttums: Zensurfelder und Arbeitsweise am Beispiel des Münchner Lektors Ulrich Crämer." *Archiv für Geschichte des Buchwesens* 62 (1968): 213–26.

Jens, Inge. *Dichter zwischen rechts und links: Die Geschichte der Lektion für Dichtkunst der Preussischen Akademie der Künste dargestellt nach den Dokumenten.* Munich: Piper, 1971.

Joerden, Rudolf. "Dreimal Bibliothekar: Eine Abschiedsrede." *Bücherei und Bildung* 19 (1967): 135–39.

Jung, Ottmar. "Der literarische Judenstern: Die Indizierung der jüdischen Rechtsliteratur in nationalsozialistischen Deutschland." *Vierteljahrshefte für Zeitgeschichte* 54 (2006): 25–59.

Jungmichl, Johannes. *Nationalsozialistische Literaturlenkung und Bibliothekarische Buchbe-sprechung.* Berlin: Deutscher Bibliotekarsverband, 1974.

Jütte, Werner. "'Volksbibliothekar im Nationalsozialismus': Einige Bermerkungen zum Beitrag von Adolf von Morzé." *Buch und Bibliothek* 39 (1987): 345–48.

Kaas, Harald. "Der faschistische Piccolo: Arnold Bronnen." In *Intelleltuelle im Bann des National-sozialismus.* Edited by Karl Corino, pp. 136–49. Hamburg: Hoffmann und Campe, 1980.

Kamenetsky, Christa. *Children's Literature in Hitler's Germany: The Cultural Policy of National Socialism.* Athens: Ohio University Press, 1984.

Kannengiesser, Gertrud. *Die Bibliothek der Technischen Universität Braunschweig, wie ich sie erlebt habe 1928–1962.* Braunschweig: Technische Universität, 1967.

Kast, Raimund. "Der deutsche Leihbuchhandel und seine Organisationen im 20. Jahrhundert." *Archiv für Geschichte des Buchwesens* 36 (1991): 165–349.

———. "Die Leihbibliotheken im Nationalsozialismus." In *Bibliotheken während des National-sozialismus.* Edited by Peter Vodosek and Manfred Komorowski, vol. 1, pp. 515–28. Wiesbaden: Harrassowitz, 1989.

Kästner, Erich. "Bei Durchsicht meiner Bücher." In *Gesammelte Schriften für Erwachsene*, vol. 8, pp. 198–200. Zürich: Atrium, 1969.

Kellerhoff, Sven Felix. *Der Reichstagsbrand: Die Karriere eines Kriminalfalls.* Berlin: Be-bra, 2008.

Kerr, Alfred. "Gerhart Hauptmanns Schande." In *Exil: Literartur und politische Texte aus dem deutschen Exil 1933–1945.* Edited by Ernst Loewy, pp. 218–22. Stuttgart: J. B. Metzlersche, 1979.

———. *Die Welt im Licht.* Berlin: Kiepenheuer und Witsch, 1961.

Kershaw, Ian. *Hitler 1889–1936: Hubris.* New York: W. W. Norton, 1999.

Kettel, Andrea. *Volksbibliothekare und Nationalsozialismus: Zum Verhalten führender Berufs-vertreter während der nationalsozialistischen Machtübernahme.* Cologne: Pahl Rugenstein, 1981.

Kiaulehn, Walther. *Mein Freund, der Verleger: Ernst Rowohlt.* Reinbek bei Hamburg: Rowohlt, 1967.

Kirchner, Joachim. "Schrifttum und wissenschaftliche Bibliotheken im nationalsozialist-ischen Deutschland." *Zentralblatt für Bibliothekswesen* 50 (1933): 514–25.

Klapper, John. *Stefan Andres: The Christian Humanist as a Critic of His Times.* Bern: Peter Lang, 1995.

Klee, Ernst. *Das Kulturlexikon zum Dritten Reich: Wer war was vor und nach 1945.* Frankfurt am Main: S. Fischer, 2007.

Klepper, Jochen. *Briefwechsel 1925–1942.* Edited by Ernst G. Riemschneider. Stuttgart: Deutsche Verlags-Anstalt, 1973.

———. *Unter dem Schatten deiner Flügel: Aus den Tagebüchern der Jahre 1932–1942.* Edited by Hildegard Klepper. Stuttgart: Deutsche Verlags-Anstalt, 1956.

Klotzbücher, Alois. "Städtische Bibliotheken im Ruhrgebiet während des Nationalsozialismus." In *Bibliotheken während des Nationalsozialismus.* Edited by Peter Vodosek and Manfred Komorowski, vol. 2, pp. 53–89. Wiesbaden: Harrassowitz, 1992.

Koch, Hugo. "Die Bekämpfung des schädlichen und unerwünschten Schrifttums." *Jahrbuch des Grossdeutschen Leihbuchhandels 1941,* pp. 138–50.

Koch, Richard. "Die Neuordnung der Beratungsstellen." *Die Bücherei* 1 (1934): 18–20.

Kolbenheyer, Erwin Guido. *Stimme: Eine Sammlung von Aufsätzen.* Berlin: Georg Müller, 1932.

Komorowski, Manfred. "Die Tagungsprotokolle des Reichsbeirats für Bibliotheksange- legenheiten." *Bibliothek: Forschung und Praxis* 16 (1992): 66–98.

———. "Die wissenschaftlichen Bibliotheken während des Nationalsozialismus," In *Bibliotheken während des Nationalsozialismus.* Edited by Peter Vodosek and Manfred Komorowski, vol. 1, pp. 1–23. Wiesbaden: Harrassowitz, 1989

Korolnik, Marcel, and Annette Korolnik-Andersch. *Sansibar ist überall: Alfred Andersch, Seine Welt in Texten, Bildern und Dokumenten.* Munich: Edition Text, 2008.

Kriek, Ernst. "Agonie: Schlusswort zu Thomas Mann." *Volk und Werden* 5 (1938): 121–25.

Kroll, Frank-Lothar, and Rüdiger von Voss. *Schriftsteller und Widerstand: Facetten und Probleme der 'Inneren Emigration.'* Göttingen: Wallstein, 2012.

Krüger, Gerhard. "Die Parteiamtliche Prüfungskommission." *Die Bücherei* 8 (1941): 105–08.

Krüger, H. K. "Ernst Wiechert im Neuen Reich." *Der Buchhändler im Neuen Reich* 8 (1943): 35–42.

Krummsdorf, Juliane, and Ingrid Werner, eds. *Verbrannt, verboten, verbannt: Vergessen? Zur Erinnerung an die Bücherverbrennung 1933.* 2nd rev. ed. Dresden: Bibliothek beim Landesvorstand der PDS, 1993.

Kuhn, Michael, ed. *Verbrannte Bücher: Verzeichnis der Bücher, die 1933 aus dem Bestand des TH Braunschweig aussortiert und zum grössten Teil vernichtet wurden.* Braunschweig: Universi- tätsbibliothek der Technischen Universität Braunschweig, 1993.

Kummer, Bernard. "Nationalsozialismus und Volksbüchereiwesen." *Die Bücherei* 2 (1935): 319–25.

———. "Das wissenschaftliche Bibiliotheksweisen im nationalsozialistischen Deutschland." *Zentralblatt für Bibliothekswesen* 55 (1938): 399–413.

Kunze, Gerndt. *Hermann Stresau und Max Wieser: Zwei Beispiele bibliothekarischen Zeitgeistes während der Nazidiktatur.* Hannover: Laurentius, 1990.

Kutsch, Arnulf, ed. *Zeitungswissenschaft im Dritten Reich: Sieben biographische Studien.* Cologne: Studienverlag Hayit, 1984.

Labach, Michael. "Der Verein Deutscher Bibliothekare während des Nationalsozialismus." In *Bibliotheken während des Nationalsozialismus.* Edited by Peter Vodosek and Manfred Komorowski, vol. 2, pp. 151–68. Wiesbaden: Harrassowitz, 1992.

Lämmert, Eberhard. "Beherrschte Prosa: Poetische Lizensen in Deutschland zwischen 1933 und 1945." *Neue Rundschau* 86 (1975): 404–21.

Lange, Horst. *Tagebücher aus dem Zweiten Weltkrieg.* Edited by Hans Dieter Schäfer. Mainz: V. Hase und Koehler, 1979.

Langenbucher, Hellmuth. "Deutsches Schrifttum 1937—politisch gesehen." *Nationalsozia- listische Bibliographie—NSB,* no. 2 (February 1938), 3. Beilage, pp. i-xx.

———. *Die deutsche Gegenwartsdichtung: Eine Einführung in das volkhafte Schrifttum unserer Zeit.* Berlin: Junker und Dünnhaupt, 1939.

———. "Schrifttumspflege in neuen Deutschland." *Börsenblatt für den deutschen Buchhandel,* no. 114 (May 18, 1935): 24–30.

———. *Volkhafte Dichtung der Zeit.* 3rd rev. ed. Berlin: Junker und Dünnhaupt, 1937.

———. *Die Welt des Buches: Eine Kunde vom Buch.* Ebenhausen bei Munich: Wilhelm Langwiesche-Brandt, 1938.

Langendorf, Peter. "Die neuen Massstäbe bei der Buchauswahl in der politisch-historischen Literatur." *Die Bücherei* 1 (1934): 270–81.

Langgässer, Elisabeth. "Schriftsteller unter der Hitler-Diktatur." *Ost und West* 1 (1947): 36–41.

Laufhütte, Hartmut, ed. *Hans Carossa: Dreizehn Versuche zu seinem Werk*. Tübingen: Max Niemeyer, 1991.

"Das Leben des Juden Heinrich Heine." *Der deutsche Schriftsteller* 5 (1940): 79.

Lehmann, Hartmut, and Otto Gerhard Oexle, eds. *Nationalsozialismus in den Kulturwissenschaften*, 2 vols. Göttingen: Vandenboeck and Ruprecht, 2004.

Lemberg, Margret. *Verboten und nicht verbrannt*, 2 vols. Marburg: Universitätsbibliothek, 2001.

Leonhard, Joachim-Felix, ed. *Bücherverbrennung: Zensur, Verbot, Vernichtung unter dem Nationalsozialismus in Heidelberg*. Heidelberg: Heidelberger Verlagsanstalt, 1983.

Leppmann, Wolfgang. *Gerhart Hauptmanns Leben, Werk und Zeit*. Bern: Scherz, 1986.

Lerchenmüller, Joachim. *Die Geschichtswissenschaft in den Planungen des Sicherheitsdienstes der SS: Der DS-Historiker Hermann Löffler*. Bonn: J. H. W. Dietz, 2001.

———. "Die 'SD-mässige' Bearbeitung der Geschichtswissenschaft." In *Nachrichtendienst, politische Elite und Mordeinheit: Der Sicherheitsdienst des Reichsführers SS*. Edited by Michael Wildt, pp. 160–89. Hamburg: Hamburger Edition, 2003.

Leske, Monika. *Philosophen im "Dritten Reich": Studien zu Hochschul- und Philosophiebetrieb im faschistischen Deutschland*. Berlin: Dietz, 1990.

Lexikon des gesamten Buchwesens. 2nd ed. Stuttgart: Anton Hiersemann, 1987.

Link, Werner, ed. *Schriftsteller und Politik in Deutschland*. Düsseldorf: Droste, 1979.

Linthout, Ine van. *Das Buch in der nationalsozialistischen Propagandapolitik*. Berlin: Walter de Gruyter, 2012.

———. "'Dichter schreibt Unterhaltungsromane!': Der Stellenwert der Unterhaltungsliteratur im Dritten Reich." In *Im Pausenraum des "Dritten Reiches": Zur Populärkultur im nationalsozialistischen Deutschland*. Edited by Varsten Würmann and Ansgar Warner, pp. 111–24. Bern: Peter Lang, 2008.

Loerke, Oskar. *Tagebücher 1903–1939*. Edited by Hermann Kasack. Heidelberg: Sambert Schneider, 1956

Loewy, Ernst, ed. *Exil: Literarische und politische Texte aus dem deutschen Exil 1933–1945*. Stuttgart: J. B. Metzlersche, 1979.

———. *Literatur unter dem Hakenkreuz: Das Dritte Reich und seine Dichtung: Eine Dokumentation*. Frankfurt am Main: Europäische Verlagsanstalt, 1966.

Lohner, Edgar. *Dichter über ihre Dichtungen: Gottfried Benn*. Munich: Heimeran, 1969.

Lokatis, Siegfried. *Hanseatische Verlagsanstalt: Politisches Buchmarketing im "Dritten Reich."* Frankfurt am Main: Buchhändler Vereinigung, 1992.

Longerich, Peter. *Hitlers Stellvertreter: Führung der Partei und Kontrolle des Staatsapparats durch den Stab Hess und die Partei-Kanzlei Bormann*. Munich: K. G. Saur, 1992.

Losch, Sebastian. "Klare Haltung." *Grossdeutsches Leihbüchereiblatt* 1 (1939): 209–10.

Lundgreen, Peter. *Wissenschaft im Dritten Reich*. Frankfurt am Main: Suhrkamp, 1985.

Magenau, Jörg. *Gottfried Benn*. Berlin: Kunstverlag, 2010.

Manasse, Peter M. *Verschleppte Archive und Bibliotheken: Die Tätigkeit des Einsatzstabes Rosenberg während des Zweiten Weltkrieges*. Translated by Georg A. Pippig. St. Ingbert: Röhrig, 1997.

Mank, Dieter. *Erich Kästner im nationalsozialistischen Deutschland 1933–1945: Zeit ohne Werk?* Frankfurt am Main: Peter Lang, 1981.

Mann, Thomas. "Essays." Vols. 5 and 6. Frankfurt am Main: S. Fischer, 1997.

Mann, Thomas et al. *Ein Streitgespräch über die innere und äussere Emigration*. Dortmund: W. Crüwell, 1946.

Manning, Molly Guptill. *When Books Went to War: The Stories That Helped Us Win World War II*. New York: Houghton Mifflin, 2014.

Manthey, Jürgen. *Hans Fallada in Selbstzeugnissen und Bilddokumenten*. Reinbek bei Hamburg: Rowohlt, 1963.

Marhoff, Lydia. "Von der 'kameradschaftlichen' zur 'gesunden' Sexualität: Frauenliteratur der dreissiger und vierziger Jahre zwischen Frauenbewegung und Nationalsozialismus." In *Banalität mit Stil: Zur Widersprüchlichkeit der Literaturproduktion in Nationalsozialismus*. Edited by Walter Delabar et al., pp. 179–98. Bern: Peter Lang, 1999.

Maurer, Warren R. *Understanding Gerhart Hauptmann*. Columbia: University of South Carolina Press, 1992.

Mendelssohn, Peter de. *Der Geist in der Despotie: Versuche über die moralischen Möglichkeiten des Intellektuellen in der totalitären Gesellschaft*. Frankfurt am Main: Taschenbuchverlag, 1987.

Menz, Gerhart. *Der Aufbau des Kulturstandes: Die Reichskulturkammergesetzgebung, ihre Grundlagen und ihre Erfolge*. Munich: C. H. Beck, 1938.

Mirbt, Karl-Wolfgang. "Theorie und Technik des Camouflage: Die Deutsche Rundschau im Dritten Reich als Beispiel publizistischer Opposition unter totalitärer Gewalt. *Publizistik* 9 (1964): 3–16.

Mitchell, Allan. *The Devil's Capitain: Ernst Jünger in Nazi Paris 1941–1944*. New York: Berghahn, 2011.

Mittenzwei, Werner. *Der Untergang einer Akademie oder die Mentalität des ewigen Deutschen: Der Einfluss der nationalkonservativen Dichter an der Preussischen Akademie der Künste 1918 bis 1947*. Berlin: Aufbau, 1992.

Molo, Walter von. *So wunderbar ist das Leben: Erinnerungen und Begegnungen*. Stuttgart: Verlag deutscher Volksbücher, 1957.

———. "Was ist nordisch?" *Deutscher Kulturwart* (June 1939): 49–52.

Mörchen, Helmut. "Gegenaufklärung der Unterwerfung: Tendenzen der Essayistik im Dritten Reich." In *Die deutsche Literatur im Dritten Reich: Themen, Traditionen, Wirkungen*. Edited by Horst Denkler and Karl Prümm, pp. 224–39. Stuttgart: Philipp Reclam, 1976.

Morze, Adolf von. "Verlust des Bildungsreiches: Volksbibliothekare im Nationalsozialismus." *Buch und Bibliothek* 39 (1987): 106–26.

Müller, Georg Wilhelm. *Das Reichsministerium für Volksaufklärung und Propaganda*. Berlin: Junker und Dünnhaupt, 1940.

Müller, Hildegard. "Die Universitätsbibliothek Heidelberg im Dritten Reich." In *Bibliotheken während des Nationalsozialismus*. Edited by Peter Vodosek and Manfred Komorowski, vol. 1, pp. 343–58. Wiesbaden: Harrassowitz, 1989.

Nassen, Ulrich. *Jugend, Buch und Konjunktur 1933–1945*. Munich: Wilhelm Fink, 1987.

"Neuordnung der Volksbibliotheken in Sachsen." *Die Bücherei* 1 (1934): 171–72.

Noakes, Jeremy. "Philipp Bouhler und die Kanzlei des Führers: Beispiel einer Sonderverwaltung im Dritten Reich." In *Verwaltung contra Menschenführung im Staat Hitler: Studien zum politisch-administrativen System*. Edited by Dieter Rebentisch and Karl Teppe, pp. 208–36. Göttingen: Vandenhoeck and Ruprecht, 1986.

Paetel, Karl Otto. *Deutsche Innere Emigration: Anti-nationalsozialistische Zeugnisse aus Deutschland*. New York: Friedrich Krause, 1946.

Paret, Peter. *An Artist against the Third Reich: Ernst Barlach 1933–1938*. New York: Cambridge University Press, 2003.

Patutschnick, Karl Helmut. "Die rechtliche Stellung der Parteiamtlichen Kommission zum Schutze des NS-Schrifttums." *Deutsches Recht* 5 (1935): 444–46.

Payr, Bernhard. *Das Amt Schrifttumspflege: Seine Entwicklungsgeschichte und seine Organisation*. Berlin: Junker und Dünnhaupt, 1941.

———. "Aufgaben des Amtes Schrifttumspflege." In *Die Welt des Buches*. Edited by Hellmuth Langenbucher, pp. 203–07. Ebenhausen bei Munich: Langewiesche-Brandt, 1938.

Pechel, Rudolf. *Deutsche Rundschau: Acht Jahrzehnte deutschen Geisteslebens*. Hamburg: Ritten und Loening, 1961.

———. *Zwischen den Zeilen: Der Kampf einer Zeitschrift für Freiheit und Recht*. Wiesentheid: Droemerische Verlagsanstalt, 1948.

Pedersen, Ulf. *Bernhard Rust: Ein nationalsozialistischer Bildungspolitiker vor dem Hintergrund seiner Zeit*. Braunschweig: Gifthorn, 1994.

Peters, J. "Das Werk Ernst Wiecherts." *Die Bücherei* 7 (1940): 1–28.

Petersen, Klaus. *Zensur in der Weimarer Republik*. Stuttgart: J. B. Metzler, 1995.

Petzold, Joachim. "Das Büchereiwesen der NSDAP unter besonderer Berücksichtigung der wissenschaftlichen Spezialbibliotheken." *Zentralblatt für Bibliothekswesen* 55 (1938): 524–33.

Peukert, Detlev. "Der Schund- und Schmutzkampf als 'Sozialpolitik der Seele': Eine Vorge-schichte der Bücherverbrennung." In *"Das war ein Vorspiel nur . . ." Bücherverbrennung*

Deutschland 1933: Voraussetzungen und Folgen. Edited by Hermann Haarmann et al., pp. 51–63. Berlin: Medusa, 1983.

Pfoser, Alfred. "Die Leipziger Radikalkur in Wien: Die Wiener städtischen Büchereien im Nationalsozialismus." In *Bibliotheken während des Nationalsozialismus*. Edited by Peter Vodosek and Manfred Komorowski, vol. 2, pp. 91–100. Wiesbaden: Harrassowitz, 1992.

Pfoser, Alfred, and Friedrich Stadler, eds. *Die verbrannten Bücher 10.5. 1933*. Vienna: Institut für Wissenschaft und Kunst, 1983.

Piper, Ernst. *Alfred Rosenberg: Hitlers Chefideologe*. Munich: Karl Blessing, 2005.

Popp, Karl Robert. "Das gute Jugendbuch." *Börsenblatt für den deutschen Buchhandel*. No. 104 (May 7, 1935): 358–59.

Prinzhorn, Fritz. *Die Aufgaben der Bibliotheken im nationalsozialistischen Deutschland*. Leipzig: Eichblatt, 1934.

Pritzsche, Peter. *Life and Death in the Third Reich*. Cambridge, Mass.: Harvard University Press, 2008.

Raddatz, Fritz Joachim. *Gottfried Benn: Leben—niederer Wahn: Eine Biographie*. Berlin: Propyläen, 2001.

———. *Die Nachgeborenen: Lesererfahrungen mit zeitgenössischer Literatur*. Frankfurt am Main: S. Fischer, 1983.

Rang, Bernhard. "Hermann Hesse und das gegenwärtige Deutschland." *Die Bücherei* 9 (1942): 23–26.

Rantzau, Otto Graf zu. *Das Reichsministerium für Wissenschaft, Erziehung und Volksbildung*. Berlin: Juncker und Dünnhaupt, 1939.

Raphael, Lutz. "Radikales Ordnungsdenken und die Organisation totalitärer Herrschaft: Weltanschauungseliten und Humanwissenschaftler im NS-Regime." *Geschichte und Gesellschaft* 27 (2001): 5–40.

Razum, Christine. "Der deutsche Verband Evangelischer Büchereien (DVEB)." In *Bibliotheken während des Nationalsozialismus*. Edited by Peter Vodosek and Manfred Komorowski, vol. 1, pp. 501–07. Wiesbaden: Harrassowitz, 1989.

Reichmann, Felix. "The First Year of American Publications Control in Germany." *Publishers' Weekly*, November 14, 1946, pp. 2810–12.

Reichsführer SS. *Leitheft no. 2: Buchhandel*. Berlin, 1937.

———. *Leitheft no. 5: Verlagswesen*. Berlin, 1937.

———. *Leitheft no. 30: Schrifttumswesen und Schrifttumspolitik*. Berlin, 1937.

Reichsministerium für Volksaufklärung und Propaganda, Abteilung Schrifttum. *Das Buch ein Schwert des Geistes: Erste Grundliste für den deutschen Leihbuchhandel*. Leipzig: Verlag des Börsenvereins für den deutschen Buchhandel, 1940.

———. *Liste der für Jugendliche und Büchereien ungeeigneten Druckschriften: Stand vom 15. Oktober 1940*. Leipzig: Verlag des Börsenvereins für den deutschen Buchhandel, 1940.

———. *Verzeichnis englischer und amerikanischer Schriftsteller*. Leipzig: Verlag des Börsenvereins für den deutschen Buchhandel, 1942.

Reichsministerium für Volksaufklärung und Propaganda, Fachbuch-Zentrallektorat. *Arbeitsrichtlinien für den Fachbuch-Lektor*. Berlin: Wilhelm Limpert, 1941.

Reichsschrifttumskammer, *Liste 1 des schädlichen und unerwünschten Schrifttums. Stand vom Oktober 1935*. Berlin: Reichsdruckerei, 1935.

———. *Liste des schädlichen und unerwünschten Schrifttums. Stand vom 31. Dezember 1938*. Leipzig: Ernst Hedrich, 1938. (Reprint: Vaduz, Liechtenstein: Topos, 1979.)

Reichs- und Preussischer Minister für Wissenschaft, Erziehung, und Volksbildung. "Richtlinien für das Voksbüchereiwesen." *Die Bücherei* 5 (1938): 39–46.

Reiner, Guido. *Ernst Wiechert im Dritten Reich: Eine Dokumentation*. Paris: G. Reiner, 1974.

Reinhardt, Stephan. *Alfred Andersch: Eine Biographie*. Zürich: Diogenes, 1990.

Reinhold, Ursula. *Alfred Andersch: Politisches Engagement und literarische Wirksamkeit*. Berlin (Ost): Akademie-Verlag, 1988.

Reuter, Emil. "Dichtung als Lebensmacht: Wozu brauchen wir noch eine Dichtung?" *Der deutsche Schriftsteller* 7 (1942): 134–36.

Richards, Pamela Spence. " 'Aryan Librarianship': Academic and Research Librarians under Hitler." *Journal of Library History* 19 (1984): 231–58.

———. "Die technisch-wissenschaftliche Bibliothek während des Nationalsozialismus." *Bibliotheken während des Nationalsozialismus.* Edited by Peter Vodosek and Manfred Komorowski, vol. 1, pp. 529–48. Wiesbaden: Harrassowitz, 1989.

"Richtlinien für die Bestandsprüfung in den Volksbüchereien Sachsens." *Die Bücherei* 2 (1935): 279–80.

"Richtlinien zur Neuordnung des Bestandes der ostmärkischen Büchereien." *Ostmark-Bücherei,* vol. 1, no. 3 (June 1939): 14–16.

Richter, Hans. "Wo finde ich den Juden?" *Börsenblatt für den deutschen Buchhandel,* no. 205 (September 3, 1936): 761–63.

Riemschneider, Ernst. *Der Fall Klepper: Eine Dokumentation.* Stuttgart: Deutsche Verlagsanstalt, 1975.

Rischer, Walter. *Die nationalsozialistische Kulturpolitk in Düsseldorf.* Düsseldorf: Michael Triltsch, 1972.

Ritchie, J. M. *German Literature under National Socialism.* London: Croom Helm, 1983.

Ritter, Gerhard. "The German Professor in the Third Reich." *Review of Politics* 8 (1956): 242–54.

Rose, Jonathan, ed. *The Holocaust and the Book: Destruction and Preservation.* Amherst: University of Massachusetts Press, 2001.

Rosenberg, Alfred. *Das politische Tagebuch Alfred Rosenbergs aus den Jahren 1934/35 und 1939/41.* Edited by Hans-Günther Seraphim. Göttingen: Musterschmidt, 1956

———. *Portrait eines Menschlichkeitsverbrechers nach den hinterlassenen Memoiren des ehemaligen Reichsministers Alfred Rosenberg.* Edited by Serge Lange and Ernst von Schenk. St. Gallen: Zollikofer, 1947.

Röska, Günther. "Walter Hofmann und der Nationalsozialismus: Auseinandersetzung um das Leipziger Volksbüchereiwesen." *Buchhandelsgeschichte* (Beilage zum *Börsenblatt für den deutschen Buchhandel,* December 12, 2000), B 172–B 175.

Rothfeder, Herbert P. "Amt Schrifttumspflege: A Study in Literary Control." *German Studies Review* 4 (1981): 63–78.

Röttig, Sabine. "'. . . bleiben Sie wie bisher in Dichters Landes und nähren Sie sich redlich': Der Gustav Kiepenheuer Verlag 1933–1949." *Archiv für Geschichte des Buchwesens* 58 (2004): 1–139.

Rühle, Gerd. *Das Dritte Reich: Dokumentarische Darstellung des Aufbaus der Nation,* 3 vols. Berlin: Hummel, 1934–35.

Rust, Bernhard. *Das nationalsozialistische Deutschland und die Wissenschaft: Heidelberger Reden.* Hamburg: Hanseatische Verlagsanstalt, 1936.

———. "Noch heute!" *Die Bücherei* 1 (1934): 11–13.

Sarkowicz, Hans. *Hitlers Künstler: Die Kultur im Dienste des Nationalsozialismus.* Frankfurt am Main: Insel, 2004.

———. *Literatur in Nazi-Deutschland: Ein biographisches Lexikon.* Hamburg: Europa, 2000.

———. *Schriftsteller im Nationalsozialismus.* Berlin: Insel, 2011.

———. "Zwischen Sympathie und Apologie: Der Schriftsteller Hans Grimm und sein Verhältnis zum Nationalsozialismus." In *Intellektuelle im Bann des Nationalsozialismus.* Edited by Karl Corino, pp. 120–35. Hamburg: Hoffmann und Campe, 1980.

Sarkowski, Heinz. *Springer-Verlag: History of a Scientific Publishing House.* Translated by Gerald Graham. Vol. 1: 1842–1945. Berlin: Springer, 1996.

———. "Opposition or Opportunism: Günter Eich's Status as an Inner Emmigrant." In *Leid der Worte: Panorama des literarischen Nationalsozialismus.* Edited by Jörg Thunecke, pp. 176–87. Bonn: Bouvier, 1987.

———. "'Saint Joan before the Cannibals: George Bernard Shaw in the Third Reich." *German Studies Review* 16 (1993): 435–61.

Sarkowski, Heinz, and Wolfgang Jeske. *Der Insel Verlag 1899–1999: Die Geschichte des Verlags.* Frankfurt am Main: Insel, 1999.

Sauder, Gerhard, ed. *Die Bücherverbrennung: Zum 10. Mai 1933.* Munich: Carl Hanser, 1986.

———. "Der Germanist Goebbels als Redner bei der Berliner Bücherverbrennung." In *Das war ein Vorspiel nur . . .": Berliner Colloquium zur Literaturpolitik im Dritten Reich.* Edited by Horst Denkler and Eberhard Lämmer, pp. 56–81. Berlin: Akademie der Künste, 1985.

Saur, Klaus G., and Martin Hollender, eds. *Selbstbehauptung, Anpassung, Gleichschaltung, Verstrickung: Die preussische Staatsbibliothek und das deutsche Bibliothekswesen 1933–1945.* Frankfurt am Main: Vittorio Klostermann, 2014.

"Schädlinge des Volkes." *Börsenblatt für den deutschen Buchhandel.* No. 285 (December 8, 1936): 1073.

Schaefer, Oda. *Auch wenn du träumst gehen die Uhren: Lebenserinnerungen.* Munich: Piper, 1970.

Schäfer, Hans Dieter. *Das gespaltene Bewusstsein: Über deutsche Kultur und Lebenswirklichkeit 1933–1945.* Rev. ed. Göttingen: Wallstein, 2009.

Schidorsky, Dov. "Das Schicksal jüdischer Bibliothekare im Dritten Reich." In *Bibliotheken während des Nationalsozialismus.* Edited by Peter Vodosek and Manfred Komorowski, vol. 2, pp. 189–222. Wiesbaden: Harrassowitz, 1992.

Schlecht, Hein. "Parole 1940." *Grossdeutsches Leihbüchereiblatt* 2 (1940): 1.

Schlegel, Werner. *Dichter auf dem Scheiterhaufen.* Berlin: Verlag für Kulturpolitik, 1934.

Schlösser, Manfred. *An den Wind geschrieben: Lyrik der Freiheit 1933–1945.* Munich: Deutscher Taschenbuchverlag, 1962.

Schmidt, Roderich, ed. *175 Jahre Deuerlichsche Buchhandlung: Eine Chronik mit Dokumenten und Bildern.* Göttingen: Deuerlichsche Buchhandlung, 1982.

Schmidt-Leonhardt, H. *Das Schrifttumsgesetz vom 4. Oktober 1933 nebst den einschlägigen Bestimmungen.* 2nd ed. Berlin: Carl Heymann, 1938.

Schmollinger, Annette. *"Intra muros et extra": Deutsche Literatur im Exil und in der Inneren Emigration, Ein Exemplarischer Vergleich.* Heidelberg: C. Winter, 1999.

Schnell, Ralf. *Dichtung in finsteren Zeiten: Deutsche Literatur und Faschismus.* Reinbek bei Hamburg: Rowohlt, 1998.

———. *Literarische Innere Emigration: 1933–1945.* Stuttgart: J. B. Metzler, 1976.

Schoeps, Julius, and Werner Tresi. *Orte der Bücherverbrennungen in Deutschland 1933.* Berlin: Georg Olms, 2008.

Schöffling, Klaus, ed. *Dort wo man Bücher verbrennt: Stimmen der Betroffenen.* Frankfurt am Main: Suhrkamp, 1983.

Scholz, Kai-Uwe. "Chamälen oder Die Vielen Gesichter des Hans-Friedrich Blunck: Ampassungsstrategien eines prominierten Kulturfunktionär vor und nach 1945." In *Dann waren die Sieger da: Studien zur literarischen Kultur in Hamburg 1945–1950.* Edited by Ludwig Fischer et al. Hamburg: Dölling und Galitz, 1999.

Schonauer, Franz. *Deutsche Literatur im Dritten Reich: Versuch einer Darstellung in polemischdidaktischer Absicht.* Freiburg im Breisgau: Walter, 1961.

Schönwälder, Karen. *Historik und Politik: Geschichtswissenschaft im Nationalsozialismus.* Frankfurt am Main: Campus, 1992.

Schrader, Bärbel. *"Jederzeit widerruflich": Die Reichskulturkammer und die Sondergenehmigungen in Theater und Film des NS-Staates.* Berlin: Metropol, 2008.

Schrieber, Karl-Friedrich. *Das Recht der Reichskulturkammer: Sammlung der für den Kulturstand geltenden Gesetze und Verordnungen, der amtlichen Anordnungen und Bekanntmachungen der Reichskulturkammer und ihrer Einzelkammern.* Berlin: Junker und Dünnhaupt, 1935–37.

———. *Die Reichskulturkammer: Organisation und Ziele der deutschen Kulturpolitik.* Berlin: Junker und Dünnhaupt, 1934.

Schriewer, Franz. "Kampf den Leihbüchereien!" *Bücherei und Bildungspflege* 13 (1933): 100–13.

Schröder, Jürgen. "Benn in den dreissiger Jahren." In *Intellektuelle im Bann des Nationalsozialismus.* Edited by Karl Corino, pp. 48–60. Hamburg: Hoffmann und Kampe, 1980.

Schroeder, Werner. ". . . eine Fundgrube der Schrifttumsinformation": Die Leipziger 'Arbeitsstelle für Schrifttumsbearbeitung beim Sicherheitshauptamt (SD)' und die SD-Verbindungsstelle an der Deutschen Bibliothek. In "Arisierung" in Leipzig: Annäherung an ein lange verdrängtes Kapitel der Stadtgeschichte der Jahre 1933 bis 1945.* Edited by Monika Gibas, pp. 116–51. Leipzig: Leipziger Universitätsverlag, 2007.

Schulz, F. O. H. "Von Heine bis Stalin." *Der deutsche Schriftsteller* 7 (1942): 98.

Schulz, Gerd. "Die Machtergreifung im Börsenverein: Aus dem historischen Archiv des Börsenvereins." *Buchhandelsgeschichte* 4 (1985): B 98–B 101.

Schulz, Hans Ferdinand. *Das Schicksal der Bücher und des Buchhandel: System einer Vertriebskunde des Buches.* 2nd ed. Berlin: de Gruyter, 1960.

Schulz, Kurd. "Schundkomplex und Leihbüchereien." *Bücherei und Bildungspflege* 13 (1933): 297–305.

Schulze. "Beratungs- und Prüfungsstelle für astrologisches und verwandfes Schrifttum." *Der deutsche Schriftsteller* 1 (1936): 40.

Schuster, Wilhelm. "Bücherei und Nationalsozialismus." *Die Bücherei* 1 (1934): 1–9.

———. "Erklärung und Aufruf des Verbandes Deutscher Volksbibliothekare." *Bücherei und Bildungspflege* 13 (1933): 97–98.

———. "Masse und Volk, Gruppe und Einzelne in ihren Beziehungen zur Volkserziehung und Bücherei." *Die Bücherei* 2 (1935): 97–105.

———. "Die Neuordnung des Preussischen Büchereiwesens." *Die Bücherei* 1 (1934): 9–17.

———. "Der Stand des deutschen öffentlichen Büchereiwesens." *Die Bücherei* 2 (1935): 242–51.

———. "Die Volksbücherei im neuen Reich." *Die Bücherei* 1 (1934): 342–48.

Schütz, Erhard. "Ein Geruch von Blut und Schande." *Juni: Ein Magazin für Literatur und Politik* 24 (1996): 139–55.

Schwarz, Egon. "Hermann Hesse und der Nationalsozialismus." In *Hermann Hesse: Politische und wirkungsgeschichtliche Aspekte.* Edited by Sigrid Bauschinger and Albert Reh, pp. 55–71. Berlin: Francke, 1986.

Schwarz, Falk. "Die gelenkte Literatur: Die 'Neue Rundschau' im Konflikt mit den Kontrollstellen des NS-Staates und der nationalsozialistischen Bewegung." In *Die deutsche Literatur im Dritten Reich: Themen, Traditionen, Wirkungen.* Edited by Horst Denkler and Karl Prümm, pp. 66–82. Stuttgart: Philipp Reclam, 1976.

Schwilk, Heimo. *Ernst Jünger: Ein Jahrhundertleben der Biographie.* Munich: Piper, 2007.

Sebald, Winfried Georg. *On the Natural History of Destruction.* Translated by Anthea Bell. New York: Random House, 2003.

Seier, Hellmut. "Kollaborative und oppositionelle Momente der inneren Emigration Jochen Kleppers." *Jahrbuch für die Geschichte Mittel- und Ostdeutschlands* 8 (1959): 319–47.

Seifert, Otto. *Die grosse Säuberung des Schrifttums: Der Börsenverein der deutschen Buchhändler zu Leipzig 1933 bis 1945.* Schkenditz: GNN, 2000.

Siebenhaar, Klaus. "Buch und Schwert: Anmerkungen zur Indizierungspraxis und 'Schrifttumspolitik' im Nationalsozialismus." In *"Das war ein Vorspiel nur . . .": Bücherverbrennung Deutschland 1933, Voraussetzungen und Folgen.* Edited by Hermann Haarmann et al., pp. 81–96. Berlin: Medusa, 1983.

Simon, Gerd. "Germanistik und Sicherheitsdienst." In *Nachrichtendienst, politische Elite und Mordeinheit: Der Sicherheitsdienst des Reichsführers SS.* Edited by Michael Wildt, pp. 190–203. Hamburg: Hamburger Edition, 2003.

Sims, Amy R. "The Unsettling History of German Historians in the Third Reich." In *Flight of Fantasy: New Perspectives on Inner Emigration in German Literature.* Edited by Neil H. Donohue and Doris Kirdchner, pp. 277–304. New York: Berghahn, 2003.

Soenke, Jürgen. *Studien über zeitgenössische Zensursysteme.* Frankfurt am Main: Moritz Diesterweg, 1941.

Sommer, Kurt A. "10 Jahre Parteiamtliche Prüfungskommission zum Schutze des NS-Schrifttum: Zur Entwicklung der NS-Bibliographie." *Zentralblatt für Bibliothekswesen* 60 (1943): 354–56.

Sprengel, Peter. *Der Dichter stand auf hoher Küste: Gerhart Hauptmann im Dritten Reich.* Berlin: Propyläen, 2009.

Staatliche Landesfachstelle für Volksbüchereiwesen Sachsen. "Richtlinien für die Bestandsprüfung in den Volksbüchereien Sachsens." *Die Bücherei* 2 (1935): 279–80.

Stapel, Rudolf. *Die literarische Vorherrschaft der Juden in Deutschland: 1918–1933.* Hamburg: Hanseatische Verlagsanstalt, 1937.

Stefen, Rudolf, ed. *Gesamtverzeichnis der von der Bundesprüfstelle indizierten Bücher, Taschenbücher, Broschüren, Comics und Flugblätter.* St. Augustin: Asgard, 1989.

Steinweis, Alan E. *Art, Ideologie and Economics in Nazi Germany: The Reich Chamber of Music, Theater and the Visual Arts*. Chapel Hill: University of North Carolina Press, 1993.

Stieg, Margaret F. *Public Libraries in Nazi Germany*. Tuscaloosa: University of Alabama Press, 1992.

Stollberg, Jochen. *Die Rothschild'sche Bibliothek in Frankfurt am Main*. Frankfurt am Main: Vittorio Klostermann, 1988.

Strätz, Hans-Wolfgang. "Die studentische 'Aktion wider den undeutschen Geist' im Frühjahr 1933." *Vierteljahrshefte für Zeitgeschichte* 16 (1968): 347–72.

Stresau, Hermann. *Von Jahr zu Jahr*. Berlin: Minerva, 1948

Strothmann, Dietrich. *Nationalsozialistische Literaturpolitik: Ein Beitrag zur Publizistik im Dritten Reich*. Bonn: Bouvier, 1985.

Studentowski, Werner. "Partei und Volksbücherei." *Die Bücherei* 4 (1937): 285–91.

Suchenwirth, Richard. "Der deutsche Schriftsteller in Dritten Reich." *Der deutsche Schriftsteller* 1 (1936): 3–4.

Sywottek, Jutta. "Die Gleichschaltung der deutschen Volksbüchereien 1933 bis 1937." *Archiv für Geschichte des Buchwesens* 24 (1983): 386–535.

Taupitz, Karl. "Der Aufbau des Büchereiwesens in Sachsen seit der nationalsozialistischen Revolution." *Die Bücherei* 4 (1937): 243–58.

———. "Parteibibliotheken oder Volksbüchereien?" *Die Bücherei* 2 (1935): 545–50.

Terwort, Gerhard. *Hans Fallada im Dritten Reich*. Frankfurt am Main: Peter Lang, 1992.

Thiess, Frank. *Jahre des Unheils: Fragmente erlebter Geschichte*. Vienna: Paul Zsolnay, 1972.

Thunecke, Jörg, ed. *Leid der Worte: Panorama des literarischen Nationalsozialismus*. Bonn: Bouvier, 1987.

Töteberg, Michael, and Sabine Buck. *Hans Fallada: Ewig auf der Rutschbahn. Briefwechsel mit dem Rowohlt Verlag*. Reinbek bei Hamburg: Rowohlt, 2008.

Toussaint, Ingo. *Die Universitätsbibliothek Freiburg im Dritten Reich*. 2nd rev. ed. Munich: K. G. Saur, 1984.

———. *Die Universitätsbibliotheken Heidelberg, Jena und Köln unter dem Nationalsozialismus*. Munich: K. G. Saur, 1989.

———. "Wissenschaftliche Bibliotheken im Dritten Reich: Ein vorläufiges Resümé." In *Bibliotheken während des Nationalsozialismus*. Edited by Peter Vodosek and Manfred Komorowski, vol. 1, pp. 385–88. Wiesbaden: Harrassowitz, 1989.

Trawny, Peter. *Die Autorität des Zeugen: Ernst Jüngers Politisches Werk*. Berlin: Mathes und Seitz, 2009.

Trenkler, Ernst. *Geschichte der Österreichischen Nationalbibliothek, Part II: 1923–1967*. Vienna: Brüder Hollinek, 1973.

Triebel, Florian. "Die Meldungen aus dem Reich als buchhandelsgeschichtliche Quelle." *Archiv für Geschichte des Buchwesens* 58 (2004): 197–209.

Tuchel, Johannes. "Alfred Andersch im Nationalsozialismus." In *Sansibar ist überall: Alfred Andersch—Seine Welt in Texten, Bildern, Dokumenten*. Edited by Marcel Korolnik and Annette Korolnik-Andersch, pp. 31–41. Munich: Edition Text, 2008.

Urban, Regina, and Ralph Herpolsheimer. "Franz Alfred Six." In *Zeitungswissenschaftler im Dritten Reich*. Edited by Arnulf Kutsch, pp. 169–214. Cologne: Studienverlag Hayit, 1984.

"Verbotenes und unerwünschtes Schrifttum." *Der Buchhändler im neuen Reich* 2 (1937): 41–42.

Verweyen, Theodor. *Bücherverbrennungen: Eine Vorlage aus Anlass des 65. Jahrestages der "Aktion wider den undeutschen Geist."* Heidelberg: Universitätsverlag, 2000.

Vieregg, Axel. *Der eigenen Fehlbarkeit begegnen: Günter Eichs Realitäten 1933–1945*. Eggingen: Klaus Isele, 1993.

Vodosek, Peter, and Manfred Komorowski, eds. *Bibliotheken während des Nationalsozialismus*. 2 vols. Wiesbaden: Harrassowitz, 1989–92.

Volckmar-Frentze, Theodor. *In den Stürmen der Zeit: Zur Geschichte des Hauses Volkmar 1829–1954*. Stuttgart: K. F. Koehler, 1954.

"Vom Wesen der Leihbücherei." *Der Buchhändler im neuen Reich* 2 (1937): 79–82.

Vondung, Klaus. "Autodafé und Phönix: Vom Glauben an den deutschen Geist." In *"Das war ein Vorspiel nur . . .": Colloquium zur Literaturpolitk im Dritten Reich.* Edited by Horst Denkler and Eberhard Lämmer, pp. 89–104. Berlin: Akademie der Künste, 1985.

Wagener, Hans. *Stefan Andres.* Berlin: Colloquium, 1974.

Walberer, Ulrich, ed. *10. Mai 1933: Bücherverbrennung und Folgen.* Frankfurt am Main: S. Fischer, 1983.

Wallenborn, Markus. "Schreibtisch im Freigehege: Der Schriftsteller Erich Kästner im Dritten Reich." In *Im Pausenraum des "Dritten Reiches": Zur Populärliteratur im nationalsozialistischen Deutschland.* Edited by Carsten Würmann and Ansgar Warner, pp. 215–28. Bern: Peter Lang, 2008.

Wallrath-Janssen, Anne-M. *Der Verlag H. Goverts im Dritten Reich.* Munich: K. G. Saur, 2007.

Weber, Albrecht. "Widersprüche harmonisiert? Hans Carossas Leben als Werk." In *Hans Carossa: Dreizehn Versuche zu seinem Werk.* Edited by Hartmut Laufhütte, pp. 97–116. Tübingen: Max Niemeyer, 1991.

Wecht, Martin Johannes. *Jochen Klepper: Ein christlicher Schriftsteller im jüdischen Schicksal.* Düsseldorf: Uwe Nolte, 1998.

Weidermann, Volker. *Das Buch der verbrannten Bücher.* Cologne: Kiepenheuer und Witsch, 2008.

Weinreich, Paul. "Das politische Buch im nationalsozialistischen Staat." *Börsenblatt für den deutschen Buchhandel,* no. 49 (February 27, 1934): 185–87.

Weisenborn, Günther. *Der lautlose Aufstand: Bericht über die Widerstandsbewegung des deutschen Volkes 1933–1945.* Reinbek bei Hamburg: Rowohlt, 1953.

Weiss, Albert Maria, and Engebert Krebs. *Im Dienst am Buch.* Freiburg im Breisgau: Herder, 1951.

"Der Widerstand in den Büchereien." *Die Tat* 26 (1934/35): 314–16.

Wiechert, Ernst. "Die Aufgaben des deutschen Buchhandels im nationalsozialistischen Staat: Hat der Buchhandel versagt?" *Börsenblatt für den deutschen Buchhandel.* No. 294 (December 19, 1933): 979–80.

———. *Häftling nr. 7188: Tagebuchnotizen und Briefe.* Edited by Gerhard Kamin. Munich: Kurt Desch, 1966.

———. "Das 'Ja' und 'Nein' der deutschen Dichter und Schriftsteller." *Börsenblatt für den deutschen Buchhandel.* No. 292 (December 16, 1933): 971–74.

———. "Jahre und Zeiten: Erinnerungen." In *Sämtliche Werke,* vol. 9. Munich: Kurt Desch, 1957.

———. "Der Totenwald." In *Sämtliche Werke,* vol. 9. Munich: Kurt Desch, 1957.

Wild, Reiner, et al., eds. *Dennoch leben sie: Verfemte Bücher, verfolgte Autorinnen und Autoren: Zu den Auswirkungen nationalsozialistischer Literaturpolitik.* Munich: Edition Text und Kritik, 2003.

Wildt, Michael, ed. *Nachrichtendienst, politische Elite und Mordeinheit: Der Sicherheitsdienst des Reichsführers SS.* Hamburg: Hamburger Edition, 2003.

Wilk, Werner. *Werner Bergengruen.* Berlin: Colloquium, 1968.

Williams, Jenny. *More Lives than One: A Biography of Hans Fallada.* London: Libris, 1998.

Williams, John Alexander. *Hiking, Nudism and Conservation: 1900–1940.* Stanford, Calif.: Stanford University Press, 2007.

Williams, Rhys W. "Survival without Compromise? Reconfiguring the Past in the Works of Hans Werner Richter and Alfred Andersch." In *Flight of Fantasie: New Perspectives on Inner Emigration in German Literatur 1933–1945.* Edited by Neil H. Donohue and Doris Kirchner, pp. 211–22. New York: Berghahn, 2003.

Willrich, Wolfgang. *Säuberung der Kunsttempel: Eine kunstpolitische Kampfschrift zur Gesundung deutscher Kunst im Geiste nordischer Art.* Munich: J. F. Lehmann, 1937.

Wismann, Heinz. "Bekanntmachung der Reichsschrifttuskmammer vom 24. Juli 1935." *Börsenblatt für den deutschen Buchhandel.* No. 184 (August 10, 1935): 649.

———. "Dank des Schrifttums." *Der deutsche Schriftsteller* 1 (1936): 50.

———. "Schrifttumsförderung." *Der deutsche Schriftsteller* 1 (1936): 121–244.

Wistrich, Robert S. *Who's Who in Nazi Germany.* New York: Bonanza, 1984.

Witte, Karsten. "Politik als Nebenhandlung: Zu einer Theorie des faschistischen Films." *Politik und Kultur* 2 (1982): 32–41.

Wolf, Yvonne. *Frank Thiess und der Nationalsozialismus: Konservativer Revolutionär als Dissident.* Tübingen: M. Niemeyer, 2003.

Wolfrum, Edgar. *Geschichte als Waffe: Vom Kaiserreich bis zur Wiedervereinigung.* Göttingen: Vandenhoeck und Ruprecht, 2001.

Wulf, Joseph. *Literatur und Dichtung im Dritten Reich: Eine Dokumentation.* Frankfurt am Main: M. Ulstein, 1989.

Zachau, Reinhard K. *Hans Fallada als politischer Schriftsteller.* New York: Peter Lang, 1990.

Zeck, Wilhelm. "Die Bekämpfung unerwünschtes Schrifttums im nationalsozialistischen Staat." *Deutsche Verwaltung* 11 (1936): 349–50.

Ziegler, Edda. *100 Jahre Piper: Die Geschichte eines Verlags.* Munich: Piper, 2004.

———. *Verboten—verfemt—vertrieben: Schriftstellerinnen im Widerstand gegen den Nationalsozialismus.* Munich: Deutscher Taschenbuchverlag, 2010.

Ziegler, Hans Severus. *Praktische Kulturarbeit im Dritten Reich: Anregungen und Richtlinien für eine gesunde Volksbildung.* Munich: Franz Eher, 1931.

Ziesel, Kurt. *Das verlorene Gewissen: Hinter den Kulissen der Presse, der Literatur und ihrer Machtträger von heute.* Munich: J. F. Lehmann, 1962.

Zuckmayer, Carl. *Geheimreport.* Edited by Gunther Nickel and Johanna Schrön. Göttingen: Wallstein, 2002.

Zweck, Lily. "Reichslisten für Volksbüchereien: Im Auftrage des Reichserziehungsministerium herausgegeben von der Reichsstelle für volkstümliches Büchereiwesen." *Die Bücherei* 3 (1936): 337–38.

INDEX

CPSIA information can be obtained
at www.ICGtesting.com
Printed in the USA
BVHW041140280620
582403BV00001B/2

9 780197 524282